The Mother in the Age of Mechanical Reproduction

The Mother in the Age of Mechanical Reproduction

Psychoanalysis, Photography, Deconstruction

Elissa Marder

FORDHAM UNIVERSITY PRESS

NEW YORK 2012

This book has been published with the assistance of a subvention from Emory University.

Library of Congress Cataloging-in-Publication Data

Marder, Elissa.
The mother in the age of mechanical reproduction : psychoanalysis, photography, deconstruction / Elissa Marder. — 1st ed.
p. cm.
Includes bibliographical references and index.
ISBN 978-0-8232-4055-5 (cloth : alk. paper) —
ISBN 978-0-8232-4056-2 (pbk. : alk. paper)
1. Motherhood in literature. 2. Human reproduction in literature. 3. Human body in literature. 4. Technology in literature. I. Title.
PN1650.M68M37 2012
809'.9335252—dc23

2011030873

Printed in the United States of America

14 13 12 5 4 3 2 1

First edition

For Geoff

and

In memory of D.

CONTENTS

Acknowledgments ix

Introduction: Pandora's Legacy 1

PART ONE: PSYCHOANALYSIS AND THE MATERNAL FUNCTION

1. The Sex of Death and the Maternal Crypt 19

2. Mourning, Magic, and Telepathy 37

3. The Sexual Animal and the Primal Scene of Birth 53

4. Back of Beyond: Anxiety and the Birth of the Future 77

PART TWO: PHOTOGRAPHY AND THE PROSTHETIC MATERNAL

5. On Psycho-Photography: Shame and Abu Ghraib 91

6. Avital Ronell's Body Politics 111

7. *Blade Runner*'s Moving Still 130

8. Nothing to Say: Fragments on the Mother in the Age of Mechanical Reproduction 149

PART THREE: PHOTO-READINGS AND THE POSSIBLE IMPOSSIBILITIES OF LITERATURE

9. Darkroom Readings: Scenes of Maternal Photography 163

10. The Mother Tongue in *Phèdre* and *Frankenstein* 195

11. Birthmarks (Given Names) 214

12. Bit: Mourning Remains in Derrida and Cixous 229

Notes 251

Bibliography 285

Index 301

ACKNOWLEDGMENTS

This book was born over a long period of time. While most of the texts contained in it were composed fairly recently, a few of them were written long ago. Looking back, I recall that many years ago, after a lecture I had given on *Blade Runner* at the University of Rochester, my dear friend Sharon Willis asked me to explain what I meant by the term "mother." At the time, I was unable to articulate why I found the uncanny, photographic image of the mother to be so fascinating and so central to the film's concerns. In many ways, this book is the belated response to that question.

Given the long and complex genesis of the book, it is impossible for me to thank everyone who participated in all of its various stages over the years. I would like to thank a number of people, however, whose help and generosity were crucial to its emergence as a book. I am deeply grateful to the entire team at Fordham University Press. Helen Tartar, my editor, has been supportive and enthusiastic about the project from the very beginning. Thomas Lay oversaw the whole process with diligence and care. I would also like to thank Gregory McNamee for his sensitive and judicious copy editing of the manuscript. Kelly Oliver and David Wills both read the entire manuscript and offered generous and helpful suggestions for revisions. Hélène Cixous, Peggy Kamuf, and Avital Ronell offered continued inspiration and support. Elizabeth Rottenberg provided intellectual encouragement, keen insight, and warm friendship throughout the process. Several of the pieces in this book started off as invited lectures and/or contributions to journals and collected volumes. I would like to thank the following organizers and editors (some of whom are also friends) for including me in their various projects: Jennifer Bajorek, Jeanne Wolf Bernstein, Bruno Chaouat, Diane Davis, Mark Dawson, Karen Jacobs, Martin McQuillan, Steven

Miller, Michael Naas, Nicholas Royle, Eric Prenowitz, Marc Redfield, Marta Segarra, Ashley Thompson, Charles Shepherdson, Philippe Van Haute, and Emily Zakin. Numerous other friends and colleagues discussed many of the ideas in the book with me. In particular, I would like to thank Branka Arsić, April Alliston, Eduardo Cadava, Cathy Caruth, Tim Dean, Rindala El Khoury Grizard, Lalitha Gopalan, Emma Henderson, Tom Keenan, Jill Robbins, Deborah Elise White, Sarah Wood, and Ewa Ziarek. Ariel Ross provided welcome assistance with the preparation of the final manuscript. I am deeply indebted to the graduate students at Emory University with whom I have worked over the last decade for their curiosity, generosity, and intelligence. Many of them will find responses to their inspiring and fascinating work embedded in these pages. I would also like to thank Deans Robin Forman, Robert Paul, and Lisa Tedesco at Emory University for their generous support of this project: Emory provided the press with a publication subsidy and gave me a valued research leave that afforded me the time necessary to complete it. I received constant encouragement from my family throughout. Dorothy Marder, my photographer-mother-who-didn't-like-to-be-identified-as-a-mother, died while I was finishing this book and watches over it in her inimitable way. Finally, my greatest thanks go to Geoffrey Bennington, whose love and support make the impossible possible for me.

Earlier versions of many of the chapters in this book were previously published in scholarly journals and edited collections, and I am grateful to all of the presses for permission to reprint them here. A version of Chapter 1 was published as "The Sex of Death and the Maternal Crypt," *Parallax: Inscr(i/y)ptions* 15, no. 1 (2009): 5–20. The first section of Chapter 2 was originally presented as a lecture at the American Comparative Literature Association in April 2008, as part of the collective seminar "Jacques Derrida and the Singular Event of Psychoanalysis"; an earlier version of the chapter was published as "Mourning, Magic and Telepathy," *The Oxford Literary Review* 30, no. 2 (2008): 181–200. A portion of Chapter 3 was published as "The Sexual Animal and the Primal Scene," in *Sexuality and Psychoanalysis: Philosophical Criticisms*, ed. Jens De Vleminck and Eran Dorfman (Leuven: Leuven University Press, 2010), 121–137. An earlier version of Chapter 4 was published as "Back of Beyond: Anxiety and the Birth of the Future," *Philosophy Today: Selected Studies in Phenomenology and Existential Philosophy* 50 (2006): 98–105. An earlier and significantly shorter version of Chapter 5 was published as "On 'Psycho-Photography': The 'Case' of Abu Ghraib," *English Language Notes* 44, no. 2 (2006): 231–242. A version of Chapter 6 was published as "Avital Ronell's Body Politics," in *Reading Ronell*, ed. Diane Davis (Champaign: University of Illinois Press, 2009), 94–112. Chapter 7 was first published, in substantially the same form, as "*Blade Runner*'s Moving Still," *Camera Obscura* 27 (1992): 89–107, and is reprinted by permission of the publisher, Duke University Press. At that time, *Blade Runner* had not yet attained the status of cult film and postmodern noir classic that it holds today. Since that time, the critical literature on *Blade Runner* has exploded. Because my essay had an impact on much of the later scholarship, for the most part, I have decided not to update it here in light of that later work. A version of Chapter 8 was published as "Nothing to Say: Fragments on the Mother in the Age of Mechanical Reproduction," *L'Esprit Créateur: Writing One's Own Death* (Spring 2000): 25–35. A version of Chapter 9 was published as "Dark Room Readings: Scenes of Maternal Photography," *Oxford Literary Review* 32 (2010): 231–270. A version of Chapter 10 was published as "The Mother Tongue in Phèdre and Frankenstein," *Yale French Studies* 76 (1989): 59–77. Much of the thinking in this book began with it, and Chapter 10 is dedicated to the memory of Mary Quaintance, who was there at its inception. A version of Chapter 11 was published as "Birthmarks (Given Names)," *Parallax* 13, no. 3 (August 2007): 49–61.

The Mother in the Age of Mechanical Reproduction

Introduction: Pandora's Legacy

The Maternal Function

This book grows out of a long-standing fascination with the uncanny status of the mother in literature, psychoanalysis, philosophy, film, and photography. Sigmund Freud famously derives the psychoanalytic notion of the uncanny (the disturbing convergence of what is most familiar and most strange) from the etymology of the German word "*Unheimlich*" (or "unhomelike") and associates this figure with the passage through the mother's body in the event of being born.[1] This book explores the meanings (psychic, cultural, political, philosophical, and literary) that become attached to the maternal body as it emerges as an uncanny figure for the primal (and perhaps even radically unthinkable) relation to our own birth. This book aims to show that the uncanny maternal body is itself a conceptual matrix that demands to be read.

Whereas the "Mother" has often traditionally been represented as a quintessentially "natural" figure (even as the very figure of "Nature" itself, as in "Mother Nature") and birth is often assumed to be an incontestably empirical and knowable event, in the pages that follow I propose to show that far from grounding the notion of a stable origin, the concept of the mother in fact challenges it. Although the physical act of bearing children may be construed (and experienced) as a "natural act," the place accorded to the mother in culture and history, and the philosophical, political, and psychological *meaning* of what I shall call "the maternal function" is anything but natural. More specifically, this book explores why the figure of human birth is so often expressed in strikingly nonhuman terms. I have chosen to use the term "maternal function" here in order to highlight the technological, and non-anthropomorphic aspects that are often latently inscribed within the concept of birth.

In the chapters that follow, we will find that the uncanny properties of the "maternal function" often become manifest through disturbances of time and space. The event of birth becomes associated with instances of uncontrollable mechanical repetition and images of strangely animated containers whose contours defy the confines of any determinable spatial location. By examining the uncanny properties of the "maternal function," I explore how, throughout history and culture, humankind has attempted to reconcile the conceptual abyss between the apparently self-evident materiality of the maternal body and the radical unthinkability of the event of one's own birth. Attempts to account for the event of birth have simultaneously troubled existing systems of representation and provided a fertile source for alternative, nonmimetic, nonlinear conceptions of time and space. The more closely one looks at the act of giving birth and the event of being born, the stranger the maternal function becomes.[2]

Unlike the traditional conception of the "Mother" who ostensibly grounds a specifically human separation between nature and culture, the maternal function operates at the very outer limits of the human. It opens up a strange space in which birth and death, *bios* and *techné*, the human and the nonhuman are brought into an intimate and disturbing proximity with one another. From the beginning of human history, the privileged figure of the maternal function has always been that of an ambiguous "container" (the womb) that fails to contain the unruly contradictions at work in the concept of birth. The "womb" that holds the body before the beginning of life is structurally indistinguishable from the "tomb" that holds the body after the end of life. Indeed, in mythology, literature, and art, the womb is often depicted in strikingly technological terms: It is associated with artisanal boxes of all sorts including chests, caskets, jars, and, as we shall see, even with the camera obscura of photography that gives birth to embodied images through mechanical reproduction.

Furthermore, in contrast to the paternal function (the cultural meaning of which has traditionally occupied a pivotal role in the founding narratives of cultural institutions of all kinds including religion, anthropology, psychoanalysis, politics, and the law), with the maternal function a number of compelling paradoxes emerge. The figure of the mother tends to be both excluded from the realm of representation on the grounds that she is "natural" and simultaneously inscribed into representational practices as the very name for that which cannot be represented. In other words, the "mother" is often the philosophical name given to that which cannot be thought philosophically.[3] Likewise, although giving birth is depicted as the epitome of a purely natural act, the very act of childbearing (labor) has also been obliquely recognized as the first defining instance of human work. As such, the maternal function implicitly haunts the figure of work itself. As the originary matrix for all other reproductive acts, the maternal body tends to become associated and confused with other forms of cultural labor that are defined (at least in part) by their reproductive capabilities. By examining cases in which the reproductive capabilities originally attributed to the maternal function become conceptually linked to other modes of cultural production (in forms as diverse as dreams, memory, myths, agriculture, kitchen appliances, writing, translation, landscape paintings, theater, photography, factory labor, and the news media), we discover traces of an anxiety that appears to stem from the unacknowledged, uncomfortable proximity between childbearing and *principles of reproducibility* more generally. In this sense, the specific parameters of the "maternal function" and the repercussions of the confusions that subtend this conceptual figure have remained relatively unthought.[4]

It should be clear from what I have said thus far that the "maternal function," as I am invoking it here, refers neither to "mothers" in any simple sense nor to any of the many important symbolic, psychic, and cultural activities performed by mothers. Indeed, there is a vast bibliography of important recent work by (mostly feminist) scholars in philosophy, literature, and psychoanalysis devoted to many important aspects of mothers and mothering. Although that work is of great interest to me and provides an important context for many of the discussions in this book, my focus here is slightly different. I have chosen to explore the concept of birth and the "maternal function" independently of the role of the mother as a real person in the life of the child. There are several reasons for this decision. As feminist scholars have argued for decades, the conceptual categories of "woman" and "mother" are notoriously difficult to separate.[5] But by subsuming women too quickly into the category of "mothers" (or potential mothers), women are assigned to a particular, symbolically loaded place within the culture: the place of "home," "origin," "certainty," and "nature," indeed the very place of "place" itself. While I would certainly not want to contest the fact that real mothers may (or may not) provide great comfort to their children through the various acts of mothering they proffer (and endowing them with a secure sense of place may indeed be of particular importance in this regard), the consequences of defining the cultural concept of "Mother" as the symbolic place-holder for "home" as stable point of origin remain not only problematic but also inherently untenable.

This is so, I suggest, in part because the very concept of the "Mother" (as bearer of human birth), is haunted, from the beginning, by a radical confusion concerning the possibility of discerning between birth and death, and between presence and absence. However much we might want to lay claim to having a unique relation to the singularity of the event of our own birth, we have no direct access to it. We remain both bound to and exiled from our own birth. As an event, birth accrues and produces psychic meanings long before there is anyone "home" in the self who would be able to attempt to read those meanings. In this sense, the event of our birth is not our own, even if it is profoundly and uniquely addressed to us.[6]

This is further complicated by the fact that not only are we not able to be "present" to the event of our own birth, but someone else, the mother, is there at the scene—in our place—without being there as our witness, proxy or representative. There is something radically incommensurable and asymmetrical about the relation between mother and child in the event of birth. Unlike the child to whom she gives birth, the mother can potentially have an experience of the event. For the one who is being born, however, birth is on the other side of life; it can never be experienced as part of life, although it will always already have left traces on all future life experiences. As an event, therefore, birth is both shared and not shared with the mother who makes it possible. Although, by necessity, she had to have been "there" (in some sense, at any rate) at the very place where the one born can never go, the mother was "there" in her radical difference from the child to whom she gives birth. The mother's presumed "presence" at the scene of our birth strangely accentuates the paradoxical fact that we ourselves are radically excluded from it. Furthermore, to the extent that the mother is "present" at the scene at all, she is not entirely "present" to herself, since she is there in two very different capacities: as a human being with a history of life experiences and a set of expectations (both conscious and unconscious) about the birth in which she participates, and as the incarnation of a reproductive capability of the maternal body. Depending on the particularities of the circumstances and the person involved, these two different modes of being may be more or less aligned with or alienated from one another. But the very fact that these two registers can (and sometimes do) operate independently—and indeed at times conflict—indicates that the "maternal function" exceeds the limits of the mother's subjective capacity to contain the many meanings that the event of giving birth carries for her and for the child she bears.[7] The meanings of birth produce indelible psychic traces that return throughout one's lifetime in the form of *mechanical reproductions* that to some degree remain radically indecipherable.

Unable to be present to the event that is closest to us, we attempt to return to it and account for it individually and collectively. Although it is well known that the fantasy of returning to the mother's body often finds expression in dreams, myths, and literature, in this book I explore how anxieties concerning the uncanny properties of the maternal function turn up in unexpected places within contemporary culture. The book examines manifestations of mechanical reproduction in a diverse variety of cultural realms (including psychoanalysis, photography, politics, media culture, philosophy, literature, and war) and shows how they can be related to one another through their (sometimes latent) expressions of unease about the maternal function. Anxiety is central to many of the discussions in the book because the missed encounter with the event of birth is itself a primordial source of anxiety. Psychoanalytic theory has defined anxiety as an automatic psychic reaction to a missed encounter in the past (modeled after the missed encounter with the event of birth) that is then mechanically reproduced and projected onto an unknown future in order to forestall the effects of an unforeseen event. Given this description, it is not surprising that events, situations, and images that conjure up the temporal volatility of the maternal function often trigger anxious reactions.

This book is divided into three parts that correspond to three different spheres of cultural meaning in which the maternal function has produced legible and significant effects: as a troubling figure within psychoanalytic theory, as an unacknowledged reference point for modern technology, and as a productive literary figure. Part I, "Psychoanalysis and the Maternal Function," introduces the concept of the maternal function through an examination of the paradoxical place that Freud accords to the mother and the status of the event of birth within the organizational structure of the psyche. By looking closely at texts in which Freud grapples with the psychic meaning of birth, we discover that in his attempt to provide a theoretical account for birth's impact, he is led into the murkiest and most challenging regions of psychoanalytic theory. The figure of the mother becomes associated with many of the most unruly and enigmatic concepts within psychoanalysis: the uncanny, anxiety, the primal scene, "deferred action" (*Nachträglichkeit*), shame, *déjà vu*, telepathy, magical thinking, and various forms of failed mourning. On the basis of close readings of Freud's texts, I claim that the uncanny mother ultimately undermines his patriarchal accounts of the Oedipal complex as a foundation for human culture. Having established that the maternal function poses a critical problem for traditional Freudian metapsychology, I turn to Jacques Derrida's work on mourning and the notion of the crypt (as first defined by psychoanalysts Nicolas Abraham and Maria Torok) to show how his thinking both challenges traditional psychoanalytic descriptions of the maternal function and provides a compelling alternative to it.

Part II, "Photography and the Prosthetic Maternal," makes use of some of the psychoanalytic insights developed in Part I in order to explore how the reproductive properties of modern media technologies such as photography and the telephone often mobilize anxieties about the maternal function. This section opens with a chapter devoted to an analysis of the Abu Ghraib photographs, in which I argue that there is a formal connection between the temporality of anxiety, the psychic structure of shame, and the photographic medium itself. In this chapter, "On Psycho-photography: Shame and the Abu Ghraib photographs," I show how the forms of mechanical repetition and spatial indeterminacy that we found to be constitutive of the maternal function and the psychic structure of anxiety in Part I take on new social and political meanings when they collaborate with photography's potential to violate the boundaries between public and private spheres on account of its inherent propensity for uncontrollable reproduction and uncontainable exposure of images and events. In the next chapter, by working with Avital Ronell's important analysis of the invention of the telephone as a fantastic, fetishistic extension of the maternal body,[8] I continue to explore how the relationship between technology and the maternal function establishes legible lines of communication between the psychic affects that are mobilized through specific technologies (such as "photographic shame" and "telephonic fetishistic denial of loss") and the related political effects that can come to be associated with these affective disturbances. In the final two chapters in this section, through close readings of Ridley Scott's 1982 film *Blade Runner* and Roland Barthes's book *Camera Lucida* (which is famously both a theoretical study of photography and an autobiographical elegy to his dead mother), I show how the photographic medium is often represented as a prosthetic maternal body that is simultaneously defined by and contrasted to the body of the biological mother. In both *Blade Runner* and *Camera Lucida*, photography's presumed capacity to reproduce the world referentially tends to become epistemologically associated with the maternal body as the locus of undeniable certainty and the source of the meaning of human birth. Throughout all four chapters in this section, I trace the points of contact between technology and psychoanalytic theory as the two converge through the prosthetic maternal function. To the extent that these technologies aim to usurp the maternal function, they are often deployed as a means of regulating or warding off anxieties that are provoked by the inevitable experience of loss that real separation from the mother invariably demands.

Part III, "Photo-Readings and the Possible Impossibilities of Literature," picks up where Part II leaves off and returns to Barthes's *Camera Lucida* in order to show how, when photography relinquishes its referential aims, the photographic maternal body becomes a source of literary writing. By proposing that Barthes's *Camera Lucida* is not merely a book *about* photography, but also, more radically, a book that invents a kind of *photographic writing*, I extend the reflections about photography and psychoanalysis from the earlier sections to include a discussion of the specifically literary (or fictional) dimension of the maternal function. In this section, I examine a selection of literary works (by Jean Racine, Mary Shelley, and Hélène Cixous) in which the maternal function occupies a central place, in order to show how the figure of the mother challenges referential uses of language and even becomes a fertile source of the foreignness of language itself. In these literary texts, the mother does not bring us back to a stable origin, but serves instead as a figure for our first relation to language. As such, the mother figure, *as literary figure*, opens us up to the strange and uncanny relation we have, as speaking beings, to our ultimately unspeakable birth. The writings of Hélène Cixous figure prominently here. Cixous's writing produces a space that provides a source of inventive alternatives to the concept of life as naturally defined. In her writings (and in Derrida's writings on her writings) death is not opposed to life, it is part of life. Literature, after all, has the capacity to give birth to forms of life for which the distinction between life and death does not hold. In the literary texts examined here, the maternal function emerges as an uncanny, ambiguous vessel that contains uncontainable events, ideas, temporalities, and that paradoxically creates a space for the birth of futures that may have otherwise remained unimaginable.

However, given that its fundamental supposition is that the maternal function resists codification and containment, this book also resists linear presentation of its major themes and claims. Each chapter highlights some particular aspect of the maternal function through close readings of a particular text or conceptual question. These close readings in turn generate the multiple threads or *motifs* that then become woven into different patterns throughout the book. Like the productive properties of the dream (to which the maternal function has a privileged relation), the web of motifs produces multiple sets of associations. As I hope the reader will discover, like the figure of Pandora's jar to which I will turn in a moment, the maternal function is an uncanny vessel that bears both terror and hope.

Pandora and the Technological Birth of Birth

Although this book is primarily dedicated to an examination of the maternal function in the era of modern technology, one of its basic premises is that the uncanny technological conception of the maternal function is not a new phenomenon. Indeed, I would argue that the maternal function is as old as human history itself even if it takes on new forms and different cultural meanings in "the age of mechanical reproduction." I invoke this phrase (in an obvious allusion to Walter Benjamin's famous essay about how the invention of photography changes the cultural and political work performed by the work of art) to follow Benjamin in underscoring the idea that the maternal function (like the principle of reproducibility with which it is intimately associated) has always been operative throughout human history even if, in an earlier historical moment, it may have operated less visibly or even very differently. By way of illustration of this claim, I propose to take a brief detour by way of the ancient world in order to show that the uncanny maternal function is as least as old as one of humankind's oldest and most influential stories about the origin of human history itself.

According to the legend that comes to us from an ancient Greek text by Hesiod, Pandora, the first woman, was artificially produced rather than naturally born from any mother or mother figure.[9] Commissioned by Zeus and fabricated by Hephaestus out of clay and water, this first woman, first of the race of all future "human" women, is a manufactured product. In today's parlance, we might call her an android, a robot, or a replicant. Pandora's paradox—that she is the "matrix" of human birth even though she is neither born from a mother nor can even be considered strictly human—has rendered her a particularly fascinating figure for modern readers. Over the last thirty or so years, a number of eminent classicists including Jean-Pierre Vernant (who dedicated his final book, *La première femme*, to her), Pietro Pucci, Nicole Loraux, Geneviève Hoffman, and Froma Zeitlin have reopened Pandora's case and have offered illuminating and provocative new ways of understanding the implications of this ancient text for contemporary discussions of politics, gender, and the meaning of cultural myths more generally.[10]

Because I am not trained as a classicist, my remarks about the specific textual dimension of Hesiod's text will by necessity be somewhat limited. Nonetheless, I propose to take up the ancient myth of Pandora from the vantage point of a contemporary reader (assisted by the work done by those scholars) as a way of showing that the concept of "the mother" has always been paradoxical and that the idea of human birth has always already been marked by *technological* figures, fears, desires, and anxieties.

As is well known, Hesiod tells the story of the creation of Pandora, the "first woman," twice, in two very different texts: the *Theogony* and *Works and*

Days. Despite the very great differences between them, in both texts the story of Pandora marks the culmination or endpoint of a larger narrative that provides an account for how "man" became human in the first place. As the story goes, in the golden age before the invention of woman, there were already men, and those men lived openly together with the gods. Those early men were born of the (Mother) Earth rather than from any woman. In those happy days before woman was made, there was no illness, no misery, no toil, no death, hence no birth, and no children. The invention of the first artificial woman puts an end to that prehistorical era and inaugurates the dawn of human time and human history. Human history, therefore, begins with Pandora's arrival into the world of men; she brings "death," "birth," and sexual difference with her in addition to all the other "ills" associated with mortal life.

Even before we look more closely at the texts in question, we are already confronted with a number of striking paradoxes. Man's fall into the human condition apparently requires the intervention of "woman," but the invented woman who engenders the first principles of human nature is neither natural nor fully (and perhaps not even partially) human herself. In other words, although she inaugurates the birth of the human race (either directly through her own actions or indirectly through the consequences that ensue because of her actions depending on how one reads the text), it is never entirely clear that she is part of the human race that she founds. Moreover, despite the fact that the very purpose of this story has been commonly understood as an attempt to provide a mythic explanation for why there must be two sexes (instead of one) and for how sexual difference becomes implicated in human reproduction, the story itself is remarkably opaque and poetically suggestive regarding the link between sexuality and reproduction, the role of the mother in childbirth, and the specific properties associated with the maternal body.

Let me provide a brief summary of how Pandora's story is told in each of Hesiod's texts. In the *Theogony* (which tells the story of the creation of the universe through the birth of the gods), the creation of the "first woman" comes about as the final gesture in an ongoing feud between Zeus and the titan Prometheus. The story begins with a contest of wits and cunning between Zeus and Prometheus. Prometheus tricks (or attempts to trick) Zeus by butchering an ox and dividing it into two shares: He places the bare bones under the ox's skin and hides the delicious meat inside the ox's disgusting belly pouch and then asks Zeus to pick a share. Pretending to be deceived, Zeus picks the pile of bones instead of the share with the meat and decides to retaliate against Prometheus by punishing man. The punishment consists in taking divine fire away from mortals. In response, Prometheus steals fire from the gods and hides it in a hollow fennel stalk and delivers it to man. Finally, Zeus puts an end to the conflict and makes man pay the price for Prometheus's transgressions by creating an artificial woman, adorned by the gods and goddesses; this "beautiful evil" is designed to trick men into entering into the economic hardships and trials of marriage. Here is how the first woman is described:

> For from her comes the race of female women; for of her is the deadly race and tribe of women, a great woe for mortals, dwelling with men, no companion of baneful poverty, but only of luxury. (590–594)

In this version of the story, the first woman is not given a name. According to Nicole Loraux, she has no body either.[11] She is an image, the mere appearance of a woman who is designed to deceive men and to exploit their productive labor. While he toils in the fields, she consumes his food at home. He produces everything. She produces nothing other than "the race of womankind, the deadly female race and tribe of wives." It is not clear from the text whether or not this "race" of womankind comes into being via an act of procreation or of mechanical reproduction. According to some critics, this first woman must (implicitly at least) be construed as a mother as well, since "from her comes all the race of womankind." For Loraux, however, these lines are precisely the indication that the first woman is anything but a mother in the traditional sense as she is alienated from reproduction. She writes:

> Indeed, unless we butcher the text, we must resign ourselves: whether we call her Pandora or not, the first woman of the *Theogony* is not "the mother of humanity." She is the "mother of women." Thus, this "necessary evil" takes us far from the reproductive woman. The tradition is born in heterodoxy, and the founding text situates the race of women in an original state of separation.[12]

Loraux's analysis of this passage implies that Pandora's function appears to be exactly the opposite from what one might expect: she inaugurates a radical (and presumably permanent) separation between "men" and the evil and debased "race of women" rather than serving as the principle through which men and women come together in the production of children. But whether or not we accept Loraux's compelling reading, the text still leaves us with a curious dilemma about how to conceptualize human reproduction as we are confronted with two mutually exclusive but equally unsatisfactory explanations for how the human race first began to reproduce itself. If we reject Loraux's reading and insist instead that this first artificial woman must also logically become the first mother of "humankind," then what happens to the related assumption that the maternal body is quintessentially "natural"? If, however, we accept Loraux's interpretation, we are confronted with a situation in which we must imagine that the first woman replicates herself parthenogenetically without being involved in any kind of sexual reproduction. Regardless of which alternative we choose, we are left with a fundamental confusion about how to account for the maternal function. In either case, that function is fundamentally marked as "technological" rather than natural.

If we now turn to the second text in which Hesiod writes about the first woman, *Works and Days*, Pandora's relationship to maternity becomes arguably even more complicated. In this text, a didactic poem that explains the *mores* of the world and provides instruction for how to live a moral life, Hesiod once again recounts the story of the first woman as the denouement of a drama between Zeus and Prometheus. Here the story unfolds as follows: The gods hide the fire of divine life from men in seeds so that men will be obliged to work. Men must sow the seeds in the earth, plow the land and harvest the grain in order to gain access to the divine life force that is hidden within the seeds. Zeus hides the divine fire because he was angry with Prometheus for having deceived him. In retaliation, Prometheus steals the fire back from Zeus and then hides the fire in a hollow fennel stalk and gives it to men. To settle the matter once and for all, Zeus gleefully resolves to give men a "gift" so evil that it makes them choose to love the very thing that steals their life force from them. That gift is woman.

Unlike the *Theogony*, which more or less ends this narrative unit with the creation of woman, *Works and Days* provides many additional details concerning the fabrication, the delivery, and the consequences of this beautiful, evil, gift. In making this artificial woman, Hephaestus copies the divine beauty of the goddesses. She is then given "gifts" by all the gods and with them, the name "Pandora." Although she is beautiful, she is also monstrous because she combines divine, animal and supposedly human qualities: she possesses godlike beauty, a bestial, insatiable appetite for food and sex, a thieving, "bitchlike" character, and a seductive voice that speaks only in lies. This artfully designed, artificial creature that specializes in artifice is sent to beguile Prometheus's slightly retarded brother, Epimetheus (Afterthought), into marriage. Although Prometheus (Forethought) had anticipated Zeus's gesture and had therefore warned his brother not to accept any gifts from the gods, Epimetheus only belatedly recognizes Pandora as the gift he was supposed to avoid. He welcomes her into his home only to discover, too late, that it is too late to save mankind from the calamities she brings with her.

Despite all her gifts, Pandora, it seems, is still not enough of a technological calamity on her own. In order to carry out her divine mission to destroy mankind, she also comes equipped with a technological accessory, a food storage jar (presumably made of the same matter as she: clay and water) and, by opening the lid of that deadly container, she unleashes death and devastation into the world and disperses invisible evils everywhere. Then, following Zeus's orders, she quickly snaps the lid of the jar shut, enclosing only Elpis inside. Although *elpis* has often been traditionally been translated as "hope," Vernant and other recent scholars advise that it can mean "fear" as well. In the recent Harvard Loeb edition, Glenn Most translates *elpis* as "anticipation." Given the specific mixture of "fear," "hope," and "futurity," "*elpis*" conjures up a powerful connection to anxiety as well.

Several questions arise at this juncture: What is the meaning of Pandora's jar, and what is her connection to it? Why does she even need this technological prosthetic supplement to help her fulfill her nefarious function, given that she is already so well endowed with evil powers? Critics have proposed several different kinds of responses to these questions. Some have pointed out the resemblance between Pandora and the jar. Both are duplicitous creations: They are beautiful on the outside while being disgusting, evil and debased on the inside. In both cases, the alluring external attributes conceal internal destructiveness. This scene has also often been read as an allegory of childbearing in which the jar (the object that traditionally holds the household stores of "seeds") represents the female womb that receives man's "seeds." However, even among those critics who want to propose that there may be some sort of connection between Pandora, the jar, and the act of reproduction, there is little consensus about how to understand the precise mechanisms involved.

The problems arise when trying to determine the status of the jar: Is it a "natural" representation of the womb as a natural place, or some kind of cultural tool or technological prosthesis?[13] In spite of all of the textual emphasis on Pandora's artificial, technological nature, some critics have continued to insist, nonetheless, that the jar is a figure for earth and hence must be read as a natural image of fertility thereby implicitly rendering Pandora capable of "natural childbirth." In a nuanced modification of this view, Jean-Pierre Vernant has proposed that the "grain" associated with the story of Pandora must be understood in its relation to the theme of agriculture. As such, it is "cultivated" and therefore belongs to culture rather than simply being part of nature. He writes:

> Pandora corresponds to *bios*, the cereal food that Zeus "hides" when he also hides his celestial fire, just as Prometheus hid the food in the form of meat in the *gastēr*, and the seed of stolen fire in the hollow stem. The belly of the woman which man must plough if he wishes to have children, is like the belly of the earth that he must plough if he wishes to have wheat since Zeus has hidden the *bios* in it.[14]

Implicit in this reading is the notion that producing children is a cultural activity rather than a natural act. However, as part of culture, it is essentially man's work. While he plows the fields, sows the seeds and harvests the grain, the earth (and the female womb with which it is here associated) remains the passive natural ground upon which he performs his cultural labor.

In contrast, for Nicole Loraux, Pandora has nothing to do with fertility: she is the very antithesis of sexual reproduction. Writing about the *Theogony*, she asserts:

> If the text implies that with the appearance of woman comes marriage—and therefore reproduction—then the "function of fertility" is certainly hidden from sight. Nothing indicates that the woman is designed to "imitate the earth" as she is in the orthodox tradition of Greek representations of fertility. And we should not be too quick to seek the motif of Mother Earth in the *parthenos*, as some scholars have done.[15]

Picking up on Loraux's work, Froma Zeitlin explores the implicit contradictions and inherent tensions within the representation of Pandora's relation to her jar. For Zeitlin, the image of Pandora's jar represents the uterus and the figure of Elpis conjures up the hopes and fears associated with the birth of a future child:

> But taken as an image that embodies an idea, the Elpis that is left in the jar corresponds most closely to the child (or the hope of a child) who resides inside his mother's womb. . . . Throughout the Hippocratic corpus and the works of the later, more sophisticated anatomists, the woman's uterus is likened to an upside-down jar, furnished with two ears or handles. . . . The jar/uterus is modeled on features of human anatomy. It too has a mouth and a neck. This nomenclature is also pertinent to the widespread idea of a correlation between woman's sexual and oral appetites, emphasized in the Hesiodic text as located below in the rapacious belly (*gastēr*) that fills up on man's substance. . . . The analogy continues in the notion of a seal or stopper that is needed to prevent entry, with the aim of preserving virginity or, conversely, of retaining the seed deposited in it to allow a successful pregnancy to occur. What does it mean, then, that Pandora comes equipped with her own jar, and that she removes the lid to open it, releasing a swarm of ills that now wander silent and invisible all over the world, leaving only Hope within?[16]

In response to this last question, Zeitlin contends that Hesiod's text manifests anxiety about the power of woman's reproductive capabilities and the economic consequences of bearing too many children thereby depleting the store of household grain. She proposes that Hesiod separates the image of household jar (*pithos*) of stored goods from the image of the *pithos* as feminine uterus in order to contain his fears about the latter. She ultimately concludes that Pandora's function is to suppress, rather than express, the link between women and reproduction:

> This woman, as argued earlier, is hardly represented as a "bringer of fertility" and the "principle of reproduction," as most interpreters like to insist—or, to put it another way, to the extent that she is, the text suppresses these functions as much as possible.[17]

Although, as we have seen, the critics above disagree on many points, they do appear to agree that the maternal function in reproduction is a natural act. The critics who argue that Pandora is a principle of fertility automatically associate her with the earth and thereby with traditional Greek notions of Mother Earth as the primordial figure of Nature. The critics who dispute Pandora's reproductive capabilities do so, in part, by pointing out that she is not a natural woman, but rather a technological creation. In both cases, however, the link between reproduction and nature in the maternal function is never questioned. Thus, for example, when Zeitlin compares Pandora's jar to a uterus, the jar, as technological object, is understood to be in an analogous and mimetic relation to the body it represents. In other words, according to the classical anatomists that Zeitlin invokes, the jar "imitates nature" by representing the uterus. Although the analogy between "jar" and "uterus" seems to work on a general basis, as Zeitlin herself points out, it seems to present specific problems in Pandora's case.

But what if Pandora's jar (and its relation to the maternal function) were even more unsettling than has been hitherto suspected? What would happen if we were to understand the jar as a *mechanical reproduction* of the womb rather than as a *representation* of it? The jar, then, would have to be understood as a fabricated replica of Pandora's fabricated duplicitously empty body. As a prosthetic, externalized replication of Pandora's womb (within which lurks a figure of "Anxiety," here bearing the name Elpis), the jar opens up the disturbing possibility that the maternal function is not a natural operation and that it cannot be so easily contained. This book explores the uncanny consequences that are released with that thought.

PART ONE

Psychoanalysis and the Maternal Function

ONE

The Sex of Death and the Maternal Crypt

> I wish her to be buried in her wedding dress, with white shoes, and a wreath. Her hair is to be spread about her shoulders. Three coffins, one oak, one mahogany, one of lead.
>
> — FLAUBERT, *Madame Bovary*

> When the face without face, name without name, of the mother returns, in the end, one has what I called in *Glas* the logic of obsequence. The mother buries all her own. She assists whoever calls herself her mother, and follows all burials.
>
> — JACQUES DERRIDA, *The Post Card: From Socrates to Freud and Beyond*

Mourning and Femininity

"Mourning women." The phrase reverberates and conjures up the many names of women who have become known to us (in myth, literature, history, philosophy) by their celebrated acts of mourning. "*Andromache, je pense à vous!*" "Andromache, I think of you," writes Baudelaire in the opening lines of "The Swan."[1] Or perhaps one thinks first and foremost of Antigone, philosophy's darling token feminine figure and arguably the most scrutinized and theorized mourner in the history of Western philosophy.[2] Or of Electra, who mourns her father by plotting to murder her mother.[3] Or of Niobe, who weeps eternally over the loss of her dead children: the seven sons and seven daughters murdered by a god as punishment for her excessive maternal pride.[4] The history of Western culture is saturated, inundated, drenched with the tears of mourning women. And, with very few exceptions (notably mothers who sometimes mourn for daughters), the most famous mourning women are those women who mourn for men. The widow Andromache mourns for her husband. The sister, Antigone, mourns for her brother. The daughter, Electra, mourns for her father. Only Niobe, the mourning mother, mourns for daughters as well as sons and husband.

Moreover, Nicole Loraux reminds us that in the ancient world mourning was uniquely a feminine activity.[5] It was practiced only by women, and, like the women themselves, mourning was kept inside the home (*oikos*) and away from the public, political space (*agora*) of the city.

Mourning women. The phrase always seems to refer to mourning *by* women, rather than mourning *of* women. But what happens if we change the inflection of the phrase and ask about how women have been mourned rather than how they have mourned? Mourning women: Who mourns for women? And who are the women who have been mourned? Mourned, I mean, symbolically, and publicly, and given a proper name in being mourned rather than being celebrated as a "mother" or collective maternal or paternal figure such as a queen or a head of state. How often has a particular, individual woman been recognized by a monument to her enduring accomplishments, an elegy to her art, a symphony, or any other collective cultural expression of posthumous remembrance? Surprisingly, the question has not been asked very often. And, according to Nicole Loraux, in the ancient world, it was unthinkable. In the opening pages of *Tragic Ways of Killing a Woman*, Loraux explains that, historically speaking, real women living in ancient Greece were excluded from receiving even the most minimal mourning rites. Their lives were destined to be unremarkable, and their deaths were condemned to remain radically unmarked. Unlike their famous fictional sisters in tragedy, such as Antigone, to name the most often-cited example, real woman had no claims whatsoever on death rites. And, like their lives, women's deaths belonged entirely to the domestic space; they were acknowledged only by their husbands and commemorated only by their husbands' memories of them.[6]

Let me begin again. For reasons that I hope will become clear later, I think it might be useful to situate the remarks that follow in the context of a certain history of the changing concerns within feminist work in psychoanalysis. Thinking back to the first major encounters between psychoanalysis and feminism from the mid-1970s onward, some general themes emerge. Despite the often-cited differences between and among American, British, and French feminists working in or around psychoanalysis at that time, the general focus of debate concerned questions of sexual difference and sexuality.[7] Some feminists explicitly engaged in a return to Freud in order to appropriate his work for feminism (here I think of Juliet Mitchell) while others did so in order to challenge his assumptions about feminine sexuality and to repudiate his conclusions (here I think of Luce Irigaray). These rereadings were mostly focused on Freud's writings explicitly devoted to feminine sexuality and female sexual development. The question of sexual difference also provoked the substantial and productive feminist attention given to the Dora case history and to questions of hysteria more generally.[8] In some sense, much of the work from this period was devoted (in one way or another) to what we might now call "The Enigma of Woman," in the wake of Sarah Kofman's important reappropriation of Freud's phrase; texts from this period (by Sarah Kofman, Luce Irigaray, and Shoshana Felman, among others) elucidated Freud's lifelong fascination with the question of feminine desire as well as his repeated failures to provide a viable theoretical account for it according to the Oedipal narrative.[9] A dialogue with Lacan was implicit in most of these readings as well. Some feminists (Juliet Mitchell, Jacqueline Rose, Jane Gallop, and perhaps even Kristeva) chose to engage with Lacanian terms in the interest of feminist ends while others (Irigaray, Cixous) rejected them. And, at the risk of deforming a history that was certainly much richer than my description of it, the next major locus of work was focused on the mother.[10] Some of the work treated the erasure of the mother from the Oedipal paradigm and proposed new forms of maternal relations (Irigaray), while that of others (here Kristeva comes to mind) insisted on the importance of pre-Oedipal relations with the mother. All of this is surely very familiar.

Nonetheless, it is perhaps worth adding here that there may be something of a conceptual disconnect between the kinds of questions asked by practicing psychoanalysts with feminist concerns and those posed by feminist theorists who turn to (or against) psychoanalysis for specific political or philosophical motivations that may ultimately be external to it. Analysts tend to respond to material that arises from what they see and hear on the couch. Thus, however "repressed" or "annihilated" the mother might be in theoretical accounts, her psychic presence emanating from the unconscious looms large in case histories for most patients regardless of sex or sexual orientation. Thus, in a paper from 1993 entitled "Woman's Social Status as a Reflection of the Internal Relationship to Mother and Father in Both

Sexes," Janine Chasseguet-Smirgel presents case material in order to support her hypothesis that there is an inverse relationship between the power of the maternal image in the unconscious of both men and women and the lack of power accorded to real women in the real world. She writes:

> The maternal power is in the unconscious considered to be so great, that women must strictly be confined to it. The difficulty within the socio-cultural field, in accepting an integrated bisexual functioning in women, is linked, to a large extent, to a fear of the primitive maternal representation.[11]

I cite this passage here not so much in order to agree or disagree with it, but rather to highlight two specific points: First, it is imperative not to confuse unconscious representations of feminine figures with actual women, and second, there may indeed be a relationship between unconscious representations of feminine figures and the place assigned to women in social and political life, but that relationship is neither transparent nor mimetic. Simply put, what this means is that it is not only important not to confuse the figure of the woman with the figure of the mother, but also that it is important not to confuse the conscious mother or the mother as person with unconscious psychic representations and manifestations of the maternal function. Again, according to Chasseguet-Smirgel's account, greater power accorded to the maternal imago in the unconscious of both sexes often translates into a loss of access to positions of power and a lower sense of entitlement for actual women in the world.

As it happens, and as I more or less indicated earlier, I am not exactly sure that I entirely agree with this formulation. Nonetheless, I find it extremely useful for its value as a cautionary tale against assuming that we know what we are talking about when we use the word "mother" in relation to the unconscious processes. Here it might be advisable to add that I am making an implicit distinction between what I am calling the maternal function (a name for the psychic account for how babies are made) and discussions of the maternal body as it operates as the first love object for the infant. My focus here is not on infant attachment to the maternal body as such, but rather to the ways in which the very fact of being born is expressed in the psyche. At the risk of jumping ahead of myself, I would like to suggest that the place of the maternal function—as it is articulated in Freud's metapsychology—may turn out to be a lot stranger and even more uncanny than has been generally acknowledged up until now. Furthermore, although it does appear to be incontestable that the mother is largely absent from the Oedipal narrative, she does emerge consistently and significantly as a *concept* in Freud's writings about dreams, literature, art, fetishism, mourning, and death.[12]

Indeed, as I hope to argue in the pages that follow, some of Freud's most interesting and provocative notions about sexual difference are to be found not only in his writings about sexuality but also in his many different and sometimes divergent attempts to provide a psychoanalytic account for death. As we shall see, the concept of death is itself sexed in Freud's writings. Like the ancient Greeks, who had two distinct and very different figures for death, one designated male (*Thanatos*) and one female (*Kere*),[13] Freud inscribes two different (and perhaps mutually exclusive) articulations to explain how death is represented in the psyche. I would like to suggest that by approaching sexual difference through the question of the sexual difference of death, it may be possible to open up some new ways of thinking about the repercussions that psychic representations can produce on social and political life. Finally, although I would insist on the lack of transparency between psychic figures and social reality, I do believe that there is a latent but vital relation between them that can be opened up and altered through various kinds of analytic and interpretative acts.

I would like to begin this approach to the sex of death obliquely by telling a story about a case that was much in the news in France in recent years. It is a true story—the kind of story that the French call a *fait divers*. In French, the term *fait divers* refers to stories in which ordinary people become newsworthy by becoming agents or victims of events that command media attention and captivate public fascination. Enhanced by media magnification and repetition, *faits divers* are often purveyors of modern myths. They assume a function roughly analogous to a contemporary fairy tale in which the actors are larger than life, events are stranger than fiction and the story recounted poses a question about the basic tenets and beliefs of human experience. Such is the case in this case. For at first glance, this *fait divers* presents itself as an exemplary "case." It enters the public sphere first and foremost as a legal case, but it is also clearly a psychological case, and perhaps even a religious case. Furthermore, as I would like to suggest here, this exemplary "case" about women and maternity may actually turn out to be more of a crypt than a case. For unlike a case, which (in principle) aims to disclose general truths by using the power of example as illustration, this "case" fails to be "opened up" through analysis. Instead, it powerfully enacts a set of enigmatic questions concerning the difficulties of understanding what "mother" means in the psyche and challenges the limits between life and death. As we shall see, embedded within this tragic and disturbing case about a mother's violent refusal to accept her maternal position lurks an uncanny anxiety about a form of failed mourning that is itself encrypted within the maternal function.

So here is the story. I will call it "The Case of the Freezer" for now.

The Case of the Freezer

One day in July 2006, a forty-year-old French businessman living with his thirty-eight-year-old French wife and their two children in a middle-class neighborhood known as "little France" in Seoul, South Korea, went to put something into the freezer located in the kitchen of their home. When he opened the freezer, the man discovered the corpses of two frozen babies wrapped in plastic there. Shocked and appalled, he went to the police. The man told the police that he believed it was an industrial revenge operation. He volunteered immediately for DNA tests. The couple denied any knowledge of the babies, and they returned to France. Several months later, DNA results determined that these two people were indeed the parents of the dead babies. On October 11, 2006, the wife, Véronique Courjault, admitted that she had been pregnant twice, first in 2002 and then again in 2003. She said that she hid both pregnancies from her husband, gave birth to the babies in her home, strangled them, and put them in the freezer. When the couple moved during that time, she put the babies in a freezer bag and transported them to the freezer in the kitchen of her new home. She then also admitted that she had killed a third baby in 1999 in France. She had hidden that pregnancy as well. She still claims that her husband never knew she was pregnant. No one in her immediate circle, none of her friends or family, knew that she was pregnant.

Since the revelation of the "Courjault affair," several new cases of denial of pregnancy and infanticide have become exposed in the news. According to psychoanalytic and psychiatric experts interviewed in the wake of the revelation of the Courjault case, it appears that this story is not as unusual as it might seem. Apparently, the phenomenon of "denial of pregnancy" (in which the woman successfully hides her pregnancy from herself, her partner, and others) coupled with infanticide is not so uncommon. Several experts said that they too had encountered cases in which babies were killed and put into the freezer.[14]

But what is a freezer? Any interpretation we might be tempted to make of this case (and, at this point I hope that it goes without saying that I am treating this case as a text—that is to say, a cultural phenomenon made available for public scrutiny and analysis via media diffusion rather than as an analysis of the individual psyche of the person here involved) depends upon how we understand the function of the freezer and the woman's relationship to it. The freezer is the enigmatic question at the heart of the case. Had this woman killed her babies and disposed of them, we could recognize her action as a "simple" case of infanticide—if one could ever consider infanticide as simple. But by putting her dead babies into the freezer, transporting them from one home to another, keeping them in a freezer located in the kitchen—in the hearth of her home—and hence in direct proximity to the storehouse of the family foods, and guarding the dead babies in this frozen state over several years, Véronique Courjault invites us to look more closely at the freezer and to wonder about how it might be related to larger questions of motherhood, death, and mourning.

A freezer is, after all, itself a particular kind of a case—a technologically enhanced object designed for holding, containing, or preserving something (normally food) against the ravages of time. A freezer is designed to keep something safe, protected, and near. In this sense, it is the opposite of a disposal site; it retains, contains, and safeguards the objects that are confined in it. It is also the opposite of an oven. Following this association, dead babies in the freezer might be read as a reversal of the common image of the pregnant woman who has "buns in the oven." Here it might be important to recall that Freud insists throughout his writings that all references to containers relate to the maternal function. For example, in a sentence added to *The Interpretation of Dreams* in 1909, he writes: "Boxes, cases, chests, cupboards and ovens represent the uterus."[15] So a woman who denies and conceals her pregnancy, gives birth to babies at home, kills the babies in secret, and then preserves them indefinitely in the heart of her home seems to be asking some fundamental questions about what it what mean to be a mother—what it means to "give birth" and to "give death" and whether or not there is a relationship between the two. For the freezer, like the frozen babies contained within it, is an ambiguous and ambivalent figure of both life and death: It is simultaneously a womb, a tomb, a stomach, and a crypt.

The babies are preserved in their newly born and newly dead state; the event of their death almost coincides with the moment of their birth. The freezer accentuates this radical confusion between birth and death. Moving directly from being contained in the womb to being contained in the freezer, the babies are suspended in a time of perpetual birth-death. As such, the freezer can be read as a replacement for and extension of the mother's body. As an external, prosthetic womb, the freezer might be understood as a continuation of maternity by other means.

From this perspective, Véronique Courjault's act might then be read as an unconscious attempt to "outsource" the maternal function to the freezer and would thereby indicate that she herself was profoundly unable to identify with the figure of a mother or to assume that place. The freezer seems to safeguard and secure some kind of unconscious belief system about motherhood and death. Whatever else one might want to say about this story, its haunting horror seems to stem from the fact that it is a mutely tragic case of radically failed mourning. Indeed, during and after her confession, the woman was unable to find anything to say about why she did what she did. But might this pathological enactment of a profound and fundamental confusion between mothering and death be able tell us something about the so-called normal structure of mourning? Before we can reopen the question of mourning and mothering, we will first need to take a closer look at the psychoanalytic conception of death itself.

The Sex of Death (Totem Animals, Cannibalism, and Crypts)

One of Freud's most important (and least appreciated) fundamental insights concerns the extreme difficulty that the psyche undergoes in its attempts to assimilate the idea of death.[16] The knowledge of death is elusive, filled with contradictions, and by no means "natural." In fact, as Freud repeatedly points out, one of the primary tasks of culture is to teach us about death. Knowledge of death is painfully acquired over time. Religion comes into being as part of the process of learning about death and art provides a means of representing it. The difficulty with death stems from the fact that, at the level of the unconscious, it does not exist. In his 1915 essay "Thoughts for the Times on War and Death," Freud famously describes the problem as follows:

> It is indeed impossible to imagine our own death; and whenever we attempt to do so we can perceive that we are in fact still present as spectators. Hence the psycho-analytic school could venture on the assertion that at bottom no one believes in his own death, or, to put the same thing in another way, that in the unconscious every one of us is convinced of his own immortality.[17]

Throughout his writings, Freud returns again and again to the problem of the conception of death. And, although he produces almost as many explanations as he does texts devoted to the subject, there are two general strains underlying his thinking about death.

The first and more familiar version of the story about death runs parallel (and is grafted on) to the story of Oedipus. Knowledge of death comes about as a by-product of the son's murderous and ambivalent feelings toward his father. In *Totem and Taboo*, for example, knowledge about death arises in reaction to and as a consequence of the murder of the primal father by the band of brothers. After killing the father, the surviving sons learn to mourn him by reenacting the crime on a symbolic totemic substitute for him. By eating the totem animal, which both takes his place and marks the place where he once was, the sons simultaneously repeat the murder, mourn it and work through it. Unlike the real primal father—who is predominantly an object of hatred—the totem animal substitute has the power to elicit, contain, and represent coexisting murderous and loving feelings. After having fully digested the totem animal, they overcome their hatred of him and learn to love and mourn him by making him become part of themselves. And this is the story of the foundation of religion, social relations, ethics, and the law. In *Totem and Taboo*, Freud tells this version:

> The violent primal father had doubtless been the feared and envied model of each one of the company of brothers: and in the act of devouring him they accomplished their identification with him, and each one of them acquired a portion of his strength. The totem meal, which is perhaps mankind's earliest festival, would thus be a repetition and a commemoration of this memorable and criminal deed, which was the beginning of so many things—of social organization, of moral restrictions and of religion.[18]

As feminist readers of *Totem and Taboo* have long observed, in this story about the founding of religion and politics, women have no active role to play.[19] But my interest in this text is somewhat different here. I would like to suggest that the "erasure" of the maternal and the feminine with which *Totem and Taboo* famously ends is both derived from and challenged by the complicated inscription of animals, maternity, eating, and death throughout its earlier sections.

As it happens, throughout Freud's work, animals do the lion's share of the theoretical work in the metapsychology for the conceptual foundation of the idea of death, castration, and consequently the difference between the sexes.[20] Thus, in the third section of the fourth and concluding chapter of *Totem and Taboo*, Freud invokes "animals" as the privileged figure of enlightenment provided by psychoanalysis:

> Into this obscurity one single ray of light is thrown by psychoanalytic observation. There is a great deal of resemblance between the relations of children and of primitive men toward animals. Children share no trace of the arrogance which urges adult civilized men to draw a hard-and-fast line between their own nature and that of all other animals. . . . Not infrequently, however, a strange rift occurs in the excellent relations between children and animals. A child will suddenly begin to be frightened of some particular species of animal and to avoid touching or seeing any individual of that species. The clinical picture of an animal phobia emerges—a very common, and perhaps the earliest, form of psychoneurotic illness occurring in childhood.[21]

Freud goes on to explain that when animal phobias are directed against larger animals:

> It was the same in every case: where the children concerned were boys, their fear related at bottom to their father and had merely been displaced on to the animal.[22]

It is important to recognize that Freud invokes the existence of the animal phobia as proof and symptom of the fear of the father well *before* he presents the famous narrative of the primal murder at the end of the text. Freud himself calls specific attention to the importance of this animal intervention: He presents it as a "ray of light" that promises to illuminate the relationship between the primitive culture and modern civilization. More specifically, at the level of his argument, the introduction of "animal phobias" creates a textual divide, or threshold, between what he designates as prehistorical and/or primitive culture (and this includes the extraordinarily fertile pages devoted to magical thinking, animism, ghosts, and spirits as well as some explicit references to matriarchal societies and the importance of the maternal function more generally) and the infamous derivation of the murderous foundation of patriarchal "civilization" with which the text ends. The move from cultures based on "Totem" and "Taboo" to cultures bound by monotheism and patriarchal law passes thus through the animals. Here I would like to point out that *Totem and Taboo* is not the only text in which Freud conjures up the clinical example of "animal phobias" in order to attempt to bridge a conceptual divide that separates his discussions of the enigma of birth and the maternal function from his discussions of death and the father. Most notably, in *Inhibitions, Symptoms and Anxiety*, Freud inserts a discussion of "animal phobias" as preemptive proof and preparation for his later and very provocative claim that the idea of death is modeled on castration rather than the other way around.[23] As I will show in greater detail in Chapters 3 and 4, it appears that without the animals, Freud cannot account for the idea of death in the psyche. More specifically, without animal intervention, the entire Oedipal narrative that results from the primal murder of the primal father is impossible. In short, it is only by appealing to the animal phobias that Freud derives the system that leads to the last supper in which the dead father (in the form of an edible animal) can be consumed. Consumed, that is, by men and by men only it would seem. As the story is told, the women do not eat the father; they are seemingly not endowed with the powers of digestion. Along the same lines, Freud never mentions a female case of an animal phobia. However, in almost every case of a male animal phobia (here I am thinking Rat Man and Wolf Man), the phobic child *also* has a dead and unmourned sister whom he has consumed, but whose unmarked death becomes frozen in the psyche.[24]

Here I would like to pause an instant to point out that it is precisely the strange undigested status of the Wolf Man's dead sister that provokes psychoanalysts Nicolas Abraham and Maria Torok to reopen Freud's famous case history and to derive their concept of the crypt from it.[25] On the basis of their radical rethinking of the primordial relationship between mourning and eating the other, they formulate the notion that the crypt is an "intrapsychic tomb" that bears traumatic witness to an unspeakable trauma that has been "swallowed" without being digested. In their "Mourning or Melancholia: Introjection *versus* Incorporation," they write:

> The words that cannot be uttered, the scenes that cannot be recalled, the tears that cannot be shed—everything will be swallowed along with the trauma that led to the loss. Swallowed and preserved. Inexpressible mourning erects a secret tomb inside the subject. Reconstituted from the memories of words, scenes and affects, the objectal correlative of the loss is buried alive in the crypt.[26]

In this essay, Abraham and Torok draw attention to the ways in which pathological mourning always entails an act of (regressive) psychic cannibalism: The mourner attempts to counteract the primal and traumatic void of speech by swallowing the lost loved object instead. The mouth that is empty of speech stuffs itself with the dead other—who has now become transformed (within the psyche) into an edible, albeit indigestible, object. They write:

> Because our mouth is unable to say certain words and unable to form certain sentences, we fantasize, for reasons yet to be determined, that we are actually taking into our mouth the unnamable, the object itself. As the empty mouth calls out in vain to be filled with introjective speech, it reverts to being the food-craving mouth it was prior to the acquisition of speech. Failing to feed itself on words to be exchanged with others, the mouth absorbs in fantasy all or part of a person—the genuine depository of what is now nameless.[27]

This notion of the crypt—as silent witness to an unspeakable loss—runs through their work and enables them to produce many startling and compelling analyses of their patients' (hitherto) unspeakable primal traumas. However, it is interesting that although Abraham and Torok discuss at least two case histories (including the Wolf Man) in which a male patient "swallows" a dead sister, they do not appear to relate their analyses of crypt formation to questions about sexual difference or to anxieties about the maternal function. But it seems that their work on the crypt might invite reflections on another, potentially even more regressive primordial fantasy at work in the act of "swallowing" the other. Swallowing the dead other in order to keep that dead other alive within can also be read as a kind of primitive inverted confusion between giving birth, burying, and being buried. Here we might recall that even if the other is "ingested" through the mouth, it does not remain there, but must be secreted into the radical "elsewhere" of the crypt. Following this line of thought, we might say that, at the level of the psyche, the belly that receives that swallowed object now becomes haunted by the crypt, and becomes a womb-tomb. Along with its strange topography and its paradoxical function, the crypt has a foundational and conceptual relation to anxieties surrounding the maternal function. This is certainly not to say that the crypt simply determines or is determined by known gender positions, but rather that the questions raised by the crypt (concerning secret relations to the living dead others that inhabit me without my knowledge) are inextricable from the questions raised (for both sexes) concerning the strangeness of the maternal figure.

Keeping these remarks about the crypt in mind, if we now return to Freud's discussion of the derivation of the ancient psychological meanings ascribed to totem animals in *Totem and Taboo*, we discover that, first, early descriptions of the totem share certain qualities with the crypt, and second, totemism itself comes into being in response to a radical confusion about how babies are born. Following Freud (who follows an early theory of James Frazer) we discover that the function of the totem was to provide a "safe place" for the soul by removing it from the confines of the self. Thus, the primordial function of the totem was to provide "a safe place of refuge in which the soul could be deposited and so escape the dangers which threatened it. When a primitive man had deposited his soul into the totem he himself was invulnerable, and he naturally avoided doing any injury to the receptacle of his soul."[28] According to this logic, the totem is the mirror inversion of the crypt: The totem defies death and safeguards the soul by separating it from the life of the subject and placing it in an external, living, receptacle, whereas the crypt defies death by safeguarding the life of the dead other in a secret internal-external receptacle lodged deep within the recesses of the psyche. Both cases, however, are attempts to keep life safe by preserving it in a secret and inviolable container. Furthermore, in the case of the totem as in the case of the crypt there can be no mourning *as such*, because in these uncanny maternal spaces, there is no place for death; death can be neither assimilated nor represented.

In a related passage in *Totem and Taboo*, Freud clearly states that the source of the power given to totemic animals is conceived of by women.

More precisely still, the totemic animal *is conception itself*: It comes into being in order to establish a connection between the idea of conception and the belated fact of childbirth. Freud writes:

> Accordingly, the ultimate source of totemism would be the savages' ignorance of the process by which men and animals reproduce their kind; and, in particular, ignorance of the part played by the male in fertilization. This ignorance must have been facilitated by the long interval between the act of fertilization and the birth of the child (or the first perception of movements). Thus totemism would be a creation of the feminine rather than of the masculine mind: its roots would lie in the "sick fancies of the pregnant woman."[29]

There would be much to say about this. I will limit myself to two quick observations: First, this text highlights not only the importance of the maternal function, but also calls attention to its opacity and its complexity. Maternity is here related to the sacred, to the magical power of thought and to a nonbiological conception of conception. Second, curiously, also, this text offers another way of thinking about the privileged relationship accorded to paternity and animal proxies. Following this thread, we might say that at the moment of conception, the animal displaces the father by taking his place, but at the moment of totemic consumption, the animal restitutes the paternal function by reincarnating him and being eaten in his place.

Bearing the Dead

But in addition to this paternal model of death, there is also another, perhaps somewhat less familiar, conception of death that runs through Freud's writings. In this version, death is radically uncanny. Associated with the maternal function, feminine death is indistinguishable from birth and is conceptualized as a traumatic repetition of it. Freud most famously explores this figure of mother-death in his essays devoted to literature such as "The Theme of the Three Caskets," (1913), "The Uncanny," (1919) and the posthumously published "Medusa's Head" (1940).[30] But we also find it at work in every level of the *Interpretation of Dreams*,[31] in his most famous case history (Wolf Man), as well as in his most bizarre and generally underrated metapsychological text, *Inhibitions, Symptoms and Anxiety*.

In "the Uncanny," for example, Freud famously associates the fear of being buried alive with the fantasy of reentering the maternal body:

> To some people the idea of being buried alive by mistake is the most uncanny thing of all. And yet psycho-analysis has taught us that this terrifying phantasy is only a transformation of another phantasy which had originally nothing terrifying about it at all, but was qualified by a certain lasciviousness—the phantasy, I mean, of intra-uterine existence.[32]

In this phantasy, "death" does not mean death; it is merely an expression of a desire for the mother's body. Buried in the conscious fear of being buried alive is an unconscious wish to *repeat* and *undo* the act of being born by copulating with the mother. It is interesting to note, in passing, that Freud supports this particular claim by referring his readers, in a footnote, to the Wolf Man case history for corroboration. There, Freud argues that the Wolf Man is haunted by an unconscious wish to reenact the scene of his own conception. But as that case history attests (and, as we shall see in more detail in Chapter 3, which is devoted to a detailed analysis of Wolf Man), that very wish is only further evidence of the fact that we can never be "present" to our own birth and therefore that the presumed incontestable "reality" of our birth is, in its own way, as remote and inconceivable to us as our future death.

In "The Theme of the Three Caskets," Freud gives one of his most elaborate and enigmatic articulations of the convergence between the idea of death and the figure of mother. In this short, rich, and deceptively simple text, Freud calls attention to a recurrent theme in literature and myth: that of a suitor who is asked to choose among three women, three sisters, or, as the essay's title indicates, three caskets made of gold, silver, and lead. Drawing upon his own theory of dream symbolism, Freud asserts that "caskets are also women, symbols of what is essential in woman, and therefore of a woman herself—like coffers, boxes, cases, baskets, and so on."[33] But what does it mean to assert that "caskets" are symbols of what is essential in woman? What, after all, is a casket? A receptacle or container, surely. But what does it contain? A casket, after all, can be a coffin as well as a breadbasket or, for that matter, a freezer.

And this is indeed the point of the figure of the "casket": like Pandora's jar, it "represents" what is "essential" in woman through a figure for a container that comes to stand in for that which cannot be contained. Throughout the little essay, Freud traces the twists, turns, and reversals that emerge as the uncanny container is repeatedly filled and voided with sets of seemingly contradictory pairs of opposite meanings; love and death, chance and necessity, womb and tomb. Although the casket always stands in for "what is essential in woman," it conjures up the so-called essential nature of "woman" by showing her in each and every possible symbolic relationship she might have with a man. Thus the casket is explicitly associated with the following female characters: beautiful brides, daughters, sisters, goddesses, and the Fates. In this strange and resonant little essay, it is important to follow the basic line of the argument in order to appreciate the oddness of its lyrical—and quasi-operatic—finale. Freud wonders why the story of the three caskets (in all of its various forms from Shakespeare to Greek mythology) involves choosing the casket that is least desirable (the one made of lead) in order to win the love of the most desirable woman. Midway through the essay, he asserts that the third leaden casket is death and goes on to ask why the myth always portrays the suitor choosing the third, and hence choosing death. "For, after all," he writes, "no one freely chooses death, and it is only by fatality that one falls victim to it." Freud then argues that man's tenacious refusal to accept the reality of death enables him to transform the fact of death into a figure of love in his imagination:

> The third of the sisters was no longer Death; she was the fairest, best, most desirable and most lovable of women. Nor was this substitution in any way technically difficult: it was prepared for by an ancient ambivalence, it was carried along a primaeval line of connection which could not long have been forgotten. . . . The great Mother-goddesses of the oriental peoples, however, all seem to have been creators and destroyers—both goddesses of life and fertility and goddesses of death.[34]

In the final two passages of the essay, Freud suggests that woman (and not just mother) is *always* a figure of death. In the penultimate paragraph, he provides a moving (and troubling) gloss of the end of *King Lear*. Freud reads the image of Lear bearing Cordelia's dead body as a figure for Cordelia as bearer of Lear's death. He writes:

> Lear carries Cordelia's dead body on to the Stage. Cordelia is Death. If we reverse the situation it becomes intelligible and familiar to us. She is the Death-goddess who, like the Valkyrie in German mythology, carries away the dead hero from the battlefield. Eternal wisdom, clothed in the primaeval

> myth, bids the old man renounce love, choose death and make friends with the necessity of dying.[35]

As a figure for death, as Death incarnate, Cordelia becomes the bearer of Lear's death. She contains it for him by rendering it intelligible and meaningful. But because she *is* Death, she herself cannot die. She has no death of her own, nor can her death be mourned. Her death gives meaning to his death. But there is another reason why she can neither die nor can she be mourned.

In the final paragraph of the essay, Freud goes one step further. He argues that the theme of the three caskets that gives rise to the drama that culminates with Cordelia becoming Death is itself an allegory of man's relationship to the mother. He writes:

> We might argue that what is represented here are the three inevitable relations that a man has with a woman—the woman who bears him, the woman who is his mate and the woman who destroys him; or that they are the three forms taken by the figure of the mother in the course of a man's life—the mother herself, the beloved one who is chosen after her pattern, and lastly the Mother Earth who receives him once more. But it is in vain that an old man yearns for the love of woman as he had it from his mother; the third of the Fates alone, the silent Goddess of Death, will take him into her arms.[36]

Following the uncanny and paradoxical logic of the argument, we discover that the casket designates the "essential nature" of all women as containers—or figures—of death. But the death here figured is not recognizable as death. It is an uncanny repetition of birth—a return to a primordial mother who gives death and thereby reclaims the birth that she had supposedly given. It should not be forgotten that this mother-death is no human figure. Ancient and archaic figure for death before the origin of religion, of politics, but not before art, the uncanny figure of mother-death's body incarnates the very threshold of all representability. Mother-death is the container for the uncontainable. But it may be that this primal figure for death haunts and inhabits the psyche of contemporary culture in strange and uncanny ways.

All of which brings us back to the questions about woman and mourning and the chilling enigma of the case of the freezer with which we began. In light of the preceding remarks, we can conclude only with a set of observations and questions rather than any answers. But we might start by observing that this singular case, horrendous and unaccountable as it is, must contain and encrypt some persistent but unmanageable contemporary belief system about women and mourning and mothers and death. The case places Véronique Courjault in the blinding light of the technological public sphere. In it, her monstrous private act becomes part of the public discourse. The recent quasi-epidemic of similar cases (as well as the fact that François Mitterand's illegitimate daughter has written a novel based upon this case) would seem to indicate that something about this story is addressed to the community at large. The case horrifies and fascinates because—in its muteness—it bears witness to some radical failure to mourn something or someone for which the culture has no name, no language, or no place. But perhaps the mute call from the no-place of this maternal crypt calls for the need to begin thinking about mourning differently in order to begin a new kind of work of mourning.

TWO

Mourning, Magic, and Telepathy

Mourning and Magic

There is no mourning without magic, Jacques Derrida will have told us in various ways in numerous texts spanning from the early 1970s up until the end and beyond. And, as we shall see, by linking mourning to magic, Derrida inaugurates a new work on mourning by questioning the very notion that mourning *should* work and by suggesting that this overinvestment in the productive labor power of mourning is too often accompanied by the concurrent need to pathologize the archaic and magical resources of the maternal crypt. When the crypt is pathologized, it becomes a repository for the kind of pathological form of failed mourning that we encountered in the last chapter. In his mourning work, by contrast, Derrida intimates that the crypt need not necessarily be understood as mourning's aberrant and pathological other and that mourning is not only a response to a death but also a figure for the birth of a different kind of subject.

Derrida begins working on mourning, perhaps one should already say "with mourning" in his three major texts of the mid-1970s: *Glas*, "*Fors*," and *Truth in Painting*.[1] This early work on mourning seemingly does something to Derrida's work. Once opened up, the work on mourning does not end. He will go on to speak about mourning, with mourning and in mourning in many of the important texts that follow. And, as he famously puts it in the interview "*Ja*, or the *Faux-Bond*," first published in 1977, mourning—or "semi-mourning" (*demi-deuil*), as he will come to call it—cannot merely be understood as some thing upon which he happens to work, but rather as that force which makes him work:

> But do we already know what mourning is or, a sharper concept that we ought to make use of, *semi-mourning*? Mourning-work as the only motif or motive that would be proper to me, as the only drive tending to reappropriate me even to my own death, but a work *on* mourning, on the work of mourning in general and all its modes (reappropriation, interiorization by introjection *or* incorporation, or between the two—once again, semi-mourning—idealization, nomination, and so forth). To work on mourning, is also, yes, to enter into a practical, effective analysis of mourning, to elaborate the psychoanalytic concept and concepts of mourning. But it is first of all—and by that very token—the operation which would consist in working *on* mourning the way one says that something functions on such and such an energy source, or such and such a fuel—for example, to run on high octane. To the point of exhaustion. And to do one's mourning for mourning.[2]

Mourning, in other words, is not an object of work, but rather its very energy source and driving force. In this sense, one can say that mourning work is what makes work itself work; it is the work of work. This is in keeping with what he says in *Specters of Marx*, for example, when he writes that "mourning is not one kind of work among others. It is work itself, work in general, the trait by means of which one ought perhaps to reconsider the very concept of production."[3] But he will also argue, in the same breath as it were, that if mourning is the work of work, it is precisely because mourning is itself impossible—mourning does not and cannot ever "work" successfully. All work is mourning, but mourning does not work.

"Semi-mourning" is the name that Derrida gives to this paradoxical double bind in the wake of *Glas* and "*Fors*." But in order to appreciate the impossible and duplicitous effects of mourning work, one must return to the texts in which he begins to elaborate it. In passing, I would like to say that there is still much work to be done on these difficult early texts; they are hardly exhausted. There certainly remains more to be said, for example, about the strange "law of obsequence," set forth in *Glas*, which traces the mother's survival as a form of remainder of that which was never present and hence escapes all ontology. One might wonder if—or how—this law of "obsequence" might underwrite mourning work in later texts and inflect the notion of inheritance (between fathers and sons) that he pursues in *Specters of Marx* and elsewhere. At the very least, it bears observing that this spectral presence of a primordial mother "watches over" all his mourning texts.

But for the purposes of this discussion, I would like to return to "*Fors*" for a moment. For it is in "*Fors*" that, arguably for the first time, Derrida borrows a set of concepts from so-called post-Freudian psychoanalysis and incorporates them into his own elaboration of the concept of mourning. Of course, the word "incorporation" is particularly loaded in this context, since it is one of the most important and elusive concepts that he imports *from* psychoanalysis in this very text. We will return to this point. For now, however, I would like to suggest that before "*Fors*," that is, in his earliest treatments of psychoanalytic texts such as "Freud and the Scene of Writing," "The Double Session," and the two Artaud texts in *Writing and Difference*, Derrida approaches Freud's texts by reading them through his own interest in the question of writing and, in so doing, he actively disengages Freud's concepts and claims from a specifically "psychoanalytic" conceptual field.[4] In "*Fors*," however, Derrida approaches the conceptual language of psychoanalysis somewhat differently. In this text, he takes up a set of critical terms and concepts found in the psychoanalytic work of Nicolas Abraham and Maria Torok ("crypt," "fantom," "introjection," and "incorporation"),[5] reworks them, and then takes them into his own writings. In other words, these words that come from encounters with these "psychoanalytic" others become inscribed into his future signature. Thus, in many of the later texts—including the *Post Card*, "Circumfession," *Memoires for Paul de Man*, *Specters of Marx*, *Aporias*, and *Faith and Knowledge* as well as many of the interviews in *Points*[6]—at critical junctures in his argument, he invokes the terms "introjection" and/or "incorporation." In so doing, he conjures up his reading of Abraham and Torok and, along with it, a certain complex and ambivalent relation to the discourse and practice of psychoanalysis itself. It should be clear by now that I am suggesting that Derrida's later complex and ambivalent stance in relation to these specific psychoanalytic terms (appropriation, ex-appropriation, introjection, and incorporation), and subsequently to the singularity of psychoanalytic concepts more generally, is itself instantiated in and through his own reading of them in this difficult and cryptic early text.

Derrida often refers back to "*Fors*" as the source for his later insistence that any notion of the subject "after deconstruction" must be thought and constituted by taking the necessity and inevitability of failed mourning into account. Thus, in an interview with Maurizio Ferraris published in 1990, Derrida explains his understanding of the necessary impossibility of mourning as follows:

> I speak of mourning as the attempt, always doomed to fail (thus a constitutive failure, precisely), to incorporate, interiorize, introject, subjectivize the other in me. Even before the death of the other, the inscription in me of her or his mortality constitutes me. I mourn, therefore, I am, I am—dead with the death of the other, my relation to myself is first of all plunged into mourning, a mourning that is moreover impossible. This is also what I call ex-appropriation, appropriation caught in a double bind. I must and I must not take the other into myself. . . . I explain this more clearly in "*Fors*," the foreword to the *Wolf Man's Magic Word* by Nicolas Abraham and Maria Torok. I suggest there that the opposition between incorporation and introjection, however fruitful it may be, remains of a limited pertinence. Faithful mourning of the other must fail to succeed/by succeeding (it fails, precisely, if it succeeds! It fails because of its success!). There is no successful introjection, there is no pure and simple incorporation. If one wants to reconstruct a concept of the subject "after deconstruction," one has to take this into account.[7]

Supposing, therefore, that one did want to reconstruct a concept of the subject "after deconstruction," what would the subject of the sentence: "I mourn, therefore I am, I am dead—with the death of the other" do with or to psychoanalytic concepts, discourse and method?

As Derrida suggests, the beginning of a response to this question can, indeed, be found in "*Fors*," assuming, that is, that one knows where to look for it and how to read it. Indeed, the question itself is plagued by a difficult relation to place, since it is inscribed in the writings on the crypt around which Derrida's own text is constructed. Here it is worth recalling that "*Fors*" begins with the question, "What is a crypt?" And his text unfolds in response to this enigmatic opening question. Throughout "*Fors*," he will turn around the question of the crypt and the far-reaching implications of its impossible location within the self. Simply put, following Derrida following Abraham and Torok, we can say that the crypt is a secret place, a non-place within the self where the self keeps a dead other safe and hidden even from itself.[8] This foreign body inhabits the self as an internal outside object, thereby destabilizing all possibilities of differentiating the self from its others or even of locating its own boundaries. Derrida writes: "The inhabitant of a crypt is always a living dead, a dead entity we are perfectly willing to keep alive, but as dead, one we are willing to keep, as long as we keep it, within us, intact in any way save as living."[9] As he suggests here, the crypt not only disrupts the concept of self and, with it, conventional ways of thinking about place, but also radically undermines any possible clear distinction between the living and the dead by showing that the living can be inhabited by dead others even as those dead others are "kept alive" artificially in secret safehouses within the self.

Although Derrida's description of the crypt is entirely and explicitly appropriated from Abraham and Torok, his understanding of it differs from theirs in some subtle ways that are important to underscore. And, perhaps by examining these differences, we will get closer to understanding why there is no mourning without magic and what the consequences of such an utterance might be. For Abraham and Torok, the existence of a crypt within the psyche is the proof that the process of "normal" mourning has failed. And, although their work challenges Freud's famous elaboration of the difference between normal and pathological mourning in "Mourning and Melancholia,"[10] they nonetheless subscribe to his notion that so-called normal mourning has a fundamentally different structure from its pathological alternatives. In "Mourning and Melancholia," Freud argues that normal mourning is a form of psychic work in which the self detaches from the world and retreats into itself so that it can, slowly and painfully, disengage the energy it has invested in a love object that no longer exists in order to be able to reclaim that lost energy for itself. In melancholia, however, the psyche refuses to accept the reality of the loss and takes the lost object into the psyche instead. In the text entitled "Mourning or Melancholia: Introjection *versus* Incorporation,"[11] Abraham and Torok modify Freud's description by suggesting that mourning always entails taking the lost object into the self in one way or another. For them, however, in successful mourning, the process they call "introjection," the departed object is successfully consumed: it is fully "ingested," "digested," and "metabolized" until it ultimately becomes assimilated into the self. The lost object is successfully mourned when it becomes an integral part of the "me" who mourns. To this healthy form of psychic cannibalism, they oppose the notion of "incorporation," in which the mourner refuses, as they put it, to swallow the reality of the loss and so swallows the person instead. The departed other, neither living nor dead, disappears, as if by magic, into the hidden crypt that the self secretly builds for it within itself. The disappearance occurs in a flash, as if by magic, and seemingly leaves no trace.

"Magic" is the word Abraham and Torok use to describe how incorporation suddenly takes hold of the psyche. It is the name they give for the way the subject transforms lost loved ones into cryptic word-things that then become inscribed into the very language of the self. They write:

> But the fantasy of incorporation merely simulates profound psychic transformation through magic: it does so by implementing literally something that has only figurative meaning. So in order not to "swallow" a loss, we fantasize swallowing (or having swallowed) that which has been lost, as if it were some kind of thing. The magical "cure" by incorporation exempts the subject from the painful process of reorganization. When, in the form of imaginary or real nourishment, we ingest the love object we miss, this means that we refuse to mourn and that we shun the consequences of mourning even though our psyche is fully bereaved. . . . The fantasy of incorporation reveals a gap within the psyche: it points to something missing just where introjection should have occurred.[12]

According to Abraham and Torok, however much the ersatz mourning of incorporation mimics the process of introjection, they are adamant that the two functions are distinct and must be kept apart. Incorporation, they insist, is a pathological response to an early trauma that cannot be assimilated by the self. In attempting to repair the damage done to it by an early trauma, the self opens up a secret space within into which the internalized living dead are encrypted and kept safe. Safe, that is, from both life and death, since the purpose of incorporation is to make sure that nothing happens to either the self or its incarcerated others.

Throughout "*Fors*," Derrida retraces the distinction between introjection and incorporation made by Abraham and Torok and dismantles it. Meticulously, and through careful argument, he repeatedly shows that however much one might want to maintain a rigorous separation between the two terms, that distinction is untenable. For example, he explains:

> I pretend to keep the dead alive, intact, safe (save) inside me, but only in order to refuse, in a necessarily equivocal way, to love the dead as a living part of me, dead save in me, through the process of introjection, as happens in so-called normal mourning. The question could of course be raised as to whether or not "normal" mourning preserves the object as other (a living person dead) inside me. This question—of the general appropriation and safekeeping of the other *as other*, can always be raised as the deciding factor, but does it not at the same time blur the very line it draws between introjection and incorporation, through an essential and irreducible ambiguity.[13]

In other words, Derrida is here suggesting that in both so-called normal mourning (in which I integrate the lost other into myself) and so-called pathological mourning (in which I keep the other alive within me) there is an irreducible confusion concerning who is preserved or kept alive at the expense of the other. He will go on to argue that these two structures are not only not mutually exclusive but also are implicated in and through one another. He shows that there can be no pure introjection that would remain untouched by the possibility of incorporation, and no pure incorporation without some potential element of introjection.

One reason for this is the word "magic." Indeed, Derrida's divergence from Abraham and Torok can be traced back, in part, to his insistence on elaborating some of the consequences of their derivation of the psychic power of magic words. In his restatement of their claims, via a kind of transvaluation of the word "magic," he asserts not only that "magic" is key to incorporation, but also that incorporation itself calls for a rethinking of magic:

> Faced with the impotence of the process of introjection (gradual, slow, laborious, mediated, effective), incorporation is the only choice: fantasmatic, unmediated, instantaneous, magical, sometimes hallucinatory. Magic (the Wolf Man himself will resort to a "magic word" to silently commemorate—his word is also a word-thing and a "mute word"—the act of incorporation)—magic is already recognized, in the 1968 article, as the very element of incorporation. Anasemia of reading: The new concept of incorporation thus tells us more about magic than the ordinary conception of magic—which everyone thinks he is sure of—reveals about an aspect of incorporation.[14]

What, therefore, does incorporation tell us about how magic works? And why is this work of magic critical to the formation of the so-called subject and ultimately to the notion of work itself? Although I cannot do justice to these questions, I would like to sketch out some provisional lines of thought. If incorporation tells us something about magic, it is because it tells us something about the various ways in which language works or does not. The crypt, after all, is magically made of words that no longer simply signify. Made up of bits of words that resemble hieroglyphs, "magic" words do not function "properly": They violate the distinction between literal and figural, they cannot be gathered up and contained under any proper name and, perhaps most significantly, they bear witness to alternative realities without representing them. As Derrida carefully points out, the words that constitute the crypt neither connote nor denote a given reality; instead, they are the poetic traces of an event that was never "present." He writes: "The referent is constructed in such a way as never to present itself 'in person,' not even as the object of a theoretical discourse within the traditional norms. . . . The 'narrated' event, reconstituted by a novelistic, mythico-dramatico-poetic genesis, never appears."[15] Another way of saying this is to say that magic words work the way literature works and, like literature, they displace the categories of the status of an event, the notion of place, the separation between the possible and impossible, and they open up a divide between that which can be scientifically verified and that which is "poetically true."

At this juncture it might be helpful to recall that throughout "*Fors*," Derrida calls particular attention to the way in which *The Wolf Man's Magic Word* is written "like a novel, a poem, a myth, or a drama, the whole thing in a plural translation, productive and simultaneous."[16] He then goes on to point out that the proliferating and polyvocal literary production at work in the writing of the case is inextricable from its analytic work. And that analytic work is therefore only made possible by magic. In order to work on magic words, one must work magic with words as "magic words" do not lend themselves to interpretation, they cannot be deciphered, exactly; they do not constitute a code that can be cracked by any unlocking key. The only way to approach these anasemic word things is by a singular act of reading. And that singular act of reading would therefore also necessarily be a singular act of writing the words of the other in translation. This is the basis of all reading; without magic words, there is no language of the other, hence no reading as such, and no subject to be read. Moreover, as Derrida insists throughout "*Fors*," the anasemia at work in the crypt cannot be understood as a pathological accident that happens to an already constituted subject, rather it is its very condition of possibility. By the same token, the discovery of the crypt cannot be limited to exceptional or pathological cases; instead, it calls for a radical displacement of all familiar topologies of the self and disrupts the metaphysical underpinnings of traditional Freudian metapsychology.

Incorporation, therefore, and the magical proclivities of language associated with it are not exceptional and pathological occurrences; they are the processes out of which something like a subject comes into being. The subject "after deconstruction" is produced by the crypt and remains inhabited and haunted by its innumerable unnamed and unnamable encrypted others. This is why the subject who emerges from the crypt says, "I mourn, therefore I am—I am dead with the death of the other." As we have seen, however, this necessarily impossible mourning is made possible by the work of magic. Magic is not only a name for the force that keeps death alive, but it is also a name for that magic force that works to make another kind of life possible. That is, moreover, what Derrida suggests in *H.C. for Life, That Is to Say*,[17] where he returns to Freud's writing on animism in *Totem and Taboo* to conjure up a poetico-performative magical form of writing that, in the very act of doing the impossible also bears witness to impotence and vulnerability; such a writing writes life before life and beyond life, and writes of a mode of living that would neither be defined in opposition to death nor be compelled to exclude it. But if all work is mourning, and there is no mourning without magic, then magic itself would have to be rethought as a force—indeed perhaps something like a drive—a drive that does the impossible, without force, without power, and unbound by any known economy.

The Magic of Telepathy

Magic appears in almost every text in which Derrida speaks about psychoanalysis after "*Fors*," Magic shows up in particularly interesting ways surrounding the question of the "work of mourning" in the Marx book. It is also ubiquitous in the texts on Freud after *The Post Card*: "Telepathy" and "My Chances/Mes Chances: A Rendezvous with Some Epicurean Stereophonies."[18] In these texts, as is well known, Derrida demonstrates how despite Freud's attempts to banish both magic and literature from his metapsychology, his work is continuously haunted by both. In this sense, literature and magic are exemplarily excluded from a certain traditional psychoanalytic model of the psyche.

But let us recall here that "*Fors*" is not merely "about" how mourning and magic constitute the crypt: the text of "*Fors*" is itself a crypt of sorts. This powerfully occult work occupies an eccentrically central place in the Derridean corpus. As we have said, in the years immediately following "*Fors*," Derrida increasingly devoted his attention to psychoanalysis by writing a series of major texts on it beginning, most notably, with *The Post Card* but also including important occasional pieces such as "Telepathy," "My Chances/Mes Chances," "Me—Psychoanalysis," and "'Geopsychoanalysis' and the Rest of the World."[19] Although these latter texts were originally published separately as articles or chapters in collective volumes, they were subsequently gathered together and published in *Psyche*. They were all reprinted except "*Fors*." This exceptional text (whose title, the French word "*Fors*," means "except for") remains one of the very few major texts written by Jacques Derrida that was never published or reprinted in a book bearing his signature in the place of the author. The only published incarnation of "*Fors*" is as the preface to the book signed by Nicolas Abraham and Maria Torok. Within that book, Derrida's text functions something like an internal outside, or a "foreign body."

The strange shared textual space produced by the relation between Derrida's "exceptional" preface and the text by Abraham and Torok produces some strange effects and seemingly exerts an uncanny influence on the fate of that particular book, as well as more generally on the future work of all concerned. The book entitled *Le verbier de l'homme aux loups* is haunted by the various ways in which Derrida's prefatory text lies both *inside* and *outside* the ongoing psychoanalytic practice of its primary authors. Moreover, this haunting effect becomes even more visible when, in the English translation, two new texts are added to the already strange body of the original book: a long translator's introduction, by Nicholas Rand, and a new "Afterword" by Maria Torok.[20] According to Torok's account, this afterword makes use of newly available archival material (from the Freud-Ferenczi correspondence) that sheds new light on her reading of the Wolf Man case history by establishing a link between the actual person "Sergei Pankeiev Wolf Man" and Freud's account of the case of the patient called

"Mr. P" in the (fake) lecture entitled "Dreams and Occultism."[21] As we shall see, it is no accident that she makes these new discoveries about the case via an interpretation of Freud's discussion of "Telepathy."

At this juncture, it is important to point out a number of curious details concerning the relation between the original French text of *Le verbier de l'homme aux loups* and its 1986 English counterpart, *The Wolf Man's Magic Word*). First, the original French book included an extra (detachable) text by Derrida known in French as the "*prière d'insérer*." Although this text disappears from subsequent French editions, a short excerpt of it does appear on the back cover of the original French text. An even shorter excerpt of it appears as a blurb on the back cover of the English translation. However, on the back cover of the 1998 French paperback Champs Flammarion edition, Derrida's text magically disappears entirely. Second, in its place is a blurb by Abraham and Torok's English translator, Nicholas Rand. In the English translation of the book, Derrida's "preface," "*Fors*: Les mots anglés de Nicolas Abraham et Maria Torok," is now called a "foreword" and the word "foreword" is magically incorporated into the text's new title: "Foreword: *Fors*: The Anglish Words of Nicolas Abraham and Maria Torok." The supplementary English word "foreword" now comes *before* the cryptic French word "*Fors*" in the text's title and "Foreword" appears as the "titular header" of every page of the translation. Furthermore, Derrida's "Foreword," which comes *before* the translator's "Introduction" to the book as a whole, is in fact not translated by Nicholas Rand, but by Barbara Johnson. This is so because her translation of Derrida's text appeared in *The Georgia Review* in 1977 and hence was published nine years prior to (and separately from) Rand's subsequent English translation of the rest of the book. Third, Maria Torok explicitly presents her "Afterword" to the book by explaining its genesis as follows: Her text is a translation of an article originally published in French in 1983 based on a lecture originally given in England, in 1981, at a conference devoted to the topic of "Telepathy."

Thus, the English book is not merely a translation of the French work; it is also a transformation of it. The French book is simultaneously incorporated and encrypted within the new foreign body of the translation. The new book contains new material (the added texts by Rand and Torok) and new voices (via the translations and translator's notes by both Rand and Johnson) and has a new formal structure. *The Wolf Man's Magic Word* now opens with the "Foreword" by Jacques Derrida and closes with the

"Afterword" by Maria Torok, thereby establishing a formal symmetry between the two. But what lines of communication (if any) are opened up between these two liminal "words"? On one level, it might appear that the relation between these two texts is purely contingent, as Derrida never mentions telepathy in his "Foreword" on the crypt, and Torok never mentions Derrida in her "Afterword" on telepathy. Nonetheless, as we will see, these two texts are profoundly and obscurely connected, precisely through "Telepathy." Furthermore (and this is the premise for the remarks that follow), the "telepathic" link at work between these two particular texts is itself an inevitable consequence of, and corollary to, the notion of the crypt as Derrida described it in "*Fors.*" At the risk of sounding too cryptic, we might say that Derrida's interrogation of the subject of the crypt anticipates—or even *foretells*—Torok's later invocation of the subject of telepathy; the "foreign body" that haunts the subject from the external inside of the crypt obeys the same occult logic as the "foreign body" that Freud explicitly invokes in his discussion of telepathy in "Dreams and Occultism."[22]

At this point, perhaps it would be a good idea to take a closer look at how Maria Torok explicitly conjures up this Freudian "foreign body" to explain both why she works on telepathy and how she puts "Telepathy" to work in her clinical case presentation of the Wolf Man. Torok writes:

> At a colloquium held in England in 1981 at Brunel University on the topic of telepathy, I put forward the idea that *telepathy* was probably the name Freud unwittingly gave to a foreign body within the corpus of psychoanalysis, a foreign body that retains its own individuality, walls, and partitions. At that time I stated hopefully, "One day perhaps the Freud-Ferenczi correspondence, which is being kept in this country in some (outer) safe, will say with precision what the two friends Ferenczi-Freud were looking to read in each other through the *medium* called telepathy. It will then be possible to recognize the words of a secretly kept story, hidden elsewhere and by a beyond, in a hitherto unknown psychic topography and in a hitherto undiscovered dynamics. Telepathy could thus be seen as the precursor to a type of research that dares to regard the imagination as regards oneself and others, that refuses to be imprisoned in systems, mythologies, and universal symbolic equivalents. Telepathy would be the name of an ongoing and groping research that—at the moment of its emergence and in the area of its relevance—had not yet grasped either the true scope of its enquiry or the conceptual rigor of its elaboration." Today I think I am in a better position to begin to explore the contents of this

> foreign body, the unique formation awaiting analysis: a crypt that threw psychoanalysts, Freud included, into confusion in the 1920s. The Freud-Ferenczi correspondence—which I hoped would one day emerge from its safe—has now become available to me, and the words of a secret story concerning the case of the Wolf Man are slowly regaining their power in and for speech.[23]

In this passage from the "Afterword," Torok refers back to her earlier 1981 lecture in order to elucidate her analytic method. "Telepathy," she claims, is Freud's name for a strange "foreign body" emanating from *within* psychoanalysis that threatens to destabilize its methods and trouble its borders. But where Freud attempts to keep this "foreign body" out of psychoanalysis so as to contain its disruptive effects, Torok proposes to open up psychoanalysis to the hidden potential of its uncanny internal outcast. More radically still, she proposes to put telepathy to work *for* psychoanalysis by drawing upon the force of its occult magic for analytic practice. Psychoanalysis, she suggests, needs to work with telepathy in order to free itself from the confines of rigid models of the psyche so that it will become able to account for the reality of certain kinds of hidden and powerful psychic events that have hitherto eluded its purview. She therefore proposes that telepathy should become the name for a new form of analytic interpretation capable of unleashing the power of the imagination in order to uncover the secret forces that have forged occult pathways to forgotten crypts buried alive deep within the psyche.

Furthermore, in the passage from the "Afterword" cited before, Torok's discussion of the power of telepathy is curiously reenacted at the level of the text itself. She cites her former self predicting a future role for telepathy in psychoanalysis as a kind of retroactive prescient validation of the importance that telepathy will have played in her new analysis of the Wolf Man's case. But who is speaking here in the name of what sort of knowledge? Torok's text becomes strangely divided against itself by the two voices at work within it: Her earlier speaking voice calls out to telepathy to discover an unknown and secret future for psychoanalysis, whereas her current written voice invokes telepathy as a medium through which she becomes able to uncover hidden secrets and reveal hidden truths. In other words, Torok's telepathic text seems to conjure up the power of telepathy in two very different ways: On one hand, telepathy appears as an occult force that troubles known categories by forging new and inventive associative relations, while on the other hand, it seems to become something like a super power tool capable of opening up sealed crypts and cracking safes in order to expose the secrets locked within.

It is important to distinguish between these two different incarnations of telepathic power as they correspond to two very different approaches to the act of reading itself. Simply put, at stake is the difference between understanding the magical power of telepathy as a deconstructive poetics and as a psychoanalytic hermeneutics of interpretation. In the latter instance, telepathy runs the risk of losing touch with its "occult" nature by transforming its magic into a form of revelatory power that claims the capacity to produce new discourses of truth and knowledge. Deployed in this way, telepathy grants itself the power to unlock secrets hidden in the psyche by exposing them to the light of interpretation. Recalling our earlier discussion of the magical work of mourning in Derrida's "*Fors*," we might describe a deconstructive approach to telepathic reading as an encounter with an uncanny foreign body that forever remains inaccessible—not because it was ever hidden, but because the singular event of its literary inscription resists any translation into any known or knowable language. For Derrida, the necessity for this kind of "telepathic" reading emerges as an ineluctable consequence of the structure of the crypt and is put to work in every true encounter with any literary text. Although we can find different elaborations of this approach to reading virtually everywhere in Derrida's writings, he explicitly establishes the connection between the crypt and the act of reading in the following passage on Baudelaire's prose poem, "Counterfeit Money," in *Given Time*:

> The interest of "Counterfeit Money" like any analogous text in general, comes from the enigma constructed out of this crypt which gives to be read that which will remain *eternally* unreadable, absolutely indecipherable, even refusing itself to any promise of deciphering or hermeneutic.[24]

I would suggest that Maria Torok's deliriously ingenious "Afterword" to *The Wolf Man's Magic Word* vacillates between deconstructive reading and psychoanalytic hermeneutics and engages elements of both. However, to the extent that she is adamant about having "solved" the mystery of the identity of the patient "Mr. P" from "Dreams and Occultism" by proving—via telepathy—that he *is* indubitably Wolf Man Sergei Pankeiev, her text paradoxically loses some of its magic.

At this point, I would like to return to the question asked earlier regarding the "telepathic" relation between Torok's "Afterword" and Derrida's "Foreword." As I have already remarked, Torok makes no mention of Derrida in her writing on telepathy. Torok's text, however, manifests a close and uncanny telepathic connection to Derrida's writings. As fate would have it, in 1981, the year in which Maria Torok first gave her lecture on "Dreams and Occultism" at the conference on telepathy in England, Jacques Derrida published a text on telepathy in French, called "*Télépathie*,"[25] that was, like Torok's "Afterword," devoted to a close reading of Freud's "Dreams and Occultism." Like Torok, Derrida is also fascinated with Freud's discussion of the "foreign body" in the text and with the mysterious patient known as "Mr. P." And, in the closing passages of "Telepathy," Derrida writes:

> Who was Mr. P.? Plato the master thinker [*maître-penseur*], the postmaster [*maître des postes*], but still, soothsayer [*devine*], at that date. . . . So psychoanalysis (and you're still following the fold line) resembles an adventure of modern rationality set on swallowing and simultaneously rejecting the foreign body named Telepathy, assimilating it and vomiting it up without making up its mind to do one or the other. Translate all that in terms of the politics—internal and external—of the psychoanalytic state (c'est moi). The "conversion" is not a resolution or a solution, it is still the speaking scar of the foreign body.[26]

Despite the fact that there is no overt link between Torok's "Afterword" and Derrida's "Telepathy" or any way of knowing (from the texts themselves) whether or not there was any conscious communication between the two writers regarding their respective readings of "Dreams and Occultism," there is an uncanny, telepathic connection between these two texts that resembles something like a comic, long distance conversation. "Who is Mr. P.?" asks Derrida's text and Torok's text promptly responds: "Mr. P. is Sergei Pankeiev Wolf Man."[27] But what makes this exchange so funny—and so interesting—is the way in which this telepathic communication becomes paradoxically productive through the irreducible distance and disconnection between the two parties concerned. In other words, although both Derrida and Torok appear to speak *to* each other through their common question, "Who is Mr. P?" the telepathic nature of this conversation produces a different kind of encounter between them. This encounter is paradoxically made possible by its very failure to establish open lines of communication. In this sense, Derrida and Torok speak together "telepathically" in the many ways in which they speak *through* each other's magic words. Thus, if we return to Derrida's text, we can discern Abraham and Torok's encrypted absent-presence in "Telepathy" through his description of telepathy's relation to psychoanalysis in the very cannibalistic language that he first derives from their psychoanalytic concepts of incorporation and introjection in "*Fors*":

> So psychoanalysis . . . resembles an adventure of modern rationality set on swallowing and simultaneously rejecting the foreign body named Telepathy, assimilating it and vomiting it up without making up its mind to do one or the other.

Furthermore, as Derrida's readers know well, the text of "Telepathy" is itself something like a crypt.[28] As he explains in its inaugural footnote, this text (comprising a series of "postcards" dated from July 9 to July 15, 1979) was apparently accidently misplaced and therefore was omitted from its intended place as part of the "Envois" section of *The Post Card*. As a remainder of the *Post Card* that can never recover its lost place within the economy of that book, "Telepathy" both incarnates the nowhere topology of the crypt, and obeys the telepathic logic that forges unknown paths of communication between unknowing subjects. Moreover, it should be clear by now that telepathy is not simply located *inside* "Telepathy," nor can it be contained within the borders of any single text. It is a name for the strange way in which texts speak through each other's secret languages. Therefore, as I have been suggesting from the beginning, there is no telepathy without a crypt, no crypt without telepathy. The "foreign body" of telepathy comes into being from the haunted recesses of the crypt. If the crypt is the figure for the "subject after deconstruction," then telepathy is a name for the language of that subject. The telepathic language of the crypt cannot be located anywhere, but its traces haunt every subject, every literary text, every utterance, and it works—by magic.

THREE

The Sexual Animal and the Primal Scene of Birth

The Wolf Man's Afterlife and the Primal Scene of Birth

If the case history popularly referred to by the animal nickname of his most famous patient, "the Wolf Man," remains Freud's most notorious clinical case, it is in part because it has never been closed.[1] On the contrary: not only has this case resolutely resisted all forms of closure (clinical, theoretical, textual), but "the Wolf Man" also continues to thrive in what can only be described as an unprecedented clinical and textual afterlife. Since Freud first prematurely declared his patient "cured" in 1914, Wolf Man has both been the object of numerous clinical and theoretical papers in psychoanalysis (by Freud himself as well as by numerous others) and provided influential material for work in a wide variety of disciplines other than psychoanalysis, including philosophy, literary theory, literary criticism, art history, and studies in gender and sexuality.[2] In his many returns, Wolf Man has continued to spawn new clinical approaches to psychoanalysis, new metapsychological theories, and new literary conceptions of topics ranging from narrative temporality to insights on dreams, fairy tales, and various forms of haunting, trauma, and failed mourning.

Sergei Pankeiev, the biographical person behind the psychoanalytic construct "Wolf Man," died in 1979 at the age of ninety-two after having survived two world wars, Nazi control of Austria, financial ruin, exile, and the suicides of his sister and his wife. He lived much of his long life, however, as "the Wolf Man," having famously appropriated the persona of his psychoanalytic avatar for his own financial, libidinal, and professional ends, even choosing to write and publish his own memoirs under the hybrid animal name given to him by psychoanalysis rather than in his own name. During his long career as a psychoanalytic patient, "the Wolf Man" underwent multiple (and sometimes recurring) treatments: two analyses with Freud (the first conducted in 1910–1914 and the second in 1923), a follow-up analysis with Freud's disciple Ruth Mack Brunswick (who originally published her account as "A Supplement to Freud's 'History of an Infantile Neurosis'" in 1928, and then subsequently supplemented her own supplement with a further update in 1945), and a parapsychoanalytic engagement with Muriel Gardiner (who in 1971 edited a volume under the title *The Wolf Man by the Wolf Man* in which his own autobiographical writings and personal reflections on his analytic history first appeared in English translation—unreadable for him—alongside Ruth Mack Brunswick's clinical report as well as other documents pertaining to the case).[3]

The collection of texts in Muriel Gardiner's edited volume also provided much of the primary source material for Nicolas Abraham and Maria Torok's provocative and innovative textually based clinical reassessment of the case that was first published in French as *Le verbier de l'homme aux loups* in 1976, and then again in an expanded English translation under the title *The Wolf Man's Magic Word* in 1986—nearly a decade after the deaths of Abraham and of the patient known as Wolf Man. As we have already indicated in the previous two chapters, Abraham and Torok derive their radical reconception of failed mourning and the concept of the crypt (which they understand as a "magical" incorporation of an undead and unmourned other who becomes secretly entombed within the structure of the psyche) in large part through their retroactive reworking of untreated primal material from Freud's case.

As Abraham and Torok point out (and as all other readers of the case know well), Freud himself returned repeatedly and obsessively to the material in this case up until the very end. More or less explicit references to Wolf Man can be found in "The Occurrence in Dreams of Material from Fairy Tales" (1913), "*Fausse reconnaissance* (Déjà Raconté) in Psychoanalytic Treatment" (1914), "Remembering, Repeating, and Working Through" (1914), "Repression" (1915), "The Uncanny" (1919), *Inhibitions, Symptoms and Anxiety* (1926), "Analysis Terminable and Interminable" (1937), and the posthumously published unfinished paper, "Splitting of the Ego in the Process of Defense" (1941). This list, however, is hardly exhaustive. Tracking latent traces of the Wolf Man in Freud's writings has fascinated many of Freud's readers. In *The Wolf Man's Magic Word*, for example, Abraham and Torok present a compelling case for the idea that Wolf Man also served as the model for the patient, described by Freud in the "Fetishism" essay, whose fetishistic interest in a "shine on the nose" (*Glanz auf der Nase*) had to be heard as an utterance with meaning in multiple languages and hence translated in order to be interpreted.[4]

Because the Wolf Man raises many (if not all) of psychoanalysis's most tricky technical questions and intractable conceptual stumbling blocks, it is perhaps no accident that Freud returns to this case repeatedly in many of his very final papers. Most notably, he tacitly alludes to the Wolf Man's status as his most obstinately interminable case in the title he gives to his 1937 paper "Analysis Terminable and Interminable" as well as in the paper itself where he openly acknowledges his longstanding fascination with this case in a striking passage that has become justifiably famous:

> When he left me in the midsummer of 1914, with as little suspicion as the rest of us what lay so shortly ahead, I believed that his cure was radical and permanent. In a footnote added to this patient's case history in 1923, I have already reported that I was mistaken. . . . Thanks to the skills of one of my pupils, Dr. Ruth Mack Brunswick, a short course of treatment has on each occasion brought these conditions [attacks of illness] to an end. . . . In other attacks, however, the pathogenic material consisted of pieces of the patient's childhood history, which had not come to light while I was analyzing him and which now came away—the comparison is unavoidable—like sutures after an operation, or small fragments of necrotic bone. I have found the history of the patient's recovery scarcely less interesting than that of his illness.[5]

But what if the long history of the Wolf Man's interminable "recovery" (as Freud wishfully puts it)—marked as it is by the tenacity of intractable primal matter that does not in fact fall away like necrotic bone, but rather persists and asserts its stubborn claims on the patient as well as on all his analysts—were inscribed in the very structure and foundations of the case itself?

At this point, it is important to recall that the actual title of this case is, of course, not "Wolf Man" but rather *From the History of an Infantile Neurosis*. Freud's explicitly stated aim in the case is to analyze a primordial *infantile* neurosis retroactively by reconstructing the childhood illness through the residual traces, sediments, and recollections that have been deposited in the psyche and that later become manifest in the adult during the treatment. Freud's rather astonishing working premise in this case is this: In order to gain the maximum access possible to the earliest psychic material, it is preferable to *increase* (rather than decrease) the quantity of time separating the original childhood trauma from its subsequent analysis. In an extraordinary passage from the opening pages of the case, Freud writes:

> Analyses which lead to a favourable conclusion in a short time are of value in ministering to the therapist's self-esteem and substantiate the medical importance of psychoanalysis; but they remain for the most part insignificant as regards the advancement of scientific knowledge. Nothing new is learnt from them. Something new can only be gained by analyses that present special difficulties, and to the overcoming of these a great deal of time has to be devoted. Only in such cases do we succeed in descending to the deepest and most primitive strata of mental development and in gaining from there the solutions for the problems of later formations. And we feel afterwards that, strictly speaking, only an analysis which has penetrated so far deserves the name. Naturally, a single case does not have all the information that we should like to have. Or, to put it more correctly, it might teach us everything, if only we were in a position to make everything out, and if we were not compelled by the inexperience of our own perception to content ourselves with a little.[6]

To recapitulate: Short analyses make the analyst feel good because they tend to produce anticipated and desired results. They are of limited value, however, because they restrict their scope of inquiry to known material and knowable problems. "Something new" can be learned only by cases that present special difficulties. Those cases have a special relationship to time: they take more time—indeed perhaps even an interminable amount of time—because they succeed in descending into "the most primitive strata of mental development." Freud seems to be suggesting that there is an inverse relationship between the time of the treatment and the depth of the analysis: as the treatment moves forward in time, the analysis recedes inexorably into the shady mists of a time out of time—to a prehistoric past that constitutes the (otherwise) inaccessible and unknowable deepest and most primitive strata of the psyche.

Given what we have just said, it follows that *From the History of an Infantile Neurosis* (also called "Wolf Man") is a very special case indeed. It also follows that all of the technical questions concerning the duration of the treatment in the original case as well as in its various sequels (ranging from Freud's initial decision to examine the childhood trauma via the adult patient to his decision to impose a deadline on the analysis in order to attempt to put an end to it) are inextricably bound up with the treatment of the question of time itself. But if this case is as special as it seems to be, exactly what is the "something new" that can be learned from it? Judging from the amount of time that this special case has already demanded, it would seem, following the logic presented above, that this case leads us to the deepest strata of the psyche imaginable. Or indeed perhaps even deeper still.

The name that Freud famously gives to this encounter with the most primitive strata of the psyche in this special case is, of course, "the primal scene." Although I will explore the complexities of this difficult temporal concept in greater detail later in this chapter, I would like at this point to propose some general ways of thinking about the significance of the primal scene both for this case and as a conceptual figure that is central to the overall concerns of this book as a whole. At its most basic level, the psychoanalytic term "primal scene" generally refers to an early, traumatic, formative event during which a young child witnesses his parents copulating at an age when he is too young to understand what he has seen. In Freud's exposition of the primal scene in this special case, however, the concept becomes considerably more complicated: on the basis of a dream about wolves that the child/patient has several years after the fact (and that in no way explicitly depicts the actions of the scene in question), Freud retroactively reconstructs the existence of the earlier event of coitus despite the fact that the only witness to that event comes in the form of a dream and that the event itself can never be made available to memory.

Before turning to a close reading of the primal scene in Freud's text, I would like to sketch out some preliminary propositions about how I am thinking about it here. More specifically, I would like to suggest that Freud's convoluted elaboration of the primal scene in *From the History of an Infantile Neurosis* can be read according to three separate (but related) conceptual paradigms:

A Fabulous Fable. The primal scene is a fabulous fable that enables Freud to provide an account for the emergence of a specifically *human* subjectivity that is born from an animal-like infantile sexuality but that is nonetheless distinct from the realm of natural animal sexual instincts. Like the fable of the origin of religion (via the primal murder and consumption of the primal father's totem) that Freud recounts in *Totem and Taboo* and which he wrote and published during the years that Wolf Man was in treatment with him, the function of the fable of the primal scene is to provide a story about how humans became human through the birth of the unconscious.

A Fantasmatic Image. Whereas in *Totem and Taboo* Freud provides us with a narrative—a Kiplingesque "just-so" primal myth that recounts the story of how, once upon a time, the whole of human culture was born—in *Wolf Man*, by contrast, he presents us with something analogous to a psychic "snapshot" (in the form of the dream about wolves) of the precise moment in each human infant's life during which he or she becomes born as a human subject. As we shall see, the crucial piece of evidence on which the entire case hinges is a special kind of dream image that operates more like a magical psychic photographic apparatus than it does like a normal dream. Freud presents his documentary dream text in two ways: through a verbal description of the dream image and by reproducing a famous picture of the wolf dream, drawn by the Wolf Man himself, which lurks in the pages of Freud's text like a photographic foreign body.[7] As purveyor of the primal scene, the dream image not only bears witness to an event that the dreamer himself is unable to see (as it happened before he was "born" as a subject), it also precipitates his subsequent passage into subjectivity.

A Fantastic Figure for the Interminability of Birth. From what we have already said (and on the basis of the very temporal structure of the primal scene itself) it follows that birth cannot be confined to the moment of our biological entry into the world nor can its status as psychic event be located there. By looking at the primal scene as a fantastic figure for birth itself, the event of birth emerges as interminable and uncanny process that haunts us throughout our lifetime, speaks to us through its mechanical repetitions, and whose meaning only makes itself known to us retroactively.

Before moving on to a closer look at the text of the Wolf Man case, I would like to make one final remark about its "special" status. As we have already intimated, this case is not merely the textual site of Freud's most radical articulation of the concept of the primal scene *in* psychoanalysis, the case itself constitutes something of a primal scene *for* psychoanalysis as well. Indeed, this uncontainable case paradoxically "contains" traces of all of psychoanalysis's most unresolved issues, enigmatic claims, and essential insights regarding: infantile sexuality, hysteria, constitutive bisexuality, dreamwork, screen memories, anal eroticism, masochism, splitting, mourning and melancholia, animal phobias, castration, somatic compliance, fantasies of intrauterine existence, primal phantasies, and primal repression. In short, special case that it is, the case of Wolf Man is something like a fantasmatic dream text that amalgamates the entire metapsychological apparatus and many of the papers on technique into a fabulous narrative. Seen in this way, *Wolf Man* resembles something like a repository for all the ideas and concepts for which Freud is unable to find a suitable resolution through theoretical argumentation or clinical proof. Unmoored from a metapsychology that cannot account for them, these errant figures of psychoanalytic thought return in the many fantastic forms of fiction that appear in this interminable case. In other words, *Wolf Man* repeats and recapitulates the primal scene of the birth of psychoanalysis itself.

Sexual Animals and the Primal Scene

In Freud's case history, the animals are primal. In contrast to the folkloric figure of the Werewolf, which depicts man as capable of becoming or returning to animal life, in *Wolf Man* Freud grapples with the inverse problem: How, why, and when does the animal-like substratum of the human psyche, sexuality, give birth to human subjectivity? Throughout the case, Freud attempts to grapple with the fact that the specificity of human subjectivity is grounded in a relation to sexuality that renders us simultaneously too close and too far from the realm of animals. Although animals populate virtually every page of *Wolf Man*, however, very little has been said about the status of the animal as such.[8] Indeed, it may be almost impossible to speak about the animal "as such," precisely because the many animals and animal figures in the case operate at so many different and mutually exclusive levels of reality and psychic organization. There is in fact a vertiginous array of fauna, a veritable bestiary in the text. Aside from the famous wolves, there are important references to: sheep, sheep-dogs, flies and beetles, caterpillars, snakes, horses, a wasp, goats, a fledgling bird, a giant caterpillar, a snail, and, finally, a swallow-tail butterfly that, we discover, is a second animal incarnation of the same anxiety that produced the famous wolf dream. Some of these animals are representations that come from fairytales and picture books, some are produced as dream images, and some are animals encountered in the world. And some are animals that stand in for humans. In short, the animals are not always, or not simply, animals. More problematically still, it seems that animals can move from one status to another with remarkable flexibility. Animal figures operate at every level of the case and intervene in complicated ways in its conceptual framework. Indeed, in what follows, I hope to demonstrate that animals occupy a critical, albeit somewhat obscure, role in many if not most of the major theoretical issues raised by the case. These would include: the temporal status of the primal scene and the structure of *Nachträglichkeit*, the relationship between primal scene and primal fantasies, the specificity of infantile sexuality, primal repression and the formation of the unconscious, castration and sexual difference, and the grounds for establishing the distinction between "animal" instinct (*Instinkt*) and "human" drive (*Trieb*).[9]

Before going any further, I want to make it clear that I am certainly not arguing in favor of an unproblematic continuity between human and animal realms. On the contrary, I hope to argue that, paradoxically, the animals in the text serve as strange indices to the very specificity of the human psyche. My aim in looking more closely at them is to bring the enigma of human sexuality and subjectivity more clearly into focus. Bizarrely, in what follows, it will emerge that one of the defining traits of being human is the incorporation of animal figures within the psyche; these internal animal figures are uncanny traces of our radical alterity and separation from animals.

Let me begin by returning to the famous primal scene itself. In an attempt to demonstrate the fundamental role played by infantile sexuality in individual psychic life, Freud dedicates his entire case to the derivation and discussion of the strange event he calls the "*Urzene*," the primal scene. As readers of Freud know well, the term "primal scene" refers to Freud's reconstruction of an early, traumatic event: an act of coitus witnessed by the patient when he was too young to comprehend what he was seeing. On the basis of a subsequent childhood dream about wolves, analyzed as part of a treatment of the adult patient, Freud meticulously reconstitutes the existence of the traumatic event, the presumed date of its occurrence, and the precise details of the sexual content in the scene. In order to understand why this scene is so important for Freud, it is important to keep in mind that the precipitating event can never be recovered by memory because it occurred before the infant had developed the capacity either to remember it or to understand it. The dream that the child produces two and a half years later therefore serves both as a belated recognition of the meaning of the scene and as a psychic response to it.

In thinking about the primal scene, it is important not to lose sight of the fact that the scene itself happens "twice," as it were, and involves at least two different events. In the first instance, there is the "real" external event witnessed by the infant. Because the precipitating event was "seen" without being assimilated, traces left by the images that were not understood from the first scene reappear, belatedly, in the dream about wolves that takes place several years later. The first, traumatic event is both represented *in* the dream and reactivated *by* it. What this means is that the dream is not only a belated reproduction of the initial scene, but also that the dream itself constitutes a new event as well.

The "primal scene" must thus be understood as the relationship between these two limit events. The first, ostensibly "real" event is something that happens to the infant *before* the development of the unconscious, while the second event, the wolf dream, is not only entirely produced *by* the unconscious but is also evidence of its prior formation. Both events are traumatic in nature: The initial event overwhelms the infant and in so doing *activates* the psychic mechanisms from which the unconscious will be formed, whereas the dream about wolves is the psychic trace of an overpowering anxiety coming from within.

Almost all of the determining events in the case history take place during the time between these two traumas. Indeed, the "reconstructed" chronology that Freud helpfully provides in a footnote at the end of the text confirms that all of the relevant action in the case concerns events (both "real" and "psychic") that take place during this early childhood period. As we have already suggested, it appears that one of the uses Freud makes of the concept of the primal scene is as an attempt to render unconscious processes and events *visible*. However, none of the many "images" associated with the case (i.e., the original scene of coitus, the original dream, the Wolf Man's drawing of the dream, and Freud's narrative retelling of the Wolf Man's dream text) can be considered to be visual images in any simple sense. Even the Wolf Man's drawing which seems to be a "real picture" (and on one level of course it is) nonetheless remains, paradoxically, a nonvisual image as it is merely a *real* picture of a purely *fantasmatic* image. After all, the drawing is purported to be a depiction of the original *dream images* rather than a mimetic representation of the actual events of the primal scene itself. This is why the drawing shows the scene in such distorted form. Like a dream text, the drawing of the dream functions more like a *transcription* of the word-pictures (or rebuses) from which dreams are made rather than as a visual rendering of something that ever could be available to perception. Furthermore, the very fact that the Wolf Man is capable of "drawing" the dream as an adult, on the basis of traces of an ancient memory of a childhood dream, implicitly endows the drawing with uncanny quasi-photographic powers. Acting more like a photograph than like the memory of a prehistoric childhood dream, the Wolf Man's drawing is presumably capable of retrieving impressions from the childhood dream that have been perfectly preserved and, despite years of dormancy, it ostensibly faithfully develops and reproduces the original dream images into the form of the drawing made decades later. Later in this book, in the chapters explicitly devoted to photography, I will offer some further thoughts about how the specifically photographic quality of the primal scene image is directly related to and a function of its traumatic nature.

By using the two traumatic poles of the primal scene in order to provide a temporal frame for the childhood events through which psyche and sexuality take shape, Freud is able to provide a means of *showing* the impact of "infantile sexuality" without relying exclusively on biological or developmental paradigms. Regardless of how fantastic or fictive the image of the primal scene may appear to be, its aim is to document how an individual infant becomes marked as fully "human," as it were, *during* early childhood and in response to specific infantile sexual events. Thus, from this perspective as well, we find once again that the primal scene functions like a photographic apparatus: It captures the impossible moment at which the psyche comes into being. It comes into being, that is, as a specifically *human* psyche—hence susceptible to perverse fixations, phobias, and hysteria. Paradoxically, however, the child's dream about wolves is the sign that he has become fully "human." The very event of the wolf dream is evidence both of the fact that he is now suffering from a specifically human conflict and that his psyche is now capable of registering and processing that distress by making a dream out of it.

At this juncture (and this will become significant later on), it is interesting to note that the wolf dream does not resemble a *typical* child's dream precisely because of the degree of distortion involved in it. As Freud explains in the third chapter of the *Interpretation of Dreams*, typical children's dreams are literal and literal-minded. They are the pure, undistorted expression of a simple wish:

> The dreams of young children are frequently pure wish fulfillments and are in that case quite uninteresting compared with the dreams of adults. They raise no problems for solution; but on the other hand they are of inestimable importance in proving that, in their essential nature, dreams represent fulfillments of wishes.[10]

It is not accidental that Freud concludes his discussion about typical children's dreams by invoking a speculative analogy between them and animal dreams:

> I do not myself know what animals dream of. But a proverb, to which my attention was drawn by one of my students, does claim to know. "What" asks the proverb, "do geese dream of?" And it replies: "Of maize." The whole theory that dreams are wish fulfillments is contained in these two phrases.[11]

Of course, as Freud knows perfectly well, and as he then goes on to argue in the following chapter, dreams are not merely wishes, but manifestations of *unconscious* wishes. It is precisely because of the unbreachable divide between conscious and unconscious registers that the dreamwork (including condensation, displacement, distortion, and so on) becomes necessary.

The comparison between children's dreams and animal dreams is merely one instance of Freud's more general and common claim that children and animals are especially close to one another. But the precise rationale for this particular proximity is arguably more complicated than it might appear to be at first glance. On one hand, Freud often suggests or implies (as in the passage from the *Interpretation of Dreams* cited earlier) that children are close to animals because they *resemble* them. According to this logic, children are similar to animals because, like animals, they are governed by instinctual or biological needs. But Freud also regularly suggests that children are close to animals not because they resemble the animals themselves, but because they resemble primitive man and hence share his predisposition for engaging in totemic practices. But proximity to animals based on instinctual continuity and biological similarity is qualitatively different from proximity based on totemism, because where the first case presumes the existence of genuinely shared traits, the second one posits instead a representational structure (the totem) founded upon a "misrecognition" or denial of species difference. Thus, following the logic of totemism, primitive people are especially close to animals not because they are actually *like* them, but rather because of their inability to recognize the difference between them. This failed recognition of difference is apparently linked to the origin of representation itself, since identification with totem animals seemingly gives rise to the need to make use of animals as symbolic substitutes for humans. However, it should be remembered that this particular form of failure to recognize the difference between humans and animals is, after all, the very hallmark of human culture. Animals do not seem to display the same profound need or propensity for interspecies identification. In other words, in general, we do not suspect that wolves commonly dream of little boys even if little boys commonly dream of wolves.

Keeping this in mind, let us now return to the wolf dream. As we have already observed, the wolf dream is not merely a simple "representation" of the observed act of coitus, but rather a psychic repetition and reenactment of it. When reactivated in and by the dream, the primal scene conveys new information to the psyche about the event as well as new psychic effects. But if we look more closely at the specific meaning that Freud attributes to it in Part IV of the case history, we discover that the wolf dream combines, condenses, and confuses three related questions concerning three different kinds of (sexual) differences: the difference between children and adults, the difference between men and women and the difference between humans and animals. Through the medium of the dream, Freud explains, the child simultaneously "discovers" the existence of the vagina and develops a wolf phobia in function of that traumatic discovery.

> The activation of the primal scene in the dream now brought him back to the genital organization. He discovered the vagina and the biological significance of masculine and feminine. He understood now that active was the same as masculine, while passive was the same as feminine. His passive sexual aim should now have been transformed into a feminine one, and having expressed itself as "being copulated with by his father" instead of "being beaten by him on the genitals or on the bottom." This feminine aim, however, underwent repression and was obliged to let itself be replaced by fear of the wolf.[12]

But the very discovery of "sexual difference" (the existence of the vagina) that is revealed *by* the dream is expressed *in* the dream through the substitution of animals in place of human figures. In the dream (re)activation of the earlier scene during which the child ostensibly witnessed *sexual* difference without understanding it, here multiple wolves (who are not sexually differentiated from one another) become the telltale indicators of human sexual difference. In other words, the only way *human* sexual difference can be perceived or represented in the scene is through the mediation and substitution of animal figures for human ones. The subsequent emergence of the symptom of the wolf phobia (which is an effect of the dream rather than part of its explicit narrative content) indicates both that sexual difference has been recognized and that it has been repressed.

Although the questions raised by the wolf phobia are extremely important (and I will discuss them briefly later on), for the time being I would like to continue to look even more closely at how the observation of sexual difference in the primal scene is predicated upon yet another set of confusions between humans and animals. In his famous reconstruction of the act of coitus that the infant must have seen, Freud is adamant about one precise and indispensable detail: the specific postures adopted in the sexual act. He famously (and repeatedly) uses the Latin phrases, "*more ferarum*," "in the manner of the animals," and "*a tergo*," "from behind," to describe these postures. As he will go on to explain, Freud's case is predicated upon the idea that *only animal-like sex* (or sex in the manner of animals) renders the genitals visible enough for the infant to perceive the evidence of sexual difference. It is this animal inspired "picture" of the revelation of the genitals that traumatizes the young child and triggers the belated production of the dream images of the wolves. Here is how Freud describes how this picture of animal-like figures gives rise to the dream of the primal scene:

> What sprang into activity that night out of the chaos of the dreamer's unconscious memory-traces was the picture of copulation between his parents, copulation in circumstances which were not entirely usual and were especially favourable for observation.
>
> When he woke up, he witnessed a coitus *a tergo* [from behind], three times repeated; he was able to see his mother's genitals as well as his father's organ; and he understood the process as well as its significance.
>
> We will first proceed with the study of the relations between this "primal scene" and the patient's dream, his symptoms, and the history of his life; and we will trace separately the effects that followed from the essential content of the scene and from one its visual impressions. By the latter I mean the postures which he saw his parents adopt—the man upright, and the woman bent down like an animal [*die aufrechte des Mannes und die tierähnlich gebückte der Frau*].[13]

These passages come from Part IV of the case history. At this point in his argument, Freud presents this detailed and precise visual description of the "pictures" witnessed by the infant during the primal scene in order to substantiate his claim that the event in question really "happened," and that what the child saw was an act of copulation between his two parents. But it is striking that in Freud's derivation of the scene, the child comes into contact with human sexuality and confronts sexual difference only when the humans involved do not appear to act like humans, but like animals. Once again, human sexuality becomes visible only when humans behave like animals. In the dream of wolves, therefore, the animal figures are distorted substitutes for human figures that are themselves imitating animal postures.

But there is still another detail in Freud's description that further complicates the scene. Throughout the case history, Freud not only insists that the sexual act was performed (three times) from behind, but he also places great emphasis on the difference between the posture adopted by the woman and that assumed by the man. He specifies that the man is upright, but the woman is "bent down like an animal." Although both figures are engaged in animal-style sex, they are "animal-like" to different degrees: The man is erect and upright like a human figure, whereas the woman is explicitly compared to an animal in the language of the text. Thus it would seem that the figure of the woman is more of an animal than the figure of the man. The animal sexual act in which they are both engaged erases all traces of her "human" status whereas there is some confusion concerning the species status of the upright man. It would appear that these images not only convey information about sexual difference, but also information about species difference at the same time. In others words, the picture in the scene seems to show that to be a woman is to be more like an animal than a man.

These "postural" differences play a crucial role in Freud's interpretation of the case as he will go on to insist that although the wolves in the dream represent both his father and his mother, the wolf figure that gives rise to the boy's wolf phobia is a symptom of his repressed desire for his father and is related to him alone. According to Freud, the initial scene witnessed by the boy aroused his desire for his father and elicited identification with his mother and with her animal posture. In the wake of the dream, however, and in response to the "discovery" of castration and sexual difference conveyed by it, the boy's desire for the father becomes repressed and the father himself becomes transformed into a terrifying wolf. But not just any kind of scary wolf: The wolf in the phobia is an erect and humanlike upright wolf. This wolf does not live in the "real world" and therefore cannot be observed in it. A wolf such as this exists only in the imagination: it is a product of the mind and can only be found there or in picture books.

The "imaginary" nature of the source of this animal phobia deserves some attention as it potentially troubles some of the assumptions and claims that Freud makes more generally regarding the function and meaning of animal phobias. As we saw in Chapter 1, for Freud, the emergence of animal phobias in young boys is always a symptom of fear of castration by the father. The function of the phobia is to contain the internal conflict (fear of castration by the father) by isolating and externalizing it. Through the phobia, the fear of a seemingly omnipotent and omnipresent father is displaced onto an external animal substitute for him. In this way, the phobia insures both that the fear-inducing animal father figure can be mostly avoided, and that the real human father can be tolerated. Freud makes this general argument in several texts, but the metapsychological stakes of the discussion of animal phobias appear perhaps most notably in *Totem and Taboo* and *Inhibitions, Symptoms and Anxiety*. He explicitly invokes the *Wolf Man* alongside of his other famous case of infantile neurosis, *Little Hans*, in both of these texts in order to derive and explain the existence of castration anxiety and its essential link to the concept of death and fear of the father.

Here is how he describes the mechanism in *Inhibitions, Symptoms and Anxiety*:

> We have said that as soon as the ego recognizes the danger of castration it gives the signal of anxiety and inhibits through the pleasure-unpleasure agency (in a way which we cannot yet understand) the impending cathetic process in the id. At the same time the phobia is formed. And now the castration anxiety is directed to a different object and expressed in a distorted form, so that the patient is afraid, not of being castrated by his father, but of being bitten by a horse or devoured by a wolf. The substitute formation has two obvious advantages. In the first place it avoids a conflict due to ambivalence (for the father was a loved object, too) and in the second place it enables the ego to cease generating anxiety. For the anxiety belonging to a phobia is conditional; it only emerges when the object is perceived—and rightly so, since it is only then that the danger-situation is present. There is no need to be afraid of being castrated by a father who is not there. On the other hand, one cannot get rid of a father; he can appear whenever he chooses. But if he is replaced by an animal, all one has to do is to avoid the sight of it—that is—its presence—in order to be free from danger and anxiety.[14]

Although Freud's understanding of the *structure* of the animal phobia is fairly straightforward, its metapsychological status is more problematic as he seems to vacillate between two semi-tautological positions: sometimes he seems to *prove* the theory of castration anxiety based on his analysis of the clinical example, and sometimes he posits castration and then *explains* the phobia on the basis of the theory. And sometimes he seemingly does both at once by arguing that although the specific connection between the animal phobia and castration is *innate* and thereby possesses a privileged relation to the prehistory of the psyche, this "predisposition" only produces a phobia in function of specific childhood psychic "sexual" events.

But the argument that the animal phobia is *both* a function of prehistoric knowledge of castration *and* a specific response to childhood events depends, once again, on the presumption of an ambiguous "special proximity" between boy children and large animals, and the specific psychic malleability of the figure of the animal itself. This double function is particularly evident in Freud's offhand allusions to "totemic thought" in his presentation of the case of "little Hans" in *Inhibitions, Symptoms and Anxiety*:

> What made it a neurosis was one thing alone: the replacement of his father by a horse. It is this displacement, then, which has a claim to be called a symptom. . . . Such a displacement is made possible or facilitated at "Little Hans's" early stage because the inborn traces of totemic thought can still be easily revived. Children do not yet recognize or, at any rate, lay such an exaggerated stress upon the gulf that separates human beings from the animal world. In their eyes the grown man, the object of their fear and admiration, still belongs to the same category as the big animal who has so many enviable attributes but against whom they have been warned because he may become dangerous.[15]

Freud is here suggesting that despite the fact that the animal phobia in question is a unique psychic response to a specific early sexual conflict, the emergence of the phobia relies upon an inborn predisposition to fear of animals based upon a heightened identification with them and with their observable (and presumably genital) "enviable attributes." In this way, the animal figure has a specifically privileged relationship to the sexual dramas of childhood; it both prepares the psyche for the experience of infantile sexuality and produces visible traces of its effects. Once again, therefore, the animal figures precede and usurp human figures in the demarcation of sexual difference. In passing, it is interesting to note that Freud explicitly clarifies that everything he says about animal phobias pertains to little boys and only to little boys. And, as the explanation of the structure of the animal phobia makes clear, the drama of castration and sexual difference is now played out between the boy, his father, and his animal father substitute. When animal figures are present, the female figures apparently disappear from the scene.

In light of these remarks, if we now return to *Wolf Man*, we discover that the treatment of animal phobias in this text seems to present some special difficulties for the general theory outlined earlier. In the first place, the source of the wolf phobia is an imaginary animal rather than an animal observed by the boy in the world. Although Freud himself acknowledges this point, his explanation of it leaves several important questions unanswered. He writes:

> This phobia was only distinguished by other similar cases by the fact that the anxiety-animal was not an object easily accessible to observation (such as a horse or a dog), but was known to him only from stories and picture-books.[16]

There are several problems with this. In the first place, the fact that the anxiety-animal is both relatively inaccessible and imaginary seems to undercut its potential ability to isolate and externalize the fear of the father inspired by it. Furthermore, according to Freud's text, the image of the dream wolves (which precipitates the phobia) is a creation of the psyche itself. The image of the dream-wolf is not merely an imaginary animal; it is the very product of the child's imagination: a composite figure composed of elements taken from fairytale wolves and goats, real dead sheep, and real sheep dogs that the child may or may not have seen copulating. Although the wolves in the fairytales and picture books provide some of the raw material for the wolf-dream, Freud himself argues that the figure of the "erect wolf" that forms the source of the phobia does not, in fact, come from the fairy tale material, but rather from the primal "real" images of the upright father in the primal scene. In other words, the picture-book wolves are merely mediating figures that provide an associative link between the traumatic primal images of the real human father and his subsequent wolf avatar. Unlike in the case of "Little Hans," however, it is the human father himself who ostensibly provides the source images according to which the anxiety-animal is subsequently chosen rather than the other way around. As Freud points out, the critical element in the phobia is not the figure of the wolf itself, but its "erect posture":

> The wolf that he was afraid of was undoubtedly his father; but his fear of the wolf was conditioned upon the creature being in an upright position. His recollection asserted most definitely that he had not been terrified by pictures of wolves going on all fours or, as in the story of "Little Red Riding-Hood," lying in bed. The posture which, according to our construction of the primal scene, he had seen the woman assume, was of no less significance; though in this case the significance was limited to the sexual sphere.[17]

As it happens these two different sexual "postures" or positions determine and correspond to two different and competing psychic positions concerning the status of sexual difference in the life of the patient. Freud makes it clear (and this point will be of interest later to Lacan) that although the wolf phobia (and the erect male posture in it) is presumably a sign that the patient has "understood" sexual difference, he also continues to "deny" or "disavow" both castration and sexual difference. He maintains a lifelong identification with his mother through the bowels as well as a powerful sexual fixation on women who assume a posture "bent down like an animal" proffering the buttocks. Freud will return to this patient's famous "disavowal" of sexual difference in his paper "Fetishism." But there is also a third, hidden, element in this scene that further fractures the patient's split "understanding" of sexual difference. That third element is death and, like sexual difference, it is conveyed through animal mediation in the material that arises from the primal scene and determines the dream. Although this topic exceeds the scope of this discussion, I would simply like to point out here that the child's quest for sexual knowledge coincides and crosses with evidence of the existence of death throughout the case. Here is how Freud announces it in Part IV:

> There were several conclusions, too, to be drawn from the raw material which had been produced by the patient's first analysis of the dream, and these had to be fitted into the collocation of which we were in search. Behind the mention of the sheep-breeding, evidence was to be expected of his sexual researches, his interests in which he was able to gratify during his visits with his father, but there must also have been allusions to a fear of death, since the greater part of the sheep had died of the epidemic.[18]

If I mention the dead sheep at this juncture, it is in part in response to a rather astonishing assertion that appears in several of Jean Laplanche's rigorous and provocative treatments of this case history. In two of his more recent essays (most notably in "The Unfinished Copernican Revolution" and "Seduction, Persecution, Revelation"), Laplanche invokes *Wolf Man* in order to rethink the status of seduction and the meaning of a "primal scene." For Laplanche, the importance of the primal scene lies in the inherently traumatic nature of the enigmatic sexual messages that are exchanged between adults and children. He argues that a primal scene is never something simply related to sexual content but rather arises from the parents' active (and unconscious) communicative participation in the scene. However, in both of those essays, he not only argues that Freud overlooks the role played by the parents but also specifically suggests that the father actively takes the young boy to the sheep fields in order to expose him to the sight of animals copulating. In both instances in which Laplanche invokes this imagined (and arguably invented) scenario, his own rhetoric becomes strangely excessive. In "The Unfinished Copernican Revolution," for example, he writes himself into the scene by describing it in the first person: "What is it this father wants of me by showing me, letting me see this primal scene, even if only by taking me to a field to witness animal coitus?" and in "Seduction, Persecution, Revelation" he produces a truly extraordinary association in the footnote that accompanies his reference to *Wolf Man*. Laplanche writes:

> When the Wolf Man's father takes the child to watch the animals copulating, are we really to imagine that nothing but an innocent stroll is intended?[19]

But in the footnote to this suggestive claim about the suggestive stroll, Laplanche adds the following:

> What could be less innocent than a stroll? I remember that, during the occupation, the few French words the German soldiers knew were "Promenade, mademoiselle?" a sexual invitation, coded as such.

Although Freud's text does clearly specify that the boy's visits to the sheep fields with his father were a particular source of pleasure for him, the text never indicates that the father explicitly or directly exposed him to the sight of animals copulating. Furthermore, and I think this is significant, Laplanche never mentions the role that is played by the animal in the transmission and production of this specific "enigmatic message" nor the fact, emphasized repeatedly by Freud, that the (beloved) sheep die from an epidemic and hence, by implication, that the father was unable to save them or somehow participated in their death. Curiously, Laplanche has not only erased the importance of the animal from the scene but also inserted a peculiarly overdetermined personal memory from the German occupation of France into it. Laplanche's rendition of the scene transforms the encounter between a father, his son, and some animals that may or may not be copulating but some of which are certainly dying into a sexual encounter between a man and a woman who do not speak the same language. Given his commitment to the importance of the irreducibly enigmatic nature of "primal scenes," it is understandable why Laplanche might be inclined to downplay the importance of the animal figures. However, I am suggesting here that the animals in Freud's text are not merely the brute instinctual and biological alternative to human sexuality (as Laplanche tends to imply), but rather that they might turn out to play a critical role in the production and transmission of "enigmatic messages" between humans. In other words, I am arguing that Laplanche's "enigmatic messages" may not be enigmatic *enough*, and that, paradoxically, the animal figure comes to stand in for something in the human sexual experience that cannot be translated, transferred, or communicated at all.

Thus far, I have not yet come to many of the central—and, indeed most famous—questions concerning the critical importance of the animal element in the *Wolf Man* as I have focused almost exclusively on Part IV of Freud's text, "The Dream and the Primal Scene." This is the chapter in which Freud analyzes the wolf dream and derives the reality of the primal scene from it. However, as readers of *Wolf Man* know well, the text does not end with the derivation of the primal scene. Instead, in the fifth section of the case history, Freud famously produces an alternative explanation for the event that gives rise to the primal scene. In this version, the traumatic images of coitus between the child's parents are the product of a retroactive fantasy projection based upon real images of an observed act of coitus performed by animals, not humans. And then, in the remaining four sections of the text, Freud simultaneously argues that the fact that the coitus may have been performed by animals is not significant for his essential understanding of the structure and meaning of the primal scene and presents "new" material that ostensibly substantiates his initial hypothesis that the primal scene was a real, witnessed, event of coitus between his parents.

Although I cannot take on a full analysis of the complexity of Freud's twisted argument in the concluding sections of *Wolf Man* here (indeed, no "full analysis" of this case is possible, since it has always proven to be "interminable"), I would like to indicate, albeit telegraphically and suggestively, three matters emerging from my reading of Freud's text that merit further analysis: the reality of the event, the nature of the butterfly, and the animal analogy of human sexuality.

The Reality of the Event

Although Freud does present two versions to explain the structure of the primal scene (real event vs. fantasy), it is interesting to note that the status of the "reality" of the event also determines the status of the "reality" of the animals in question. In other words, if the primal scene is "real," then the animals (wolves) in the scene are imaginary, but if the scene itself is a fantasy, then the animals are necessarily real (child observes dogs copulating).

The reality of the "event" of copulation is never put into question, merely the species status of the performers in the sexual scene. The section in which Freud introduces the two versions of the scene is section V. This is the precise midpoint of the text and of Freud's convoluted argument. Furthermore, the meaning of the roman numeral "V" will later be introduced as material in the case history. The arguments *in* section "V" of the text are retroactively inflected by Freud's discussion of the meaning of the roman numeral "V" in conjunction with another animal phobia, the phobia of the "swallowtail" butterfly.

The Butterfly

The central importance of the butterfly emerges in section VIII. Through an analysis of the memory of the phobia of the butterfly, Freud discovers "new material" on the basis of which he claims to have proven the reality of the primal scene. In section VIII, Freud explains that throughout the analysis, the patient produced a recurrent childhood memory of chasing a beautiful big butterfly covered with yellow stripes. When the butterfly settled on a flower, the patient became seized with a terrible anxiety. From the evidence provided by the anxiety provoked by the movement of the butterfly's wings (that formed a "V") along with the multilingual verbal associations produced by the image of the yellow stripes, Freud and the patient reconstruct the memory of an ancient and hitherto unremembered primal memory: the scene of seduction with "Grusha." According to Freud, this scene (in which the young boy, just over two years old, responds to the sight of "Grusha" scrubbing the floor on her hands and knees by urinating in excitement) provides the earliest evidence of the psychic traces produced by the primal scene. According to Freud, the movements by Grusha in the scene awaken the dormant image of the primal scene and provoke a reenactment of it. Paradoxically, however, Freud bases his proof of the irrefutable reality of the irretrievable primal scene on the reconstructed, recovered memory of a repetition of it in the second scene. By uncovering traces (or afterimages) of the primal scene in its first *repetition*, Freud claims to have finally truly "corroborated" the reality of the first one. In this sense, the primal scene "really" occurs not once, but twice; each time, it is associated with an animal phobia. In this instance, however, the animal is not an *imaginary* wolf, but a *real* butterfly. The butterfly, however, is an animal that the patient has explicitly marked as "feminine." Freud writes:

> It then appeared that his fear of the butterfly was in every respect analogous to his fear of the wolf; in both cases it was a fear of castration, which was, to begin with, referred to the person who had first uttered the threat of castration, but was then transposed on to another person to whom it was bound to become attached in accordance to phylogenetic precedence.[20]

Once again, there is ambiguity concerning the nature of the link between castration and animal phobias. Here, the animal producing the phobia is marked as feminine, the person who supposedly uttered the threat of castration is feminine, nonetheless, Freud will argue that the butterfly phobia, like the wolf phobia, is both a response to the primal scene (via its repetition in the scene with Grusha) and a reincarnation of the earlier wolf phobia. The wolf and the butterfly are therefore merely two different *animal* forms of the same "human" idea: fear of castration by the father. Furthermore, for Freud, the fact that the wolf turns into a butterfly does not deter him from arguing for the determinant "precedence" of the "phylogenetic" meaning of the animal phobia according to which the father is central to the scene and the mother is absent from it.

The Animal Analogy

In the final paragraphs of *Wolf Man*, Freud's argument takes a final and enigmatic twist. After having vigorously argued for the essential role played by individual infantile sexuality throughout the entire case, and therefore for the radical specificity of human sexuality (as opposed to animal instinct), Freud famously ends his case by invoking a form of sexual knowledge in humans that is something "like" instinctual animal knowledge about sex. Although these passages have been the object of compelling and complex commentary by Jean Laplanche, I suggest that perhaps it is the very status of the "animal analogy" that needs to be further explored here. What Freud actually says, however, is that he is unable to find an adequate representative form or a conception for this deepest and most foundational stratum of human sexuality. And here, once again, when he struggles to convey the idea of that which is most foundational and "primal," he introduces an *animal figure* to stand in for what cannot be conceived otherwise:

> If one considers the behaviour of the four-year old child towards the re-activated primal scene or even if one thinks of the far simpler reactions of the one and a half year old child when the scene was actually experienced, it is hard to dismiss the view that some sort of hardly definable knowledge, something, as it were, preparatory to an understanding, was at work in the child at the time. We can form no conception of what this may have consisted in; and we have nothing at our disposal but the single analogy—and it is an excellent one—of the far-reaching *instinctive* knowledge of animals.[21]

In this final picture of *Wolf Man*'s "primal scene," via the last resort of this unique yet "excellent" animal analogy, sexual difference and human subjectivity come into being, through each other, in an absolute and obscure proximity to the very animality from which they are born.

FOUR

Back of Beyond: Anxiety and the Birth of the Future

> The trauma remains traumatizing and incurable because it comes from the future. For the virtual can also traumatize. Trauma takes places when one is wounded by a wound that has not yet taken place, in an effective fashion, in a way other than by the sign of its announcement. Its temporalization proceeds from the to-come.
>
> —JACQUES DERRIDA, *Rogues*

Beyond the Pleasure Principle

Beyond the Pleasure Principle (1920) is often thought to be Freud's most philosophical work. It is not then surprising, that philosophers have devoted so much critical attention to it. As Jacques Derrida points out in his famous reading of *Beyond* in *The Post Card*, Freud's most ambitious "metapsychological" work attempts to ground psychoanalysis philosophically while refusing to acknowledge its debt to philosophy.[1] Many psychoanalysts, however, and particularly Americans, have regarded this book of "philosophy" as a bizarre aberration in Freud's thinking and have excluded it from the accepted canon of psychoanalysis. One of the reasons that philosophers have found the book so interesting is that it offers a radical account of trauma and temporality in the form of "repetition compulsion." Cathy Caruth's important work on trauma, largely derived from a close reading of Freud's description of the belated temporality of the repetition compulsion, has helped inspire a new field of trauma studies and has contributed to *Beyond the Pleasure Principle*'s becoming the principal point of reference for many recent readers of Freud.[2]

As most readers of *Beyond* know well, Freud introduces his description of trauma by telling a story. The story that Freud tells is about how some people suffer terrible illnesses (what is now known as PTSD, or posttraumatic stress disorder) after surviving war, railway disasters, and other near-death experiences. Surprisingly, however, Freud uses these stories of near-death experiences in order to argue that the illnesses suffered are *not* caused by the actual threat of death, but rather by the element of surprise itself. People become traumatized, Freud claims, not because they have a close encounter with death, but because they become overwhelmed by fright produced by their encounter with an experience for which they are not prepared. Freud is adamant on this point: Trauma cannot be directly correlated to an external threat to life, no matter how real the threat may be. Rather, trauma is caused by a rupture in the experience of time itself caused by the state of fright. The repetition compulsion that accompanies trauma is an automatic, uncontrollable, and belated attempt to repair the rift in time caused by the unpreparedness of fright. Because the psyche is overwhelmed by fright, it misses the very experience that provoked the fright. The repetition of the experience is an attempt to prevent the missed event from having happened in the past by preparing for its future recurrence.

In *Beyond the Pleasure Principle*, Freud defines the specific nature of trauma by comparing it to other potential affective responses to situations of danger. He writes:

> "Fright" [*Schreck*], "fear" [*Furcht*], and "anxiety" [*Angst*] are improperly used as synonymous expressions; they are in fact capable of clear distinction in their relation to danger. "Anxiety" describes a particular state of expecting the danger or of preparing for it, even though it may be an unknown one. "Fear" requires a definite object of which to be afraid. "Fright," however, is the name we give to the state a person gets into when he has run into a danger without being prepared for it; it emphasizes the factor of surprise. I do not think that anxiety can produce a traumatic neurosis. There is something about anxiety that protects its subject against fright and so against fright-neuroses.[3]

According to Freud here, all three terms (fright, fear, and anxiety) describe possible responses to a given situation of danger. A situation of danger—even extreme—can produce fear, anxiety, or fright. But only "*Schreck*" ("fright") produces trauma because it and it alone is determined by the element of surprise. Fear does not produce trauma because it has a known and knowable source. When we are afraid of something, Freud suggests, we do not become overwhelmed by surprise because we know *what* we fear even if it is something genuinely fearful.

While the distinction between "fright" and "fear" seems fairly clear, Freud's description of the case of "anxiety" introduces new difficulties. "Anxiety," Freud asserts, is the inverse of fright. By means of the feeling of anxiety, the psyche prepares itself to expect an unknown threat so as to avoid the experience of "fright." In "fright," the psyche responds "too late" to danger—and the experience of the event is marked by this "belatedness." In anxiety, the psyche anticipates the experience of an event and responds to it before it happens. To the extent that the psyche "responds" to something before it happens, one can say that in anxiety, the psyche's response comes "too soon." By producing a feeling of surprise in advance of and in preparation for the unknown danger to come, anxiety protects the psyche from trauma. For this reason, Freud claims that fright and anxiety are mutually exclusive: "Fright" produces trauma, whereas "anxiety" prevents it.

The Return of Trauma and the Birth of Anxiety

Six years later, in *Inhibitions, Symptoms, and Anxiety*, Freud returns to the relationship between trauma and anxiety and substantially revises his story.[4] Like *Beyond the Pleasure Principle*, the latter book is one of Freud's major "metapsychological" undertakings. Unlike *Beyond the Pleasure Principle*, however, aside from a few notable exceptions, *Inhibitions, Symptoms, and Anxiety* has not attracted sustained philosophical attention. Furthermore, whereas *Beyond the Pleasure Principle*'s many ambiguities and complexities have stimulated philosophical interest in the text, the inconsistencies, inconclusiveness, and internal contradictions of *Inhibitions, Symptoms, and Anxiety* have largely been dismissed by readers who tend to minimize the extent to which it resists being reduced to a coherent narrative of determinable and stable claims.[5]

Even French psychoanalyst Jean Laplanche, who is arguably one of the most subtle philosophical readers of Freud, considers that in *Inhibitions, Symptoms, and Anxiety*, Freud retreats from the daring conceptual leap he had made in *Beyond the Pleasure Principle*. In a paper provocatively entitled "A Metapsychology put to the test of Anxiety," Laplanche writes,

> In this rich and exciting but rather ambiguous and even contradictory book, a fruitful trajectory seems to be deflected, indeed turned back on itself in an alarming way; I mean the line of thought which reached its apex with *Beyond the Pleasure Principle*.[6]

According to Laplanche, the problem with *Inhibitions, Symptoms, and Anxiety* is that it goes "back" rather than "beyond." It interrupts the "fruitful trajectory" of *Beyond the Pleasure Principle*—a trajectory that was taking Freud's thinking "beyond"—and sends it back in the wrong direction. For Laplanche, in the "backward" thinking of *Inhibitions, Symptoms, and Anxiety*, Freud turns his back on himself and his own thinking. In this "rich and exciting but rather ambiguous and even contradictory book," Laplanche is "alarmed" to find that Freud's thinking is "turned back on itself," and he implies that Freud's text is an *example* of anxiety rather than an *analysis* of it. One might even go so far as to say that he implicitly asserts that the book itself is an anxious defense against the anxiety provoked by the step beyond of *Beyond the Pleasure Principle*.

But what would it mean to accept Laplanche's *description* of the movement of Freud's text without accepting his conclusions about it? I would like to suggest that the interest of Freud's text lies precisely in various ways in which it thinks about what it means to "step back." Furthermore, I would like to raise the possibility that by following the tortured and contorted movement of Freud's text, we may find that in the very moments in which Freud seemingly turns against himself and his own thinking, he goes "beyond" himself. By attending to the many inconsistencies and ambiguities that comprise *Inhibitions, Symptoms, and Anxiety*, we may find that in this curious "step back," Freud might offer us some of his most powerful thinking about the future. Thus, paradoxically, perhaps the only way to go "beyond" the step taken in *Beyond the Pleasure Principle* is to take a step back. Freud himself almost says as much in the famous concluding lines: "*Was man nicht erfliegen kann, muss man erhinken*"—What we cannot reach flying, we must reach by limping.

Therefore, as I hope to show, in *Inhibitions, Symptoms, and Anxiety*, Freud proposes a radical new way of thinking about anxiety in order to tell a rich and strange story about the temporal dimension of the human psyche.

By means of this new conception of "anxiety," Freud opens some of the most philosophically difficult regions of psychoanalytic theory by suggesting that anxiety underlies the very birth of the psyche as such and accounts for its subsequent relationship to time. More radically still, we might propose that "anxiety" is the strange and even uncanny temporal dimension of birth itself and that it gives birth to the psyche *in* time as well as the psychic conception *of* time. Unlike *Beyond the Pleasure Principle*, in which Freud tells a story about near-death experiences in order to illustrate the belated temporality of trauma, in *Inhibitions, Symptoms, and Anxiety*, Freud's exploration of anxiety leads us to rethink our relationship to birth, not death. And although the philosophical tradition has long explored the ways in which human temporality is a relationship to death, we are less accustomed to thinking about birth in unfamiliar ways.

One of the things that makes the treatment of the temporality of anxiety in *Inhibitions, Symptoms, and Anxiety* so powerful is that Freud makes "birth" itself strange to us in this text. Freud's text resists any simple biological, philosophical, or narrative explanation of birth. As we saw in the last chapter, Freud had already begun grappling with the radical strangeness of the concept of birth in *The Wolf Man* through the figure of the primal scene. In that text, however, his focus was on the birth of the individual subject's unconscious rather than on the subject of birth as such. In this text, by contrast, Freud struggles with the very idea of birth and attempts to integrate it into his general metapsychology. As we shall see, instead of presenting birth as the origin of a developmental linear trajectory that leads inexorably to death along a time-line that moves us forward from a past, through a present toward a future, Freud places "birth" at the heart of the human psyche but refuses to think of birth as an event in any simple sense. Birth is figured essentially as the birth of anxiety. And anxiety cannot be linked directly to a fear of death, but rather a fear of life that itself comes from life—that *is* life. Birth, like the primal anxiety that marks it, neither constitutes a fixed origin or "beginning," nor is it certain that it is ever completed. Birth, Freud will suggest, is a trauma in the strongest possible sense, and anxiety is always the repetition of the trauma of birth. As such, anxiety recalls the trauma of birth and in so doing, gives birth to the possibility of a future.

But perhaps we have gotten ahead of ourselves. Let us return for the moment to Freud's revised understanding of the relationship between trauma and anxiety in *Inhibitions, Symptoms, and Anxiety*. In this text, Freud discards the clear-cut distinction between "fright" (*Schreck*) and "anxiety" (*Angst*) that he had taken such pains to establish in *Beyond the Pleasure Principle* and replaces it with a new and very strange conception of "anxiety." Now it appears that anxiety is no longer simply opposed to trauma, but rather is a particular psychic manifestation of it. In fact, in *Inhibitions, Symptoms, and Anxiety*, it turns out that "anxiety" and "trauma" are actually two versions of the same thing, and Freud refers to them both by the term "anxiety." The earlier distinction he established between "fright" and "anxiety" is now recast as an uncanny drama between anxiety and itself.

At the very end of *Inhibitions, Symptoms, and Anxiety*, after numerous (seemingly failed) attempts to define anxiety, in the very last chapter of this complicated and twisted text, Freud reaches the conclusion that anxiety can be neatly divided into two types: "automatic anxiety" and "signal anxiety." "Automatic anxiety" is an uncontrollable and traumatic response to danger. In "automatic anxiety," the psyche is overwhelmed by a situation of danger and triggers an automatic repetition of an earlier trauma and reproduces it in the present situation. The trauma from the past overwhelms and annihilates the present moment, and the psyche is retraumatized. In "signal anxiety," on the other hand, the psyche responds to the perceived threat of a future danger by reproducing a feeling of anxiety from a past trauma and using it as a warning signal. The feeling of anxiety "signals" the possibility of the future danger and helps to avert the occurrence of a future experience of anxiety. A small dose of anxiety in the present prevents one from being exposed to an overwhelming dose of anxiety in the future.

Although he formalizes the distinction between these two kinds of anxiety only in the final chapter of the book, throughout *Inhibitions, Symptoms and Anxiety*, Freud struggles to derive a model for the psyche in order to establish and maintain a rigorous distinction between "automatic anxiety" and "signal anxiety." Nonetheless, despite Freud's elaborate attempts to derive and sustain the difference between them, automatic and signal anxiety constantly threaten to become confused with one another. In fact, as we shall see, they cannot be separated from one another because they are in an uncanny relationship with one another. One might even say that the very notion of the "uncanny" itself is directly linked to the double nature of anxiety. But Freud needs to maintain this distinction because without it, the boundaries of the psyche itself threaten to become irrevocably unstable. Instead, despite Freud's many efforts to contain them, the uncanny properties of anxiety permeate the text and destabilize it in particularly telling ways. As we shall see, throughout this uncanny text, Freud has great difficulty in maintaining all distinctions including those that determine the lines that should separate the inside from the outside, the past from the present, the future from the present and the past and, interestingly enough, the ego from everything that is not ego.

But perhaps we need to take another step back.

It is generally agreed that Freud's theory of anxiety undergoes a change around the time that he was writing *Inhibitions, Symptoms and Anxiety*. Roughly speaking, the shift concerns Freud's understanding of the relationship between anxiety and repression. Where Freud had once thought that anxiety was an *effect* of repression, he now believes that anxiety *causes* repression. In his former view, Freud had understood that anxiety was a by-product of inadequately or inappropriately discharged sexual energy. In *Inhibitions, Symptoms, and Anxiety*, he takes a step back from that conception of anxiety and now asserts that anxiety belongs to the ego and to the ego alone. The ego, he now argues, is "the actual seat of anxiety;" In section II he writes,

> but we may legitimately hold firmly to the idea that the ego is the actual seat of anxiety and give up our earlier view that the cathectic energy of the repressed impulse is automatically turned into anxiety. If I expressed myself earlier in the latter sense, I was giving a phenomenological description and not a metapsychological account of what was occurring.[7]

And again, in Section IV, he insists on the fact that anxiety comes from the ego and belongs to it: "It is always the ego's attitude of anxiety which is the primary thing and which sets the repression going. Anxiety never arises from repressed libido." Although many of Freud's readers have called attention to consequences of this shift, they tend to focus on what it implies for the understanding of the drives. For our purposes, however, I would like to call attention to the impact that shift produces on the ego itself. I would like to suggest that in the relocation of anxiety from the id to the ego, the ego becomes radically alienated from itself. Once anxiety can be located in the ego, the ego becomes dislocated in relation to itself. In other words, once the ego becomes the "seat of anxiety," the ego's relationship to itself becomes uncanny.

But what happens to the ego and how does anxiety make it so uncanny? Among the strangenesses of this text is the fact that the focus is, as it were, not on the ego's struggle with its privileged others, but on the ego's struggle with itself, in itself, against itself, and, most radically, *as* a self. After explaining that "the ego is the actual seat of anxiety," Freud goes on to assert, rather surprisingly, that the ego is actually not different from the id, but rather is "identical" to it:

> To return to the problem of the ego. . . . We were justified, I think, in dividing the ego from the id, for there are certain considerations which necessitate that step. On the other hand, the ego is identical with the id, and is merely a specially differentiated part of it. If we think of this part by itself in contradistinction to the whole, or if a real split has occurred between the two, the weakness of the ego becomes apparent. But if the ego remains bound up with the id and indistinguishable from it, then it displays its strength. . . . In repression the decisive fact is that the ego is an organization and the id is not. The ego is, indeed, the organized portion of the id. We would be quite wrong if we pictured the ego and the id as two opposing camps.[8]

In this view, the ego and the id should not be considered as two separate agencies or entities. The ego, Freud specifies, is not opposed to the id, it is merely a special and specialized part of it. And it is special because it is specialized. The ego, Freud tells us, is an organization. Furthermore, we might go so far as to suggest that the ego is not only an "organization," it is, in a very profound sense, a *political* organization. Therefore it is no accident that Freud, who always loves to describe psychic structures with political analogies, outdoes himself in the sections of *Inhibitions, Symptoms, and Anxiety* devoted to the structure of the ego. Indeed, these sections of the text almost read like a treatise in political theory. Finally, although I cannot fully substantiate this claim here, I would suggest that the political dimension of the ego is a consequence of its uncanny nature. Simply put, it is destined to be political because it cannot be itself, cannot found itself or define itself in relation to any other.[9]

Despite the fact that the ego is conceived of as an organization (even a *political* organization), it is important to remember that it is not a *conscious* organization, nor can it be associated with or assimilated to "consciousness" in any direct way. To the extent that the ego comes into being as a response to "anxiety," and in so much as it is *part* of the id, the ego is now redefined as an unconscious, but organized defense against anxiety. In other words, the ego's ability to separate itself from the id lies in its capacity to produce itself as an organized structure. But this structure itself only comes into being as a defensive response to internal and external stimuli. To the extent that the psyche is overwhelmed by the stimuli through trauma, it responds to the trauma by repeating it. But the repetition of the trauma is itself a signal. As a "signal," it calls for a defensive, organized response to the overwhelming stimuli. The "ego" is the name that Freud gives to this "organized" response. The strength of the ego lies in its power to defend itself from stimuli by incorporating the stimuli into its own organization. And the stronger it gets, the more it becomes capable of appropriating foreign elements and turning them into part of its complex organization. Nonetheless, anxiety remains the driving force behind all of the subsequent negotiations and defenses in which the ego ultimately engages. Each and every encounter that the ego has with anything that is non-ego is, in some sense, determined, mediated, and regulated by the ego's primordial relationship with anxiety. This brings us to one of the most fundamental paradoxes in Freud's text. The root of all anxiety is disorganization. But the home of anxiety is the ego, which is organization. To the extent that anxiety is located in the ego, that it *inhabits* the ego, anxiety is the ego's absolute other, its demonic doppelganger, as well as its raison d'être.

In order to understand why Freud makes such a paradoxical claim, we must begin to refine our understanding of anxiety itself. Anxiety, we have suggested, is both a response to primal trauma and a repetition of it. More precisely, the response is repetition. One of the ways in which Freud describes this repetition that is a response is by calling it a "signal." Anxiety is the psyche's "signal response" to trauma. The signal is both a response to the missed encounter of the past and a call to the future. But these two temporal dimensions of the signal cannot be simply separated from one another. We shall return to this temporal dimension of anxiety later, but for the time being it is important to underscore that the ego absolutely requires anxiety—its alien other—in order to function *as* an organization. Anxiety enables the ego to function because without it, the ego would be unable to assert its claims, or even to make them known, to the other agencies of the psyche. Anxiety is the primordial language of the psyche. Anxiety is always response. But a response is also always a call. Therefore, anxiety facilitates the ego by "responding" to id impulses (internal stimuli) and then the ego responds in turn by using anxiety in order to quell these impulses by compelling the id to produce repressions. This is why Freud is able to say that "anxiety" causes repression rather than the other way around.

Anxiety gives us the future, and there is no future without anxiety.

But in order to understand why this is so, we may need to step back, yet again, and take another look at Freud's text. It is worth pointing out, for example, that *Inhibitions, Symptoms, and Anxiety* is explicitly organized around his own repeated admissions that there is something about anxiety that continues to resist all of his efforts at explaining it. For example, in the opening paragraph of Chapter VIII, he writes:

> What we clearly want is to find something that will tell us what anxiety really is, some criterion that will enable us to distinguish true statements from false ones. But this is not easy to get, Anxiety is not a simple matter. Up to now we have arrived at nothing but contradictory views about it.[10]

But before we take a closer look at some of the "contradictory views" that Freud puts forth about anxiety in *Inhibitions, Symptoms, and Anxiety*, it might be useful to recapitulate some of Freud's most basic claims about anxiety. Throughout the text, there is one fundamental description of anxiety that he repeats and to which he clings tenaciously: Anxiety is a response by the ego to a situation of danger. However, despite the alluring clarity and simplicity of this utterance, it turns out that Freud's clearest definition of anxiety not only fails to define the term in question, but also reveals the extent of its inherent difficulties. As Freud's essay shows, the concept of "anxiety" destabilizes each and every one of the terms that Freud uses in order to define it. Thus, what does it mean to say that "anxiety is a response on the part of the ego to a situation of danger" when, as we have seen, anxiety alters our conception of the ego by making it radically uncanny. Similarly, we have begun to see how anxiety radically challenges our understanding of what a response is and what it means to respond. Finally, as we have suggested, even the notion of a "situation of danger" presents problems because danger cannot be assimilated to death. Furthermore, we do not know how exactly the ego assesses danger, given that, as we have seen throughout our discussion, there can be no simple correlation between the psychic experience of danger and the existence of a real, external threat.

It is around this question of "danger" that Freud's text becomes most contradictory and arguably most interesting. At the risk of oversimplifying this rich and complex text, we can say that Freud gives two parallel, competing and, I would argue, ultimately incompatible accounts of the "danger" associated with anxiety. Very simply put, anxiety is either essentially and irreducibly related to the trauma of birth as an unfinished event, or it is essentially related to a fear of loss of being separated from a loved object and hence castration and death. Freud, of course, attempts to reconcile these two accounts throughout his text. Moreover, he uses his discussion of the relationship between anxiety and phobias in order to suggest that the prototype of the danger associated with anxiety is castration. Thus, he writes:

> The anxiety felt in animal phobias is, therefore an affective reaction on the part of the ego to danger; and the danger which is being signaled in this way is the danger of castration.[11]

Furthermore, and again moving very quickly, Freud uses castration in order to argue that anxiety is a response to loss. On the basis of that assertion, castration not only becomes the privileged example of any kind of fear of loss, but also, more radically, becomes the very anchoring point of reference for the temporal model of the psyche. Thus, through "castration" anxiety, the ego negotiates all dangers and situates itself as a self in time. Castration anxiety provides the ego with a defense against the unruly repetitions of the primal trauma of birth and allows it to enter into a relationship with death that is modeled on castration. Thus, Freud writes,

> But the unconscious seems to contain nothing that could give any content to our concept of the annihilation of life. Castration can be pictured on the basis of the daily experience of the faeces being separated from the body or on the basis of losing the mother's breast at weaning. . . . I am therefore inclined to adhere to the view that the fear of death should be regarded as analogous to the fear of castration.[12]

And, indeed, most readers of Freud (with the notable exception of Lacan) tend to accept the notion that Freud fully subscribes to the notion that the danger associated with anxiety is related to the threat of separation or loss.

But this is not the only story Freud tells in this text. Throughout, Freud returns, again and again, to an understanding of anxiety based on a repetition of birth that opens up new ways of thinking about both birth and time. And now, if we return to where we began, we can hear how the traumatic nature of birth haunts Freud's description of the distinction between "automatic anxiety and signal anxiety."

> Thus we attributed two modes of origin to anxiety in later life. One was involuntary, automatic and always justified on economic grounds, and arose whenever a danger-situation analogous to birth had established itself. The other was produced by the ego as soon as the situation of this kind merely threatened to occur, in order to call for its avoidance. In the second case, the ego subjects itself to anxiety as a sort of inoculation, submitting to a slight attack of the illness in order to escape its full strength. It vividly images the danger-situation, as it were, with the unmistakable purpose of restricting that distressing situation to a mere indication, a signal.[13]

Most radically, Freud suggests that to be born is to be born into anxiety. To be born into anxiety is to be torn out of linear time. Thus the very first act of life, the cry that emanates from the heart and lungs, is itself a traumatic repetition of the signal by which anxiety calls us into time. Anxiety calls us into time traumatically; it gives time to the psyche, gives the psyche time, by ripping time open from birth. To the extent that it recalls the trauma of birth "automatically,""automatic anxiety" lies both "beyond" and "before" the ego. It lies "beyond" the ego, marks a potential beyond for the ego *because* it comes before it, precedes it, calls it into being although it remains radically other to it. Anxiety is the first "sign of life," and it is the most irreducible form of life's relationship to that which lies "beyond." Anxiety has no proper time. It comes from the unlived past of birth and opens up a future from it. It is a signal from birth that tells us that our birth will forever lie before us in a future that is yet to come. But this dislocated relation to time is, as Derrida has suggested, both a promise and a threat. Like the figure of Elpis in Pandora's jar, it is our best and only chance for a future.

PART TWO

Photography and the Prosthetic Maternal

FIVE

On Psycho-Photography: Shame and Abu Ghraib

> "The illiteracy of the future," someone has said, "will be ignorance not of reading or writing, but of photography." But shouldn't a photographer who cannot read his own pictures be no less counted as an illiterate? Won't inscription become the most important part of the photograph?
>
> — WALTER BENJAMIN, "Little History of Photography"

Although one might want to argue that all politics can be seen as an attempt to manage fear, in the aftermath of 9/11 fear has explicitly dominated prevailing political discourse and dictated U.S. domestic and foreign policies. More specifically, the decision to wage preemptive war in Iraq was justified as a reasonable and defensive response to the fear of a future attack. Since U.S. intelligence ostensibly *knew* that Saddam Hussein had weapons of mass destruction, and since we *knew* that Iraq was a breeding ground for Al-Qaeda, and since we *knew* that Hussein and Al-Qaeda were colluding to plan another surprise attack on U.S. soil, it was imperative, it was argued, to wage war on Hussein *there* in Iraq *now* in order to ward off an attack *here* in the *future*. In that heady time leading up to the Iraq war, those who refused to acknowledge the fear-provoking evidence or failed to experience the need for fear were dismissed as foolish at best and irresponsible at worst.

According to this logic, a certain understanding of and faith in the truth of "fear" was required in order to conclude that war was imminent, necessary, and inevitable. The argument that it was vital to U.S. security to take immediate action (made famously by Colin Powell at the United Nations in the spring of 2003) was predicated on the insistence that the danger to U.S. security was not only "real" and "present," but also therefore that the "fear" caused by the danger was rational and reliable. Fear, in other words, became both a measure of political reason and a justification for military action. Once launched, the logic of this politics of fear demanded not only that we *initiate* war with Iraq immediately but also asserted that (appearances to the contrary) the offensive strike in Iraq was actually (in the immortal coinage of Ronald Reagan) a "defensive retaliation." Seen in these terms, the decision to instigate war in Iraq was conceived of as a measured "response" to a palpable *future* threat in the ongoing "war on terror" based on the need to *prevent* an attack like the one the United States had already passively (and traumatically) endured on 9/11. Implicitly, the official position of the U.S. government relied upon its faith in the validity of its own capacity to register, assess, and respond to "fear" appropriately. The war in Iraq provided the Bush administration with an effective and strategic way to use fear as a motivation to take "action." Once mobilized into action, fear became deployed as a defensive weapon in the war against terror. But how are we to understand the paradoxical logic according to which "fear" was invoked as a viable defensive weapon in the "war on terror" since the aim of terror is, after all, to produce fear? How can fear be conceived of both as a protection *from* terror as well as the very sign that one has already succumbed *to* its effects?

As we saw in the last chapter, if one turns to psychoanalysis for insight here, it emerges that understanding the precise dynamics of the kind of anxious fear about the future described earlier proved to be an intractable stumbling block for Freud in the construction of the description of how the psyche is organized (what we have come to call his "metapsychology"). In the pages that follow, I propose to take a look at the traumatic temporal structure of the events surrounding the Abu Ghraib photographs in order to show how the temporality of shame anxiety participated in the production of many of the meanings that became attributed to the images and their exacerbated shameful impact. Before turning to the photographs, however, I would like to return briefly to some of salient points about anxiety that we discussed in the last chapter in order to recall the precise mechanisms of the structures involved. As we observed there, the problem

Freud confronted repeatedly (from his early work in the *Project on Scientific Psychology*, taken up again in *Beyond the Pleasure Principle* and then most saliently in *Inhibitions, Symptoms, and Anxiety*) concerned the difficulty of understanding how the psyche registers and recognizes a situation of "danger." In all of his major metapsychological texts, Freud struggles with the fact that there can be no *simple* correlation between the psychic experience of danger and the existence of a real, external threat. In *Inhibitions, Symptoms, and Anxiety*, he remarks, "Man seems not to have been endowed with, or to have been endowed to only a very small degree, with an instinctive recognition of the dangers that threaten him from without." This failure to recognize danger underlies his derivation of trauma in *Beyond the Pleasure Principle*, where he explains that people do not become traumatized because they have a close encounter with death, but rather because they become overwhelmed by fright. The fright is produced by the encounter with an experience for which the psyche is not prepared rather than by the existence of a real, external danger. Psychically speaking, it is extremely difficult, if not impossible, to locate the precise source, degree, and timing of a danger situation. Thus, although "fear" is a reliable signal of the psychic *experience* of danger, the presence of "fear" is rarely (if ever) a reliable indicator of whether the danger in question is internal or external, real or imagined or whether it is currently present, has already happened, or is anticipated in the future.

As we have also seen, although Freud attempts to establish a clear-cut distinction between fear, trauma and anxiety, ultimately he is unable to do so. While ordinary fear (if such a thing actually exists) is unproblematic from a psychic standpoint (as it is an entirely rational and conscious reaction to a real and present danger), distinguishing between trauma and anxiety is much more difficult, since both radically disrupt special and temporal parameters in similar ways. The distinction between them (such as it is) is paradoxically located in their different modes of being dislocated in time and space. Whereas trauma happens *to the psyche* when unknown danger suddenly befalls it, anxiety is a traumatic response that is produced *by the psyche* itself: In an attempt to ward off a future recurrence of a past trauma, the ego reproduces and simulates traumatic surprise as a prophylactic against traumatic surprise. There is an appealing narrative coherence to this entire account: fear is aligned with consciousness, reality, and presence, while trauma is conceived in relation to a missed past (as it is associated with the disruptive psychic effects caused by an intrusive, external event that is only retroactively registered), and anxiety is associated with a virtual future as it takes the form of an internal protective response to the anticipation of a future danger that has not yet occurred. Anxiety, however, belongs uniquely to the ego and its function is to defend the ego's aims and police its borders. By giving itself over to anxiety, the ego attempts to master overwhelming affects by internalizing them and reproducing them in "defensive retaliation" against future threats.

During the lead-up to the Iraq war, the prevailing political discourse of the U.S. government displayed all of the hallmarks of anxiety—that is, it attempted to transform an unassimilated past experience of helplessness into an active, powerful, and masterful intervention. Who can forget the promissory threat of "shock and awe"? The very name conjures up both trauma and anxiety. But the strange temporal structure of anxiety (which can never contain, locate, or even identify the very traumatic events it is attempting to master) itself insures that the self can never successfully determine its own borders or regulate them effectively. Given what we have said thus far, this is because by definition the self can never be present to itself in a moment of danger. Since every situation of danger can be experienced only as a repetition of a prior trauma, the moment of danger has an uncanny temporal status. The event "happens" (to the extent that it even "happens") only in the form of a mechanical reproduction of an earlier, latent, and to some extent "unlived" earlier trauma. The thing called a self is itself called into being by trauma and attempts to constitute its borders as a belated response to it. But no matter how vigilant or violent that self prepares itself to be in defending its borders, it will always be vulnerable, since its borders are constitutively permeable and temporally unstable. The Abu Ghraib photographs mobilized the temporal structure of anxiety and, in so doing, triggered a relay of signals between the traumatic temporality of the photographic medium on one hand and the psychic experience of shame on the other.

Psycho-Photography: Abu Ghraib and Shame

> Shame is a specific form of anxiety evoked by the imminent danger of unexpected exposure, humiliation, and rejection. Shame anxiety, like all anxiety, is twofold. Either it is a response to the overwhelming trauma of helplessness already experienced . . . or shame may function merely as a signal.[1]

On April 28, 2004, the Abu Ghraib photographs were first exposed to public view on the television news program *60 Minutes*. From their very first disclosure, the photos incited an explosion of competing discourses (some of which appear to be mutually exclusive) concerning the status and meaning of the acts photographed, the act of photographing, the photographs themselves, and the impact of their exposure.[2] Almost immediately after being exhibited, they spread like dark lightning around the world. In a matter of days, they were reproduced on a massive scale and were disseminated through the Internet, television, and newspapers. From the beginning, though, there was something unusual (and perhaps even historically unprecedented) about the way in which the graphic content of the photos accelerated the dizzying rate of their reproduction and diffusion. The fact that these images were almost immediately potentially available to be seen by anyone anywhere with access to various forms of public media only further increased their power. The impact of the Abu Ghraib photographs "shocked" the world and in so doing accorded their exposure the status of an historical event. But despite the widespread sense that the *exposure* of the images did, in fact, constitute an event of sorts, the historical and political meaning of that event, the meanings of the events depicted *in* the photographs and the meaning *of* the photographs (as photographs—whether seen as objects or acts) are still unresolved. Indeed, I would like to suggest that the "photographic events" precipitated by and depicted in the Abu Ghraib photographs remain radically unfinished and troublingly unreadable.

In the years that have elapsed since they were first made public, the photographs have been displayed in museums, art galleries, and websites; images derived from them can be found on city walls, web blogs, and in numerous other "real" and virtual public spaces.[3] Moving through and beyond the borders of the various cultural institutions that have traditionally fulfilled "archival" functions (including the museum, the courtroom and the halls of government) they have now been collected, gathered up, and placed into virtual "archives" all over the web, including one designed explicitly for the purpose of serving as an archive for them on Salon.com.[4] The political and cultural significance of the creation of these "virtual archives" has not yet been fully appreciated.

Some of the images depicted in the photographs have seemingly taken on a life of their own and have now been designated as "icons." (It is generally agreed that the two photographs that have attained "iconic" status are the image of the hooded man on the box with wires attached—the picture is known by the name "Vietnam"—and the image of Lynndie England dragging a naked man across the prison floor on a leash.) Artists from around the world have adopted these photographs as "source material" and have produced art works inspired by the images. Numerous other people (including journalists, activists, militants, intellectuals, graffiti artists) have appropriated the images and put them to work in different ways for different reasons. But the proliferation of these images does not render them any easier to read. If anything (and this is part of the argument that follows), because they produce new meanings with each reproduction, they become more difficult to read even as they continue to produce incalculable political and historical effects.

As I have already suggested, there has been little agreement about how to interpret the photographs, but from very early on there was a general consensus that the Abu Ghraib photographs are "shameful." But although many commentators have invoked the notion of "shame" in their responses to the images, the concept of shame has gone largely uninterrogated. I propose to examine the concept of shame more closely and explore how shame and photography might be related. Indeed, given that shame can be defined provisionally as an anxiety concerning the fear of unexpected exposure, it appears to have a privileged relation to the medium of photography.

In fact, one of the main arguments of this chapter is that shame can be called a *photographic affect*. Shame *is* photographic. In shame, as in photography, there is an emphasis on acts of looking and effects of exposure. Furthermore, like shame, photography violates the boundaries between private and public spheres. In both shame and photography, aspects of an inner life, individual body or personal history can become (or threaten to become) available to public view. And in shame, as in photography, intensely privately lived moments can become transformed into public spectacle. By opening up a dynamic relationship between shame and photography, I hope to explore new ways of looking at the complex set of issues surrounding the meaning, causes, and consequences of the Abu Ghraib photographs. Although they display sexually graphic, sadistic, and humiliating acts, those acts are not merely "represented" as such, but rather they were clearly staged for the camera and take the form of ritualized "scenarios," or theatrical "scenes." What does the fact that some of these images were clearly produced and used for purposes of sexual stimulation tell us about the sexuality or the stimulation involved? Should they should be considered "pornographic"? And if so, does that say anything about pornography more generally?

Opening up a dynamic link between photography and shame helps to explain how and why the Abu Ghraib photographs have been able to operate on different levels and have fulfilled multiple, complex, and seemingly radically contradictory functions. These photographs have been simultaneously treated as documentary evidence, human rights advocates, instruments of torture, and perverse enactments of pornographic fantasies.

Because photography and shame share certain formal properties, they collude in powerful ways in the public sphere. The potential for reciprocal communication between the photographic medium on one hand and the psychic structure of shame on the other enhances the power of both so that the effect of each is accentuated. When photography and shame "collaborate" in this way on the world stage, they exacerbate and exploit existing confusions between political effects and psychic affects. "Psycho-photography" is the name I am giving to the effects of this collaboration. In "psycho-photography," politics and history become imbued with mechanically reproduced images (images that are neither strictly conscious or unconscious, nor personal or historical) that produce new historical associations and political effects. In this sense, "psycho-photography" is a kind of *historical* pathology that calls for careful political analysis.

The Discursive Function of the Photographs

Let us beginning by summarizing, in a rather schematic way, some of the contradictory meanings and functions that have been ascribed to the Abu Ghraib photographs as they have circulated within political discourse since their first exposure.

Documentation

According to the documentation view, photographs are purely objective and have the status of evidence. Their function is to record and document. As such, the photographs are *external* to the events they record. Many human rights activists have adopted this position on account of their (legitimate) worry that the prurient interest provoked by the photographs might detract from the attention to the reality depicted in them. *The Road to Abu Ghraib*, a report issued by the Human Rights Watch in the summer of 2004, explicitly insists upon the importance of separating the *fact* of the abuse from the apparent contingency of its having been photographed:

> In fact, the only exceptional aspect of the abuse at Abu Ghraib may have been that it was photographed. Detainees in US custody in Afghanistan have testified that they experienced treatment similar to what happened at Abu Ghraib—from beatings to prolonged sleep and sensory deprivation to being held naked—as early as 2002. Comparable—and, indeed, more extreme—cases of torture have been extensively documented by the International Committee of the Red Cross and by journalists at numerous locations in Iraq outside Abu Ghraib.[5]

Implicitly, however, this way of looking at the photographs highlights the *physical* aspect of the abuse depicted in the images at the expense of other kinds of abuse. By emphasizing the fact that the photographs do, indeed, document physical abuse, human rights activists sought to use them as a way of drawing attention to documented (but unphotographed) cases of torture elsewhere in Iraq and in Afghanistan. While the political stakes and motivation of this position are abundantly clear (that is, this view adamantly refuted the claim made by the U.S. government that "abuse" at Abu Ghraib was an isolated incident and called attention to the lack of attention that had been given to other instances of torture), this way of looking at the photographs treats them as if they are purely "transparent" representations of an external reality. In some sense, this way of looking at the photographs renders them invisible (as photographs) by making the fact that they are *representations* irrelevant to the reality they record. This perspective also downplays and discounts the apparently "sexual" nature of the "abuse" and cannot account for the "fantasy" scenarios depicted in them. In sum, according to this view, the Abu Ghraib photographs are *facts* rather than *acts*.

Exposure

A slightly modified version of this first view would have it that photographs are not merely documents, but documents with enhanced powers of persuasion. They not only bear witness to the reality of events but also are endowed with the power to bring hidden or repressed events to public consciousness by shedding light on them and placing them in public view. When photographs expose a (previously) hidden event, they are perceived to possess and reveal a privileged truth about that event. Almost everyone who has commented on the Abu Ghraib photographs (ranging from Seymour Hersh and Susan Sontag to the *Army Times* editorial page and even Donald Rumsfeld) explicitly or implicitly shares this view.

In his book *Chain of Command*, Seymour Hersh describes how "the abuses became public because of the outrage of Specialist Joseph M. Darby. . . . Darby did what the world's most influential human rights groups could not. The International Committee of the Red Cross and Human Rights Watch had repeatedly complained during the previous year about the American military's treatment of Iraqi prisoners, with little response from the system."[6] Because, in photography, the power to document is seemingly inextricable from the act of exposing hidden realities, photography lends itself exceptionally well to what, in the domain of human rights, has been called "the mobilization of shame."[7] And certainly it would appear self-evident that to the extent that the Abu Ghraib photographs have forced an acknowledgment of abuse and torture that was previously denied and hidden, they have been and they should be put in the service of a general human rights discourse about abuse and torture of prisoners in Iraq and elsewhere. Likewise, according to Hersh, although Donald Rumsfeld presumably knew about the existence of the photographs and had been presumably briefed about them, he was "in denial" about their importance until he actually looked at them at which point he described them as depicting "acts that can only be described as blatantly sadistic, cruel, and inhuman."[8] Apparently, it would seem that only the persuasive power of photography was able to force Donald Rumsfeld to admit publicly that there had indeed been "fundamentally un-American" wrongdoing at Abu Ghraib.

Implicit in the preceding discussion is the view that photographs do not merely record events. In the act of bringing hidden realities to consciousness, the exposure of the photograph itself constitutes an event. And as an event, it actively participates in the discourse of politics and even becomes part of political history in its own right. In this sense, the photographs are not merely representations, but representational "events" that take on a (political) life of their own.

An interesting corollary to the view can be found in the idea that the very power that enables photographs to persuade can also compel them to "fade out" over time. They exhibit a paradoxical capacity to obscure the very existence of the things they represent by becoming a mediating screen that separates and distances the viewer from the "represented" reality. Mark Danner opens his important book *Torture and Truth* with the following claim to this effect:

> Indeed, as I argue in these pages, though the photographs first announced Abu Ghraib to the world and gave impetus to the investigations of what happened there, as the months passed and more evidence accumulated the images have increasingly had the opposite effect, helping to block a full public understanding of how the scandal arose.[9]

When the "power" of the image fades, the (over) exposed event becomes transformed into a nonevent. And, as Danner suggests, the actions in the photographs become isolated and severed from the ongoing and complex history that produced them.

From Event to Action

The Abu Ghraib photographs have an added dimension that complicates the structure even further. Although the decision (here attributed to SPC Darby) to expose the photographs was intended to expose the abuse depicted in them, the act of taking the photographs was not intended to expose abuse, but rather was explicitly and actively engaged in it. This is important because it means that Darby's decision to expose the photographs as abusive inevitably forced him to expose the photographers as abusers in the same gesture. In other words, Darby recognized that the photographs were not merely *documents* of abusive prisoner treatment, but also—and in the same instance—*instruments* of it.

The photographic medium lends itself uniquely to this sort of rhetorical malleability. The very same photographs can *simultaneously* function as seemingly "objective" evidence of abuse as well as "subjective" agents of it. The specific nature of photography and the photographic act necessitates a kind of doubling of the self along with a splitting of subject positions. Photographs operate according to a constant and indeterminable grammatical slippage among persons. Sometimes they seem to speak in the third person, sometimes in the first person and sometimes—like the psychic structure of fetishistic splitting that they resemble in so many ways—they simultaneously maintain a series of incompatible and mutually exclusive subject positions. Furthermore, the multilayered "subject positions" of the photographs generate (and are generated by) their own "visual" grammar and language.

One of the most disturbing aspects of the Abu Ghraib photographs is that many of them appear to be in the *second* person: They are imprinted with a blatant appeal to the voyeuristic gaze of an implied but hidden viewer. As many people have remarked, the abusing soldiers looked directly into the camera and assumed smiling poses for it. Many of the scenes depicted in the photos were clearly staged for the camera. In their ritualized and perverse sadomasochistic theatricality, these images address themselves to the complicity of a (future) viewer who lurks behind the camera's gaze and in a future moment extends the event horizon of the abusive scenes beyond the frame of the still image.

These photographs never had a stable meaning, a determinable addressee, or even a finite temporal field. Every reproduction of the photograph implies some sort of reproduction of the events depicted in the photograph. The very images that provoked SPC Darby to go to the authorities were being used by some of Darby's fellow officers in the pursuit of some form of pleasure. As Hersh describes it, the army commanders were then faced by the discrepancy between the "sensitive nature" of what was documented and exposed in the photographs and the insensitive and cavalier way in which those images were treated by the troops. Hersh writes:

> The images, it was soon clear, were being swapped from computer to computer throughout the 320th Battalion. The Army's senior commanders immediately understood they had a problem—a looming political and public relations disaster that would taint the United States and damage the war effort.[10]

Furthermore, photographs rarely fail to reflect the image of what their viewer needs or wants to see. Thus, even if it were possible to determine whether or not a particular photographic event at Abu Ghraib was intended for documentary purposes (as in the case of the "ghost detainee" who was murdered and photographed on ice) or for purposes of abuse (as in the now notorious "thumbs up" images) from the instant the images were recorded, they entered into circulation. From that point on, their function and meaning become dependent on the desires, meanings, and functions ascribed to them by the viewer. Each and every event of viewing becomes a complex subjective act of citation that now engages the conscious and unconscious desires, feelings, fantasies, perceptions, and projections of the viewer.

For example, Darby made the photographs public not only because of what he saw *in* them, but also because of *how* he saw them and how they made him feel. In some sense, therefore, the exposed photographs implicitly bear the imprinted trace of Darby's "gaze." Seen from this vantage point, the act of looking at the photographs through Darby's eyes involves looking at the "photographer-abusers" who were his fellow soldiers through his disapproving look. However, adopting this viewing position in no way prevents the viewer from also entering into a complicitous identification with the actors in the photographs or with the gaze of the photographer. Although, in some sense, the photographs compel the viewer to identify (at least partially) with the (implied) look of the (hidden) photographer, even that gaze does not simply exhaust the field of vision or saturate the possibility of maintaining multiple (and contradictory) viewing positions.

In fact, one of the things that make these photographs so strange (and so disturbing) is the way in which they seemingly generate and sustain an unstable stream of possible gazes and discursive positions. The viewer can simultaneously return the gaze of the "actors" who address the camera directly; "take in" an (objectifying) look at the bodies of the (mostly hooded or otherwise unseeing) victims; and identify with the position of the photographer who presumably took pleasure in taking the photographs and with the position of the person who exposed the photographs presumably because he himself felt "exposed" by them. In fact, one can speculate that it was precisely because Darby experienced the photographs as "shameful" when he encountered them that he decided to turn them in to military officers in part as an attempt to get rid of his own sense of shame. Although none of these viewing positions is stable, they all generate and are generated by an embodied "affective" response. Shame, like anxiety, is a bodily event that happens to and in the body. But the bodily experience of shame is abjection. Hence, defenses against shame can include attempts at mastery of the body. Such attempts at body mastery often take the form of mastering the body of the other.[11]

The Photograph as Instrument of Torture and the Question of Shame

It is important to remember that one of the explicit aims and objectives of photography at Abu Ghraib prison was as an active instrument of torture. Most of the Abu Ghraib photographs were taken expressly in order to shame and humiliate the prisoners. In this context it is interesting to note that the report issued by Major General Antonio M. Taguba, unlike the previous reports issued by the IRC (International Red Cross) explicitly and insistently includes the act of photographing in the list of tortures it documents. Taguba writes:

> I find that the intentional abuse of detainees by military police personnel included the following acts…
>
> b. (S) Videotaping and photographing naked male and female detainees;
> c. (S) Forcibly arranging detainees in various sexually explicit positions for photographing;
> f. (S) Forcing groups of male detainees to masturbate themselves while being photographed and videotaped;
> j. (S) Placing a dog chain or strap around a naked detainee's neck and having a female soldier pose for a picture;
> m. (S) Taking photographs of dead Iraqi detainees.[12]

Taguba's report remains one of the few official documents that explicitly assert that the act of taking a photograph of an abused prisoner is not merely a record of torture; it *is* an act of torture. Along these same lines (and not surprisingly), Taguba made a conscious decision not to include any reproductions of the photographs in his report:

> The allegations of abuse were substantiated by detailed witness statements (ANNEX 26) and the discovery of *extremely graphic photographic evidence*. Due to the *extremely sensitive nature of these photographs* and videos, the ongoing CID investigation, and the potential for the criminal prosecution

> of several suspects, the photographic evidence is not included in the *body* of my investigation.[13]

It is significant that Taguba explains his decision to exclude the "photographic evidence" of wrongdoing from the *body* of his report due to its "extremely graphic" and "extremely sensitive" nature. It would appear that Taguba, perhaps like Darby before him, was perhaps struggling with his own painful affects, triggered both by his exposure to the photographs and his sense that it was his responsibility to attempt to contain their effects. Furthermore, once he had concluded that the photographs had been taken for the express purpose of abuse, he could no longer simply reproduce and circulate them as if they were merely documentary evidence. It seems equally plausible to suggest that Taguba's somewhat remarkable display of discretion concerning the images can be interpreted as a *conscious* attempt, on his part, to insulate the army from the impact of exposure to the shameful images. But it also may have been an *unconscious* attempt to manage his own affective response to the photographs. He seems to have been aware that the photographs not only depict shameful acts but also are themselves purveyors of shame. In other words, Taguba's actions implicitly confirm that he was afraid of being contaminated by the photographs. He seems to have understood that the photographs are, indeed, contagious and that they carry shame in the sense that one speaks of "carrying" a disease.

The psychoanalytic literature on shame is replete with examples of the way that shame, unlike guilt, to which it is often compared, is like a communicable disease. Shame is contagious and reproduces itself in the event of its disclosure. The exposure of shameful acts usually does not succeed in making shame go away or attenuating its effects. On the contrary, when exposed, shame often ends up producing even more shame. In his book, *The Mask of Shame*, psychoanalyst Léon Wurmser describes the self-replicating aspect of shame:

> Shame may well be called the most generalizable, most quickly spreading and flooding affect of them all. . . . This process of affect flooding is further promoted by the circular nature of shame, which immediately engenders the characteristic infinite regress of "shame about shame" . . . All affects show this feeding on themselves, but because of the . . . nature of shame, this process is exponentially increased and speeded up. *Shame anxiety is*

> *specifically self-potentiating and thus especially prone to traumatic mobilization and loss of control.*[14]

The traumatic self-replicating power of shame makes it virtually uncontainable and uncontrollable. Shame can spread from a person who is shamed by another or from someone who has performed a shameful act upon another to a person or people who become exposed to the shameful revelations. Exposure to shame can suffice to produce shame, which then reproduces itself and continues to spread. This is one reason why shame is often characterized as "dirty." It contaminates and defiles anything that it touches. Precisely because shame is so contagious, defenses against the threat of shame (whether psychic or cultural) often take the form of an attempt to wall shame off with strict measures for containment, like quarantine or exile.

Put in this context, it seems clearer why Taguba, whose primary concern throughout was the "honor" of the army and the country, would be so concerned to document the abuses without allowing himself or the country to be tainted by them in turn. In somewhat similar (although markedly "less honorable") fashion, the U.S. government has repeatedly attempted (and failed) to contain the effects of the Abu Ghraib photographs. The official response to the scandal of the photographs has been to insist again and again (despite the many contradictory reports that have since emerged) that the photographs were the shameful product of a few shameful individuals; that the photographs depict shameful acts that are "un-American"; that the photographs were intended as the sick entertainment of a few sick individuals rather than as an official tool designed to be used for interrogation purposes; that improper photographing (and abuse) of prisoners was not condoned and/or ordered by the military officers, intelligence officers, and civilians in charge of the prison; that the photographs and the prisoner abuse did not in itself constitute torture and did not result in the death of any prisoners; if any wrongdoing did occur, the guilty parties have been brought to justice through the judicial system.

As we now know, virtually all of these claims have proven to be false. In the time that has elapsed since the photographs first were viewed, there have been a series of subsequent revelations of great wrongdoing on the part of U.S. soldiers, officers, and government officials in Iraq, Guantanamo Bay, and Afghanistan, to name only the most obvious examples.

Photographs of Shame, Shaming, and Shamelessness

Arguably one of the most shocking claims made by Seymour Hersh in *Chain of Command* concerns the revelation of the existence of an official U.S. governmental policy to use photographs as a weapon of shame against the Iraqis. Hersh writes:

> The notion that Arabs are particularly vulnerable to sexual humiliation had become a talking point among pro-war Washington conservatives in the months before the March 2003 invasion of Iraq. One book that was frequently cited was *The Arab Mind*. . . . The Patai book, an academic told me, was "the bible of the neocons on Arab behavior." In their discussions, he said, two themes emerged—"one that Arabs only understand force and, two, that the biggest weakness of Arabs is shame and humiliation."
>
> The government consultant said that there may have been a serious goal, in the beginning, behind the sexual humiliation and the posed photographs. It was thought that some prisoners would do anything—including spying on their associates—to avoid shameful dissemination of the shameful photos to family and friends. The government consultant said, "I was told that the purpose of the photographs was to create an army of informants, people you could insert back into the population." The idea was that they would be motivated by fear of exposure, and gather information about pending insurgency action, the consultant said.[15]

Although it may never be clearly determined whether or not the Abu Ghraib photographs were promoted either as part of a direct implementation of this policy or as an indirect consequence of it, they remain, nonetheless, a telling symptom of it. Even if this policy was never officially adopted, the Abu Ghraib photographs need to be read in light of the fact that the U.S. government workers had conceived a plan in which photography was selected as the weapon of choice in order to inflict shame on Iraqis because the Iraqis were perceived by the United States to be particularly susceptible to it. Furthermore, regardless of how abhorrent the U.S. policy may have been (or still is), it is interesting to observe how dramatically and systematically that policy backfired with the dissemination of the Abu Ghraib photographs. The very medium (photography) that was supposed to be deployed in order to shame Iraqis into supporting democracy became the medium through which shameful and undemocratic U.S. treatment of Iraqi prisoners was documented and exposed. This reversal of positions (from shamer to shamed) is yet another example of how the Abu Ghraib photographs convey meanings and produce effects in ways that are similar to the psychic mechanisms operative in shame. The photographic images that were intended to shame the other as other became transformed into a shameful self-image of American-style democracy. Like democracy, photography aspires to be transparent and neutral and to bring events to light in the public sphere. But democracy, like photography, is haunted by its unanalyzed relation to shame.

Shame, Perversion, and the Political Punctum

Thus far in this discussion, I have not yet even mentioned the most explosive defining features of the Abu Ghraib photographs: the prevalence of ostensibly sexualized and/or racialized scenes of humiliation; the fact that white women were prominent in the depictions of humiliating acts on the bodies of brown men[16]; the fact that the U.S. soldiers (male and female) depicted performing the acts of humiliation, abuse, and torture showed visible signs of enjoyment and pleasure; and the fact that these scenes of humiliation were "staged" and that the actors in the pictures seemed to be acting out "scenes" according to some kind of (preexisting?) perverse "script." These images continue to test the limits of the vocabulary available to describe them. Are they pornographic? Does concern for such designation even make sense in this context? Certainly, the Abu Ghraib images have been put to pornographic use. In her article, "Torture Culture: Lynching Photographs and the Images of Abu Ghraib," Dora Apel argues that although the Abu Ghraib photographs resemble pornography, they are not pornographic. She writes,

> Although the torture photos seem to employ the basic structuring principle of pornography—the events are real but staged for the camera in order to deliver prurient pleasure—the protocols are fundamentally different. Porno actors do not mug for the camera; they maintain the fiction of authenticity. Here there is no "fiction" of authenticity, not only because the victims are not willing actors, but because the pleasure is not meant to be found in the pruriently deployed bodies but in the exultant mastery of those who would wield power over them, representing a different cultural and political order.[17]

Whether or not one can maintain a distinction between these images and images explicitly produced for pornographic consumption, the Abu Ghraib photographs display perverse citations of common pornographic scenarios. Although, as Linda Williams (among others) has shown, pornography cannot be understood as a monolithic object or cultural practice; nonetheless, cultural debates about pornography have either tended to assert *either* that the aim of pornography is about pleasure *or* that it is about power, humiliation, abuse, and control. In these perversely pornographic images, however, the pleasure clearly appears to be inextricably derived from the humiliation. These images exhibit their perverse status by drawing upon photography's capacity to facilitate fetishistic psychic splitting by blurring perceptible differences between living and dead bodies, between involuntary scenes of real torture and staged fantasies of torture in the pursuit of sadomasochistic pleasure.

From a certain psychoanalytic perspective, this sort of eroticization of torture can be directly linked to shame anxiety. In this light, perhaps the violent and perversely sexualized acts staged by U.S. soldiers in the Abu Ghraib photographs were not merely, as has been commonly accepted, a reflection of wanton insensitive shamelessness on the part of the soldiers, but rather, and perhaps more disturbingly still, these acts should also be understood as expressions of shame on the part of the soldiers themselves. We might ask whether the soldiers are not merely shameful photographers but also have become transformed into the human embodiments of shame. In this certain sense, we might even go so far as to suggest that the photographers have themselves become human photographs. Perhaps the poses they strike are reflections of a shame that they bear within them and repeat unknowingly. From a psychoanalytic perspective, perversion is the attempt to eroticize a prior trauma: In their perverse forms of acting out, these human photographs mechanically reproduce, blindly and unconsciously, the perverse effects of a traumatic shame that lurks within the very foundations of American democracy.

If these "actors" are engaged in unconscious citation, this is because citation itself is the means by which trauma can become eroticized. In this sense, one might say that these images are, above all, fetishistic and perverse exercises of excitation. This brings us back to one of the most important and enigmatic aspects of these images: the fact that they appear to be staged citational reenactments of scenes drawn from an immense and latent archive of historical and political images. Like nineteenth-century *tableaux vivants*, the scenes in the Abu Ghraib photographs deploy live actors to recreate scenes based on well-known images. But unlike the *tableaux vivants*, the Abu Ghraib photographs appear to draw upon a politically and historically overdetermined image repertory of paradoxically highly documented but nonetheless radically *untold* events. More specifically, one of the most striking effects of these photographs in their afterlife—that is, their reception—is that they proliferate, and continue to proliferate, extremely powerful associations that vary radically according to the position of the viewer. Thus, Hazel Carby and Dora Apel, along with others (many of whom have ties to the African American community) immediately perceived references to lynching. Similarly, where Rush Limbaugh recognized images of stacked bodies in a pile as a reference to frat-house hazing, Holocaust survivors produced other associations on the basis of the same images. In a perhaps debatable appropriation of the term that Roland Barthes invented to express the power of photographic affect, I use the phrase "political punctum" to describe the mechanism by which each viewer receives the photographs by replicating their effect on the basis of an internalized image repertoire that is culturally, politically, and historically determined, and that is neither conscious nor unconscious. The images address themselves to the viewer by "reproducing themselves" internally. Each such viewing provokes an affective response and triggers a new chain of images drawn from a virtual, cultural, "psycho-photographic archive" of images to which they become attached. Thus it is not surprising that in the United States, analogies were quickly made between these photographs and lynching. In France, however, associations may have led more quickly to the Algerian war. While such readings are certainly pertinent (and even essential for political analysis), the important point here is that they are not exhaustive and they do not exhaust the problem of tracing out the historical and political associations set in motion by the reproduction of the images. This has consequences in that these images cannot be contained by any kind of spatial border, be it national or psychic, nor are they contained in time. All such images are potentially singular time bombs. In principle, each of these associations is itself a "psycho-photographic" event that in turn becomes capable of producing powerful new politico-historical constellations and effects. In this sense, it would not be inaccurate to say that these photos, like the structure of anxiety itself, are inflected with the future tense. As such, the images from Abu Ghraib are "psycho-photographical" traces of new media primal scenes: They are simultaneously nightmarish dream texts that bear traces of an unassimilated traumatic historical past and a prophetic harbinger of an unfolding political future.

SIX

Avital Ronell's Body Politics

> There is no natural, originary body: technology has not simply added itself, from the outside, or after the fact, as a foreign body. Or at least this foreign and dangerous supplement is "originarily" at work and in the place of the supposed ideal interiority of the "body and soul." It is indeed at the heart of the heart.
>
> —JACQUES DERRIDA, "The Rhetoric of Drugs"

In Your Ear

In a certain sense, one might begin by saying "she told us so," but perhaps we didn't hear her well enough. For a long time now, over many years and in her many important works ranging from the early *Dictations* to the recent *Test Drive*, Avital Ronell has been trying to open our ears to the ramifications of the politics of the body. Recent events in world history and science are only confirming what she has been telling us all along. Before AIDS, terrorism, drugs, information technology, and viruses were on everyone's lips, she was tuning in to the ways in which the question of the body opens up onto politics, ethics, religion, and war. Throughout her remarkable corpus (which is, as I write, very much alive), she has continued to show that the body calls for thinking. But to say that the body calls for thinking does not mean that the body invoked here is thinkable in any simple sense; it is not an object of thought, but rather a mode, frequency, and tonal field that can only be read to the extent that it is heard. Such thinking, Ronell tells us, begins in your ear.

And, indeed, in her inimitable voice, Ronell prefaces *The Telephone Book* with the following challenge and appeal to the reader:

> Your mission, should you choose to accept it, is to learn how to read with your ears. In addition to listening for the telephone, you are being asked to tune your ears to noise frequencies, to anticoding, to the inflated reserves of random indeterminateness—in a word, you are expected to stay open to the static and interference that will occupy these lines.[1]

Ronell's direct address to the reader is an invitation and a warning as "reading with the ears" is inherently risky: it is always both a promise and a threat. As she herself elucidates, such a reading actively "engages the destabilization of the addressee" by scrambling known pathways of sense and sound, cutting off common connections, suspending meaning. Likewise, in her reading and writing practice, Avital Ronell opens her ears to the challenge of receiving the unconscious determinations and overdeterminations of contemporary politics and culture. She engages in an analytic practice of listening for "that which resists presentation." Drawing upon literature, philosophy, and psychoanalysis, Ronell attends to the white noise of popular and unpopular culture in order to forge new lines of communication. And her texts open up a new form of analytic reading that sets forth an ethics, a politics and a practice of performative intervention for which one might be tempted to invent the neologism "techno-analysis."

At stake is nothing less than the future. As she puts it in the opening pages of *Finitude's Score*: "If I am in the position of giving you anything—and this is not clear to me—I know that one cannot hope to give anything but the future."[2] The gift of the future depends upon the ability to hear the repressed strains within the history of thought. The effects of these repressions are embodied everywhere in the materiality of daily life in all its registers. The history of what has not been thought but that calls for thinking secretes its traces and produces symptoms, effects, pathologies, waste products, and technological appliances in its wake.

When, therefore, Avital Ronell picks up the telephone in *The Telephone Book*, she takes up the task of showing that the question concerning technology is inextricable from the challenge of opening up the body as a question.

To open up the body as question entails acknowledging that the body is not the silent "other" of thought, but rather its medium, its very condition of possibility. Although she had already put the concept of the body to work in *Dictations: Haunted Writing*, in *The Telephone Book*, Ronell explicitly and systematically inaugurates her (ongoing) interrogation into the ways in which technological objects come into being as symptomatic responses to certain conceptions and repressions of the body. In its attempts to bypass the body, the history of Western thought, philosophy, and culture has repressed the body and failed to read its traces. But embedded within the history of these repressive gestures, the body continues to assert its demands differently, setting up alternative networks and pathways of meaning. Ronell borrows from psychoanalysis by burrowing into its textual complexities and its contradictions, its method, material, and madness.

As she also points out, Freud himself acknowledges the telephonic dimension of psychoanalytic interpretation by explicitly comparing the transference as a telephonic communication and the position of the analyst as a receptor of messages that arrive through unconscious telephonic networks:

> To put it in a formula: he [the doctor] must turn his own unconscious like a receptive organ towards the transmitting unconscious of the patient. He must adjust himself to the patient as a telephone receiver is adjusted to the transmitting microphone. Just as the receiver converts back into sound-waves the electric oscillations in the telephone line which were set up by sound waves, so the doctor's unconscious is able, from the derivatives of the unconscious which are communicated to him, to reconstruct that unconscious, which has determined the patient's free associations.[3]

The reader who dares to take up the challenge posed in and by the *Telephone Book* must in this sense *become* a telephone by adopting a stance of "free floating reception."[4] The reader is simultaneously placed on the line and cut off from it, since ear reading opens up an outside that folds back upon itself like the invaginated ear itself. Let us remember, as Jacques Lacan has pointed out: "In the field of the unconscious, the ears are the only orifice that cannot be closed."[5] (Lacan's gloss on the ears comes to us through *The Telephone Book*, transmitted by Ronell, who also cites Derrida citing Freud on this point.) This opening and openness of the ears renders the self open to the outside, to its others (that is, to everything that is not itself and everything that it is not) as well as to others. As such, this openness (like all openings) is also a wound and a trace of incompletion, finitude, and absence. As opening, it carves out a space that can always be left empty, filled with absence. In this sense, the ear is endowed with cryptic powers and possibilities. The specter of the absent other and/or the absence of the self always lurks within its folds.

Throughout her work, Ronell insistently calls attention to the specifically uncanny and improper properties of the ear. In *The Telephone Book* and *Finitude's Score*, she explains the significance of the difference between the ear and other bodily orifices as follows:

> Unlike the mouth, the ear needs a silent partner, a double and phantom of itself. The mouth doubles itself by metonymic displacement, getting on the shuttle to vaginal and anal sites.[6]

The ear is simultaneously strangely singular and duplicitously plural. As Ronell indicates in the preceding passage, the ambiguities of the ear(s) stem in part from the fact that although we may each be morphologically endowed with two ears, our ears do not belong to us, and we do not hear with our own ears alone. In its "communicative" function, the ear relies on being given to another and shared across other bodies. In this sense, my "other" ear belongs not to me, but to the other. It is the ear of the other.[7] Although only the ear of the other can respond to my call to be heard, the ear of the other cannot be "present to me." It is, as Ronell describes it, "a silent partner, a double and phantom of itself." By comparing the ear to the mouth, Ronell implies that while both mouth and ear are the primary organs of communication, the ear communicates only with the other and with others whereas the mouth has the capacity to retreat from the other and turn inward onto the self by establishing autoerotic lines of communication.

But because the ear is, in some sense, defenseless in its appeal to an absent (or potentially absent) other, it is the most receptive, fragile, and easily bruised human orifice. Its very constitution as an organ destines it to be dependent on and vulnerable to the response or nonresponse of the other. As Ronell insists, this means that the ear cannot live without an "other" ear, cannot function by itself, cut off from a world of others. But this also means, paradoxically, that the authentic experience of solitude begins in the ear. Only the ear knows what it means to be truly alone and bereft. The solitary ear is always in some relation to mourning, listening for lost others and its phantom twin. (If people who talk to themselves are deemed to be crazy, the madness lies not in the moment of speaking—an act that would resemble in all ways the act of speaking to another—but in the act of hearing one's own voice. For one cannot hear "one's own voice" as such: it is always the voice of the other as it comes through the ear.)

In *The Telephone Book*, Ronell listens for the special effects that the telephone produces on the way we answer (or fail to answer) the call of the other as it comes to us through the ear. "The telephone," she writes, is a "structure that is not equivalent to its technical history, the telephone . . . indicates more than a technical object. In our first listening, under the pressure of 'accepting a call,' the telephone in fact will emerge as a synecdoche of technology."[8] As "synecdoche of technology," the telephone comes into being as both a reaction and a response to the body function for which it serves as prosthesis and supplement. The telephone (like all technology) is not opposed to the body, but rather mimes, repeats, amplifies, and elaborates a certain (repressed) history of the body. Hence like the ear(s) upon which it is modeled, the telephone is radically double and duplicitous: it both incarnates and disavows the vulnerability and openness of the ear[s] to which it is addressed:

> In sum, Alexander Graham Bell carried a dead ear to his mother's house that summer. It is the ear of the Other whose identity is manifold. The telephone, whose labor pains were felt in the ear, has already in this limited example of its birthmark so complex a matrix, that the question of its placement as a thing, object or machine, scientific, gynecological, or objet d'art still bears upon us.[9]

Furthermore, the technological body in question is both feminine and maternal. As we can begin to hear in this passage, the telephone is conceived as a fetishistic extension of the body of the mother.

The Prosthetic Maternal

> If one were to set an event, a date, or a time bomb in order to see the beginning of the modern concept of technology touch off, then this event gets stirred up by the invention of condensed milk. In fact, something like the history of positive technology is unthinkable without the extension of this maternal substance into its technological other: in other words, its precise mode of preservation and survival.[10]

Among the many startling and original premises of *The Telephone Book* is the notion that the birth of the telephone has a significant relation to anxieties concerning the maternal function in the technological age and that its emergence constitutes an important event in the history of mourning. Indeed, throughout the book, Ronell demonstrates the multiple ways in which the very investment in a certain repressive concept of the mother (as the grounding and stable incarnation of "nature," "origin," "connection," "meaning," "presence," "life") is one of the critical sources of the technological drive. Paradoxically, therefore, the technological drive emerges from an attempt to (re)produce a "mother" who would and could preserve the (philosophical, masculine) fantasy of full presence, life, and unending connection. Technology is the result of a fantasy to make artificial life more lifelike than life by denying death, absence, disconnection, the improper, and sexual difference.

One way of reading *The Telephone Book*, then, is as an interpretation (in the sense one gives to the word in the phrase "interpretation of dreams") of the causal drives and the consequences of this fantasy on history, politics, and culture: a study of telephonic instincts and their vicissitudes. Because, as Ronell points out, the technological drive is most often linked to an attempt to repress the body's finitude, the technological urge aims to deny the reality of the body's vulnerability and mortality by replacing (or supplementing) it with a body that does not know death; a body of "pure life." Thus the driving fantasy of technology is the (re)production of an *Über-Mutter* capable of procreating this "pure life." "Pure life," however (as Freud explores in *Beyond the Pleasure Principle*) often resembles death more than it does "life" as it privileges preservation, immobility, and absolute resistance to change or difference. Consequently, the technological *Über-Mutter* is inherently both monstrous and repressive.

Ronell explores this structure and the effects of this dynamic throughout *The Telephone Book*. However, in the final section of the book, she performs a "techno-analysis" of the problem by providing us with a kind of case history of the birth of the telephone. Alexander Graham Bell's biography emerges as an important element in Ronell's "studies in technology." By reading this biography through the ears, she constructs a certain anamnesis of the psycho-historical investments inscribed in the telephone's conception. Ronell glosses Bell's (oto)biography thus:

> "The conception of the telephone," he adds in 1916, "took place during the summer visit to my father's residence in Brantford, in the summer of 1874, and the apparatus was just as it was subsequently made, a one-membrane telephone on either end" (M, 73). He had gone a step further there, inscribing himself in the paterno-maternalizing space of invention. In his father's house he conceived something like a child by a dead ear, conceived with or for his father, which means that he as his mother conceived his father's child—a brother collapsed into a one-membrane telephone "on either end," as he puts it, on the end of a beginning, a calendrical birthday or on the end of the end, as the other end, precisely, to which one reaches for some telespark that tells the end of the other. One membrane with two ends, giving birth to the gift of death, shouting vowels at the moment of conception, watching oneself be overcome with tracings made on smoked glass.
>
> In case you think we have forgotten about the mother's vampiric energy, it has been put into storage, left coiled up in the telephone. For if Bell conceived a telephone with his father in order to bring back the two children, he was identifying the machine with "Ma-ma!" that is, he was caught up in taking her place, multiplying her, folding her invaginated ears into those of the pair of brothers left behind in Europe.[11]

As Ronell tells it, Bell gives birth to the telephone by twice replacing the mother. He himself takes the place of the mother by transforming a dead ear into a pseudo womb quickened by his voice. The telephonic offspring that he conceives is endowed with maternal properties. Furthermore, she calls attention to the fact that the telephone is conceived "in the father's house." As she hears it, the replacement replicant mother is addressed to the father either in response to his (paternal) desire or to a fantasy of paternal desire. In either case, Bell attempts to please the father by giving him a telephonic child—a gift of life that would surpass all life by being a life-giving gift. But, as Ronell points out, the gift of a life-giving gift is actually a gift of death as it annihilates the vital distance that separates us from the other. In this sense, it "tells the end of the other." She then goes on to elucidate that the repressed mother is encrypted in this father-son exchange and her "vampiric energy" remains "put in storage, left coiled in the telephone."

From its conception, then, the telephone usurps the maternal function. But the energy bound and "coiled" in this repressed mother (who is neither living nor dead) lies encrypted in the telephone system and haunts the relations it makes possible. When mommy becomes mummified in the telephone lines, the techno-maternal figure assumes new functions in the historical/hysterical organization of the modern psyche. Roughly speaking, these new tasks concern: fetishistic forms of (failed) mourning and the amplification of a pathologically punishing, (maternal) superego. As maternal prosthesis, the telephone lends itself specifically to these two functions because it can simulate a sustained (re)connection to the other by constituting, as Ronell puts it, "the maternal cord reissued."[12] When it answers to a desire to remain permanently bound to the mother, the telephone becomes used as a fetish to ward off the experience of separation, absence, or death. And, because there can be no telephone without another telephone, the telephonic matrix binds all its units together through a techno-maternal network in which each individual number loses its singularity by becoming answerable to a symbolic collectivity. This collectivity, furthermore, reproduces itself by transmitting voices that dictate orders into the ear. The first such order of the telephone is the demand to answer its call. The call from the other that comes to us through the telephone retains something of the voice of the (undead) mother who returns, with a vengeance, to issue imperatives and regulate compliance. As Ronell puts it, "There is always a remnant of the persecuting, accusatory mother in the telephone system, suggesting that the entire dimension of the monolithic parental unit can never as such be silenced."[13] When this toxic mixture of failed mourning and superego dysfunction manifest in the sphere of the political, they most often take the form of fascism, nationalism, totalitarianism, and other repressive systems of state (remote) control.

In this context, it is interesting to note that in Roland Barthes's *Camera Lucida* (a text that we will examine closely in Chapters 8 and 9) photography usurps the maternal function in similar ways. In our reading of Barthes we will find that photography, like the telephone, can replicate aspects of the maternal function; when it does, it often colludes with state control in ways that are analogous to the arguments Ronell presents here about the telephone. In both cases, for example, the technological prosthetic maternal object easily lends itself to fetishistic denial of loss and separation. Furthermore, both of these prosthetic maternal objects operate by forging identifying "connections" to a controlling matrix ("networks" in the case of the telephone and "photo id" in the case of the camera) that can easily be appropriated by state power for its own regulatory and disciplinary ends.

However, as we shall also see when we look more closely at Barthes's text on photography, there are also important specific differences in the ways these two technological prostheses operate. Unlike the temporal restrictions of the telephone connection, photography engages traumatic temporality and creative unconscious processes in extremely convoluted ways, thereby complicating the fantasy of pure presence that is conjured up by the prosthetic maternal. In this sense, the photographic maternal differs from the telephonic structures that Ronell describes here.

But perhaps we should slow down a bit. In order to understand how and why Ronell associates the telephone with state control, we must first look more closely at how the question concerning telephonic technology is haunted by the body of the mother. In one of the densest and most difficult passages of *The Telephone Book*, Ronell establishes a connection between the advent of technology, the incommensurability of "catastrophe," and the (reactive) inability and failure to mourn the loss of the mother. She writes:

> Technology . . . is inseparable from catastrophe in a radically explicit way. Cutting lines and catastrophizing, the telephone has been associated with a maternalized force. Now, when mourning is broached by an idealization and interiorization of the mother's image, which implies her loss and the withdrawal of the maternal, the telephone maintains this line of disconnection while dissimulating the loss, acting like a pacifier. But at the same time it acts as a monument to an irreducible disconnection and thus runs like incorporation, a kind of pathology inhibiting mourning, offering an alternative to the process of introjection. In this sense the telephone operates along lines whose structures promote phantasmic, unmediated, instantaneous, magical, sometimes hallucinatory flashes. What happens to the perished Other when mourning is inhibited? The refusal to mourn causes the lost "love object" to be preserved in a crypt like a mummy, maintained as the binding around what is not there. Somewhat like frozen-dried foods, the passageway is sealed off and marked (in the psyche) with the place and date in commemoration.[14]

If mourning (of any kind) is always defined by a refusal to let go of the departed other, the work of mourning entails gradually becoming able to accept the fact that the connection with the beloved other has been irrevocably severed. And because, (as Freud famously observed), no one willingly gives up a connection to the beloved other, in its less pathological manifestations, the psyche in mourning seeks consolations and compensations for the loss of the beloved object in different ways: by becoming like the lost loved one through identification and by finding new others to love. In pathological mourning, however, as Ronell invokes it above, there is no renunciation possible; the loss is simultaneously radically disavowed and experienced as catastrophic, unendurable, and inexpressible.[15] As the incarnation of our primordial attachment to and separation from the other, the mother becomes the matrix for all future connections and disconnections. In this sense, the mother prefigures the telephone and the telephone emerges in response to anxiety about separation from the mother. But as technological incarnation of the mother, the telephone mimics the maternal function perversely by annihilating distance with the ghost of presence. As a mechanical reproduction of a (catastrophic and unbearable) lost connection to the mother, the telephone will take on the function of an auxiliary organ in the service of melancholic commemoration and cannibalistic incorporation and preservation.

In "Mourning and Melancholia," Freud explains that the pathological inability to let go of the lost object is expressed as a desire to eat the other: "The ego wants to incorporate this object into itself, and, in accordance with the oral or cannibalistic phase of libidinal development in which it is, it wants to do so by devouring it."[16] But as Ronell suggests, the telephone radically amplifies this melancholic gesture by becoming a prosthetic body part in which the eaten but undigested mother is contained and preserved. Furthermore, when swallowed by the telephone, this undigested mater becomes simultaneously inaccessible and all powerful: Her body is too deeply frozen within the psyche to be touched while her ghostly, idealized image becomes projected outward and produces "instantaneous," "magical," "hallucinatory flashes."

But if, as we have suggested, the telephone serves as a technological substitute for a lost relation to the mother, its function as prosthesis is not merely to replace the lost object, but also to repair the wounds caused by the trauma of its loss. For this reason, the telephone rewires the connections of the erogenous zones through which contact was made (and lost) with the archaic mother in order to make sure that she is now kept permanently available and on hold. The fragile orifices of ear, mouth, breast, and anus through which bodies first encounter others now become joined together through an internal network that is contained and preserved in the phone system. The telephone now regulates all access to the outside.

As replacement for source of love and nourishment, the telephone mediates relations with the other through an autoerotic body reorganization that dispenses freeze-dried food, and the fantasy of an unbreakable connection. When the mother becomes telephonically ingested, however, her imperishable mechanical voice implants itself in the psyche. The implanted voice takes over the command control of the psyche by supplanting superego functions.

At this juncture it should come as no surprise to learn that there is a substantial literature devoted to telephone perversions and pathologies within clinical psychoanalysis.[17] For the purposes of this discussion, it is worth pointing out that within the psychoanalytic context, the telephone has most generally been understood as a fetish (used either for sexual gratification or to attenuate separation anxiety or both) and as an external manifestation of a particular kind of punitive superego. For example, in his essay "The Symbol of Telephoning," Leonard Shengold suggests that when the telephone is used as a fetish, it is related to addiction and masturbation and its purpose is to regulate the connection to the other. He writes,

> The use of the telephone as a kind of addiction can, as masturbation, have a calming effect—not only in relation to castration anxiety, but as a measure against separation anxiety and even more primitive dangers. In patients who are psychotic or "borderline," the telephoning can maintain some object ties at a bearable distance, providing separation without loss and contact without fusion.[18]

In the same essay, he also reminds us that the "telephone's association with sound evokes Freud's emphasis on the special relation of the superego to the auditory. The telephone can serve as a prosthetic extension or an externalization of the conscious in order to carry out such superego functions as control and censorship."[19] From its inception, then, psychoanalysis has always (if more or less implicitly) conceived of the superego in relation to the telephone.

More recently, however, Janine Chasseguet-Smirgel has explored how the inability to renounce the primal fusion of the mother can lead to the development of an "anal-sadistic superego where the longing to become one with the mother coincides with the necessity of obeying her orders. . . . It totally (or almost entirely) takes the place of the evolved superego and has a degree of autonomy in the psychic apparatus. The subject does not simply obey orders from outside, he has internalized the necessity of complying with orders."[20] This all-powerful anal superego comes into being as a traumatic response to an ancient and archaic failure to separate from the mother and subsequent inability to mourn the loss. Chasseguet-Smirgel goes on to argue that this anal-sadistic superego is linked to a pathological hatred of anything perceived as threatening to the primal "union" with the mother. And, since all "others" are foreign, anything that cannot be absorbed into the union is perceived as "filth" that must be eliminated and annihilated at all cost. For this reason, Chasseguet-Smirgel has suggests that this anal-sadistic pseudo superego can express itself through genocidal fantasies as well as other excessive attempts at eliminating "dirt" in order to protect and purify itself from any and all outside "contamination."

In Chasseguet-Smirgel's description of the excessively punitive and uncompromising demands of this anal-sadistic superego, we hear strains of the commanding mechanical voice that Ronell discovers buried in the maternal prosthesis that is the telephone. Through its desperate and regressive attempts to simulate perfect fusion with the archaic lost object, the anal-sadistic superego takes the form of a repressive machine designed to maintain autoerotic law and order by eliminating all impurities in its system. By establishing this connection between the anal-sadistic (maternally derived) superego and the telephone, we can better understand why the telephone lends itself so easily to fascist aims. In the opening pages of *The Telephone Book*, Ronell provides an example of the ways in which the telephone can facilitate fascist ends by fabricating a synthetic form of organic unity:

> The German telefilm *Heimat* (1987) organizes part of its narrative around the erection of a telephone system. The telephone connects where there has been little or no relation, it globalizes and unifies, suturing a country like a wound. The telephone participates in the myths of organic unity, where one discerns a shelter or defense against castration. A state casts a net of connectedness around itself from which the deadly flower of unity can grow under the sun of constant surveillance.[21]

As this quotation suggests (and as we have seen in the preceding pages), the technological drive is haunted by a nostalgic, reactionary investment in perpetuating a fantasy about the unity and purity of a biological body that never was. In its regressive attempts to fabricate such a body, the telephone simulates maternal biological functions and attempts to protect itself hygienically and sustain itself through homeostasis. However, as we shall see, the attempt to eliminate the other ends up producing new and potent forms of toxic waste.

The Toxic Maternal

> The *toxic maternal* means that while mother's milk is poison, it still supplies the crucial nourishment that the subject seeks. It suggests, moreover, that the maternal is too close, invading the orifices and skin with no screen protection, as it were, no intervening law to sever the ever-pumping umbilicus.[22]

As we have already seen, the commands emanating from the (undead and unmourned) mother trapped in the telephone wires are repressive and oppressive. In its tendency to control channels of communication by wiring subjects together, making them "answerable" to a collective system, the body politics generated by the telephone system can be linked to political fantasies of national purity. But the very biotechnological drive that produces the social structure of the telephone system also produces its own allergic response to that very system. One name for that allergic response is "drugs." In *Crack Wars*, Avital Ronell extends her exploration of body technologies to show how the declaration of a "war on drugs" exposes an internal link that connects this attack on drugs to failed mourning, repressive politics, and contemporary forms of warfare. In this sense, Ronell's claims about drugs, mourning, and the pathology that she calls the "toxic maternal" in *Crack Wars* can be read as an elaboration—perhaps even an effect—of the logic that produced the telephone as maternal prosthesis in *The Telephone Book*.

In *Crack Wars*, Ronell explores how drugs make it possible for the addict to commemorate lost and absent others by numbing the pain of the loss and making oneself absent. Drug addicts transform the self into a vessel for the absence of the other. Where the telephone reflects the desire to consume and absorb the (repressed and undead) mother, the drug user metabolizes nothing.[23] Instead of eating the undead mother, the person who is wasted on drugs is actually being eaten by an unconscious relation to the other as irrevocably lost. As she so strikingly puts it in her powerful reading of Flaubert's *Madame Bovary*, "something is eating at Madame Bovary. She has a 'depraved appetite,' which is to say, she accepts as comestible what by natural or normed evaluation ought to be refused. Intricate parasitism."[24] Ronell goes on to explain that Emma Bovary's perverse eating habits and inability to nurture her own daughter are due to the fact that she is otherwise occupied in feeding an unknown, unburied other:

> Something is growing in Emma of which the repelled child, Berthe, is a symptom. The other in its absence must somehow be kept alive and preserved; this requires certain metonymies of feeding. To retain the other, the subject, wanting to satisfy its depraved hunger, follows a foreign regime, filling an emptiness that somehow leaves the subject full. The body becomes the site for exercising the rights of a missing person. This person, or parasite, as interiorized other, is imperious. It demands immediate satisfaction of a felt lack. . . . There's no giving up the other.[25]

Taken in this context, drug addiction can be understood as a symptomatic response to the overwhelming and invasive demands of the telephonic immune system. Where the telephone user denies loss and overcomes distance by simulating presence, the drug addict disconnects and drops out from the collective body politic. Ronell writes that the "drug addict offers her body to the production of hallucination, vision or trance, a production assembled in the violence of non-address. This form of internal saturation of self, unhooked from a grander effective circuit, marks the constitutive adestination of the addict's address."[26]

Thus, unlike the telephone, which simulates presence in absence, drugs promote disassociation and desocialization. In biopolitical terms, however, this disassociation and desocialization becomes expressed as a perversion of body functions regulating intake and output, production, consumption, and waste. Instead of producing waste that can be eliminated from the system as filth to be disposed of, the addict becomes an internal waste product within the economy of the social system. The self "wasted" on and by drugs produces toxic waste in place of a self. As wasted self, the addict inhabits the social order, is radically disconnected from it but cannot be eliminated from it. In this sense, the addict is doubly parasitical: He or she "hosts" an alien other within, and he or she becomes an alien other that threatens to destabilize the boundaries between inside and outside, self and other, ally or enemy. As an internal outsider who threatens the ability to draw clear boundaries, the drug addict's (self) destruction is received as a threat to the health of the collective. In an essay entitled "The Rhetoric of Drugs," Jacques Derrida describes how the parasitical status of drugs means that there is no such thing as "solitary" drug use:

> So it cannot be said that the pleasure of drug use [*la jouissance toxicomanique*] is in itself forbidden. Rather we forbid a pleasure that is at once solitary, desocializing, and yet contagious for the socius. . . . Besides, you might even say that the act of drug use is structured like a language and so could not be purely private. Straightaway, drug use threatens the social bond.[27]

As Derrida suggests in this essay, as a parasite that infects and contaminates the social body, drugs are seen to be inherently contagious. Both Derrida and Ronell explore how drugs open up the question of the body as something that cannot be contained, purified, or protected from contagion. Put another way, drugs force us to acknowledge that there is no such thing as a "healthy" body. To the extent that bodies are alive, they are always already inhabited by alien others and are vulnerable to death by contagion at every touch. Attempts to quarantine or purge the foreign bodies that lurk within the self become expressed as violent acts of war. In *Crack Wars*, for example, Ronell explicitly relates drugs to both genocide and viral infection: "indeed, it would be difficult to dissociate drugs from a history of modern warfare and genocide. One could begin perhaps in the contiguous neighborhood of the ethnocide of the American Indian by alcohol or strategic, viral infection, and then could never end."[28] Furthermore, as Ronell and Derrida both argue, thinking about politics and war must take into account how hygienic exercises to ward off foreign invasion or cleanse internal infection produce what they have called an autoimmune situation where the self turns against itself because it cannot maintain or sustain a pure boundary between itself and its others. Ronell's work, however, specifically emphasizes how autoimmune (political) responses can be linked to the technological drive and its accompanying repression of the feminine body. Throughout her writings, she examines how modern war technologies are consistently feminized as a hygienic attempt to ward off (masculine) fear about the actual power, vulnerability and irreducible otherness of the feminine body. In other words, technology is the defensive, militarized reaction to the fact that, for male culture, the feminine body remains the first threatening foreign body.

Foreign Bodies and Toxic Shock

> No liberation without appliances, no war machine without a girl's name, no desire for survival without the feminine. No mode of connectivity, in short, without the Emergency Feminine.[29]

If, as we have suggested, modern technology can (at least in part) be understood as a militant defense against the threat of the female body, we can begin to appreciate why war technology and technological warfare take the form of a particularly reactive repression and denial of the feminine. One of the leitmotifs that runs through the essays assembled in *Finitude's Score* is that the specific brutality of war in the technological age is accompanied by a symptomatic radical disavowal and denial of feminine difference. The annihilation of the enemy other is related to a simultaneous negation of the feminine and a repudiation of the body as such. War waged by techno-bodies, who embody the fantasy of triumph over life, results in a form of violence in which the death of the other is rendered totally unreal. Because the body's finitude is repressed in technological war, it produces the illusion not only that the enemy other is nobody but also that he (or she) has no body. Writing about nuclear war in an essay entitled "Starting from Scratch: Mastermix," Ronell argues that if we read with our ears, we can hear how the body that is repressed in technological war returns in the form of a symptomatic rhetorical trope:

> As everyone knows, total nuclear war cannot as such begin, it can only end—the moment it takes place, nuclear war will be over. Its taking place, therefore, constitutes an original end of sorts, the final fall of the fall, the spectacular fallout. Displacement of the body: arms have become arms that race, erasing the bodies' members, heads turned into warheads, and so on. By several rhetorical maneuvers, then, the body has already been evacuated from the site of battle, a battleground no longer being grounded as a circumscribable place where a class of warriors might engage one another in a limited, classical way. Nuclear war is conducted by no bodies: a symbolic mutation in the very concept of war that has created, I think, a condition through which every body is carrying war upon itself, now.[30]

Ronell suggests that when the body is removed from the battlefield, it itself becomes a war zone. Technological attempts to cleanse the body of its frailties and impurities end up producing endless antibodies that make war everywhere. A living body is only alive to the extent that it remains open to the outside for sustenance and hence also open to the absolute inevitability of its own death. However, when the body's openings to the outside are shut down and sealed up in an attempt to protect itself from death and alien others, these internal anxieties about the body's limits become projected outwards and are externalized as "disembodied" war zones. Ronell suggests that the pathologies of modern war can be traced back to disturbances in and of the body:

> Where does war take place? . . . Not in an imaginary outside, no longer in a firmly circumscribed space of the battlefield, but in two ways—war's atomization marks the civilian body and the language that envelopes it. I wanted to scan incorporations of war, scouring the national unconscious. The war zone extends to the intestinal tract, or begins there. If we could throw it up, we would reverse the dialectic of assimilation. It is crucial to place the battlefield, especially when it is no longer localizable as such but still relegated to a hallucinated exteriority.[31]

If, as she provocatively claims, "the war zone extends to the intestinal tract, or begins there," this is so because the intestinal tract is the body site where all material decisions about that which is other to the self (incorporation, assimilation, rejection, constipation) actually take place. And if, as she suggests, we need to "throw it up," it is in order that we be able to give up the foreign matter that has been taken in without needing to contain, preserve, or conserve it. Indeed, given our earlier discussion of how the unmourned mother is encrypted in the belly of the telephone, we might imagine that Ronell is suggesting that foreign matter that we need to vomit might also be a figure for the mother as genuinely other—that is as another living being who cannot be merely assimilated into the self or preserved there indefinitely.

Throughout *Finitude's Score*, Ronell tracks how the body's repression impacts on the war zone. Several of the essays were written during and/or in response to the war that is now referred to as the "First" Gulf War, waged under the first President George Bush as opposed to its bloody sequel, the ongoing Iraq war brought to us by Bush II. As Ronell pointed out at the time, the driving fantasy of the U.S. military during the first Gulf war was that modern technology would enable "us" ("us" being the United States) to fight and win a "bloodless war." In the essay "Activist Supplement," she relates this fantasy to a fear of feminine finitude.

> I am not an essentialist feminist, but . . . it is urgent to recognize that the body of a woman has a fundamental relationship to death and despair, to finitude—and life. While the woman's body produces the eternal return of the "bloody mess of organic matter," the cyborg soldier, located in command and control systems, exercises on the fields of denial. Intentional Reality eliminates the body as an organic, finite, damageable, eviscerable, castratable, rushable entity, thus closing off orifices and stemming leakage and excrement.[32]

Ronell is certainly not "an essentialist feminist." But if she experiences the need to make that point explicitly, it may be because there is a certain politics of reading in which the mere mention of the "feminine" or of the "body" suffices to produce familiar and predictable patterns of misrecognition. Throughout her work, however, Ronell brings us back to a thinking of the body by showing how strangely and powerfully the effects produced by the body's repression think for us and think in our place.

In the corpus discussed in these pages, we have seen how technology can be seen as a material manifestation of particular political, philosophical psychosexual failure to open the ears to the (feminine) body. Latent political investments, affects and concepts become localized in and around the orifices of the body politic and are eliminated technologically. Throughout her work, Ronell performs readings of the body that challenge our preconceptions and produce shocks of (non) recognition. Through her (non essentialist) feminine writing, we discover that the body doesn't conform to our imaginary or technological fantasies about it; rather it has powerful non-anthropomorphic resources in its absolute strangeness. Ronell's texts invite us to open our ears to the unsettling strangeness of the body. She shows that every body is always already a foreign body and asks us to grapple with the political and ethical consequences of that fact. Contrary to the ways in which it has been most often domesticated, colonized, and appropriated by philosophy, religion, and culture, no body can be reduced to the property of a self. Bodies are rent with orifices, apertures, drives, and vital functions that open up the living self to all forms of otherness. And, as she points out throughout her work, the body is not only the site of this alterity, but also the battleground for a defensive response to it. Attempts to make the body invulnerable and impermeable, to regulate its intake and output, to police its erotic zones and deny its inevitable exposure to its own finitude are played out materially and expressed as forms of technology, politics, and mourning. The body politic secretes its toxins as war.

SEVEN

Blade Runner's Moving Still

In the time that has elapsed since *Blade Runner*'s first commercial release, Ridley Scott's 1982 science-fiction film has been retroactively hailed as one of the most powerful and influential examples of cinematic postmodernism.[1] Although *Blade Runner* has achieved almost canonical status in the annals of film theory, the discomfort displayed by its earliest critics serves as a telling index of the film's subversive depiction of a posthuman condition.[2] Released in the shadow of the cozy humanism of *E.T.*, which treated the alterity of the extraterrestrial with the familiarity of a domesticated pet, *Blade Runner* alienated its original audiences. Most of the reviews were not overly empathetic. Critics were more or less in agreement with Pauline Kael who wrote: "*Blade Runner* has nothing to give the audience. . . . It hasn't been thought out in human terms."[3] *Time* reviewer Richard Corliss's rendition of Kael's lament describes the film in truly monstrous terms: "*Blade Runner*, like its setting, is a beautiful, deadly organism that devours life."[4] *Rolling Stone*'s Michael Sragow adds to the chorus with the remark that

> Scott both overdoses on atmosphere and deliberately underdevelops the emotional tension. . . . His method alienates rather than entrances, completely undercutting his drama. When signs of humanity are so fleeting in both humans and replicants, the audience has no stake in their life or death.[5]

The persistent echo from all three reviewers revolves around one common complaint—*Blade Runner* simply isn't "human" enough. Somehow more or less "human" than a human film, *Blade Runner* flunks the cultural empathy test. In *Blade Runner*'s terminology, this film is a "replicant."

And yet, these critical judgments rely on the assumptions and distinctions that the film so radically puts into question. The film posits a world in which humans are indistinguishable from androids to the naked "human" eye, in which the terms "life" and "death" are irrevocably confounded, and where a visual technological apparatus, called the "empathy test," is used to determine who can be called "human." By searching for traces of humanity in this film, the critics must blind themselves to the way in which they are implicated in the film's reflection on the difference between humans and androids. *Blade Runner* explicitly interrogates what we mean when we speak of a "human film." What, after all, about film is "human"? Can we unproblematically wish to identify those celluloid figures that are mechanically animated in and by film as "humans"? The critics' desire to witness "humanity" perfectly doubled through filmic representation is a symptomatic misrecognition—and one that *Blade Runner* explicitly exposes. The filmic metaphor of the "empathy test" frames the question of the relationship between "human" subjects and the moving pictures that purport to reproduce and represent them so faithfully.

It is therefore utterly appropriate that the "empathy test" in *Blade Runner* is, in fact, an elaborate eye examination. Because the "humans" in the film cannot identify androids as androids with the naked human eye, the bounty hunter, or blade runner, must use the empathy test as a prosthesis. The blade runner looks into a video screen that projects an image of the suspected replicant's eye. The alleged replicant is given a series of questions to answer that are designed to produce an emotional response. But the blade runner does not heed the verbal response—the true test occurs in the dilation of the replicant's pupil. The replicant's eye is thereby stripped of its power to look, and it becomes a magnified object of the blade runner's mechanically amplified gaze. In the logic of this film, the emotional nerve is directly linked to the optic nerve and emotional response can be read only by calibrating quantitative movements in the optic nerve.

Although, in the empathy test, the emotional nerve is linked to the optic nerve, the relationship between verbal and visual registers is not purely mimetic. According to the implicit logic of the film, a replicant might presumably be able to pass the verbal component of the test by providing correct answers to the narrative questions while failing the quantitative component on the basis of insufficient dilation of the pupil. Correct verbal responses do not necessarily translate into the minute involuntary reflexes of the eye that become the fragile arbiter of human emotional response. The structure of the empathy test, which stages a relationship between narrative and visual constructions of meaning, underscores the fact that these two registers of meaning cannot be collapsed. The visual components of a film cannot simply be reduced to the perfectly analogous visual expression of the film's thematics. The difference between the rhetorical and visual levels of the empathy test compels us to think how verbal and visual representations are articulated in relation to each other in film. To efface or elide this difference is to refuse to read films as films.

The questions asked by the blade runner are a set of hypothetical moral dilemmas to which the replicant must supply the correct "human" answer. Most of the questions that presume to determine humanity are framed by references to an endangered, if not extinct, animal world. The inherent irony of the empathy test is clear—humans can only determine their difference from the species that they have created (androids) by invoking their nostalgic empathy for the species that they have presumably already destroyed (animals). In the first scenario, Deckard says, "It's your birthday, someone gives you a calfskin wallet." Rachel interrupts him by quickly responding, "I wouldn't accept it. Also, I'd report the person who gave it to me to the police." But where this first question seems to establish that humanity is confirmed by concern for animal welfare, the cultural, legal and political parameters through which such concern should properly be demonstrated is left disturbingly ambiguous. For example, the final scenario that Deckard invokes—"You're watching a stage play. A banquet is in progress. The guests are enjoying appetizers of raw oysters. The entree consists of boiled dog"—is left unanswered and leaves the film's spectator at a loss to know what, precisely, the desired response ought to have been. The example of a "stage play" places Rachel in the position of spectator and stages an overdetermined relationship between what is figured as tasteless and barbaric consumption (eating boiled dog) and the representation of such an act.

Because the film's spectator is ultimately unable to determine, with precision, the difference between a "correct" and "incorrect" answer, the scenarios presented by the empathy test displace the film's spectator more than they situate for us who is human and who is not. Morality becomes reduced to mores and customs that are culturally determined become, in this context, culturally indeterminable. Rather than interrogating the morality of the replicant, these rhetorical questions interrogate the status of morality as such. They undermine the spectator's ability to establish a discrete identification with the "human" figures *in* the film, while simultaneously obliging the spectator to question the assumed essential nature of his or her moral categories. The film's spectator, who is unable to distinguish humans from androids either visually or rhetorically, must repeat and mime the confusion about these categories that the film explores. In the act of watching the mise-en-scène of the empathy test scenario, the film's spectator is compelled to see himself or herself as the static, silent, passive agent of a gaze that is manipulated and controlled by a prosthetic mechanical eye—the eye of the camera. Unable simply to identify with either androids or humans in the film while being compelled to remember that he or she has relinquished a nonmediated "human" gaze, the spectator is placed in a precarious position. The questions asked through the metaphor of the empathy test (Who is human? What does it mean to be human? And how do we know?) are addressed to the film's spectator as well. As a metaphor for the film, the model of the empathy test is a medium through which *Blade Runner* links the problem of androids and humans to questions of filmic representation.

The Empathy Test and the "Primal Scene"

Blade Runner begins with a series of nonnarrative shots that depict the city: aircars, gigantic pyramids, grotesque images of eyes in flames. The camera floats through this cityscape until it enters a room in a gigantic building that we later discover to be the Tyrell Corporation—the corporation that fabricates and markets "replicants" to be exported to "Off-World" colonies. Two men sit in a room, separated by a machine that appears to be a medical device. One of the men asks the other man to respond to a series of questions. At this early juncture in the film, the first time we see the "empathy test," we do not understand what it is, or even what is going on. But as film spectators, as soon as we see "human" figures, we assume that the narrative of the film has begun. But this initial sequence does not mark the beginning of the film's narrative. Instead, it operates like a traumatic "primal scene" that the film replays and repeats in significant ways.[6]

In order to understand how the notion of the "primal scene" functions in *Blade Runner*, let us recapitulate some of what was established in Chapter 3 regarding both the temporal structure of the primal scene and its inherently photographic nature. The opening sequence of *Blade Runner* functions like a primal scene both formally (through its attention to the filmic medium itself) and thematically (through its central anxiety about the difference between human and nonhuman subjects). As we recall, because the Freudian term "primal scene" refers to a traumatic psychic event (either real or imagined) that can neither be remembered nor represented, the reality, and meaning of that event must be reconstructed retroactively (*nachträglich*) through the traces of its effects. In *Wolf Man*, Freud contends that his patient witnessed a scene of coitus between his parents when he was eighteen months old. Freud insists, however, that if this primal event can never be "remembered," it is *not* because it was "forgotten," but rather because it occurred before the child had developed the subjective apparatus required for either comprehension or memory. One might imagine that the infant occupies a position approximately analogous to that of a video recording machine capable of recording images but bereft of the psychic technology (the unconscious) required to play them. These recorded images, while meaningless in themselves, were presumably instrumental in developing the psychic machinery that would allow them to emerge two and a half years later in the distorted form of a dream about wolves. The dream at the age of four is not so much a representation of the primal scene, but rather a reconstruction of it. For Freud, the wolf dream proves that the child has witnessed, assimilated, and understood both the fact of sexual difference as well as its consequences—the threat of castration. It is important to this analysis, however, to remember that the child's fantasmatic representation of his assimilation of *sexual* difference can be represented only by the substitution of nonhuman figures for human ones. Whereas in *Wolf Man* we saw that the wolf man acquired human status by producing a traumatic, photographic dream about wolves, in *Blade Runner* the human status of both humans and replicants will be acted out and rendered visible through their photographic relations with and to each other.

This first sequence of *Blade Runner* operates like a primal scene because it does not assume meaning or significance until it is repeated. Furthermore, through the repetition of this sequence and the meaning it retroactively claims, we are exposed to the terms through which human subjectivity is ostensibly defined throughout the film. The scene unfolds as follows: The man we later learn to be the blade runner (Holden) performs what we later learn to be an empathy test on the suspected replicant (Leon). Holden sits across from Leon, asking him preparatory questions, and then the test begins. After one or two questions, Holden demands: "Tell me about your mother, only the good things you remember." In response to this question, Leon pulls out a gun and shoots Holden. The blast from Leon's gun propels Holden not only through the wall of the room, but also out of the film's frame. Because he is unable to produce a narrative of memory traces about a mother he never had, Leon's violent response retroactively identifies him as a replicant. *Blade Runner*'s narrative begins after this moment, as if the film itself is engendered by Leon's inability to respond to the question, "Tell me about your mother." After Holden is blown away, the camera floats once again through the cityscape until it descends into the street where it closes in on a man reading a newspaper in front of a television store. The film supplies us with the images and sound cues that mark the beginning of the film's narrative: an image of and voiceover by the protagonist, Deckard, who claims to have quit his job as a "blade runner."[7] Deckard's voiceover announces the real beginning of the film, which proceeds, at least initially, in more or less classical narrative form, until this "primal sequence" is repeated.

The first repetition of the "primal sequence" occurs when Deckard goes back to the police headquarters, run by Bryant, where he used to work as a blade runner. Bryant wants Deckard to take over Holden's job—to identify and eliminate five replicants that are loose in the streets of Los Angeles.[8] The film's spectator watches Bryant and Deckard sitting in a dark room, in front of a "movie" screen, watching the scene between Leon and Holden that we took for the first narrative moment of the film. At this point, however, we remember that first scene with a difference. Because we watch Deckard and Bryant watching a "movie" of the scene we just witnessed moments before, the spectator is forced to remember that primal sequence as part of a film rather than as an event that we actually "witnessed." Where film narratives often rely upon creating the illusion that the spectator has direct and unmediated access to action as it unfolds (indeed, one thinks of the desire named by the generic category of "action film"), this sequence reminds us that what we saw "happening" did not actually "happen" in our presence, but rather that it was reconstructed for our viewing pleasure. This moment provokes the spectator to remember, however fleetingly, that we are not present to the action that appears to unfold before our eyes. In the shock of the moment that reminds us of our position as spectators, we arrest the fictional continuity of the film's narrative. In short, the "filmic" situation of the second scene disrupts the illusion of narrative purity (presence) that we may have wanted to accord the first scene. The first repetition of the "primal scene" makes us aware that the first scene was also necessarily the second one—already a replication, reproduction, replicant repetition. The dismemberment of the film into a unit that is consistently broken down and repeated disturbs the illusion of narrative continuity on which fiction films generally depend.

After the first traumatic repetition of the primal sequence (which initially disrupts the continuity of the narrative), subsequent repetitions of this scene function as a kind of filmic punctuation mark that establishes and underscores the difference between androids and humans. The primal sequence now serves as a narrative cutting device or, more precisely, as splicing device. All of the initial "human" sequences are prefaced and framed by quotations of the primal sequence whereas android sequences unfold with no contextualizing markers. For example, before Deckard and Gaff visit the hotel room that Leon had given as his address, we see Deckard flying in his aircar listening to the soundtrack of Leon's first responses to Holden from the primal sequence. After the human scene between Deckard and Gaff, the android narrative begins with Roy's and Leon's visit to Chew's eye factory. But whereas Deckard's actions appear to respond to elements in the primal sequence (that is, Leon's voice giving his address to Holden directs Deckard to Leon's hotel), the first android sequence destabilizes us by providing no narrative context for its first image: a disturbing close-up of

Roy Batty's clenched fist. After the android sequence at the eye factory, Deckard's reappearance is glossed by a playback of Leon's parting words to Holden: "Let me tell you about my mother." Deckard then returns to his apartment where he finds Rachel, a suspected replicant, waiting in his elevator to tell him about her mother. Although the narrative has begun to put the difference between humans and androids into question, the filmic structures at this point in the film work in the opposite way—they establish and maintain this difference through the alternating sequences on either side of the "repeated" preface.

This structure changes at a crucial moment in *Blade Runner*, at which point another kind of primal, traumatic image is substituted for the filmic preface—a photograph. It is around this photograph, a snapshot of the replicant Rachel with her mother, that the oppositional economy that this film has established between humans and replicants trembles and falters. This photograph is central to the film's treatment of the difference between humans and replicants and, in some sense, articulates the film's ambiguous response to the question that explodes the primal sequence: "Tell me about your mother." To read the central importance that this image has for the film, we are going to take a detour through a brief analysis of the relationship between photographs and films. By using photographs—"still images"—both thematically and structurally, *Blade Runner* analyzes the medium of film through a systematic dismemberment of its constitutive elements.

Humans and Androids: Photographs and Films

Although both photographs and films are mechanically reproduced images, they are often perceived as having entirely different functions. We consider photographs to be agents of memory while we tend to view fiction films as pretexts for oblivion. Roland Barthes's work on the distinction between photography and film enables us to begin to address the ways in which this distinction is both engaged and questioned by *Blade Runner*. In "The Rhetoric of the Image," Barthes argues that "the distinction between film and photograph is not a simple difference of degree but a radical opposition."[9] If photographs are "radically opposed" to films, it is because they do not occupy the same grammatical tense. While photographs always speak the undeniable reality of the "past perfect" (they bear witness to what

Barthes calls the "having-been-there" of the referent), film destroys the photograph's link to the referent (hence the past) by binding images to other images in the construction of a fictional present tense (what he calls a "being-there") of the thing. It is important to note, however, that the temporal disjunction that separates film from photography relies entirely upon the question of movement. In order for photography to bear witness to the pastness of the past, the referent must be preserved and embalmed through the stasis of the photographic image. In *Camera Lucida*, Barthes contends that the frozen image actually bears a material memory trace of the body of the referent. Because the referent "adheres" to the photographic image, Barthes insists that photography is fundamentally different from all other forms of representation. He writes:

> I had to conceive . . . how Photography's referent is not the same as the referent of other systems of representation. I call "photographic referent" not the *optionally* real thing to which an image or sign refers but the *necessarily* real thing which has been placed before the lens, without which there would be no photograph. Painting can feign reality without having seen it. Discourse combines signs which have referents, of course, but these referents can be and are most often "chimeras." Contrary to these imitations, in Photography I can never deny that *the thing has been there*. There is a superimposition of reality and the past.[10]

Following Barthes, we can say that photographs serve as absolute testimonies both to the pastness of an event and to its reality. They purport to frame a moment of time and a subject in a past forever frozen. We think of them as receptacles for time. We accord them the status of hyperreality; these mechanically reproduced images are perceived to be perfect "replicas" of what must have been there, if the photographic trace exists to "prove" it.

Because they prove the reality of the past, we use photographs as agents of memory. These flat, material traces serve as evidence of a "having-been-there" that can only be subjectively presumed. By remembering for us, the photograph remembers us: it remembers what we cannot, or might not, down to all of the insignificant details that, because forgotten, are further testimony to the reality of the scene exposed. An artificial eye enables us to see ourselves—and our loved ones—as real. By positioning ourselves in relation to these photographic images, we posit ourselves in space and time. We regard these photographic images as the proof or arbiter of our existence across the passage of time. As prosthetic memories, photographs transform the reality of time and existence into tangible objects. In *Blade Runner*, these flat objects become the dead proof that their bearer is still living. They are the replicants or doubles through whose lifelessness we constitute our own sense of identity, place and time. But—and this is the question that the film *Blade Runner* poses so radically—do we confer our humanity onto them or are they somehow the necessary supplements through which ours is constituted? In the film's terms, why do androids or humans *need* photographs?

For, in a sense, the photograph is the true "subject" of *Blade Runner*. This "it" that is the photograph is the site of humanity and the locus of the film's quest for origins. *Blade Runner* poses the question "where do we come from?" in every possible way. From the film's origin about origins—the primal sequence—through the detoured literalizations of this question in the father/son scene between Roy Batty (the replicant leader) and Tyrell, this question is formulated and reformulated. The question of origins is coupled with the other fundamental question posed by *Blade Runner*: "Why do humans or androids need photographs?" These two questions become the same question when asked by or about the film itself. For the film, as a film, is in some sense in search of its origin through the exposure of and insistence on the photographic image. The photograph appears to be the smallest essential unit through which a film's materiality is constructed—its DNA, to paraphrase the dialogue between Roy Batty and Tyrell. But what is the relationship between this film and its photos? For film, as material trace, is a collection of still photographs arranged in sequence. When they are put into a projector, these dead stills appear to assume life—they move and speak. From *replicas* they become *replicants*, thereby echoing from the Latin the present active particle *ans*. However, it is the very "reality" we accord these past dead images that allows us to invest in the fictionality of the fiction film. Once these images are put into time, we attempt to constitute a "present" through them. In order to follow the narrative parade of images that make up the fiction film, we must forget any other past or present in a desperate attempt to race after the "presentness" that appears to be unfolding before our eyes.

In order for this structure to constitute us unproblematically, these images must be empty receptacles—forms into which we bury and perfectly fit images of ourselves. It is this structure that *Blade Runner* puts so radically into question. Its reflection of and on the photograph necessarily alters the way in which we look both at the film and at ourselves. *Blade Runner* likens androids to photographs because they function as nonhuman receptacles for human image and memory. They are designed to reflect the human figure perfectly—to cast back an image of humanity in order to confirm our own. We look at them, as our doubles, and see our humanity refracted through our difference from them. Like photographs, replicants are mechanically reproduced and, like photographs, their likeness to us is the measure and proof of a humanity that once was, and is no longer. This humanity is no longer in the sense that androids are more physically perfect than any of their human counterparts. They are doubles of life that, in their doubling and their difference from it, carve out an image of "humanity" through which humans attempt to see themselves as human. Like photographs, replicants both testify to the real existence of the past category "human" and confirm a self-image that is no longer "present" but presumed.

The Moving Still

As I stated earlier, the primal scene or preface that splices the narrative in the first half of the film gives way to another pivotal moment in *Blade Runner*. In a way, this moment is a literal response to the sequence that culminated in the question, "Tell me about your mother." At this point, however, instead of providing us with a narrative that would tell about the mother, the film responds to this question through a single image—the image of a mother and daughter. Rachel, who has begun to suspect that she might be a replicant, goes to Deckard's apartment to prove to him that she is human by showing him a photograph of her with her mother. To understand the weight of this image, however, we must return to the earlier moment when Deckard first goes to the Tyrell Corporation. Tyrell asks Deckard to test the empathy test device on his assistant Rachel. Rachel is subjected to the test and then asked to leave the room while Deckard and Tyrell discuss the results. The test reveals that Rachel, who thinks that she is human, is, in fact, a replicant. When Deckard discovers that Rachel is not human, he asks, "How can it not know what it is?" By referring to Rachel as "it" (rather than "she") Deckard neuters Rachel in an attempt to establish a greater difference between them than that of sexual difference.

But Deckard's question about an "it" itself interrogates the status of the human subject: one cannot ask, "How can it not know what it is?" without implicitly asking, "How can I know that I am I?" As the film progresses, it becomes more and more clear that Deckard's question (which he believes to be addressed to an "other") is very much self-addressed. When Deckard asks, "How can it not know what it is?" in reference to Rachel, he does not see that he is asking the question of his own autobiography. The problem of whether any subject—any purported "I"— is or can be a personal, individual or locatable entity is what is at stake in this scene.

Although Deckard attempts to establish a radical difference between himself (as "I") and Rachel (as "it"), the very fact that Rachel can misrecognize herself as human forces Deckard to examine the fragility of his own subjective position. When Rachel appears at Deckard's apartment with her photograph, Deckard is confronted with the impossibility of sustaining a difference between himself and "it." Deckard lets Rachel into the apartment. She holds a snapshot in her hands and says, "You think I'm a replicant, don't you?" He refuses to look at her photo. Instead, he launches into an interrogation of Rachel that closely parallels the structure of the empathy test. He asks her a series of questions designed to test her memory, presumably to prove to her that her memory is not her own. But the ambiguity surrounding both the questions and the responses raises questions about whose memories are being invoked and questioned in this scene.

Deckard begins the interrogation by conjuring up a childhood scene of sexual exploration. He says, "Remember when you were six, you and your brother snuck into an open window of an empty basement. You wanted to play doctor. He showed you his, but when it came to your turn, you chickened and ran. Do you remember that? Ever tell anyone that?" Deckard's invocation of this singularly private moment is designed to probe the limits of Rachel's memory implants. He believes that Rachel could never be able to remember this moment (or one like it) because it never would have been told. This is why he repeatedly asks, "Do you remember that? Ever tell anyone that?" Because this memory would not have been narrated, it could not have been appropriated by the collective memory banks out of which Rachel's "implants" were taken. But if Deckard's exemplary "private" memory does not belong to the collective memory banks, then where does it come from? One can only assume that Deckard's "example" comes from his own, personal memory banks and that when he says "you" he means "I."

Deckard has sacrificed the specificity of his "private" memory by recasting his autobiography into the rhetorical structure of the empathy test. The very gesture that is designed to establish his difference from her results in a linguistic confusion between "I" and "you," between his memories and hers. Furthermore, it is significant that Deckard's example of a "primal human memory" (a memory too private to be told) involves a demonstration of sexual difference through the showing of private parts. Deckard insists upon invoking the childhood scene through which children show sexual difference to one another as a means to construct a difference between himself (as human) and Rachel (as android).

Deckard then begins a second narrative about a mother spider that sits with her bag of eggs in a corner of the room. This is the first mention (aside from the moment in which Rachel presents the photo) of the word "mother" since the traumatic question that inaugurates the film. Deckard's recollection of a "mother" recalls Holden's inaugural imperative, "Tell me about your mother." Instead of telling about his mother, Deckard recounts a nostalgic memory about watching a mother spider brooding over her eggs. Rachel interrupts Deckard's narration and perfectly completes "his" memory, adding the end: "And then the eggs hatched and hundreds of little spiders came out, and they ate her." If this memory once "belonged" to Deckard, once Rachel tells it, Deckard's private memory no longer belongs to him. It is no longer "his" in the sense that this memory no longer uniquely remembers him—his memories no longer unite discrete bits of a private, personal past into a unified entity, an "I" named Deckard. As Rachel remembers this past for him—she dismembers him and dispossesses him of his "I." In addition, within this shared memory is told the tale of the death of a mother. This mother spider is consumed by her children, a horde of replicant spiders, which bury her by ingesting her, incorporating her, making her part of themselves. This figure of an inhuman mother who engenders a multitude of murderous offspring foreshadows the figure of the photograph of Rachel's mother that emerges at the end of this sequence.

Deckard stops the verbal empathy test and says, "They're not your memories, they're somebody else's, Tyrell's niece's. Implants." Then he goes into the kitchen to prepare drinks. Rachel drops the photo and leaves. The photograph lies between them. Deckard returns to the place she has left and picks up the photograph. The camera does not move at this point, but rather remains still, motionless, miming the stillness of the photo. It is

Deckard's hand, holding the photo, that moves the "still" closer to the camera so that the filmic frame perfectly encases the frame of the photographic image. And then, for a split second, as the film lens is framed around the photo, the "still" itself appears to move. Both mother and daughter appear to move from within the frame. This "moving still"—the split second during which the mark between photo and film is blurred—disrupts all of the film's oppositions and puts into motion an entirely different sort of economy. Furthermore, this particular image is particularly disturbing because it is no longer particular, no longer a unique image of one person's mother. Ostensibly, this is Rachel's mechanically reproduced proof that she was naturally born of a mother. But Rachel can attempt to establish her humanity, beyond the shadow of a doubt, only by offering up the image of a mother whom one must suppose to be dead or at least irretrievably absent. Rachel attempts to prove her humanity with a photo that would claim to successfully encase, frame and contain her mother in the square space of a snapshot. But this mother is not easily buried. She, or "it," refuses to lie motionless in the frame that has been constructed to contain her. The mother, in *Blade Runner*, is no more Rachel's mother than she is anyone else's. Yet this image, this "it," disrupts and violates the boundaries of the photographic frame. It is this mother that marks the irrevocable distance between ourselves and "it" that motivates the remainder of the film. This photograph, which Rachel offers as evidence of her "human" origin, is a moving form that cannot be contained by a word, a proper name or a picture frame.

Leon's Pictures: The Doubled Photograph

The image of the "moving still" motivates the remaining segments of the film. After Rachel leaves Deckard with the photo of the mother, we see him sitting at his piano, which is littered with an enormous collection of photographs. We must assume that Deckard has retrieved his "personal" collection of family photographs. Whatever Deckard saw when he looked at the image of "Rachel's mother" provokes him to look for "his" photographic memories. But from the fragmented unrelated images that lie on the piano in front of him, we understand that Deckard's family photographs no more belong to him than Rachel's photo belonged to her. Many of the photos that Deckard retrieves appear to date from the nineteenth century—a time that he could never remember personally, a time that was never his, photos of people he never knew. These photos are memory implants for him as well.

This sequence begins as the film camera moves first to the photographs on the piano, and then to Deckard's face. The "shot-countershot" structure posits Deckard posterior to, and in function of, the images of the photographs. In this way, the camera "defines" Deckard as dependent on the photographic images, and not vice versa. This structure, which is established after the sequence of the "moving still," acquires even greater force and strangeness in the subsequent shots of this sequence. From amid the collection of photos on the piano that are supposedly "his," Deckard picks one that is explicitly not "his" and that has already been shown in the film: the photograph that Deckard had found in his visit to Leon's apartment. This photograph initially appeared to be entirely meaningless. The snapshot shows a curved elbow on one side of the frame in an otherwise empty room. Upon finding the photograph Deckard had fleetingly mused, "Family photos? Replicants don't have families. Why would replicants need photographs?" At that earlier moment of the film, this bizarre photograph seemed to function as yet another mark of the difference between replicants and humans. To the naked human eye, the image appeared to make no sense: Why would anyone want a photograph of an elbow in an empty hotel room? When we first see this photograph, the difference between humans and replicants is seemingly represented by the absence of a recognizable "human" subject. When Deckard returns to this photograph in the sequence of the "moving still" that follows, he now assumes that the photo might have a meaning. He examines the snapshot in order to find what he now believes *must be there* to be seen: a "human" subject. Deckard eventually discovers the figure of a human subject buried in the photo—but the way that he "finds" "it" renders both him and "it" suspect.

Deckard inserts this seemingly meaningless image into another prosthetic visual aid device: an incredible machine that is able to dismember the photographic image from all angles and blow up, in focus, any part of the dissected image. This machine apparently has the capacity to reenter the photographic frame, fragment the image, alter the perspective, and then to restore the new "blowup" to full plenitude. In other words, the technological apparatus that allows Deckard to change the perspective of a flat, photographic image and to find a figure hidden in a corner of the frame is literally unthinkable, even in a technological paradise. For a flat "dead" photograph—a trace of and testament to a past event—cannot shift perspectives *after the fact* and remain what we call a photograph. The machine disrupts the temporal and spatial boundaries of the photographic object. With the aid of this apparatus, the photograph ceases to be a photograph; the past image is supplemented by a present image enhanced by movement and refined perspective. Using this machine, Deckard finally "finds" an image of a woman's face, framed in an oval mirror like a portrait locket. He takes a new photo of the face and prints a copy of the photo encrypted in the photo.

But the hard copy of the image that Deckard finds imbedded in the original photograph *could never* have emerged from it. The copy could not possibly be a copy of the original. Deckard was desperately looking for a "human" face, and he has made one—projected one—onto a space where it seems no "replicant" was figured. However, in so doing, the photo becomes another sort of "moving still," an impossible, artificial "mother" that engenders a new and disturbing image of a "subject." Deckard is able to find the image of the subject in the photo because he has, in a literal sense, put it there. Deckard has conferred or projected his image of subjectivity onto the replicants. He is both obliged and able to do this only to the degree to which his own "self-image" has been disrupted by his encounter with Rachel around the image of the mother. The image of the woman's face that Deckard finds is no longer a trace from the past but an impossible animation that bears witness to the present—his present as well as "its" present. At the moment in which Deckard personally reconstructs or "remembers" the image of a face he has never seen, this woman's face, framed in the mirror, also becomes a mirror for him.

The image of the woman's face in the mirror is doubly impossible. For even if this image could have been reconstructed from Leon's photograph, the face reflected in the mirror raises another set of problems. The photographic image depicts only the reflection of the face, without the back of the head that should have cast this reflection. In other words, like the doubled photograph itself, this image is yet another copy bereft of its original. In some sense, in the face that gazes back at him from the photograph, Deckard sees his own reflection. Cast across the chasm of the mechanical apparatus that separates these two faces, that separates humans and replicants, "him" from "it," and past from present, his gaze meets hers, framed by a mirror.

In the space that is constructed between Deckard's gaze and the face in this doubled photograph, he is impossibly doubled. The difference between "him" and "it" on which Deckard's self-image had been predicated has been radically effaced. This space marks *Blade Runner*'s remodeled version of subjectivity—one that is no longer essentially "human," no longer viewed as the property of one particular "subject," but simultaneously *his*, *hers*, and "*its*."

On one level, the sequence in which Deckard "blows up" Leon's photograph and uncovers the image of the woman's face is an obvious quotation of Antonioni's film *Blow-Up*. However, the ways in which *Blade Runner*'s "blowup" sequence diverges from the analogous moment in Antonioni's film emphasize both the "impossibility" and implicit violence of this scene in *Blade Runner*. In *Blow-Up*, the photographer discovers that he had been the unwitting witness to a murder when he enlarges a photo he had taken in the park. By examining the grainy "blowup" of his photograph, which serves as proof that the crime actually "happened," the photographer isolates an image of the murder weapon. The enlarged photograph incites the photographer to return to the scene of the crime and touch the body of the corpse. The power of this sequence in *Blow-Up* depends entirely on the conventional definition of the photograph as a reliable and inherently accurate witness to a past event. Thus, while *Blow-Up* explores the relation between photographs and responsibility, it in no way puts the notion of what a photograph is, and how it functions, into question. In *Blade Runner*, however, the unthinkable apparatus that alters the photograph's initial perspective provokes us to alter our understanding of what a photograph is. Whereas in *Blow-Up* the original photograph is merely enlarged, in *Blade Runner*, the original photograph is more literally "blown up"—exploded. Furthermore, in *Blow-Up*, the photograph functions as a "memory" trace of a murder that has already taken place, whereas in *Blade Runner*, the photograph functions as the "memory" of a murder that has yet to occur.

Deckard undergoes the "blowup" sequence—in which he both projects and constructs the image of the woman's face—in order to be able to kill her. On the basis of the photograph that Deckard reconstructs, he identifies the woman as Zhora, one of the replicants he is instructed to eliminate. He uses this photograph to track her down and, when he does, he kills her. Zhora's execution, which is inextricably bound up with the problem of the doubled photograph, is the first "murder" depicted in the film. This graphic act of violence initiates a cycle of violence that does not end until all of the replicants are "dead" and the film ends. However, this explicit representation of the annihilation of "subjects" is predicated upon the implicit violence to the very notion of the "subject" that emerges through an analysis of the doubled photograph and was introduced by the primal image of the "moving still."

Indeed, the doubled photograph is the film's visual response to the questions, "How can it not know what it is?" and "How can I know that I am I?" When Deckard "reconstructs" and "remembers" Zhora's face from a photograph of an empty room, he can no longer distance himself from the image he creates or from the "it" that is the missing referent for the photograph. The photograph is no longer a sealed receptacle of a past event that assures its bearer that he is still living. All of the differentiating marks that would draw a clear line between subject and "thing," human and replicant, photograph and film, have been effaced. And yet, it is as if the absence of such differentiating marks is precisely what propels Deckard (as the "human" representative) to annihilate his replicant doubles. Because he can no longer establish what the difference is or where it lies, he must effectively remove all material trace of the "double" that puts his identity into question. This is what is at stake in the murder of Zhora. Rachel, the replicant-that-doesn't-know-what-it-is, symbolically acquires "human" status, not through the photograph of the mother, but rather by the fact that she kills another android—Leon. After Deckard kills Zhora, Leon, whom we assume had been her lover, attacks Deckard. Rachel, who witnesses the scene, expresses her love for Deckard and consummates her "humanity" by killing Leon. Thus Deckard and Rachel are joined as a couple only after they have annihilated their unbearable replicant counterparts—Leon and Zhora. *Blade Runner*'s moving still exposes as fiction the notion that "humanity" and "identity" can be possessed in the form of personal property. The violence that finally explodes between so-called subjects merely acts out the violence of and to the "subject" that this film exposes. The visual representation of this violence, which begins in the "moving still" sequence and is developed in the doubled photograph sequence, is this film's response to the question that inaugurates *Blade Runner*: "Tell me about your mother." Perhaps this question is itself unutterably violent. In *Blade Runner*, the figure of the mother refuses to guarantee that one is born, and not made, human. And what more calls the human subject into question than the responsibility of understanding that humanity cannot be conferred by a petrified image in a picture frame? For the mother, the irretrievable site from whom we have all presumably sprung, can best be figured as a "moving still," a mobile empty vessel, a thing that no word or picture could ever adequately fill.

Addendum

Like Pandora's manufactured jar, Rachel's replicant photograph is both a technological incarnation of the maternal function and an uncanny figure for the event of human birth itself. As I have suggested throughout this book (and as we shall see more clearly in the next two chapters), photography has a profoundly overdetermined relation to the maternal function because of its apparent capacity to attest to the concrete reality of events that, like the irretrievable experience of our own birth, we would like to claim as our own but that lie irrevocably outside our purview. Through readings of the photographic dimension of the primal scene and the photographic temporality of anxiety, I have also proposed that the photographic apparatus simulates mechanisms that are analogous to primal psychic structures. Photography thus not only emerges as being inextricably bound up with the birth of the psyche and the psychic representation of birth, but it also performs as a magical medium that provides us with a technological reproduction of the impossible scene of the event of our own birth. For all of these reasons, it should not be surprising that, as we shall see in the next two chapters, photography functions both as a prosthetic compensation for the loss of the maternal body and as an uncanny medium that purports to bear witness to the unverifiable primal passage through the mother's body.

EIGHT

Nothing to Say: Fragments on the Mother in the Age of Mechanical Reproduction

> As if the horror of death were not precisely its platitude! The horror is this: nothing to say about the death of the one whom I love most, nothing to say about her photograph, which I contemplate without ever being able to get to the heart of it, to transform it. The only "thought" I can have is that at the end of this first death, my own death is inscribed; between the two, nothing more than waiting; I have no other resource than this *irony*: to speak about the "nothing to say."
>
> —ROLAND BARTHES, *Camera Lucida*

> This *before* is not known, obviously, because it is there before we are. It is something like birth or infancy (Latin, *in-fans*)—there before we are. The *there* in question is called the body. It is not "I" who am born, who is given birth to. "I" will be born afterwards, with language, precisely upon leaving infancy. . . Aesthetics has to do with this first touch: the one that touched me when I was not there.
>
> —JEAN-FRANÇOIS LYOTARD, "Prescription"

Ironically, the author of "The Death of the Author" did not, in fact, touch the question of his own death in that influential essay. But in his last work—published after the death of his mother and during the short span of time during which he "awaits" his own imminent death by writing about his mother's death and photography—when he claims that he has nothing more to say, nothing to say except that he has nothing to say, Roland Barthes provides us a powerful commentary on the relationship between modernity and death. For Barthes, photography is lethal because through this uncanny medium, death is removed from the realm of language and becomes inscribed directly upon the body. After the advent of photography, it would seem, death is set loose from its moorings in language: when death can no longer be "written" writing itself begins to lose its cultural and historical force. Instead, like Kafka's depiction of the "machine" in "The Penal Colony," photography inscribes a death sentence directly upon the body of the subject. In so doing, photography destroys what Jean-François Lyotard has called "the aesthetic": the body before it is touched by language and the law.[1] Because photography operates on the body *before* language (in place of language), it both recalls and effaces our primordial ties to the maternal body. Thus, as we shall see, in writing about having "nothing to say" about the death of his mother, Roland Barthes writes to us about the death of the language of death in the age of mechanical reproduction. In the following pages, by respecting Barthes's adamant declarations of photography's "*folle vérité*," we shall attempt to trace the language of death that comes to be inscribed on and through the photographic body in *Camera Lucida*.[2]

As any reader of *Camera Lucida* knows, Barthes's reflections on the ontology of photography ultimately take the form of an autobiographical elegy to his dead mother. The author's public expression of private mourning almost appears as a contingent pretext or convenient afterthought that accompanies a quasi-philosophical meditation on the medium of photography. Thus the book can be (and has been) read either as an example of an autobiography that happens to speak about photography or as a book about photography that happens to speak about the author's relationship to his dead mother.[3] But neither of these two approaches fully captures the unthinkable link that Barthes stages between photography and the mother in *Camera Lucida*. As we shall see, the uncanny link between photography and the mother exceeds his explicit invocations to his mother: not only does he structure his text around a photograph of his deceased mother that he refuses to "reproduce" but, more radically, his text also conceives of photography as a mechanical mother that mimes, distorts, and disrupts the maternal function.

The relationship between photography and the maternal function permeates all aspects of his discussions on photography. Barthes's audacious first axiom concerning the corporeal status of the photographic referent ultimately leads him to conceive of photography as having prosthetic maternal function: It endows the modern subject with a social, codifiable, collective body. Unlike Walter Benjamin, who argues that the phenomenon of mechanical reproduction erases or diminishes the specificity of the referent,

Barthes insists that the specific force of photography derives from the physical operation it performs upon the body of the referent. He writes:

> It is as though the Photograph always carries its referent with itself. . . . In short, the referent adheres. And this singular adherence makes it very difficult to focus on Photography. . . . Each time I would read something about Photography . . . it made me furious. Myself, I saw only the referent, the desired body, the beloved body.

> On dirait que la Photographie emporte toujours son référent avec elle. . . . Bref, le référent adhère. Et cette adhérence singulière fait qu'il y a une très grande difficulté à accommoder sur la photographie. . . . Chaque fois que je lisais quelque chose sur la photographie . . . cela me mettait en colère. Car moi, je ne voyais que le référent, l'objet désiré, le corps chéri.[4]

The claim that the referent adheres to the photograph motivates almost everything else Barthes has to say about the function of photography. The entire book circles around this claim despite the fact that it remains, at bottom, resolutely unthinkable and hence almost unreadable. Reasonable critics tend to overlook how crazy this idea actually is. We can begin to appreciate the unthinkability of this utterance by looking for a moment at how Jacques Derrida grapples with it in his essay "The Deaths of Roland Barthes:"

> But should we say reference or referent? Analytical precision must here be equal to the stakes, and the photograph puts this precision to the test: in the photograph, the referent is noticeably absent, suspendable, vanished into the unique past time of its event, but the reference to this referent, call it the intentional movement of reference (since Barthes does in fact appeal to phenomenology in this book) implies just as irreducibly the having-been (there) of a unique and invariable referent. It implies this "return of the dead" in the very structure of both its image and the phenomenon of its image. . . . Though it is no longer *there* (present, living, real), its *having-been-there* now presently a part of the referential or intentional structure of my relationship to the photogram, the return of the referent indeed takes the form of a haunting.[5]

Because Derrida cannot resist the temptation to make philosophical sense of Barthes's outrageous claim, his gloss on this point is doubly instructive. On one hand, Derrida's commentary allows us to understand how Barthes' claim might make sense while suggesting at the same time that perhaps the very gesture of "making sense" of Barthes's text is not the most productive way to read it. For in order to make sense of this passage, Derrida is forced to read what Barthes meant, rather than what he actually said. Because Derrida concludes that Barthes could not really have meant that the photograph actually adheres to the body of the referent, he proposes to correct Barthes's use of the word "referent" with the more accommodating notion of the "reference to the referent" and temporarily elides the question of the body of the referent that Barthes obstinately points to in the phrase "the desired object, the beloved body." Where Barthes stubbornly insists upon "this stubbornness of the Referent in always being there," Derrida gently corrects him by rationally pointing out that "although it is no longer *there* (present, living, real, etc), its *having-been-there* now part of the referential or intentional structure of my relationship to the photogram, the return of the referent indeed takes the form of a haunting." In other words, for Derrida, although it is thinkable to claim that photographic referentiality itself refers to the very possibility of pointing to an authentic, unique and unrepeatable past occurrence, it is unthinkable to claim that the referent itself actually adheres to the photogram. To the extent that the photographic referent succeeds in pointing to the undeniable existence of the pastness of the event, it would follow that the past event haunts the present photograph like a ghost. Given this reading, it should come as no surprise that Derrida focuses on the thematics of the return of the dead in Barthes's text.

But Barthes's text refuses to speak the language of philosophy: He not only writes about the "return of the dead" but also insists, contrary to all logic and reason, that he sees, in the photograph, an actual trace of the referent itself. Through his rhetorical excesses and logical inconsistencies, Barthes contends that photography can actually conjure up the (lost) body of the referent. The power of Barthes's writing does not lie in his "thought," but rather in the wild felicity of his rhetoric. He admits this himself; he even goes so far as to flaunt it by choosing to describe the questions he asks in *Camera Lucida* as "*une métaphysique 'bête'*"—a "'stupid' metaphysics."

Barthes explicitly engages in the mute language of "stupid metaphysics" so that he can speak about the unthinkable relation that exists between the mute materiality of the maternal body and the flat stupidity of the photographic image. Stupid metaphysics is metaphysics that does not know how to speak; it can only point and touch. It presents rather than represents.

Photography, he suggests, is as unthinkable as the fact of our own birth. Almost all of the essential properties that he attributes to photography also refer to the undeniable— but "stupid"—knowledge that we have about the fact of our own birth. Death, he suggests, is the foundation of metaphysics while birth lies resolutely outside the realm of language. Neither language nor philosophy has anything to say about it. Photography is as basic and as self-evident as birth. It is both undeniable and indescribable: In the penultimate chapter of *Camera Lucida*, Barthes writes:

> The *noeme* of Photography is simple, banal; no depth: "that has been." I know our critics: What! A whole book (even a short one) to discover something I know at first glance?
>
> Le noème de la photographie est simple, banal; aucune profondeur: "*Ça a été.*" Je connais nos critiques: quoi! tout un livre (même bref) pour découvrir cela que je sais dès le premier coup d'oeil?[6]

In the simple sentence "*Ça a été*"—simply consisting of the *passé composé* of the verb "to be" loosely attached to a subject that remains amorphous and unnamed ("*ça*")— Barthes exclaims his absolute, mute, and brute astonishment in finding himself face to face with a material remainder of something that undeniably happened in the past. But the affective charge that accompanies this primal utterance "*ça a été*" can also be read as an attempt on the part of the speaking subject to bridge the unutterable divide that cleaves his body from the body of the mother. This simple phrase proclaims the fact that there is no way, in language, to articulate the unspeakable but undeniable fact that our bodies are the material residue of a prior passage through the mother's womb. Thus, while the first part of *Camera Lucida* is marked by Barthes's attempt to construct a theoretical discourse proper to photography by inventing a proliferation of baroque Latinate neologisms (the *studium*, the *punctum*, the *intersum*, the *mathesis singularis*, and so on), at the end of the book it appears that all of this brouhaha was ultimately a means toward the end of discovering (as he says) the sheer flat fact that "*ça a été*: it happened, it was."

Furthermore, Barthes presents his "stupid metaphysics" about photography in a (pseudo) philosophical vocabulary comprised of Latin words. Personally, I have always been as interested in the *fact* of Barthes's systematic invocation of Latin words as well as by what he claims to express through the terms *studium*, *punctum*, and so on. There is a perverse precision in the gesture: He derives the very technical terminology of the modern phenomenon of photography from a language that "died" centuries before photography was born. If Barthes *needs* Latin in order to define photography, it is in part due to the implied presumption of a deadness common to both Latin and photography. By using Latin terms to define photo-graphy, Barthes suggests that the only way this modern form of discourse can be made to speak at all is by translating it into a language that comes from and speaks to an archaic past.

Furthermore, implicit in Barthes's use of Latin is the notion (which we find in both Benjamin and Baudelaire) that modernity is accessible only when it is read in conjunction with the history out of which it emerges. But since Barthes claims that photography itself constitutes the irrevocable rupture between history and modernity ("it is the advent of the Photograph . . . which divides the history of the world" [88]), he needs to create a mythological history for Photography—through the materiality of the Latin language—as a means of rendering this rupture readable. In the following passage, Barthes methodically parses the word "*photographie*" by translating it first into Latin and then back into French:

> Il paraît qu'en latin "photographie" se dirait: "imago lucis opera expressa"; c'est-à-dire: image révélée, "sortie," "montée," "exprimée" (comme le jus d'un citron) par l'action de la lumière. Et si la Photographie appartenait à un monde qui ait encore quelque sensibilité au mythe, on ne manquerait pas d'exulter devant la richesse du symbole: le corps aimé est immortalisé par la médiation d'un métal précieux, l'argent (monument et luxe); à quoi on ajouterait l'idée que ce métal, comme tous les métaux de l'Alchimie, est vivant.
>
> It seems that in Latin "photograph" would be said "imago lucis opera expressa"; which is to say: image revealed, "extracted," "mounted," "expressed" (like the juice of a lemon) by the action of light. And if Photography belonged to a world with some residual sensitivity to myth, we should exult over the richness of the symbol: the loved body is immortalized by the mediation of a precious metal, silver (monument and luxury); to which we might add the notion that this metal, like all the metals of Alchemy, is alive.[7]

When it speaks the language of photography, Latin is reborn as a truly magical and uncanny medium. It not only appears as photography's primordial mother tongue but it returns us to all lost times and places. Thus the Latin definition of photography both mythically sutures the divide between antiquity and modernity and allows Barthes to imagine a prehistoric time in which photography would be able to immortalize the living body of "the beloved body." This is, indeed, magical thinking. But, once again, not only is Barthes well aware of this fact, but he actually claims that this sort of magical thinking subtends all discourses about realism and the real. With characteristic aplomb and cheerful irony, Barthes asserts that only realists, like himself, recognize the important fact that photography is magic and not art. He writes:

> The realists, of whom I am one and of whom I was already one when I asserted that the Photograph was an image without code—even if, obviously, certain codes do inflect our reading of it—the realists do not take the photograph for a "copy" of reality, but for an emanation of *past reality*: a *magic*, not an art.[8]

It is no accident that Barthes invokes the notion of "realism" in the same breath as the word "magic." In so doing, he suggests that nothing is more magical than the Real. The magical charm of photography derives from the necessary and essential reality of its referent. And it is this magic charm that distinguishes photography from all other forms of representation:

> I call "photographic referent" not the optionally real thing to which an image or a sign refers but the *necessarily* real thing which has been placed before the lens, without which there would be no photograph. Painting can feign reality without having seen it. Discourse combines signs which have referents, of course, but these referents can be and are most often "chimeras." Contrary to these imitations, in Photography I can never deny that *the thing has been there*. There is a superimposition here: of reality and of the past. And since this constraint exists only for Photography, we must consider it, by reduction, as the very essence, the *noeme* of Photography.[9]

Photography is "magic" and not "art" because it although it creates the *illusion* that it functions mimetically, its real power, Barthes explains, lies in its capacity to authenticate the presence of the referent by performing as constative speech act. Photography, he states, is a *temporal* rather than representational medium. Its force lies in its power to bear witness to the reality of an event without being able to say anything about it or to understand it in any way:

> To ask whether a photograph is analogical or coded is not a good means of analysis. The important thing is that the photograph possesses an evidential force, and that its testimony bears not on the object but on time. From a

> phenomenological viewpoint, in the Photograph, the power of authentication exceeds the power of representation.[10]

Because photography, unlike all other modes of communication, can only assert the real and necessary existence of its (prior) material referent, it resembles biological reproduction more than it does artistic representation.

If we were to read Barthes's descriptions of photography through the prism of psychoanalysis, we might state that the photograph manifests a fetishistic ability to recapture the connection to the maternal body that coincides with the moment of birth. But where the psychoanalytic fetish both asserts and disavows the presence of the mother's phallus, the photograph as fetish both asserts and disavows the subject's separation from the mother's body. Barthes's insistence that "the photograph always carries its referent with itself"[11] has the same rhetorical structure—disavowal—that is emblematic of the discourse of the fetishist. And because, for Barthes, the photograph is a palpable fetish of the maternal body, it in turn becomes endowed with a magical and uncanny power to procreate. At this point, we are finally able to appreciate the rhetorical logic that leads Barthes inexorably to the following unthinkable claim that constitutes the theoretical navel of *Camera Lucida*:

> The photograph is literally an emanation of the referent. From a real body, which was there, proceed radiations which ultimately touch me, who am here; the duration of the transmission is insignificant; the photograph of the missing being touches me like the delayed rays of a star. A sort of umbilical cord links the body of the photographed thing to my gaze: light, though impalpable, is here a carnal medium, a skin I share with anyone who has been photographed.
>
> La Photo est littéralement une émanation du référent. D'un corps réel, qui était là, sont parties des radiations qui viennent me toucher, moi qui suis ici; peu importe la durée de la transmission; la photo de l'être disparu vient me toucher comme les rayons différés d'une étoile. Une sorte de lien ombilical relie le corps de la chose photographiée à mon regard: la lumière, quoique impalpable, est bien ici un milieu charnel, une peau que je partage avec celui ou celle qui a été photographié.[12]

Here, we see how photography, whose etymology means "light writing," alchemically transforms light into flesh. In this transformation, photography becomes a maternal medium that magically reconnects the body of the viewing subject to the body of the referent by an umbilical cord. This umbilical cord, in turn, creates a new corpus that envelops both the viewing subject and the photographed object under a common skin. In the act of transforming light into skin, photography transubstantiates the body of the referent and transports it through time and space. As a mechanical maternal medium, photography has the ability to reproduce a new collective body that destabilizes the separation between past and present, subject and object.

But if in this passage Barthes presents the maternal properties of photography in an affirmative, life-giving, flesh-creating light, it is because here he looks at the maternal medium from the perspective of the subject who desires to be reunited with the body of the lost object. Through the umbilical cord of light, the body of the living can be rebound to the body of the dead. The photograph itself operates as a mediating "medium:" it links the living to the dead and the dead to the living and fetishistically disavows any separation between the two realms.

The maternal properties of photography, however, render it a profoundly disturbing and uncanny medium. The mechanical mother has as great a capacity to kill as it does to procreate. When photography is viewed from the perspective of the living subject who is subjected by its mechanical eye, photography becomes deadly. Instead of preserving the body of the cherished lost object, it petrifies the body of the living subject, who is mummified by its uncanny powers:

> In terms of image-repertoire, the Photograph (the one I *intend*) represents that very subtle moment when, to tell the truth, I am neither subject nor object but a subject who feels he is becoming an object: I then experience a micro-version of death (of parenthesis): I am truly becoming a specter.[13]

The living subject who has been photographed risks finding himself face to face with the specter of his own ghost. Because the umbilical cord, which binds the living subject to its photographic image, cannot be cut, photography seizes the body of the living subject, reproduces it, and then returns it as corpse. The living body of the subject haunts the photograph in the form of an undead body that can never be fully buried. The uncanny properties of the photographic medium suspend the body in a perpetual never-never-land between procreation and mortification:

> Now, once I feel myself observed by the lens, everything changes: I constitute myself in the process of "posing," I instantaneously make another body for myself, I transform myself in advance into an image. This transformation

is an active one: I feel that the Photograph creates my body or mortifies it, according to its caprice.[14]

Although Barthes states that photography either creates or mortifies the body according to its whim, he does allow that there is one way in which the uncanny properties of photography can be attenuated, if not completely controlled. The photographic image that is delivered by a talented photographer may still be able to preserve the life of the body if that photographer manages to capture the amorphous quality that Barthes calls "*l'air du corps*."

> Thus the air is the luminous shadow which accompanies the body; and if the photographer fails to show this air, then the body moves without a shadow, and once this shadow is severed, as in the myth of the Woman without a Shadow, there remains no more than a sterile body. It is by this tenuous umbilical cord that the photographer gives life; if he cannot, either by lack of talent or bad luck, supply the transparent soul its bright shadow, the subject dies forever.[15]

Once again, we find the image of the umbilical cord. Although the photographer cannot take the place of the absent biological mother, he can, nonetheless, occupy the position of midwife to the photographed body. The photographer attends to the birth of the image like a midwife by mediating the mechanical link between the subject and the photographed object with a watchful, caring, and maternal eye. If, however, the photographer is not a "good-enough" mother, has no talent, or if there is no photographer present, the uncanny properties of photography take over. Imagining this terrifying fate, Barthes writes:

> No doubt it is metaphorically that I derive my existence from the photographer. But though this dependence is an imaginary one (and from the purest image-repertoire), I experience it with the anguish of an uncertain filiation: an image—my image—will be generated: will I be born from an antipathetic individual or from a "good sort"? . . . If only photography could give me a neutral, anatomic body, a body which signifies nothing! Alas, I am doomed by (well-meaning) Photography always to have an expression: my body never finds its zero degree, no one can give it to me (perhaps only my mother? For it is not indifference which erases the weight of the image—the Photomat always turns you into a criminal type, wanted by the police—but love, extreme love).

> Sans doute, c'est métaphoriquement que je tiens mon existence du photographe. Mais cette dépendance a beau être imaginaire (et du plus pur Imaginaire), je la vis dans l'angoisse d'une filiation incertaine: une image—mon image va naître: va-t-on m'accoucher d'un individu antipathique ou d'un "type bien"? . . . Si au moins la Photographie pouvait me donner un corps neutre, anatomique, un corps qui ne signifie rien! Hélas, je suis condamné par la Photographie, qui croit bien faire, à avoir toujours une mine: mon corps ne trouve jamais son dégre zéro, personne ne le lui donne (peut-être seule ma mère? Car ce n'est pas l'indifférence qui enlève le poids de l'image—rien de tel qu'une photo "objective," du genre "Photomaton," pour faire de vous un individu pénal, guetté par la police—, c'est l'amour, l'amour extrême).[16]

Only the love of the biological mother can save the modern subject from the unwanted, social body that the photographic mother engenders. The mechanical mother destroys the life of the living subject by overwhelming that body with an excess of meaning. The unmediated photographic gaze places the body of the subject under arrest and hands it over to the law. The photographed body is all too legible—it destroys the sanctity of the private space because it can be read by anyone, at any time, for any purpose. Photography objectifies, embalms, and incarcerates the contemporary subject by pinning it to a static and petrified social identity. Unlike the biological mother who paradoxically protects the subject from the world, as a prosthetic mother that usurps the maternal function by substituting identity for subjectivity, photography casts the modern subject into a new body that is doomed to be stillborn.

PART THREE

Photo-Readings and the Possible Impossibilities of Literature

NINE

Darkroom Readings: Scenes of Maternal Photography

> The impossible sometimes, by chance, becomes possible as a utopia.
>
> —JACQUES DERRIDA, "The Deaths of Roland Barthes"

> I had the impression that, by focusing on these words like a photograph, one could—and the analysis would be endless—discover within them so many "things" that their letters showed by concealing themselves, remaining [*demeurant*] immobile, impassive, exposed, too obvious, although suspended in broad daylight in some dark room, some *camera obscura* of the French language.
>
> —JACQUES DERRIDA, *Athens, Still Remains*

The figure of photography as a mortifying prosthetic mother with which we ended the last chapter is only part of story that Barthes's text tells about the complex relation between photography and the mother in *Camera Lucida*. In this chapter, we will explore how photography also functions as a form of maternal writing. By looking closely at an often-overlooked passage in *Camera Lucida* (in which Barthes discusses the feeling of "déjà vu" stirred up by a nineteenth century photograph), we will uncover the latent traces of a very different kind of photographic maternal function. This photographic maternal conjures up an evocative and provocative relation to the past and takes the form of something we will come to call "photographic writing." Like the belated, nonmimetic relation between the dream of wolves and the primal scene that we have been examining throughout this book, photographic writing neither proves nor documents past events; instead, it creates fantasmatic images for primordial events (like the primal scene itself) that cannot be represented. As such, photographic writing makes possible a kind of return to the mother's body; however, this strange imaginary return is very different from the fetishistic denial of the separation from the mother that we saw at work both in the last chapter on Barthes and in Avital Ronell's writings on the telephone earlier. By working with and from Barthes's invocation of an evocative experience of uncanny photographic "déjà vu," we will encounter a form of writing that emerges from an imaginary return to the scene of one's own birth and, in so doing, paradoxically enables one to imagine a past that has never been seen before.

Second Sight: The Photographic Maternal (Barthes)

In one of the rare important passages of *Camera Lucida* that has not yet been subjected to extensive critical scrutiny, Roland Barthes invokes Baudelaire, Freud, and the maternal body in the same breath as part of a meditation on Charles Clifford's 1854 photograph *Alhambra* (see accompanying figure).

Alhambra (Charles Clifford, 1854)

Barthes's discussion of that photograph takes place in chapter 16 of *Camera Lucida* and appears at first glance to be no more than a simple illustration of his declared preference that landscapes ought to be places one desires to inhabit rather than places one wants to visit. As he contemplates Clifford's nineteenth-century image of an ancient Mediterranean urban landscape and wonders why it elicits such a powerful feeling of familiarity in him, he produces this remarkable gloss on his own response to the image:

> This longing to inhabit, if I observe it clearly in myself, is neither oneiric (I do not dream of some extravagant site) nor empirical (I do not buy a house according to the views of a real estate agency); it is fantasmatic, deriving from a kind of second sight which seems to bear me forward to a utopian time, or to carry me back to somewhere in myself: a double movement which Baudelaire celebrated in "*Invitation au voyage*" and "*La Vie antérieure.*" Looking back at these landscapes of predilection, it is as if I *were certain* of having been there or going there. Now Freud says of the maternal body that "there is no other place of which one can say with so much certainty that one has already been there." Such then would be the landscape (chosen by desire): *heimlich*, awakening in me the Mother (and never the disturbing Mother).[1]

This deceptively simple passage demands to be read closely and calls for careful thinking.

Indeed, the more closely one looks at it, the stranger it becomes. Paradoxically, this is so in part because it presents itself so emphatically (at every level) under the sign of the "familiar." After all, this chapter of the book is explicitly devoted to landscapes, home, and the mother: all three of these figures are arguably the very defining principles of "Nature," the natural, and the familiar. Read in this way, Barthes here is simply indulging in a nostalgic longing to return to the known and knowable comforts of home where the biographically familiar and biologically natural mother will watch over him. Such a reading implicitly assumes that Barthes's references to the language of poetry (via Baudelaire) and that of psychoanalysis (via Freud) are merely instrumental (or ornamental) and need not be taken overly seriously. Thus many (if not most) readers interested in the larger historical, political, philosophical, aesthetic, and deconstructive stakes of Barthes's reflections on photography simply skip over this moment in the text, preferring to ruminate instead on the seductive powers of the *punctum* and the elusive aura of the Winter Garden photograph.

Moreover, even for those readers who do take the time to look at it more closely, this passage presents special difficulties, as it is tempting to read it (and it almost asks to be read thus) according to a number of very familiar conceptual paradigms. Among the more compelling readings that have been proposed we tend to find variations on the following themes: a regressive (mythical) fantasy of a return to the (lost) and mourned biographical mother; a poetic expression of the powers of the imagination in the articulation of desire; an engagement with Freud's "Uncanny" essay as a way of thinking about photography's inherently canny/uncanny relation to the referent, the natural world, and with it the body of the mother and the *noeme* of photography; and a perverse (incestuous and murderous) relation to the maternal body accompanied by a fetishistic denial of the mother's death.

Barthes's text certainly supplies ample evidence to support all of these approaches. Several critics have offered particularly convincing and sophisticated accounts to explain why Barthes insists upon claiming that the "Mother" about whom he writes here is purely "*heimlich*" despite the fact that he knows perfectly well that such a designation verges on the meaningless, the mad or the perverse because, according to the very logic of the text by Freud to which he alludes here, the word "*heimlich*" (meaning "homelike" because comforting and familiar) can never be fully dissociated from its disturbing, unfamiliar opposite: "*unheimlich*."[2] While I do not want to contest the validity of any of these readings, I do want to suggest that they may not have fully accounted for some of the most far-reaching uncanny insights of this passage in Barthes's book. As we shall see in a moment, Barthes's handling of this photograph is critical to any reading of *Camera Lucida* not merely because of *what* he claims to find in the *Alhambra* landscape image (that is, the "*heimlich*" maternal body) but also, more radically, because of *how* he reads the image: photographically.

Although I hope to draw out some of the implications of this photographic reading process in the pages that follow, for the moment I would merely like to sketch out briefly the structure of the reading process as he describes it in the passage cited earlier. He recounts how he turns his gaze inward and observes himself recollecting certain textual images that come to him through the language of poetry (via two poems by Baudelaire) and dreamlike text-images that come to him through the language of psychoanalysis (via the quotation from Freud). On the basis of his internal reproduction of all these images in the dark reading room of the psyche, he produces a new kind of image ("fantasmatic") derived from a new kind of psychic image-writing technology ("second sight") that enables him to conjure up a new kind of temporality ("utopian time"). Barthes does not exactly seem to read the photograph; instead, the photograph reads him. It retrieves a latent image from an immemorial past within him and returns it to him as a timeless (or "*utopian*") image of his desire. The entire process is explicitly figured as a quasi-photographic operation that opens up onto a complex reflection on temporality, language, and an alternative (nonreferential) conception of writing history.

But we are not there yet. If, for now, we take out a magnifying glass to look in greater detail at how Barthes treats Clifford's photograph in his own text, we find that the image in question starts to look even stranger still. He provides little or no specific commentary about any of the visual or photographic qualities of the photograph as such. Instead of writing *about* the image, he writes *on* it, inscribing it with diverse kinds of written texts, thereby transcribing the visual components of the image into a new composite form of writing. As it figures in Barthes's text, Clifford's photographic image turns into a word-picture composed of various elements, both visual and verbal, which he carefully assembles and puts into meaningful relation with one another. The most obvious visible elements of this picture-puzzle are:

the "original" photographic image; the identifying textual markers for the photographic image ("Charles Clifford: Alhambra (Grenada) 1854–1856");

the caption, written by Barthes, that is inscribed under the image: "*C'est là que je voudrais vivre*" ("It is there that I would like to live"; translation modified);[3]

the titles of two poems by Charles Baudelaire ("*Invitation au voyage*" and "*La Vie antérieure*");

and an allusion to Freud's conception of the maternal body as primal dwelling place presented via an (unidentified) sentence fragment of Freud's writing.

This "fantasmatically" constructed composite photo-word picture operates within Barthes's text both as gloss of the "original" photograph by Clifford and as a new, quasi-photographic lexical reproduction that must now be read on its own terms. But what kind of an image is this and how is it to be read given that it is not, strictly speaking, "visible" to the naked eye? This image only becomes legible through acts of reading. Barthes himself signals its special status by gesturing toward the need for a new critical vocabulary to describe its dreamlike formal consistency and its unique (albeit virtual) powers through his use of the descriptive qualifiers: "fantasmatic," "second sight," and "utopian."

Indeed, the composite structure of this fantasmatic photo-text resembles something analogous to Freud's famous description, in *The Interpretation of Dreams*, of the "poetical phrases" of the picture-puzzle rebus that are the stuff from which dreams are made. Freud describes how the rebus should be read as follows:

> If we attempted to read these characters according to their pictorial value instead of according to their symbolic relation, we should clearly be led into error. Suppose I have a picture-puzzle, a rebus, in front of me. . . . The words which are put together in this way are no longer nonsensical but may form a poetical phrase of the greatest beauty and significance. A dream is a picture-puzzle of this sort.[4]

As is well known, this description of the dream as a "picture-puzzle" (or a rebus) occurs at the beginning of Chapter VI of the *Interpretation of Dreams* where Freud introduces the complex signifying operations that constitute the dreamwork. I would like to suggest a comparison between Barthes's "fantasmatic" image and Freud's dream rebus in this context for several reasons. First, I would like to call attention to the fact that Barthes's "fantasmatic" image (like the picture-puzzle described by Freud) demands to be actively read and interpreted precisely because its meaning is *not* located at the level of mimetic referential representation. Like the dream rebus, the "fantasmatic" photographic image constitutes its meaning by *how* it speaks—according to the laws of its own strange signifying system derived from the relations among its various elements—rather than by *what* it depicts. For Freud, dream images come from the past, but they do not belong to it. Dreams are not representations, but are psychic elaborations of (repressed) material from the past that is worked over in the darkroom of the psyche and then brought to light in the ("utopian") timeless time of the dream image. It is worth recalling here that Barthes initially defines the fantasmatic image through *negation* by comparing it to what it is *not*: He specifies that it is neither "oneiric" nor "empirical." Indeed, the very designation "fantasmatic" itself emerges, within Barthes's text, as a kind of fantasmatic dialectical resolution (or *Aufhebung*)—it springs forth as a new third term that materializes out of the negative relation between the "oneiric" and the "empirical," that is, between dream image and referential representation. Moreover, the relation between the virtual possibilities normally attributed to the "oneiric" dream image and the referential certainty normally ascribed to the realm of the "empirical" determine and haunt this passage in other significant ways as well.

This strange relation that Barthes establishes (between dream image and referential certainty) becomes somewhat more legible if we take a closer look at the sentence fragment by Freud that Barthes quotes in this passage. Leaving aside the titles of Baudelaire's poems, this fragment is the only direct quotation in this chapter of Barthes's book. The source of the fragment in question comes verbatim from the *Interpretation of Dreams* and not, as has been assumed by many of Barthes's readers, from the much later "Uncanny" essay—although, as we shall see, Freud himself essentially photocopies his own earlier passage from the dream book and reproduces it (with some slight differences) in that later text.[5] The words Barthes attributes to Freud are the following: "There is no other place of which one can say with so much certainty that one has already been there." But if we now take a closer look at the context in which these words appear in the *Interpretation of Dreams* and read them back through Barthes's discussion of landscape photography and its relation to the "fantasmatic image," both texts—Barthes's and Freud's—begin to look even stranger. Here is the passage from the *Interpretation of Dreams*:

> In some dreams of landscapes and other localities emphasis is laid in the dream itself on a convinced feeling of having been there once before. (Occurrences of *déjà vu* in dreams have a special meaning.) These places are invariably the genitals of the dreamer's mother; there is indeed no other place about which one can assert with such conviction that one has been there once before.[6]

Freud's text is, quite simply, astonishing. He begins with the fairly unremarkable observation that dreams of landscapes often awaken a particular feeling of familiarity in the dreamer. From there, however, he goes on to relate the particular feeling of familiarity (as it is "lived" in *dreams*) to the occurrence of *déjà vu* (as it is experienced in *dreams*) and then goes on to conclude (on the basis of the evidence provided by these unique instances of fantasmatic dream images) that these exceptional dream experiences (unlike the normal kinds of dream-images discussed above) are actually memory traces of a real, lived, former existence in the mother's body and that, as such, they bear witness to the primal and foundational "certainty" of that former life and, along with it, of the event of our birth. Put another way, Freud here seems to suggest that when the experience of *déjà vu* occurs in dreams, (as opposed to "lived life") it does not function like a dream image at all, but more like some kind of psychic "photograph" that provides quasi-referential evidence to support the "certainty" that we have once inhabited the body of the mother.

It is important to recognize how truly strange this argument is even within Freud's own conceptual framework. For Freud, ordinary experiences of *déjà vu* in conscious, waking life *do not* mean that one has actually seen something before; on the contrary, he explains such feelings as benign distortions of reality that are determined by unconscious subjective desires and fears.[7] Here, however, he argues something very different altogether. He suggests that when the experience of *déjà vu* occurs in dreams, it is the *mechanical reproduction* of an impossible image (the image of our birth) that was seen (but not by any subjective presence) without having been seen. *Déjà vu* in dreams really means that something real was *always already seen before*: the very fact of the repetition and reproduction of the image appears, paradoxically, to guarantee the unique status (in time and place) of the event that it ostensibly repeats. In this sense, the reproduction of the image through the dream resembles something like a photographic reproduction of an unphotographable event.

And all of this, it would seem, is made possible by a fantasmatic dream image that passes through the darkroom that is the maternal body.[8] Given the strange and uncanny convergence between "dream image" and "unique certainty" of the reality of a former life that cannot be recalled, it is no wonder that Freud returns to the uncanny properties of the maternal body in his essay on "The Uncanny." There, he writes:

> It often happens that neurotic men declare that they feel that there is something uncanny about the female genital organs. This *unheimlich* place, however, is the entrance to the former "*Heim*" [home] of all human beings, to the place where each one of us lived once upon a time and in the beginning. There is a joking saying that "Love is home-sickness"; and whenever a man dreams of a

> place or a country and says to himself, while he is still dreaming: "this place is familiar to me, I've been here before," we may interpret the place as being the mother's genitals or her body. [Here Freud inserts a footnote to his own prior text in *The Interpretation of Dreams*.] In this case too, then, the *unheimlich* is what was once *heimish*, familiar; the prefix '*un*' [un-] is the token of repression.[9]

There is something uncanny about the relationship between this passage about the uncanny status of the female genitals from "The Uncanny" essay and the earlier text about the feeling of *déjà vu* in landscape dreams from the *Interpretation of Dreams* to which it explicitly refers. Whereas in the passage from the dream book Freud insists upon the acute feeling of *recognition* provoked by the landscape dream image that seemingly reproduces an image from a former life (in the body of the mother) and returns one to it, in the corresponding passage from "The Uncanny" essay, he focuses instead on the feeling of *strangeness* produced by the image of the female genitals in neurotic men. He goes on to explain that the feeling of strangeness is actually the negative trace of the primal image of the absolutely familiar: the primal "home" that is the body of the mother. That primal image, however, can be rendered visible *only* when it is reproduced in negative form: as a "negative" image of the female genitals, displaced into a dream landscape, or even as the very image of "negation" itself. Here we might recall, in passing, that Freud's famous text called "Negation" begins with the following telling example of negation: " 'You ask who this person in the dream can have been. It was *not* my mother.' We emend this: so it *was* his mother."[10]

It bears mentioning that this unique and fantasmatic image of the maternal body is neither "natural" nor "present." Although it ostensibly provides an *absolutely unique certainty* regarding the place of origin (as Freud puts it, "there is indeed no other place about which one can assert with such conviction that one has been there once before"), the epistemological status of this claim to "certainty" is itself uncanny and paradoxically uncertain as it cannot be substantiated by either subjective memory or empirical evidence. The "unique certainty" of having passed through the mother's body is therefore spectral in nature and the uniquely "real" image that this passage produces in its wake is therefore *uniquely* unreal as well. Its fantasmatic unreality is in uncanny proximity to its unique claim on reality. The unique image of the place of origin can be rendered visible only through its fantasmatic mechanical counterpart: the birthplace makes itself "known" and leaves its mark through the reproduction of a peculiar image of "no place," or "utopia."

And it is this uncanny conception of utopia—as a fantasmatic unreal image of a place that is paradoxically impregnated with the trace of a "real" (albeit irrecoverable) primal past—that returns us, once again, to Barthes's "fantasmatic image" and the "utopian time" in Baudelaire's poetry with which he associates it. The notion of "utopian time," as Barthes derives it here from Baudelaire and Freud, need not be understood as an escape from history, but rather as an alternative approach to it. Through his inscription of "utopian time," Barthes asks us to imagine a form of photographic historical writing that would be roughly analogous to Proust's "involuntary memory," endowed as it is with the power to conjure up unconscious and forgotten traces of past lived experiences as well as unrealized latent potentials. Unlike the memory trace that constitutes the trigger for Proust's involuntary memory, however, Barthes's fantasmatic photographic dream-poem image of "utopian time" conjures up a past prior to any subjective existence and, in so doing, calls forth a thinking of a writing of historical time that reaches back into a past even more remote, and more profoundly "unconscious" than that described by Proust. But like the action of involuntary memory described by Proust, the critical power at work in "involuntary remembering" does not lie in the capability to document known past events, but rather in its capacity to create new temporalities that unfold from dormant histories that are embedded in its inscriptions. "Utopian time," therefore, is a writing of history that unfolds as an unfurling of latently inscribed future potentialities. For this reason, "utopian time" is expressed in both past and conditional tenses: it is neither purely past nor strictly speaking future. Barthes explicitly calls attention to the photographic qualities of this doubled time by referring to it as "a second sight which seems to bear me forward to a utopian time, or to carry me back to somewhere in myself: a double movement." He also inscribes the doubled temporality of this "second sight" in his caption to the Alhambra photograph, where he rewrites Baudelaire's famous avowal of recognition of an impossible past "*C'est là que j'ai vécu!*" (It is there that I lived) into an affirmation that links that immemorial past to a potential future created by desire: "*C'est là que je voudrais vivre!*" (It is there that I would like to live).

The temporality of history as opened up by "utopian time" is neither linear nor purely located in the world of consciously lived experiences.

However, even if this "fantasmatic image"—which is both a product of and produced by "utopian time"—does not conform to reality as it can be consciously known, it nonetheless cannot be conceived of as purely imaginary or subjective. Its creative potentials are "real" in the sense that they "realize" or bring into being latent possibilities in the form of new configurations. Like dreams, these "utopic" configurations must be read or interpreted to disclose their relationship to an unknown (and perhaps even unknowable) past and their potential impact on the thinking of what is or is not possible. The utopian time conjured up by the *Alhambra* photograph, which is, in some sense, derived from the photographic potentiality of the maternal body (even as it cannot be construed as a "photograph" of the mother in any simple sense) opens up a new way of approaching the question of the writing of history through the lens of this impossible possibility.

For most readers of *Camera Lucida*, when one invokes the figure of an impossible but "utopically real" photograph of the mother, it is most common to think immediately of the famous "winter garden photograph." The image that goes by this name refers to an unreproduced photograph that Barthes describes of his mother as a five year old girl, with her seven-year-old brother, under the palms of the winter garden in the house in which she was born. After the death of his mother, Barthes searches unsuccessfully for an image of her in which he might be able to recognize the person he had known and loved. In this image, the "winter garden photograph," that is, in an image of his mother as he never could have "known" her in any literal sense, he ultimately finds her again and recognizes her absolutely. As the unique quality of this impossibly "utopic" recognition is uniquely singular to him and to him alone, he refuses to reproduce this image as a photograph in the book. In his essay, "The Deaths of Roland Barthes," Jacques Derrida calls attention to the motif of "utopia" in *Camera Lucida* as it emerges in Barthes's invocation of the "winter garden photograph." Glossing Barthes's commentary about the "truth" of this impossible image, Derrida writes:

> The impossible, sometimes, by chance, becomes possible: as a utopia. This is in fact what he said before his death, though for him, of the Winter Garden Photograph. Beyond analogies, "it achieved for me, utopically, *the impossible science of the unique being*" [*Camera Lucida*, 71]. He said this uniquely, turned toward his mother and not the Mother. But the poignant singularity does not

> contradict the generality, it does not forbid it from having the force of law, but only arrows, marks, and signs it. Singular plural. Is there, then, already in the first language, the first mark, another possibility, another chance except the pain of this plural? And what about metonymy? And homonymy? Can we suffer from anything else? But could we speak without them?[11]

As he picks up on Barthes's insistence upon the "utopically" "unique" and "singular" quality of the Winter Garden photograph, Derrida points to the latent structure of repetition, and hence plurality, that underwrites and paradoxically renders possible the poignant singularity of the image that Barthes so cherishes. For Derrida, the very singularity of this chance event in which an impossibility (the true image of a unique being is encountered after her death) utopically "becomes possible," and can only become "possible," as it were, because of the doubled temporality and essentially written status of this utopic scene of recognition. In other words, to say that "the impossible, sometimes, by chance, becomes possible: as a utopia," implies that the photographic image in question is a form of writing and that as writing it has the latent potential to inscribe "utopian time." But it is only when photography relinquishes its dominant referential powers and loosens its grasp on documentation, information, cognition, and consciousness and returns to its "first language" as "mark" or as writing that it opens itself up "utopically" to its impossible possibilities. As he continues his discussion of the Winter Garden photograph, Derrida repeatedly emphasizes the term "utopically" and its relation to writing and to death:

> What we might playfully call the *mathesis singularis*, what is achieved for him "utopically" in front of the Winter Garden Photograph, is impossible and yet takes place, utopically, metonymically, as soon as it marks, even "before" language. Barthes speaks of utopia at least twice in *Camera Lucida*. Both times between his mother's death and his own—that is, inasmuch as he entrusts it to writing: "Once she was dead I no longer had any reason to attune myself to the progress of the superior Life Force (the race, the species). My particularity could never again universalize itself (unless) utopically, by writing, whose project henceforth would become the unique goal of my life."[12]

Although Derrida alludes (somewhat cryptically here) to a mark "before" language and with the mention of that mark implicitly conjures up the figure of birth and the maternal body, his focus here is the marked space of writing that Barthes himself explicitly opens up between two deaths: his mother's past death and his own future death.[13] Indeed, as Barthes himself famously and wryly observes in *Camera Lucida*, the book itself is conceived as a form of "waiting" between those two deaths: "The only "thought" I can have is that at the end of this first death, my own death is inscribed; between the two, nothing more than waiting."[14] In the passage by Derrida cited above, he (Derrida) associates "utopia" with this time of writing that has given up on life's "possibilities" and hence given itself over to a temporality marked by death. And indeed, much of Derrida's essay on Barthes is devoted to the relation between writing, death, and mourning. And this is certainly not surprising given that Barthes's book is most explicitly a book of mourning and death is everywhere in it.[15]

Neither Derrida nor Barthes overtly acknowledges the striking inverse connection between the "utopian time" of a past *before birth* conjured up by the Alhambra photograph and the utopic encounter *after death* occasioned by the discovery of the winter garden photograph. This is somewhat surprising given Derrida's explicit interest in the motif of "utopia" and its relationship to what one might call, following his text, the "singular plural" of and at the origin. In any case, as should be clear by now, these two "impossible" photo-images of the "mother" are uncanny doubles of one another. Furthermore, temporally, they are in a photographically "negative" relation to one another. As we have already seen, the "utopic" impossible possibility of the Alhambra photograph recalls the trace of the Mother (and it is important to note that Barthes capitalizes the word "Mother" here) prior to any subjective or personal incarnation, and thus prior to any simple inscription into human, historical time. In the winter garden photograph, by contrast, the "utopic" impossible possibility turns around the fact that the image that Barthes discovers of his mother is an absolutely unique, singular, and particular being, and in that absolute singularity (be it plural or not), the image cannot be rendered legible within the constraints of human, historical time. Neither image is "visible"; both images rely upon radically unconscious processes of reading and writing. Read in this light, the winter garden photograph, for all its uniqueness, is not merely an impossibly "utopic" scene of "recognition"—it is more like an uncanny scene of "*déjà vu*." And "*déjà vu*," as I have been trying to develop it here, does not refer to the repetition of something that one has seen before, but rather refers to the photographic recurrence of that which was *never* seen before. As such, *déjà vu*, understood in this sense, returns us to the question of how the photographic maternal bears witness to an unphotographable event. Derrida himself invokes something like this conception of "*déjà vu*" as impossible witness to an unknowable event when, in *Athens, Still Remains*, he writes of the image-sentence-phrase, "we owe ourselves to death" (*nous nous devons à la mort*) that comes to him, photographically, "like an original—or a negative without origin."

This conception of "*déjà vu*" as a photographic witness to an unconscious trace of an unknowable event returns us to the question of history and the place of the mother within that question. While a certain classical philosophical tradition would place the maternal function on the side of "nature," biology, and "prehistory," in the preceding pages I have been trying to suggest that the figure of the "photographic maternal" challenges the very temporal field through which one establishes a clear distinction between "nature" and "history," between "prehistorical" and "historical" events, or between conscious documentation and unconscious latent possibilities.[16] It bears mentioning at this point that, on one level, this derivation of the "photographic maternal" from Barthes's text might seem somewhat perverse, if not downright nonsensical, given that, throughout *Camera Lucida*, Barthes insists emphatically upon the hyperreferential character of photography (via the famous pivotal assertions that "the referent adheres" to the photograph and that the *noeme*—or essential truth— of photography can be expressed as: "it-was-there" (*ça-a-été*) and resolutely aims to preserve and protect the image of his own beloved mother from the deadening socializing properties of photographic documentation.

Certainly, this attention to the excessively referential power of photography is, without a doubt, one of the most important tenets of Barthes's book. Indeed, when writing about photographic "certainty," he asserts that the excessive force of photography's power to "ratify" past presence overwhelms and cancels out the more fragile power of memory and, for this reason, he suggests that photography and writing are, to some degree, mutually exclusive:

> The Photograph does not necessarily say *what is no longer*, but only and for certain *what has been*. This distinction is decisive. In front of a photograph, our consciousness does not necessarily take the nostalgic path of memory (how many photographs are outside of individual time). But for every photograph existing in the world, the path of certainty: the Photograph's

> essence is to ratify what it represents. . . . No writing can give me this certainty. It is the misfortune (but also perhaps the voluptuous pleasure) of language not to be able to authenticate itself. The *noeme* of language is perhaps this impotence.[17]

Barthes suggests that the uncanny power of photographic certainty lies in the fact that it is not merely "conscious," but superconscious —more conscious than consciousness itself: consciousness devoid of and indifferent to memory, subjectivity, and, I would suggest, even history. The paradox that Barthes points to throughout *Camera Lucida* is that precisely *because* photography is endowed with an excessive power to document the "reality" of pastness itself, it is incapable of language, of speech, of memory, of writing and of history. Recalling, once again, Proust's distinction between voluntary and involuntary memory, we might say that Barthes implies that photography's capacity for this overvoluntary memory renders it incapable of telling a story, or creating a permeable associative field in which events can be ordered and reordered in relation to one another. Barthes himself says explicitly that the photograph "does not invent" and that it "possesses an evidential force, and that its testimony bears not on the object but on time."[18] For Barthes, this capacity for super-certainty predetermines photography's propensity to be used as an extension of the police as its "default" rhetorical position is that of "proof" or "evidence." In an attempt to convey the alienating anxiety produced by this evidentiary power, he recounts the following anecdote:

> One day I received from a photographer a picture of myself which I could not remember being taken, for all my efforts; I inspected the tie, the sweater to discover in what circumstances I had worn them; to no avail. And yet, *because it was a photograph* I could not deny that I had been *there* (even if I did not know *where*). This distortion between certainty and oblivion gave me a kind of vertigo, something of a "detective" anguish (the theme of *Blow-Up* was not far off); I went to the photographer's show as to a police investigation, to learn at last what I no longer knew about myself.[19]

Curiously, this description of an uncanny and disturbing convergence between "certainty" and "oblivion" regarding the undeniable status of a place ("*there*") where I "know" that I have been before, but that I cannot remember, recalls and negates the scene of familiar recognition of the primal home in the maternal body that was conjured up by the Alhambra photograph. In both cases, there is a sense of "certainty" of "having been there before" that cannot be corroborated by any subjective act of memory. In the case cited earlier, however, there is only one possible resolution to the crime drama in which Barthes finds himself: In one way or another, he must produce a conscious correspondence between himself and the image of himself with which he is confronted. The relationship between those two images will be relegated to "consciousness" even if he ultimately remains unable to recall his prior presence at the scene of the photographic event in question. Photography's power thereby subjects him to its implacable objectification, to which he must give himself over willingly. But in the case of the Alhambra photograph, "certainty" is detached from any referential or evidentiary "photographic" power; it creates a temporal field whose claim on reality is entirely dependent on the fragile and mobile fate of its unconscious traces of *déjà vu* that are brought to light by singular acts of reading and writing.

These two scenes, however, are related to one another. By reading them through one another, an important (but somewhat latent) aspect of Barthes's book becomes somewhat more legible. From what we have seen, Barthes inscribes (at least) two different kinds of photographic principles in his book: the first is superconscious, referential, visible, and "powerful." This photographic principle fixes events in time by freezing time into the living death of a preserved past. Following the analogy with Proust, we might call this "voluntary photography." However, alongside this principle, there is also another photographic principle: it is a nonreferential, rebuslike, and profoundly "unconscious." It mobilizes temporality but, like the form of writing that it is, its claim on factual authenticity remains, as Barthes describes the *noeme* of language: "impotent." This photographic principle does not, in fact, represent; instead, it activates the temporality of *dejá vu* and, at the risk of being too schematic, we might call it "involuntary photography."

It is important to clarify at this juncture that this "Proustian" inflected reading of these two photographic principles in Barthes's book might appear to go "against the grain" (and even actively contradict) his own explicit statements about the photograph's nonrelationship to Proustian time. He says, explicitly, for example: "The Photograph does not call up the past (nothing Proustian in a photograph). The effect it produces upon me is not to restore what has been abolished (by time, by distance) but to attest that what I see has indeed existed."[20] Or this: "In the Photograph, Time's immobilization assumes only an excessive, monstrous, mode: Time is engorged . . . Not only is the Photograph never, in essence, a memory (whose grammatical expression would be the perfect tense, whereas the tense of the Photograph is the aorist), but it actually blocks memory, quickly becomes a counter-memory."[21] It is important to note that in all of these emphatic (and non-negotiable) assertions, Barthes is referring to the specifically visible, tangible object that he calls "The Photograph." And indeed, everything that he says regarding this thing he calls "The Photograph"—(be it as phenomenological experience or ontological entity)—remains determined by his attempt to account for the various forms of "power" inherent in the nonverbal, excessively referential force of what I have been calling "voluntary photography." Furthermore, at the end of the book, Barthes follows the path of this excessive referential power to the point of arriving at its limit, which he calls "madness."

> Here is where the madness is, for until this day no representation could assure me of the past of a thing except by intermediaries; but with the Photograph, my certainty is immediate: no one in the world can undeceive me. The Photograph then becomes a bizarre *medium*, a new form of hallucination, so to speak, a modest, shared hallucination (on the one hand, "it is not there," on the other "but it has indeed been"): a mad image, chafed by reality.[22]

At the end of the book, Barthes argues that the excessive certainty of "The Photograph" destines it to become received as either "mad" or "tame." When "mad," "The Photograph" becomes tactile: it allows the dead to touch and be touched and the name that Barthes gives for this impossible loving embrace is "Pity": "In the love stirred by Photography (by certain photographs), another music is heard, its name, old-fashioned: Pity." When tame, "The Photograph" becomes omnipotent and "crushes all other images by its tyranny."[23] In both cases, however, either as "mad" or as "tame," "The Photograph" uses it power of certainty to disable the latent potentialities of language: it neither reads nor writes.

Nonetheless, despite all of Barthes's numerous claims regarding the excessive referential certainty of "The Photograph," there is, as we have already seen in our reading of the Alhambra photograph, another story (and another history) regarding photographic writing inscribed within his book. Certainly, in his text, photography and writing are not simply opposed to one another. *Camera Lucida* is not simply a book "about" photography; it is itself a book of "photographic" writing. And this is so on many levels, beginning with the fact that, from its very first sentences onward, Barthes conjures up various kinds of word-images that are "photographic" even if they do appear in the form of actual photographs. Among the most striking examples, we find the following pictorial "explanation" of the relationship between the Photograph and the referent:

> It is as if the Photograph always carries its referent with itself, both affected by the same amorous or funeral immobility, at the very heart of the moving world; they are glued together, limb by limb, like the condemned man and the corpse in certain tortures; or even like those pairs of fish (sharks, I think, according to Michelet) which navigate in convoy, as though united in eternal coitus.[24]

Furthermore, there are many (ostensibly real, but who knows?) photographs in the book that Barthes chooses to reproduce verbally rather than photographically. In one of the most famous (and arguably self-consciously "Proustian") passages in the book, Barthes presents a theory of "History" as a temporal field constituted by his (implicitly partly unconscious) relationship to the time that his mother was alive before him—that is, to the time *before* his own conception and birth.[25] He punctuates this theory with a description of a scene in which he contemplates a photograph of himself as a child, in his mother's arms; by looking at the photograph, he becomes able to awaken the long dormant (and presumably otherwise irretrievable) memory traces of the feel of the texture of her dress and the smell of her powder:

> Thus the life of someone whose existence has somewhat preceded our own encloses in its particularity the very tension of History, its division. History is hysterical: it is constituted only if we consider it, only if we look at it—and in order to look at it, we must be excluded from it. As a living soul, I am the very contrary of History, I am what belies it, destroys it for the sake of my own history (impossible for me to believe in "witnesses"; impossible, at least to be one; Michelet was able to write virtually nothing about his own time). That is what the time when my mother was alive *before me* is—History (moreover, it is the period which interests me most, historically). No anamnesis could ever make me glimpse this time starting from myself (this is the definition of anamnesis)—whereas, contemplating a photograph in which she is hugging me, a child, against her, I can waken in myself the rumpled softness of her crêpe de Chine and the perfume of her rice powder.[26]

These sensory memories, resurrected by the photographic scene, do indeed enlarge the field of his memory beyond the scope of his subjective, conscious memory. Here the photograph appears (in some sense) to "bear witness" to something that would have otherwise remained temporally inaccessible: the time *before* him in his mother's life. In other words, this photograph (utopically and impossibly) opens up and extends the field of anamnesis from the time that "starts from me" to the time *before* me. In this scene, something is transmitted, through the latent inscriptions of what Benjamin might call an entire "image world" that is embedded in "her crêpe de Chine" and the perfume of her rice powder. Furthermore, for this "awakening" to occur, it would appear that the narrator must, in some sense, allow himself to reproduce the photograph in his own psyche. Only by responding "photographically," as it were, to this image—that is, by giving himself over to the unconscious photographic capacities within his own psyche, can these latent inscriptions of the lost life (and perhaps the life is neither strictly his nor hers) be awakened. It is no accident that Barthes conjures up this scene of "involuntary photography" in the context of a discussion of the limits of the possibility of writing "History" and writing historically. In this context, it is also important to recall—and perhaps to take seriously—that the question of "History"—specifically the question of how to write history after the advent of photography—is, arguably, the central conceptual concern of *Camera Lucida*. (For this reason, perhaps, Michelet appears like something of a nineteenth-century proxy for Barthes throughout the book). Many—if not most—of the most important critical images (reproduced as photographs or not) in the book *come from* or *point to* obscure aspects of nineteenth-century desires, events, and traumas. It is easy to lose sight of the importance of Barthes's reflections on history in *Camera Lucida*, since this question is easily overshadowed by his inimitable narrative of mourning the mother through writing about photography. Throughout this book, however, I have been trying to suggest that photography and the mother are not accidentally related and that the specific links between photography and the maternal function are themselves central to Barthes's reflections on writing history. Furthermore, as we have seen through our reading of the "Alhambra image," Barthes's most compelling insights about the possibilities and limits of writing history may not be immediately visible. They are inscribed, from the beginning, latently, within the photographic scene of his own writing.

Let us recall that the opening lines of *Camera Lucida* recount the narration of a very striking photographic scene:

> One day, quite some time ago, I happened on a photograph of Napoleon's youngest brother, Jerome, taken in 1852. And I realized then, with an amazement I have not been able to lessen since: "I am looking at eyes that looked at the Emperor." Sometimes I would mention this amazement, but since no one seemed to share it, nor even to understand it (life consists of these little touches of solitude), I forgot about it. My interest in photography took a more cultural turn.[27]

Although this opening image has received relatively little critical attention, it establishes, from the beginning, the complexity of the reflections on history that also bind writing to photography and the mother throughout the remainder of the book.[28] It is a vertiginously uncanny scene of "*déjà vu*." The first person narrator verbally reproduces an ostensibly forgotten memory of an earlier image of himself looking at a photograph (taken during the Second Empire, in 1852, under the rule of Napoleon III) that bears witness to a witness (Napoleon's youngest brother Jérôme) to the Emperor himself and through him to the last historical political period that predated any possible photographic historical documentation.[29] This moment, which opens the book and then is explicitly "forgotten" by its narrator, who fails to engage the attention of his entourage, inaugurates attentiveness to the latent, but untold, legacies of the nineteenth century. Here, as in the passage we just read, in which Barthes reads the image of himself with his mother, the narrator both writes about photography and writes photographically. This "photographic writing" cannot show anything directly; it animates a potential field of associations through which the time "before" is awakened otherwise and, when read, brings the *déjà vu* of a possible, impossible future to life.

Photo-readings in Hélène Cixous: The Will to Photography and Darkroom Writing

In the preceding pages, we have begun to explore how photography might be linked, from the beginning, as it were, to the body of the mother and to the maternal function as it operates within the psyche. When looked at in this light, "photography" becomes something other than its capacity to document or record something known or knowable. Indeed, as we have seen through our reading of the various "unrepresented" (or utopic) photographs in Barthes's text, a certain "truth" of photography operates at the very limits of what can be imagined as "visible" or even "possible." When photography loosens its grasp on its various referential conscious powers (to know, to prove, to document) and gives itself over to be read as a form of writing, it calls for a mode of reading (of events, texts, and the world) that is neither conscious nor unconscious as conventionally understood. And, as we have begun to see through our reading of these photo-text-images in Barthes's text, this mode of photographic reading is intimately connected with the figure of the mother both *in* photographic writing and *as* photographic writing.

In order to pursue how photographic writing works as a primal figure for untold histories, I would like to turn briefly to the relationship between photography and the maternal function in some of Hélène Cixous's recent writings. Over the last two decades or so, a period during which her works have become more explicitly marked by her ongoing readings of Proust, Hélène Cixous has increasingly (and perhaps not coincidentally) inscribed reflections on the negative powers of photography and the impossible possibilities of photographic writing into her works. In the shelter of her solitary chamber, Cixous develops her readings of Proust and puts them to work otherwise in her own writing. The traces of these Proustian photo-readings are inscribed just about everywhere in the recent texts, but they become particularly visible in the scenes that turn around the mother, the grandmother, and the photographic maternal function.

The Will to Photography in So Close

To be sure, however, from a certain point of view, photography is Hélène Cixous's declared enemy.[30] This is, indeed, what she says explicitly in the inaugural scene of her recent novel, *So Close* (*Si près*), where she writes: "Photography I've always thought is the enemy, my enemy exactly, the adversary, one can't take photos and write, I say to myself."[31]

As we shall see, Cixous specifies that photography is the "adversary" and "exactly" her enemy because it remains at once too far and too close to writing. It is no accident, however, that photography, in all its capacities, conscious and otherwise, casts such a large shadow over the writing in and of this particular book. In this novel, Cixous tells the story of her ambivalent return to Algeria, her birthplace and the place to which she vowed for decades that she would never return. The narrator's powerful ambivalence about the possibility or the impossibility of her return to Algeria is reflected, in part, through her powerful expressions of negativity regarding the ambiguous powers of photography. Throughout *So Close*, the narrator punctuates the story of this impossible-possible return to the place of her birth with ongoing reflections on what it means for her to take (or not to take) a photograph of her mother, in a bathing suit, on her ninety-fifth birthday.

From its opening scene onward, in which the narrator catches herself in the act of taking a "mental photograph" of her mother on her birthday, the novel presents the photographic act as actively and violently opposed to the life given by writing: that is, it is both writing's negative image and the very negation of its mode of being. As the inaugural scene unfolds, the narrator carries on a continuous, reflective diatribe against photography. Within this long speech detailing why photography is the negation of writing, she even goes so far as to negate her own negative argument by recounting how her friend says "exactly the opposite, there is writing in photography, he says." Nonetheless, despite his objections, she continues her rant as follows:

> in the idea of taking a photograph technically everything frightens me, the idea of "taking" whereas in my opinion the camera cuts, out of a photograph, the infinite flux of the untakeable, whereas writing takes nothing at all, writing dreams of not stopping what is in the process of being lost, nothing more powerless and desperate, thus nothing more faithful to the infidelities of life I say to myself.[32]

Photography, she tells herself, takes too much. Its capacity to "take" is overwhelmingly powerful—excessively powerful—as it seizes hold of everything including even the "untakeable" itself: the very part of "life" that is truly vital and hence "untakeable" precisely and paradoxically because it is all too "takeable." It imposes its powerful will on life by stripping it of all its movement and precious precariousness. Its power is nefarious: it competes with death by anticipating it, and thus precipitously makes it come too soon. Its precociousness is brutal. Throughout *So Close*, the narrator tries to defend herself against this negative power of photography by countering it point by point with precise negations and denials. At every turn, she disavows any and all relation to photography. On numerous occasions, as if in response to an unspoken query, she repeatedly asserts that she "never took a photo." At other moments, she insists that she has no movie camera either and continues to protest (as if countering an opposing force) that she has never taken a photo, not *ever*. Well into the book, the narrator says:

> I have no movie camera. I have never had a movie camera in my whole life I have never taken a photo, I have never taken anything, I have pushed the "you shall make for yourself no graven image" to the height of extremes, I have never taken a photo of my beloved, there are no photos of our life, not a single image, I did not take photos of our children, I did not take my brother, or my women friends, or my friend J.D. I never fought off a desire to photograph or to film, I never had the sudden urge to keep a visual trace, I should have perhaps sometimes I will never know if I did the wrong thing I can't I can no longer look back it's too late.[33]

But at the very moment when she affirms that "it is too late" even to regret *not* having taken all the photos that she never took, it is already "too late" once *again* because she herself has already been taken by an unexpected and unpredictable desire to film her mother. And it's done. The decision is made in a photographic flash, instantaneously. Nevertheless, throughout the negative speech she makes against photography, and despite its manifest content, she finds herself looking for her friend Ruth Beckermann's movie camera (which she had left in her office), and hence the film of her mother that she had never wanted to make is already underway, despite her conscious intentions to the contrary:

> I have never touched a movie camera. I have never put an apparatus for looking between desired subjects and the retinas of my soul. Without explanation, I came running back down. My mother was already in her film. In the film in which she is the subject, the cause.

> Je n'ai jamais touché une caméra. Je n'ai jamais mis un appareil à regarder entre des sujets désirés et les rétines de mon âme. Sans explication. Je suis redescendue en courant. Ma mère était déjà dans son film. Dans le film dont elle est le sujet, la cause.[34]

If we look at the excessively negative declarations in *So Close* more closely, it appears clear (and one does not need to avail oneself of what, in French, is the astute gaze known as "*l'oeil américain*," the American eye, to see it) that these denials regarding photography are not simple affirmations of negative feelings; they are psychic disavowals—and, as such, they bear the trace of unavowed or unavowable desires that can *only* be expressed in the negative. In other words, the negative declaration *against* photography is itself photographic in form; its negative inscription precedes and makes possible the development of a latent future image. We will return to this point later on.

But if, for the time being, one looks at this passage even more closely, this time by moving from the meaning of the words to their sounds of the words as they are written in French, we can hear, at the level of their repeated and insistent sounds, an auditory image that corresponds in another way to this photographic signifying effect. The narrator incessantly repeats the French phrase "*je n'ai, jamais*" ("I have, never"). In the repetition of the auditory syllables: "*je n'ai*" (negation of the verb "*avoir*," to have) one can hear the distant echo of an affirmation of birth ("*je nais*," "I am born"). There is only a little negative, a little step (*pas*), between *naître* and *ne pas être*, between birth and the negation of life. Now, *So Close* plays constantly on the potential confusion between the various forms of the verb *naître* (to be born) and all the negative possibilities of the verb *être* (*not* "to be"). Here, for example, is how the phonemes intersect in the following passage:

> I had just written "I was born in Algeria" and once again I felt that I didn't know what I was saying, what this sentence was saying to me, I don't know what it was thinking by saying "in Algeria" or borninAlgeria or what I thought of being born in without being of, being of nothingness, not being of Algeria, but with Algeria nonetheless. I felt this uncanny and exhilarating strangeness that has the gift of repeating itself, reigniting itself with each interrogation.
>
> Je venais d'écrire "je suis née en Algérie" et une fois encore je sentis que je ne savais pas ce que je disais, ce que me disait cette phrase, je ne sais pas ce qu'elle pensait en disant "en Algérie" ou néenalgérie ni ce que je pensais d'être née sans en être, d'être du néant, de ne pas être d'Algérie, mais avec Algérie néanmoins. J'éprouvai cette inquiétante et enivrante étrangeté qui a ce don de se répéter, se rallumer, à chaque interrogatoire.[35]

One could even say that the question "*naître ou ne pas être*" (to be born or not to be) in Algeria is one of the obsessive preoccupations of *So Close*. This question haunts the book at several levels. At one moment, for example, the narrator asks the friend she calls by the name "Telephone:" "If I say to you *Né* [born], I say to the Telephone, what is it?" A little later, she asks, "How do you write '*Né*,' I say to my mother. *Née* Klein, says my mother. —The other one, I say. When you say '*Né*' on the telephone when you talk to your sister." Refusing to recognize the narrator's insistence on the negative possibilities inscribed within the birth word, "*Né*," her mother replies: "It is not written at all. It is also not said." But after the daughter's repeated objections, the mother clarifies the matter as follows: "One says it but you can't write it. Perhaps it's said in our district of Osnabrück. But as for me, I say *Nein*. No, I don't say *Né*."[36] In these two examples, there is an ambiguous tension (which makes itself heard specifically when the place of birth is mentioned) between the affirmation of birth on the one hand and the expression of a negative linguistic power on the other. The narrator cannot say "I was born in Algeria" (*je suis née en Algérie*) without by the same token denying this birth in Algeria, while the mother explains that in spite of the fact that one *can* say "*Né*" to mean "no" in her native city, Osnabrück, she herself does not say "*Ne*" but "*Nein*." Whereas the mother affirms her negation clearly, the daughter denies the possibility of declaring her birthplace.

On this commentary about telephonic exchanges, let us recall that at the beginning of the book the narrator affirms that her love for the telephone is precisely the counterpart of her aversion for photography:

> Here is an odd thing: my love for the Telephone is equal in intensity to my antipathy for the camera. That's because the Telephone is you. The camera is a prosthesis, it's a pair of optical pliers, an ocular harpoon, an avid prolongation of me.[37]

Although the author here declares her opinion that the telephone respects the alterity of the other, whereas photography is merely a narcissistic and mortiferous weapon of the self, it is not so clear that her book entirely accords with this judgment. The telephone, defined against photography, presented as its positive negative, as it were, is itself implied in the photographic structure of the book and subject to its obscure law. And, apparently against the will of the author, the writing of the book is marked by photographic effects.

Now the traces of the obscure, duplicitous and contradictory laws of photography are at work from the very first pages of *So Close*, and perhaps even before. Although the book begins with the announcement of a verbal "blow," involuntarily inflicted by the narrator on her mother on the anniversary of her birth, we discover immediately that this verbal blow is in fact merely the aftereffect of a primordial image that appears for the first time before the beginning of the book, and on the basis of which the narrative gets going. The image in question reappears in the text in the form of a detailed description of a mental photograph of the mother, in a bathing suit, taken by the daughter on the former's ninety-fifth birthday. The text has us see the photo of the mother as it develops progressively in the eyes of the daughter, who watches herself watching her mother in the bathing suit and finds herself caught up in her avid desire to take a picture of her. She says:

> My gaze was busy mentally photographing the desired face, the face of her birthday, I wanted to imprint in I know not what immortal wax my dearly beloved's features when she turned ninety-five years old. . . . I was given over entirely to this secret attempt to steal a picture taken from my mother in a bathing suit [*ma mère en maillot*], I was hoping that she was totally unaware of it, I was hoping to absorb her figure, the muscular drive of prey that makes its nest in me was brooding over this face in transformation.
>
> Maman changes so quickly, I say to myself, this mobility is like that of a five-year old child, I realize that this predatory passion keeps me captive myself, I want to take and I am taken by the need to take, it's a frenzy that devastates me, it's exhausting to want to hold on to what is passing, I am haunted by a mental camera, I who have never taken a photo in my life. Photography I've always thought is the enemy, my enemy exactly, the adversary, one can't takes photos and write, I say to myself.[38]

But if the narrator is caught up in this drive that condemns her to want what she has never wanted, namely to take a photo of her mother, this is because photography claims to be able to deny nothingness by offering a desired image in the place of the unimaginable. So if she lets herself be taken by photography at the beginning of the book, this is the sign that she is already haunted by the anticipation of an intolerable image. In other words, the very event of the unexpected appearance of the mother in a bathing suit on which the book opens is always already marked by the negative of that image, the image of her future disappearance.

As we have already seen, according to the narrator photography is the enemy of writing, since it is too powerful, too grasping, too conscious.

She reproaches it in particular with its authoritarian and excessive *will.* By declaring herself untouched by any photographic desire, she is trying to protect herself against the grip of that will. But, paradoxically, it is in seeing herself become involuntarily transformed into a psychic camera that she discovers, unbeknownst to herself and against her will, that there is another aspect of photography, something that can here be called provisionally (recognizing the strong presence of Proust who haunts every line of the text and following our reading of Barthes) *involuntary photography.*

The uncanny power of involuntary photography is inscribed throughout *So Close,* but is declared clearly in the scene where the mother is filmed in a two-piece bathing suit. This scene, which follows the long passage of denials about photography quoted above ("I have no movie camera. I have never had a movie camera in my whole life I have never taken a photo") reproduces, but differently, the first image of the mother. This time, after having defended herself verbally against photography, the daughter gives in to the sudden desire to film her mother with the camera she never wanted to have. And, seeing herself obey the obscure will of involuntary photography, she suddenly sees her mother, for the first time, otherwise:

> The idea occurs to me that perhaps it's not she who obeys, but I who am obeying a will external to my will which has taken over my will by a trick, it may be that it's my mother's will, hidden to herself or on the contrary hidden by herself, silent, powerful, of unquestionable authority, which dictated to me this abrupt and crazy decision: to film my mother in a purple two-piece. I filmed. But what did I film? My mother's will. I thought: Maman's will and testament. . . . Now: I see my mother. It is: the first time. I see and I see that I see. I see my mother in painting. I see what I have as yet never seen what I will never see. I take the camera and I paint my mother with large brush strokes, I have never seen my mother I say to myself I have never seen her so close.[39]

The film of the mother in her bathing suit (*en maillot*) does not take the mother's life. To the contrary, the act of filming gives birth for the first time, and after the fact, to a primordial vision of a vital and secret life that her daughter could never have seen otherwise. The scene is punctuated by several figures of birth. The word "*maillot,*" after all, refers to the swaddling of the newborn. But the film sequence of the mother "*en maillot*" or "*au maillot*" also implicitly refers to the birth of the daughter herself. In the sentence that precedes the beginning of the film of the mother, the narrator says, "The greatest illusion is to think that what is passed is finished, I say to myself." Here we might note in passing, as though by coincidence, that the greatest film on the first World War (the period of the mother's childhood), namely *La grande illusion*, came out in 1937, the year of Hélène Cixous's birth. The film shot by the daughter gives birth to this mother who is already "in her film" (*dans son film*), and this maternal filming in turn gives birth to the daughter. At the end of this sequence, the filmic act gently transforms itself into a gesture of painting, and the vital image that comes back at this moment of grace gives access to the vision of another reality of life—life lived differently, as one encounters it in art, a dream, or literature.

It is not by chance that the mother is at the center of this photographic vision. Throughout Hélène Cixous's work, the mother is always on the side of photography. She takes photos, she loves them, and she expresses her loves through them. On this point, let us note this passage from *Osnabrück* in which Cixous, speaking of her mother, writes: "Eve takes photos. It's through love. She loves flowers in photos. She plants in photos."[40] But the link that attaches the mother to photography is still more complex. This link is a knot, an obscure navel of Hélène Cixous's writing. As we have already begun to see, this knot is comprised of a number of principal strands: the history of the maternal line in its relation to the history of cities; the reading of Proust; the photographic conception of the unconscious; the primal scene of writing. In several of Cixous's recent books, these four preoccupations are woven together through the inscription of the dark powers of photography and establish secret relations between them.

Darkroom Writing

Before concluding, I would like to turn very briefly to one more striking example of how "involuntary photography" comes to assume an important place within Cixous's writing. Photography, it seems, is not simply the "enemy" of her writing, it also inhabits and haunts her texts as a ghostly, unknowing and unconscious ally of her efforts to tell certain kinds of stories that will always remain, at least to some extent, both untellable and untold. In a novel published in 2001, which to my knowledge has not yet been translated into English, *Benjamin à Montaigne: Il ne faut pas le dire* (Benjamin to Montaigne: It Must Not Be Said), Cixous places a photograph of a character, Benjamin, at the dark center of the novel's labyrinthine narrative. Benjamin's repressed and latent story develops "photographically" against the backdrop of the narrator's mother's narrative of returning, with her sister, to Osnabrück, the birth city in Germany from which she was exiled during the war. Throughout the book, Cixous refers repeatedly to a number of cherished writers, including Stendhal, Rimbaud, and Montaigne. But through the conjunction of the motifs of photography, reading, and the figure of the grandmother, she establishes a special connection to Proust's writings on, about, and through photography.[41]

In this context, it might be helpful to recall that one of the most famous depictions of the perverse power of photography in Proust concerns the narrator's grandmother who has herself photographed before her death, hoping thus to be able to lessen the future suffering of her grandson by the consoling image of her face. But the beloved expression of the grandmother's face is spoiled by the grandson during the sitting because he does not understand that she wants to have herself photographed. His belated understanding of the meaning of the photo provokes reflections on the place occupied by the dead in our memories and our hearts. Cixous explicitly invokes Proust in *Benjamin à Montaigne: Il ne faut pas le dire*, when she mentions her need for a room of her own for the four occupations necessary for writing: reading, daydreaming, tears, and pleasure.[42] But she also alludes implicitly to Proust through the thoughts provoked by stories about photos.

Now, we must pay great attention to the word "*histoire*" (which means both "history" and "story" in French) in this context. In general in Cixous's work, photos are not endowed with memory, they have no relation to so-called reality; they do not represent history and they are not representatives of history. On the contrary, they are almost always negative histories or negatives of history because they occupy the place of what is deprived of memory or experience and that runs the risk of being lost forever. On this point, one thinks, for example, of the violence of the scene in which the narrator of *Reveries of the Wild Woman: Primal Scenes* takes imaginary photos of her childhood classroom in Algeria in order to "inexist" (her word) the lying and violent world of "frenchalgeria":

> Whereupon I took my father's camera, broken beyond repair, which my mother had thrown in the trash but which I fished out even though beyond repair.

> And I made it into a tool for fabricating ghosts. I forced it on the classroom. With the vacant camera I snapped pictures of the teachers. Dozens of nonexistent snapshops. So I inexisted them. All. One after another. I gazed at them from the point of view of the absence of a gaze.[43]

One thinks too of the famous statement of Gregor, the fictive lover of *Manhattan*, who says "here take my picture" to prove that he really exists, whereas the photo constitutes the very proof of the contrary.[44] In *Benjamin à Montaigne*, however, photos are at the navel of the story. Set off against the main story of the belated visit of the two old German-Jewish sisters (Selma and Jennie) to their native city Osnabrück, one discovers the shadow cast by the story of a photo of the grandmother. Here, in contrast to Proust, it is not a photo taken *of* the grandmother, but a photo kept *by* her. The maternal grandmother of the narrator, Omi, keeps an image of her little brother Benjamin, who was expelled from the family and exiled in the United States, where he died. The family no longer speaks about Benjamin; Omi does not speak about her photo, but she keeps it safe. Omi, the grandmother, retains the image of Benjamin, the one omitted (*l'omis*) from the family history. Suddenly, in the middle of the book, the history of this Benjamin who disappeared bursts violently from the frame of the photograph in which it had been sleeping silently for years. In a passage in which the narrator is speaking to her mother and her aunt of their trip to Osnabrück, she describes the process of photographic awakening as follows:

> Suddenly I needed Benjamin and this story about which one never speaks because it is precisely the story about which one never speaks which is the key to the stories that one tells. Each time long ago that I had asked Omi my grandmother who is this Benjamin she had always answered it's my little brother while looking at the photo with a love that was intimidated regretful and distracted from herself. . . . He was put on the boat and immediately after he died in Cincinnati, her childhood brother born nine months from her, the very early dead one whose photo she never let go. In Oran Benjamin reigned alone in the dark dining-room surrounded by frames where there were no longer the large photos of relatives lost between Dresden and Oran. He had survived the moves and the *Seelige Vater und Mutter* had perished. This Benjamin had always been unreadable. He was the photo of the undecipherable, I told myself.[45]

And then her mother adds:

> I don't know why this idea of Benjamin whom one never spoke about anymore suddenly came up in the train. The greatest error is to think that the story about which nobody speaks for seventy years is a finished and decomposed thing. And the greatest surprise is how a story like that suddenly comes back, as if the joltings of the train had dislodged a dormant kidney stone.[46]

The paradoxical power of the photo of this Benjamin resides in the fact that it has never illuminated anything. On the contrary, it is, as the narrator says, "the photo of the undecipherable." Thus, by showing nothing of the history that it secretly preserves, the photo keeps the very old lost history of Benjamin safe from the ravages of the passage of time. The photo of Benjamin is merely a negative trace of that history. But through this negative inscription it safeguards the fragile possibility of its potential future survival. In other words, this photo remains in the primitive state of a prehistory that has never been "developed"; it never emerged from the darkroom of its birth. Here we might recall that in "Freud and the Scene of Writing," Jacques Derrida reminds us that Freud uses photographic language to define the structure of the unconscious and to explain resistance and the return of the repressed.[47] For Hélène Cixous, following Proust, Freud, and Derrida, it is within such darkrooms that writing is born. As she writes in a passage from *L'amour du loup* (Love of the Wolf) about the darkrooms from which writing emerges:

> Shelters are not on earth, they are subterranean . . . places where books incubate. Or else they are elevated caves, water closets, small rooms that protect the four solitary and delicious occupations to which Proust gives the generic names—reading reverie tears pleasure. These four occupations set writing into motion. But all these rooms are the places of origin of primal *visions*. They are cameras (*Kamera*, *Kammer*), cases for making images.

> Les abris ne sont pas sur terre. Ils sont souterrains . . . lieux où couvent les livres. Ou bien ce sont des cavernes en étage élevé, des cabinets, de petites pièces qui protègent les quatre occupations solitaires et délicieuses dont Proust donne les noms génériques—la lecture la rêverie les larmes la volupté. Ces quatre occupations sont des embrayeurs d'écriture. Mais toutes ces pièces sont les lieux d'origine des visions primitives. Ce sont des caméras (Kamera, Kammer) des boîtes à fabriquer des images.[48]

This uncanny original darkroom is housed in the body of the photographic maternal function. It is there, in the utopic space of that *camera obscura* to which we can only return in the images we make of it in dreams and in writing, that we have the chance to encounter the latent traces of as yet unwritten future histories. Writing photographically, both Barthes and Cixous bear witness to the world as it was never seen before, but as it is brought to life out of the primal images that are fabricated into a special kind of "historical fiction" in the dark womb of photography.

TEN

The Mother Tongue in *Phèdre* and *Frankenstein*

My poor mother, how strange was your love.

—EURIPIDES, *Hippolytus*

Apparently, *Phèdre* and *Frankenstein* make strange bedfellows. Racine's tragedy is the exemplary text of seventeenth-century French drama while Mary Shelley's horror tale has been read as a gloss on the English Romantic imagination. Although *Phèdre* is written in French and *Frankenstein* in English, these two texts speak to each other through a haunting figure for the foreignness of language itself. Both authors supplement the body of their texts with prefaces that recount the genesis of their works and name sources of foreign origin. Racine acknowledges his debt to the *Hippolytus* of Euripides, and Shelley attributes the inspiration of her tale to French translations of German ghost stories, but these explicit references to foreign sources are only traces of a tacit obsession common to both texts. By speaking about foreign origins, these two texts both speak about language in terms of errancy and exile: To speak about origins is to speak one's alienation from them. *Phèdre* and *Frankenstein* speak to each other through the echoes of a common obsession with the relationship between the question of origins and that of language; these two questions converge in a figure that, through the marks of its absence, becomes curiously central.

The question of origins and the implicit impossibility of speaking about them is articulated through the figure of an absent mother who dictates and engenders the texts that circumscribe her absence. Both texts are haunted by the specter of a mother who is ultimately unspeakable. The horror that permeates these texts emanates from the figure of a mother confronting the indelible trace of an offspring that she engenders but that is also foreign to her. Both works stage scenes of monstrous or unnatural childbirth that simultaneously recall and obliterate the strange affiliation between the mother and language.

To be born is to be born into language and to be exiled from the mother. In this sense, the word "mother" is profoundly meaningless and can be read only as a figure of speech, even as the figure from which speech necessarily springs. How can the word "mother" speak the unaccountable event of our birth, which we can neither remember nor bear to forget? In *Phèdre* and *Frankenstein*, the desire to speak stems from an impossible desire to account for the mother and from an attempt to efface the mark of this unaccountability. The desire to speak recalls an impossible desire for the mother, a desire that she bear the burden of our birth by remaining the silent witness to a time we can only imagine but never know, a time before we needed to speak our alienation from her. In both texts, however, the mother's legacy is not the safe haven of prelinguistic plenitude, but rather the strange exile of speech itself.

The Mother's Legacy

"*Par où commencer?*" Where to begin? So Phèdre says as she begins to break the silence around which the drama unfolds. This question interrupts Phèdre's first dialogue with Oenone, which is characterized by verbal detours that circumscribe the unnamed cause of her silence. Phèdre's response to this question seems at first like one more circumlocution. Instead of beginning to speak about her own illicit desire, she speaks about her mother and her mother's desire. Phèdre's allusion to her mother, however, is only apparently a refusal to speak. She might well ask, "Where to begin?" for the story of her still unspoken woe and the language with which she could tell that story both, in a sense, precede her. Her question leads her inexorably to the question of the mother.

To begin to speak is to begin to speak about the mother. But to speak about the mother is to enter into a labyrinth of discourse and desire from which there is no exit:

> O haine de Venus! O fatale colère!
> Dans quels égarements l'amour jeta ma mère!
>
> Oh hatred of Venus! Oh fatal wrath!
> Into what aberrations did Love cast
> My mother![1]

Between the lines of Phèdre's allusion to her mother lurks the monstrous figure of the Minotaur. In an attempt both to conceal and to contain this monstrous effect of Pasiphaë's "unnatural" desire, the labyrinth was constructed. Phèdre's reference to the "*égarements*" that her mother endured evokes the errancy of the desire that engendered the Minotaur as well as the necessity for the circuitous detours of the structure in which he was incarcerated. In order to speak her transgressive desire for Hippolyte, she must begin by speaking about her mother's transgressive desire for the bull. She both reproduces the discourse of that desire and becomes herself "lost" in that labyrinth of speech. The mother's legacy is a discourse of desire that Phèdre recalls and reproduces.

Where to begin, indeed? In a desperate attempt to exit from this labyrinth of speech and desire, Phèdre chooses to remain silent. Oenone accuses her of an "inhuman" silence: "*Mourez donc et gardez un silence inhumain*" (227) (Die then, and keep an inhuman silence). But this inhuman silence does not, and perhaps cannot, remain unspoken. Before Phèdre begins to speak of her mother's love and of her own, these stories have already begun to speak through her. Phèdre's silence speaks—not through words, but through the pains in her moribund body:

> Ah! s'il vous faut rougir, rougissez d'un silence
> Qui de vos maux encore aigrit la violence. (ll. 185–186)
>
> Oh! If you must blush, blush at a silence
> Which ever sharpens the violence of your pains.

The aural double meaning of "*maux*" (pains) and "*mots*" (words) suggests that Phèdre's unspoken words are incorporated as pains through which her silence speaks. This active silence threatens to destroy her; the word "*violence*" follows "*silence*" like an echo that this silence has produced. Phèdre is the bearer of a maternal legacy that cannot be silenced, a mother tongue passed on to the daughter by way of the body. What is so unspeakable in this maternal legacy? Where is the cause for horror? Phèdre can only respond to the lethal "*maux*" produced by her inhuman silence by uttering the "*mots*" of a transgressive desire that produces monstrous effects.

We can read the traces of what is horrifying, violent, or unspeakable in the figurative language through which this unspeakability is spoken. Oenone attempts to force Phèdre to name her crime, but the mark of her crime is that its horror exceeds any name one might assign it. After Oenone violates Phèdre's injunction against speaking Hippolyte's name in her presence, another discourse about the crime emerges. Oenone, Phèdre's nurse, serves as the midwife to an appalling figure of speech that interrogates Phèdre's unspoken desire:

> Et quel affreux projet avez-vous enfanté
> Dont votre coeur encor doive être épouvanté? (ll. 223–224)

> To what awful project have you given birth
> Which must still horrify your heart?

In the felicitous precision of this figure everything has already been said. Here Phèdre's crime is animated through a figure of a monstrous childbirth. Once again, as in the case of Phèdre's allusion to Pasiphaë, transgressive desire is marked by a maternal figure.

It is precisely at this juncture that Racine departs from *Hippolytus*. Up to this point, the dialogue in the Racinian play has followed the Euripidean tragedy almost word for word. Here, however, Racine strays from his near-translation of the "original" text by emphasizing a maternal figure who produces a child that is not a child. In the Euripidean text, the Nurse invokes Phaedra's love for her children and Phaedra acknowledges this love. The interrogation continues, leaving the question of "children" behind. But in the Racinian text, the question of childbirth and childbearing produces a monstrous figure that expresses precisely what cannot be said: an unspoken crime is compared to the birth of an offspring that horrifies the mother. Phèdre's "actual" crime, that she loves Hippolyte, perhaps could not engender more horror than the strange figure that Oenone employs to elicit her confession.

This figure both recapitulates the mythical maternal legacy and prophesies the outcome of the drama. In a question that posits Phèdre's unnamed crime as a monstrous childbirth, we cannot help hearing echoes of Pasiphaë. The figurative language that is used to account for a drama that is supposedly unfolding in the present speaks metaphorically of past transgressions that are passed down along the maternal line. Thus, before there are even words to "name" Phèdre's crime, it has already been articulated as a repetition of her mother's reproduction. This repetition is itself a figure for reproduction. The figure invoked by Oenone is monstrous because it is a child that is not a child. The fact that Phèdre can engender something other than literal children, and that desire does engender a child that is not a child, produces horror. For the very literal status of children is put into question. Hippolyte is a peculiarly appropriate object of this desire, since he himself is a child that is not a child—that is, his status as Phèdre's stepson blurs the distinction between her "actual" children and other children, both literal and figurative, that could come to take their place. The horror engendered by the "*project affreux*" is that a discourse of desire and one of childbirth converge in the same figure. If this play is about incest, it is not simply because Hippolyte occupies the place of Phèdre's "son," but, more, because maternity and desire cohabit the same figure. Phèdre has become a vessel who has been figuratively impregnated by the mother's desire, which she expresses as love for her stepson.

The Thread of Desire

The confusion between Phèdre's actual son and Hippolyte, her stepson, emerges as the motivating and inevitable force behind her infamous declaration of love to Hippolyte. Phèdre demands to see Hippolyte in order to speak to him about the fate of her son; but through a metonymic slippage, a discussion "about" her son leads directly to a confession of love for her stepson. Phèdre herself is utterly confounded by the inexorable logic of the discourse that leads her to this conclusion:

> Que dis-je? Cet aveu que je te viens de faire,
> Cet aveu si honteux, le crois-tu volontaire?

Tremblante pour un fils que je n'osais trahir,
Je te venais prier de ne le point haïr.
Faibles projets d'un coeur trop plein de ce qu'il aime!
Hélas! je ne t'ai pu parler que de toi-même. (ll. 693–698)

What am I saying? Can you believe that this
Confession I have just made to you—this
So shameful a declaration—is voluntary?
Trembling for a son whom I dared not betray,
I came to beg you not to hate him.
Feeble projects of a heart too full of what it loves!
Alas, I could only speak to you of yourself!

"Trembling for a son," Phèdre can speak only about her love for her stepson; Phèdre's mother tongue conceives of maternal love as desire. Any words that she utters, no matter how veiled, can only speak in a language of desire. Phèdre tries to silence the transgressive element in this discourse by speaking about the two figures whom she can love legitimately: her son and her husband, Theseus. She attempts to conceal the hidden referent of her desire by circumscribing her love for Hippolyte in circumlocutions about her husband.[2] These detours lead her to the figure of the labyrinth. At the end of this labyrinthine discourse, Phèdre irrevocably utters her desire for Hippolyte:

Par vous aurait péri le monstre de la Crète,
Malgré tous les détours de sa vaste retraite:
Pour en développer l'embarras incertain,
Ma soeur du fil fatal eût armé votre main.
Mais non: dans ce dessein je l'aurais devancée;
L'amour m'en eût d'abord inspiré la pensée:
C'est moi, prince, c'est moi, dont l'utile secours
Vous eût du Labyrinthe enseigné les détours.
Que de soins m'eût coûtés cette tête charmante!
Un fil n'eût point assez rassuré votre amante:
Compagne du péril qu'il vous fallait chercher,
Moi-même devant vous j'aurais voulu marcher;
Et Phèdre au Labyrinthe avec vous descendue
Se serait avec vous retrouvée, ou perdue. (ll. 649–662)

You would have been the monster's killer then,
In spite of all the windings of his maze.

To find your way in that uncertain dark
My sister would have armed you with the thread.
But no! In this design I would have been
Ahead of her, my sister! Me, not her,
It would have been whom Love at first inspired;
And I it would have been, Prince, I whose aid
Had taught you all the Labyrinth's crooked ways.
Oh, how I would have cared for this dear head!
A single thread would not have been enough
To satisfy your lover's fears for you.
I would myself have wished to lead the way
And share the perils you were bound to face.
Phaedra, into the Labyrinth, with you
Would have descended, and with you returned,
To safety, or with you have perished!

At the critical moment when Phèdre finally confesses her love for Hippolyte, when she finally says the unspeakable, her declaration of love is framed as a hallucinatory attempt to rewrite the history that has led them both to this place. But in Phèdre's revision of the story, the last word is "*perdue*" (lost). The mother's legacy is a threadlike speech that leads back into the labyrinth and not out of it. Phèdre can do nothing other than bear the thread of this discourse, which draws her back into the past of her mother's transgression and her sister's abandonment. In her futile attempt to conceal her love for Hippolyte through verbal detours, this love emerges as the transgressive offspring of the mother tongue.

After Phèdre confesses her love to Hippolyte, she tells Oenone:

J'ai dit ce que jamais on ne devait entendre.
Ciel! comme il m'ecoutait! Par combien de détours
L'insensible a longtemps élude mes discours! (ll. 742–744)

I have said that which never should be heard nor understood.
Oh heavens, how he listened! How,
For such a long time, my speech eluded that
Unfeeling one!

"*Discours*" (speech) rhymes with "*détours*" and leads its interlocutor along labyrinthine paths. Because Phèdre speaks in detours, the listener who follows her discourse becomes himself lost in it. The power of this speech derives not merely from what is said, but also from the fact that what is said is heard and understood (*entendre*). Through his understanding of her discourse, the listener is implicated in Phèdre's transgression. Phèdre's utterance, "I have said that which never should be heard," displaces her culpability onto her interlocutor. Despite repeated attempts to silence Phèdre's discourse, Hippolyte is drawn into the labyrinthine detours of this speech and is lost in them once he understands.

If Hippolyte "hears" and "understands" what he should not—what Phèdre is saying—it is because he realizes, ultimately to his own horror, that he speaks her language. Hippolyte himself is the recipient of a mother tongue that speaks a language of desire. In his prior declaration of love to Aricie, Hippolyte refers repeatedly to his "foreign," "wild," and "barbaric" mother, Antiope. He asserts that the words he uses to express this love are not his, but, rather, are spoken in a "foreign tongue":

> Peut-être le récit d'un amour si sauvage
> Vous fait, en m'écoutant, rougir de votre ouvrage?
> D'un coeur qui s'offre à vous quel farouche entretien!
> Quel étrange captif pour un si beau lien!
> Mais l'offrande à vos yeux en doit être plus chère:
> Songez que je vous parle une langue étrangère;
> Et ne rejetez pas les voeux mal exprimés,
> Qu'Hippolyte sans vous n'aurait jamais formé. (ll. 553–560)

> Perhaps this tale of passion so uncouth
> Makes you, in hearing me, blush at your work.
> How wild a way to offer you a heart!
> How strange a captive for so beautiful
> A leash! But dearer to your eyes should be
> This offering. Believe I speak a tongue
> Unknown to me! Do not reject these vows
> So ill-expressed, indeed, which, but for you,
> I never would have formed at all.

Like Phèdre, Hippolyte displaces the responsibility for this discourse of desire onto the listener. He claims that his speech is spoken in a foreign tongue and that it is in fact Aricie's "work" (*ouvrage*). The words in this foreign tongue that connote foreignness ("*sauvage*," "*farouche*," "*captif*") recall Hippolyte's maternal legacy. These words remind us that, in the act of speaking his desire, Hippolyte is his mother's son—son of a wild, barbaric huntress. The mother tongue is a foreign language. This language of desire is always already a foreign language from which its speaker is exiled and in which he or she is lost.

Although Hippolyte is seduced by the savage joy that he experiences when he expresses his desire for Aricie, this joy turns to horror when he is compelled to hear Phèdre's declaration of love. For both of these confessions of love are bound by a common law. They both lead to a labyrinth of speech from which there is no exit. Phèdre's declaration stuns Hippolyte into a horrified silence. Hippolyte's name now rings with the echo of the epithet, "*interdit*," which Théramène uses to describe him. "*Interdit*" means both silenced and outlawed:

> Théramène: Est-ce Phèdre qui fuit, ou plutôt qu'on entraine?
> Pourquoi, Seigneur, pourquoi ces marques de douleur?
> Je vous vois sans épée, interdit, sans couleur?
> Hippolyte: Théramène, fuyons. Ma surprise est extrême.
> Je ne puis sans horreur me regarder moi-même.
> Phèdre . . . Mais non, grands Dieux! qu'en un profond oubli
> Cet horrible secret demeure enseveli! (ll. 714–720)

> Theramenes: Is that Phaedra in flight? Or rather dragged
> By someone off? What mean these signs of grief?
> I see you without color, sword, or speech.
> Hippolytus: Let us fly, Theramenes! Extreme
> Surprise confounds me. I can look
> No more except with horror on myself.
> Phaedra . . . But no, great Gods! Let this be kept
> This horrible secret forever dark.

From this point on, Hippolyte remains silent—but his silence only speaks further against him. Accused and condemned of trying to seduce his stepmother, he is banished by his father and dismembered by a monster from the sea. Struck by the force of a discourse of desire in which he himself is implicated, Hippolyte can only look at himself with horror. Hippolyte's desire to remain silent is articulated as a desire to bury the secret of what has been spoken. But like the monster at the center of the labyrinth, this secret cannot be buried, but only immured in detoured walls of discourse.

Hippolyte's desire to silence the horrifying offspring of the mother tongue recalls Oenone's response to Phèdre's allusion to her maternal lineage:

> Oublions-les, madame; et qu'à tout l'avenir
> Un silence éternel cache ce souvenir. (ll. 251–252)
>
> Let us forget such stories, Madame
> And may an eternal silence forever hide this memory.

Oenone's imperative implies that she believes that this legacy can in fact be silenced. But the very urgency with which Oenone pleads for this forgetting reveals that she has heard the terrifying implications in Phèdre's invocation to the mother. As the end of her line, Phèdre is condemned to be the bearer of the mother tongue, the *porte-parole* of this maternal legacy, which cannot be silenced.

The Effacement of the Mother

Oenone's question, "*Quel affreux projet avez-vous enfanté*" might well have served as an epigraph for Mary Shelley's *Frankenstein*. This vertiginous text stages at least two extraordinary scenes of "monstrous" childbirth. As Barbara Johnson demonstrates, "*Frankenstein* . . . can be read as the story of the experience of writing *Frankenstein*."[3] In her preface to *Frankenstein*, Mary Shelley describes the book as her "hideous progeny" and recounts the story of how she, "then a young girl, came to think of and to dilate upon so very hideous an idea."[4] In the novel, Shelley's fictive character, Frankenstein, creates a being that, once given life, horrifies his creator. Like *Phèdre*, this text is obsessed with questions of maternity, the mother tongue, and desire. But it is as if this text responds directly to Oenone's wish that the maternal legacy be effaced and forgotten. *Frankenstein* can be read as the attempt to "forget" the mother's legacy entirely, to circumvent the necessity of passing through the mother in order to give birth and to be born.[5]

The most striking feature of *Frankenstein* is that it attempts to conceive of an entirely immaculate conception, one in which there is no place for the mother or her body.[6] But the figure of the mother, along with the attendant worries of the relationship between maternity, femininity, and desire, are doubly effaced in *Frankenstein*. The text provides us with a series of family units in which every mother figure is absent, either entirely unaccounted for or dead. While *Phèdre*'s maternal legacy is the story of the mother's unspeakability, *Frankenstein* supplies us with a detoured narration of convoluted genealogies in which biologically "natural" mother/daughter ties are virtually nonexistent and in which the daughter has been, albeit indirectly, responsible for the mother's death. Like unhallowed ghosts, these dead mothers return incessantly to haunt the novel and its characters. The importance of these figures, as well as the critical role they play in *Frankenstein*, is obscured by the fact that their stories are embedded in the inner recesses of the novel's many narrations and narrators. Not only are these mothers themselves motherless but they are almost all foreign and therefore irrevocably cut off from their mother tongue.

A simple enumeration of the "family history" of the female characters in *Frankenstein* produces a stunning narrative. Caroline, Victor Frankenstein's mother, is initially described as the doting daughter who nurses her father on his deathbed. There is no mention of her mother. She marries her father's best friend, Alphonse, and produces Victor, who recounts: "My mother had much desired a daughter, but I continued their only offspring." One day, in Italy, Caroline stumbles upon a young orphan, Elizabeth, who lives with a peasant woman: "She was not her child, but the daughter of a Milanese nobleman. Her mother was a German and had died on giving her birth." Caroline adopts Elizabeth, who becomes Victor's "more than sister" and to whom he is later betrothed. Elizabeth contracts scarlet fever and recovers, but the disease spreads to Caroline, who dies from it. Elizabeth has thus indirectly killed both her "real" mother and her surrogate mother. On her deathbed, Caroline instructs Elizabeth to "take her place" as mother of the family. In addition to Elizabeth, the Frankensteins bring another adopted daughter, Justine, into the family. Justine, the only female character in the book who has lived with her "natural" mother, is forced to leave her home because "her mother could not endure her." Justine's mother eventually dies, like all the mothers in this book, but not before she accuses her daughter of having been responsible for the deaths of her brothers and sister. The monster's adopted family, the De Laceys, are also motherless. The family consists of a father and two children: a son, Felix, and a daughter, Agatha. Even Safie, Felix's bride, the daughter of a Turkish father and an Arab mother, bears the legacy of a dead mother.

Although Safie's story occupies the most obscure and parenthetical place in the novel, her relationship to her mother and her mother's legacy is the most enigmatically explicit example of a vital dialogue between mother and daughter. But this dialogue takes place in Arabic, and through the many translations that it endures, the meaning of this maternal legacy is garbled and almost lost in the endless passages of the stories by which it is circumscribed. It is the only example of an instructive and affirmative relationship to the mother, and, perversely, it is the only place in *Frankenstein* where the question of a woman's role in society is addressed directly:

> The young girl spoke in high and enthusiastic terms of her mother, who, born in freedom, spurned the bondage to which she was now reduced. She instructed her daughter in the tenets of her religion and taught her to aspire to higher powers of intellect and an independence of spirit forbidden to the female followers of Muhammad. This lady died, but her lessons were indelibly impressed on the mind of Safie, who sickened at the prospect of again returning to Asia and being immured within the walls of a harem, allowed only to occupy herself with infantile amusements, ill-suited to the temper of her soul, now accustomed to grand ideas and a noble emulation for virtue.[7]

Strangely, it is in the mouth of Safie's Arab mother that we find the clearest traces of Mary Shelley's maternal legacy. Speaking through the translated and accented voice of Safie's mother, all but buried in the cacophony of *Frankenstein*'s many languages and voices, we hear distinct echoes of Mary Wollstonecraft's literary legacy.[8] This legacy, which is relegated to a peripheral figure in the book, emerges as the repressed but "indelible" trace of a possible relationship between mother and daughter. Apart from this brief reference to the history of a minor character, mothers and daughters appear to be mutually exclusive, even mutually destructive. It would seem that the figure of the mother is so inherently horrifying that no mother can take an active, living role in the story. Mothers appear as benevolent only when dead and daughters are guilty of being born.

Although Caroline, Victor's mother and Elizabeth's surrogate mother, plays only a minor role in the text when living, she is nonetheless a central figure, and an active one after her death. Her portrait is the ostensible pretext for the monster's first crime, William's murder. Elizabeth blames herself for the crime because she allowed the boy to wear their mother's portrait. The following description of Elizabeth's reaction to

William's death is recounted by Alphonse Frankenstein in a letter to Victor:

> She was very earnest to see the corpse. At first I attempted to prevent her, but she persisted, and entering the room where it lay, hastily examined the neck of the victim, and clasping her hands, exclaimed, "Oh, God! I have murdered my darling child!" She fainted, and was restored with extreme difficulty. When she again lived, it was only to weep and sigh. She told me that that same evening William had teased her to let him wear a very valuable miniature that she possessed of your mother. This picture is gone and was doubtless the temptation which urged the murderer to the deed.[9]

The force and extent of Elizabeth's self-accusation is staggering. Not only does she blame herself for William's death, but she also asserts that she herself has murdered him. Like all of the monster's victims, William has been strangled. When Elizabeth examines the corpse, however, she is apparently more horrified by the absence of the portrait of the mother than by the "print of the murderer's finger . . . on his neck." In a curious substitution, the murderer's mark takes the place of the mother's portrait. Through this substitution, William is metaphorically strangled by his mother's portrait. It is almost as though Elizabeth is horrified (and rendered temporarily lifeless) by the fact that she has placed the burden of the mother's legacy around William's neck. This hallucinatory and imagined infanticide is double. Caroline accidentally causes her son's death from beyond the grave by the very presence of her image; Elizabeth, William's surrogate mother, assumes the blame for having provided "her" child with the image of his natural mother. Like Elizabeth, Justine accuses herself of the crime. But unlike Elizabeth, Justine, who is found in possession of the portrait of the mother, is condemned and executed for William's murder. Mere possession of the portrait of the mother is, in the eyes of the accusers, tantamount to guilt; but Justine incriminates herself beyond redemption by confessing, in her confusion, to this crime that she did not commit. She explains the circumstances of this false confession as follows: "Ever since I was condemned, my confessor has besieged me; he threatened and menaced, until I almost began to think that I was the monster that he said I was." In some sense, Justine condemns herself because she is called a "monster." The mention of this particular word, which "names" the real murderer, seemingly corresponds to Justine's self-image, and propels her to confess that she did in fact murder William. The name "monster" is invoked to describe that moment where the image of the mother is linked to that of a surrogate daughter by the murder of a child. We shall see how the relationship between Justine's indictment and the portrait of the mother is curiously explained and validated by the monster himself.

Speaking in Foreign Tongues

If the figure of the mother is thematically repressed in *Frankenstein*, the confusions and contradictions evoked by this figure operate on the most primal level of the novel, in the novel's discussion of its own literary origins as well as in the language of the text. Although, in the preface, Mary Shelley alludes to her literal precursors, her parents, the literary inspiration for *Frankenstein* apparently derives from a translated text that is twice removed from her mother tongue: "Some volumes of ghost stories translated from the German into French fell into our hands."[10] *Frankenstein* itself is, strangely, written in translation. While the outermost "frame" of the novel is Walton's letter to his sister, which is composed in English, the bulk of the narrative is recounted by Frankenstein to Walton in English tinged with a "foreign accent." English is not spoken by any of the book's central characters; the fact that their stories have been transparently "translated" goes largely unnoticed because of the novel's imbricated structure.

The insistence upon translations between German, French, and English returns at a crucial moment in *Frankenstein*: when the monster learns to read and speak. The acquisition of language by that motherless creature takes place in the interstices of many languages. The monster learns about translation—about the foreignness of language—before he acquires a "mother tongue." He initially learns to speak by observing the De Laceys, a French family exiled in Germany. Following along with the French lessons that Felix gives Safie, the Arabian girl, the monster gradually masters the language. But before he even understands the language that they are both being taught by the De Laceys, the monster understands the concept of translation—he understands that Safie speaks a foreign mother tongue that the others do not understand:

> I soon perceived that although the stranger uttered articulate sounds and appeared to have a language of her own, she was neither understood by nor herself understood the cottagers.[11]

For the monster, language is, originally, foreign language. Bereft of a mother as well as a mother tongue, the monster learns first that language is foreign, that it expresses primally that which cannot be said.[12] Although Safie cannot communicate in words to the cottagers, she speaks to them in music. The monster is deeply moved by this foreign music which seems to him like a sublime expression of nature: "She sang, and her voice flowed in a rich cadence, swelling or dying away like the nightingale of the woods."[13] Because the monster learns language simultaneously with Safie, who yearns to express her love for Felix, he learns that language can be used in order to express desire.

Just as the monster learns that speech is originally translation, he learns to read in translation. He finds and studies three books in French, each originally written in another language: "Fortunately the books were written in the language, the elements of which I had acquired at the cottage; they consisted of *Paradise Lost*, a volume of Plutarch's *Lives*, and the *Sorrows of Werther*. The possession of these treasures gave me extreme delight."[14] These literary primers are literally translations; the monster learns about literature and history as translation. He is unable to distinguish between fact and fiction and finds his origins in *Paradise Lost*, which he reads as a true story, the translation of his life story. Reminiscent of Mary Shelley, who, in the preface, "gives birth" to the book *Frankenstein*, the monster finds his roots in literary history.[15]

If the monster identifies his creation so thoroughly with a literary work, it is in part because the word "mother," along with the concept of maternity, is initially omitted from his education. Before Safie arrives in the De Lacey family, the monster teaches himself a handful of basic words. The first words learned by this creature who has no name are the names given to family members as well as their "given" names:

> I discovered the names that were given to some of the most familiar objects of discourse; . . . I learned also the names of the cottagers themselves. The youth and his companion had each of them several names, but the old man had only one, which was "father." The girl was called "sister" or "Agatha," and the youth "Felix," "brother," or "son."[16]

Having neither father nor mother but only a creator, the monster in his first words describes those very experiences and relationships from which he is irrevocably exiled. He is unable to distinguish between proper names and the names of relationships. In the enumeration of names for family relationships that the monster learns, there are two obvious omissions: that of "mother" and "daughter." Where "Felix" is referred to as "brother" or "son," Agatha is referred to simply as "sister." The omission of the term "daughter" is the mark that the relationship that is most systematically effaced in *Frankenstein* is that which occurs between daughter and mother. Just as there is no name to describe the monster's place in this family unit, there is no name to describe the place of the mother, who in the De Lacey family not only is absent, but also seemingly was never present at all. On the level of the plot, the fact that the monster does not learn the name for "mother" is accounted for by the fact that there is no mother in the De Lacey family. But this does not explain why, on the textual level of *Frankenstein*, there is no mention of the mother at the moment when family relationships are invoked as the first linguistic referents in the acquisition of language. Given the central contradictions and confusions that surround the figure of the mother in the text as a whole, we might say that if there is no "mother" in the De Lacey family, it is perversely because there is no word for "mother"; no word can name what she is, or delineate her place within the family.

The confusion that surrounds the mother's name, image, and function in *Frankenstein* spreads to all of the definitions of family relationships in the book. Although Victor, unlike the monster, is blessed with both a mother and a loving family, he has more difficulty than the monster in learning the names of the relationships between family members. In his attempt to define and describe his relationship to Elizabeth, Victor uses a provocative figure of speech, one in which the absence of a word is associated with procreation:

> We called each other familiarly by the name of cousin. No word, no expression could *body forth* the kind of relation in which she stood to me—more than sister, since till death she was to be mine only.[17]

Victor and his betrothed call each other "familiarly" by family names. It would seem that the name of "lover" or "beloved" does not exist in the Frankenstein family lexicon. The strange and almost unreadable phrase "body forth" seems to denote the missing relationship that would be neither familiar nor familial. The phrase "body forth" evokes the image of giving birth physically to a word or expression of desire. In the resonances of this obscure figure of speech, the function of maternity is obliquely associated with the absent discourse of desire. In *Frankenstein*, the effacement of the figure of the mother is accompanied by the omission of a discourse of desire.

Although the mother is systematically "effaced" in *Frankenstein*, we discover that the mother's "face" is endowed with the threatening capacity to engender a discourse of desire in the character that beholds her image. As he strangles her child, the monster is aroused by the portrait of Caroline that he finds around William's neck:

> As I fixed my eyes on the child, I saw something glittering on his breast. I took it; it was a portrait of a most lovely woman. In spite of my malignity, it softened and attracted me. For a few moments I gazed with delight on her dark eyes, fringed by deep lashes, and her lovely lips: but presently my rage returned; I remembered that I was forever deprived of the delights that such beautiful creatures could bestow and that she whose resemblance I contemplated would, in regarding me, have changed that air of divine benignity to one expressive of disgust and affright.[18]

It is only through the eyes of the monster that the reader is finally provided with a vivid and sensual description of the infamous portrait of the mother. In the language of the monster's description of this image, we finally hear the unmistakable, albeit unfamiliar strains of a discourse of desire. Looking at the portrait of the mother makes the monster think of sex. He laments that he is "forever deprived of the delights that these beautiful creatures could bestow." As he beholds the lifeless picture of Caroline, the monster fantasizes her back to life, but his sexual fantasy turns into a nightmare when he discovers that his amorous gaze is met by a look of horror, not desire. Given, however, that the effacement of the mother coincides with the repression of a language of desire in *Frankenstein*, the horrifying encounter between the desirous monster and the benignly dead mother seems to mask an even more horrifying scenario: that the mother who is associated with a language of desire might, once animated, respond to a look of desire with desire, and not horror.

The text hints at this possibility when, after the monster is aroused and spurned by the image of the dead Caroline, he turns his amorous gaze to her surrogate daughter, Justine. After the monster has beheld the portrait of the mother, he suddenly finds words (the very ones that Victor does not know) to express his sexual feelings for these two women:

> A woman was sleeping on some straw; she was young, not indeed so beautiful as her whose portrait I held, but of an agreeable aspect and blooming in the loveliness of youth and health. Here, I thought, is one of those whose joy-imparting smiles are bestowed on all but me. And then I bent over her and whispered, "Awake, fairest, thy lover is near-he who would give his life but to obtain one look of affection from thine eyes; my beloved, awake!" The sleeper stirred.[19]

The monster addresses Justine as "beloved" and calls himself her "lover." Inspired by the portrait of Caroline that he holds in his hands, he transfers his desire for the mother onto her surrogate daughter, who is not dead, but merely sleeping. This time the monster fantasizes that Justine is capable of a "look of affection," but he is enraged by the fact that this imagined look is not directed at him. But the line "the sleeper stirred" indicates that Justine may be at least partly aroused by the monster's speech. This would help to account for Justine's extreme confusion concerning her role in the crime as well as her surprising confession. In any case, the monster perceives that Justine, as a potentially desiring creature, is the "source" of his crime and he judges that she should justly pay for it:

> —Not I, but she, shall suffer; the murder I have committed because I am forever robbed of all that she could give me, she shall atone. The crime had its source in her; be hers the punishment![20]

The monster transfers not only his desire for the mother onto Justine, but also his guilt in the murder of the mother's child. Justine becomes a substitute for both mother and monster; she becomes the recipient of the monster's desire for the mother and pays for the infanticide that accompanies this desire.

The portrait of the dead mother is benignly oblivious to the desire that it arouses but once animated by the monster's fantasy, the mother is horrified by his amorous gaze. This moment of the text is haunted, however, by the missing corollary: the specter of a potentially desiring mother. The suppressed image of a desiring mother reappears in the terrifying figure of the female monster that Frankenstein begins to "body forth" and then destroys.

Throughout *Frankenstein*, the monster's narrative has been subsumed and translated. Victor tells the monster's story to Walton in English. But in the final pages of the novel, after Frankenstein dies, the monster encounters Walton and finally speaks for himself. Paradoxically, at the moment when the monster tells his own tale, he speaks in a language that is utterly foreign to him. There have been repeated references to the fact that the monster speaks only French and Walton understands only English. With his final words, spoken in a foreign tongue, the monster calls himself an "abortion." Deprived of the prospect of a mate, and bearer of a discourse of desire, the monster has been aborted. But the book *Frankenstein* is brought to term. The time that elapses between Walton's first letter to his sister and his last is exactly nine months.

ELEVEN

Birthmarks (Given Names)

> Songez que je vous parle une langue étrangère.
>
> — RACINE

Birthmarks: Primal Passion

Hélène Cixous's writings are, to some degree, radically untranslatable. Not so much because they are written in French, but because they are not. If Hélène Cixous's texts resist translation it is because, as we shall see, they are originally written in a foreign tongue and hence are always already marked by something like a prior, primordial "translation." One might even say that this "original translation" is not a translation from French, but within and into French. Born from the French language, this foreign tongue inhabits it the way, say, a tapeworm inhabits its host. From French it borrows many (but not all) of its constituent parts—its seminal sounds, letters, grammar, syntax, and even to some degree its lexicon, but this inner tongue remains estranged from French. In its intimate proximity to French, it is infinitely removed from French. Cixous's texts invent, discover, and uncover a forgotten language that lies embedded within French's inner reaches and untold depths—in the secret passages that it never knew it had and therefore never knew it lost. She mines the French language for its hidden treasures, extracting "gold" (*or*) from its seminal sounds. All of Hélène Cixous's writings (albeit each uniquely and in its own singular idiom) bear the mark of this "original translation" and are born from it. All of Hélène Cixous's texts are signed with this primal "Birthmark."

"*Il faut que sonne une étrangère langue dès les premiers mots.*"[1] Eric Prenowitz (whom I thank here for the courage, sensitivity, and precision of his translations) translates this sentence thus: "A foreign tongue must ring from the first words." The translation is accurate, and I can suggest no better alternative. But if I here insist upon the miniscule breach that separates the Cixous sentence from its translation, it is certainly not to find fault in the translator, but rather to invite us to hear the strange resonances in the original phrase. This sentence is an invocation, an incantation, and an invitation. We should receive its first three words, "*il faut que*," as a kind of primordial commandment. The commandment entreats us to open our ears to the strange relations that inhabit language before it is claimed by the familiar laws of culture.[2] By placing the word "*étrangère*" (foreign) before the word "*langue*" (tongue), Hélène Cixous entreats us to hear the savage sounds, pulsions, and passions that pulsate in the tongue before it is domesticated and regulated by the law of the language. Inside both the word "*étrangère*" (foreign) and the word "*langue*" (tongue), we can find the scattered letters of the word "*ange*" (angel). As she affirms throughout her texts, this angel lies within—the "*ange*" is "en je." The "*étrangère langue*" is doubly inhabited by angels or perhaps inhabited by two angels as the angel within me is not the same me but another me. By opening our ears to the secret angel dispersed within the tongue, we open ourselves to it. We become porous. By lending and bending our inner ear to the secret angel tongue within, we uncover new and ancient foreign relations. These relations are familiarly unfamiliar. They are given to us and call to us through our first names. The names given to us though our first names recall the manifold and multiplying potential beings that inhabit us before we are subjected to the laws of the proper name. She writes:

> Je note, je veux écrire, avant, au temps encore en fusion d'avant le temps refroidi du récit. Quand nous sentons et ça ne s'appelle pas encore. La scène est dans les entrailles avec tumulte, élans. Les genoux s'entrechoquent, le coeur prend feu, une grande répulsion, une grande attraction, plus tard ça s'apaisera

> en nom. Mais d'abord c'est la passion. . . . Je veux peindre notre âme souterraine. Il y déjà des mots. Mais pas encore des noms propres. D'ailleurs, ici, rien n'est propre. Voilà pourquoi mes livres sont sans titre. Donner un titre est un acte d'appropriation.
>
> I note, I want to write before, at the time still in fusion before the cooled off time of the narrative. When we feel and there is not yet a name for it. The scene is in the entrails with turmoil, élans. Knees knock, the heart catches fire, a great repulsion, a great attraction, later it will be pacified into a name. But first it is passion. . . . I want to paint our subterranean soul. There are already words. But not yet proper names. Here, by the way, before, nothing is proper, nothing is of its own. This is why my books have no titles. Giving a title is an act of appropriation.[3]

The scene described herein is a scene of primal passion. The bowels of the subterranean soul teem with words engaged in unspeakable acts of love. In the darkest obscurity of the subterranean soul, in the time "before" the name, Cixous describes how nameless words couple and copulate and spawn:

> Et ce que font les mots entre eux, ces accouplements, ces hybridations, c'est du génie. Un génie érotique et fertile. Une loi de vie préside à leurs croisements. Seuls les mots qui s'aiment sèment. Sémantique clandestine. . . . Un mot nouveau-né nous émeut. Un mot né de l'amour de deux mots n'est pas un concept. Pfeilige. Internité. C'est seulement un individu poétique.
>
> And what words do between themselves—couplings, matings, hybridizations—is genius. An erotic and fertile genius. A law of life presides over their crossbreedings. Only words in love sow. Clandestine semantics. . . . A newborn word moves us. A word born out of the love of two words is not a concept. Pfeilige. Internity. It is only a poetic individual.[4]

This "primal scene" is a scene of creation and conception. New words are newly born in this fecund and fertile magma. But these newly conceived words are not concepts. Not concepts because they are "before" the law and hence not yet subject to it. Still attached to the primal "law of life," they are not yet bound to the restrictions and regulations of the law of the proper name. Furthermore, because these newborn words answer only to the call of life (*il faut que*), they do not recognize the language of the law and they do not respond to it. They do not respect the incest taboo (they couple with their own word siblings and offspring), nor are they bound by the laws of reason (they are overdetermined and signify promiscuously and indiscriminately). These newborn words are proliferating monstrosities spun together into multiplying metonymic chains that weave magnificent webs of sexed text. They are homophonetic hybrids that rhyme in homosexual sounds and demonic anagrams that expose contradictions and cross meanings through irreverent inversions of letters. Each one of these newly born words is, as Cixous says, a "poetic individual." Each one is unique, unrepeatable, untranslatable.

But if, for Hélène Cixous, words come "before" the beginning, writing itself begins in the name. Like the wellspring of words from which writing draws its source, the name is never "proper." And always resolutely not proper. "Not proper" even in its relation to itself. For the name inscribes its singular and site-specific nonproperties in unique and varied ways in each text. Not proper also because each name that gives birth to writing calls the other into being in the act of naming. Moving very quickly, we might say that a name that doesn't call doesn't name; it kills. In *Or*, for example, she writes: "*Mais tout commence par le nom propre. Je te désire et je te garde et je te tiens solidement au-dessus du néant par ton nom, je te tire de la fosse par la tresse de nom*" (But everything begins with the proper name. I desire you and I keep you and I hold you solidly above the void by your name; I pull you from the grave by holding on to you by the braid of your name).[5] Naming is thus an act of incalculable intimacy as well as one of potential violence. It is a pact and bond between beings. (In the novel *Or*, for example, the narrator recounts a very sad story about a cat with no name. One day the cat wanders off. Having no name, she cannot be called back and so she vanishes, without a trace, never to return. This loss is irrecuperable.) For Cixous, names that call from the other in me to the other who is not me are the infinite source from which writing springs. And, as her readers know well, the name almost always calls from and to the name of an irrevocably lost, but intimately familiar, place or person.[6] Thus "Oran," the name of her native city, her birthplace, is one of the first names that Hélène Cixous gives to the birth of her writing:

> Le premier de mes trésors fut le nom de ma ville natale qui était Oran. C'était ma première leçon. J'ai entendu le nom d'Oran, et par Oran je suis entrée dans le secret de la langue. J'en suis sortie entrée. J'ai découvert que ma ville faisait fruit par la simple addition de moi. Oran-je—Orange. J'ai découvert donc que le mot avait le mystère du fruit. Elle est devenue une porte magique ouvrant sur l'autre monde.

> The first of my treasures was the name of my native city, which was Oran. It was my first lesson. I heard the name of Oran and though Oran I entered into the secret of the tongue. I came out of it into it. I discovered that my city made fruit by the simple addition of me. Oran-je, Oran-I—Orange. I discovered thus that the word had the mystery of fruit. It became a magic door opening onto the other world.[7]

Cixous here recounts how, in the encounter between "Oran" and "je," the name bears fruit and becomes fertile. This "fruit" (which is, of course the source of *Vivre l'orange* as well as numerous other texts) feeds the body of writing. By eating the secret and forbidden fruit in the name, writing leaves one world and opens a door onto another. Writing the name is the way she discovers a secret door—a hidden passage and passageway—that leads to other worlds, and other lives. These other worlds and other lives do not belong to us, but they are "ours" in the deepest sense. They are all of the lives—the infinite potential lives—that we live unbeknownst to ourselves. In them, love and hate relations are revealed that might bind us to each other differently. Through them, we might invent other ways of living together and could imagine communities not restricted by the laws of nationality, identity, citizenship, gender, or proper names.

Given Names: Familial Epics and Primal Scenes

> Our life, it can be said, is a muscle strong enough to contract the whole of historical time.
>
> Walter Benjamin

During the decade following 1991, Hélène Cixous embarks on a series of epic journeys that recount a series of reencounters with her most intimate familial names. 1991 is the year during which *L'ange au secret* was published.[8] It is also, perhaps not accidentally, the year during which Hélène Cixous promises publicly never to write about her mother during her lifetime.[9] Later, she does. But that is a slightly different story. If I now want to insist upon this ten-year period, it is because it strikes me that during these years, Cixous's writing takes a marked and distinctive turn, a different turn inward and outward from what comes before. The texts that she writes during these years take the form of an auto-analysis or even as an auto-odyssey. (It goes without saying, of course, that were we to look backward from the vantage of this turning point, we could not fail to see, in retrospect, that virtually everything—perhaps even down to every last event and detail—that "happens" in the texts dating from this specific period was always already present in the texts that came before it. Thus one could argue that *Or* was already present in *Dedans* and that *Osnabrück* was inscribed in *Les commencements* and so on. That this is so changes nothing and should not surprise us. This is especially so because the texts around which I am turning are themselves all explicitly described as "primal scenes," and hence they demand to be read retroactively. As such, the "events" in them are all real fictions and fictional realities.)

At the heart of this auto-odyssey we encounter the three books that constitute its primordial, triangulated triliad: *Or: Les lettres de mon père* (*OR: My Father's Letters*), *Osnabrück*, and *Rêveries de la femme sauvage (scènes primitives)* (*Reveries of the Wild Woman: Primal Scenes*).[10] At its most basic level, these three books make up a primal family drama in which *Or* is the book of the father (George), *Osnabrück* is the book of the mother (Eve), and *Rêveries* is the book of the children (Pierre and the narrator, "Hélène"). But Cixous transposes this familiar story of familial characters into a primal drama in which the ostensibly "real" lives of these biographical and/or autobiographical characters are, paradoxically, brought to life, another life, through writing. More specifically, each book derives its own language from the characters—the letters of the given name—of each of its four, fundamental figures. Thus although the "story" may appear familiar, the books themselves transform the known story into something infinitely and wonderfully strange. Each one invents its own new language for life and each one gives birth to its own, unique, inimitable foreign tongue. Therefore, although they can be read together, indeed, they must be read together, there is a specific pleasure and gift to found in attempting to respect the idiomatic specificity of each individual book as it separates itself from the others. Paradoxically, each book differentiates itself from its kin through their common family resemblances. Each book is written in its own dialect of "Cixousian." Although they all find their source in the same set of primal signifiers derived from the sounds and letters of the family's "given names," this finite set of signifiers engenders an infinite permutation of nuanced inflections and accents. They demand translation precisely because they defy translation. In order to move across the borders that separate them, one must unearth the secret passages through which these intimate languages communicate with one another. Such a translation, however, cannot take place at the level of signification but rather through the corporeal power of the primal signifiers. Neither purely motivated nor entirely unmotivated, the primal signifiers of the given name become "placeholders" for the text. They are its "*oikos*" and "*khora*."

In what follows, I will highlight some of the differences between these texts by isolating some of the secret passages through which they communicate with one another. I will begin, therefore, with a brief discussion of the relation between *OR: Les lettres de mon père* and *Osnabrück*. In *L'amour du loup*, Hélène Cixous tenderly recounts how both books were particularly unwanted. She describes *OR* as the book she didn't want to write and *Osnabrück* as the book she emphatically really didn't want to write. In the first instance, she didn't want to write another book to her dead father because, as she explains, she had already written a book to him and about his haunting presence in her life.[11] She also didn't want to write another book to her father because she had never written a book to her mother and, indeed, had sworn never to do so during the mother's lifetime. But, as Cixous tells it, these two books adamantly refused not to be written. They triumphed over her explicit objections and interdictions, denied her authority, and wrote themselves anyway. Furthermore, not only are both books written in spite of their author, they are also both specifically addressed to the very people who are unable to read them: The father cannot read his own letters as they are returned to him through his daughter because he is dead, and the mother cannot read the book written to her because she does not read. Not because she can't read, but because she is the incarnation of reading's absolute antithesis. As we shall see, she is life itself, and as life itself she has no interest in reading, no time for it, doesn't need it, doesn't understand it, doesn't want it. But in both cases, what matters is that the book belongs neither to the author nor to the intended addressee. The book is a gift given to the author that belongs to no one. And thus to everyone. Because of this basic fact, these hyper "autobiographical" books are not autobiographies in the usual sense. Nor are they fictions, exactly. They are instances of a new kind of "life writing." A form of life that is only possible in writing and that only writing makes possible.

OR: Les lettres de mon père is a book about letters and rereading. It tells the incredible, suspenseful story of how, one fine day, out of the blue, the narrator's brother appears on her doorstep holding a Bébéconfort box filled with six hundred lost but preserved letters written by the children's father to their mother during their engagement. That is to say, the letters bear witness to the world as it was before the children are born. But, of course, the world before the children are born is also the world into which they are potentially never born or even, more radically, in which they might become unborn. This return to a time we never could have known but which is intimately ours nonetheless goes to the heart of the desperately complicated temporality of the "primal scene." *Or* is a book about the ways time, like letters, can be inverted and read backward. Although the father is dead, the letters from the man who was not yet the father are immortal and return to be read by the daughter who was not yet conceived at the time they were written. The book also tells the story of the father's death by tuberculosis and the series of fateful accidents and misreadings without which the children indeed would not have been born. Had he known that he was ill, he wouldn't have married and hence would not have had the children who must now receive and read (belatedly) the latent and repressed legacy of his death, his life and his afterlife as it returns to haunt them through the letters that survive him.

But *Or* is also a book about reading and letters in a different sense. It is a book that is a veritable gold mine of anagrams that are strewn throughout its inner recesses and buried in its archaeological depths. The primal enigmatic signifier that motivates the book is the name of the father. Is his name Georges? Or Georg? In what language is the father's given name written? What is the language written with the letters of the father's name? But because the narrator has never swallowed the death of the father, she swallows the letters of his name instead. Thus the letters of his name become lodged in her throat. Georges becomes gorge. She has a throat full of George: "*Parfois j'ai le rire de mon père dans la gorge, il se moque de moi dans ma propre gorge*" (Sometimes I have my father's laugh in my throat; he makes fun of me in my own throat). Her father's laugh mocks at her through her own, or rather disowned, throat. For, indeed, throughout this book, letters can only betray. They cross and double-cross. They can be reversed, substituted, lost, and through their endless substitutions, they decimate known certainties by secreting secret meanings through which time is sent spinning and identity unwoven. Toward the end of the book, the children part ways because they discover that they do not read the legacy of the father's letters in the same way. The first person present tense of the verb *être* (*je suis*) becomes impossibly tangled up with the verb *suivre* (*je suis*) and the present tense of the verb *perdre* (to lose). The verb *on perd* (one loses) becomes a homophone of the noun for father (*père*). Despite their common wish to respect the father's wishes, the two aging children who follow him are divided by his letters:

> Notre désir est le même: ne pas désobéir à celui des deux qui est le bon. Nous nous suivons. On se suit. Et SI C'ÉTAIT LE TIEN? JE SUIS LE MIEN. JE NE SUIS PAS MON FRÈRE. ET SI C'ÉTAIT LE SIEN? On se perd. Je suis mon père, j'en suis sûre, je ne le vois pas, je le suis, ou peut-être je suis dans sa poche dorsale, ou peut-être je suis une lettre. Je ne veux pas trahir l'inconnu, j'ai l'amour ouvert à qui que tu sois, je sonne à ta porte, je ne sais qui ouvrira.
>
> Our desire is the same: not to disobey the right one of the two. We follow each other. One is oneself following. AND IF IT WAS YOURS? I FOLLOW (AM) MINE. I DON'T FOLLOW (I AM NOT) MY BROTHER. AND IF IT WAS HIS? One loses oneself. I follow (am) my father, I'm sure of it, I do not see him, I am (follow) him, or perhaps I am in his back pocket, or perhaps I am (following) a letter. I do not want to betray the unknown one, my love is open to whoever you are, and I ring at your door. I do not know who will open.[12]

Perhaps I am a letter, the narrator wonders. Or perhaps I follow a letter. But if a child is a letter, or can be read as a letter, one of the most telling passages of this book concerns the belated reading of a letter from a bastardized, mute, animal substitute for an unborn child.

At the end of the book's convoluted narrative—a narrative that might be said to resemble a shaggy dog story—the narrator suddenly realizes that she had failed to read a letter that was there along—and here the narrator pauses to recall the story of Fipps, the dog. Fipps's name, it turns out, is the bearer of one of the most deeply buried secrets in the book. The mother's secret prior knowledge of the father's impending death and her repressed rage at him for dying is inscribed, we discover, in the strange, foreign, name that she imposes on the dog:

> Fipps aussi, ce nom, cet étranger, cette créature coupée et collée, cette histoire accrochée dans le musée fermé, un fossile vieux de cent quinze millions d'années qui vient d'être découvert hier, sur le site des lettres de mon père. Il est la preuve ce nom, ce fragment de calcaire que je ne soulevai jamais jusqu'à hier. Au bout de cinquante ans soudain hier je trouve une plume. Je me lève. Je la montre à ma mère et je dis: "Fipps. Pourquoi Fipps?" Il était huit heures, les choéphores versent du café sur la tombe sans pleurer, le malheur qui torture

le coeur est dissipé, j'aimerais savoir la vérité. "*Fipps der Affe*" dit ma mère elle sourit il n'y a ni ombre ni alarme et pourquoi y en aurait-il. L'âme de ma mère a gardé sa virginité. —Fipps le singe, comme enfant d'Allemagne, on lisait ses aventures.

—Tu as donné à ce chien un nom de singe?—C'est tout ce qui me venait à l'idée, dit ma vièrge. Posée. Ma mère unie, perpétuelle, une personnalité intérieure en cristal.

Fipps too, this name, this foreigner, this cut and pasted creature, this history hung in the closed museum, a one hundred and fifteen million year old fossil which has just been discovered yesterday, on the site of my father's letters. This name is the proof, this limestone fragment I couldn't lift until yesterday. After fifty years suddenly yesterday I find it's become a feather. I get up. I show it to my mother and I say: "Fipps. Why Fipps?" It was eight o'clock, the libation bearers pour coffee on the grave without weeping, the unhappiness that tortures the heart is dissipated, I would like to know the truth. "*Fipps der Affe*" says my mother she smiles there's no shadow no alarm and why would there be. My mother's soul has kept its virginity.—Fipps the monkey, as a child in Germany we used to read his adventures.—You gave this dog a monkey's name?—That's all I could think of, says my virgin. Composed. My smooth mother, perpetual, an inner crystal personality.[13]

In an instant, the knowledge that passes through the dog's name becomes an event. In a lightning flash, the entire family history is suddenly rewritten as it becomes retroactively reread through the meaning of Fipps's name. Although, at the level of the narrative, the event that takes place at this moment is presented as an event in the book, we might also say that this event is produced by the book itself. As she writes the book that we are reading, the narrator is being read by the very book that she is writing. As she writes, the book reads back to her and forces her to read the family history backwards. In this instant, the narrator discovers that the name "Fipps"—which she had always blindly accepted as the "given" name of her Algerian surrogate brother dog—was not, in fact, a name at all, but an anti-name or a "denunciation" —because behind the name "Fipps," lurked the uneasy and shady history of a strange ape, an exiled and orphaned child of Germany. He never had a chance to be an Algerian dog, that Fipps, as he was condemned to carry out the repressed legacy of the German name he never knew he had but that spoke through him nonetheless. Moreover, the "*signe*" of the name "Fipps" is not a sign at all, but a "*singe*." The letters in the word "*signe*" can always be reversed, read backward, and turned around. The sign for a name can always be turned into an "ape," an imposter, a denunciation, and a betrayal.

Although we could go on to say much more about this moment, I cite it here for another reason. In the passage about Fipps's name, something else is also at stake: it is our first substantial encounter with Eve, the mother virgin. This encounter (which takes the form of a dialogue—or interrogation—of the mother by the daughter) can be read like a hidden door, a trap door, or an underground secret passageway that serves as a border or frontier between this book and the two books that follow it. But the mother virgin who bears the "given" name "Eve" in *Osnabrück* does not speak the same language as the unnamed mother-virgin-widow-midwife who appears in *Rêveries de la femme sauvage*. Although both of these incarnations of the mother are, in some sense, announced in the preceding exchange between mother and daughter, these two characters are radically distinct from one another. And although they will display certain common traits, the mark of their irreducible difference from one another can be read through their distinctly different relations to the inscription or erasure of the "given name."

In *Osnabrück*, the name "Eve" is defined as distinctly other than a *nom* (noun): It is a divine verb, which, like the word of God, is a self-referential imperative "'*Je suis moi' dit Eve*" ("I am myself," says Eve) that creates and acts upon the world:

> Elle ne pense pas, ne calcule pas. Donne la vie sans intention de la donner. Une bonté flottante, sans charité, sans compassion, sans pitié, elle ne s'identifie à personne. Cela est sans nom. Eve n'est pas un nom. C'est son impératif. Elle s'obéit.

> She doesn't think, she doesn't calculate. Gives life without intending to. A floating benevolence, without charity, without compassion, without pity, she identifies with no one. It is without name. Eve is not a name or noun. She is her own imperative—which she obeys.[14]

But whereas the incalculable mother-virgin "Eve" of *Osnabrück* is a radiant and divine manifestation who appears under the sign of her name, the miscalculating "sage-femme" of *Rêveries* instantiates all of the aberrant miscarriages of acts of naming that are subsumed under the monstrous misnomer of the violating negating ape-sign "Algériefrançaise."

In *Rêveries*, there are no given names. The book is written under the sign of two letters "r" and "v" that have been amputated and severed from the absent parental sources "Georges" and "Eve." These consonants excised from the parents' names reassemble themselves in this book of exile to form the seminal roots of the words from which the book is generated.[15] But they also spell the letters of *envers* (the other side). Indeed, the world of everything is inside out and upside down in *Les rêveries de la femme sauvage*. The violence of the language of the social world constructed by "Algériefrançaise" manifests itself as name-sickness beginning with the tainting of the name "*Algérie*," which becomes afflicted with a "maladie algérie" ("Algerian disorder") that in turn becomes truncated into the expression "*malgérie*." Language is sick in this disordered world and language is sickened by it. All names are transformed into pseudo-names that violate and soil those whom they touch. These false names appropriate and objectify the beings they hold in their thrall. The unique and beloved "Aicha" is not called "Aicha." Fatma's name is not Fatma, but Barta and so on. The mother's voice becomes muted, and the name "Eve" is never openly pronounced in the text. But it is muffled within it as the sound of the name "Eve" is veiled by the word for the veiled widow (*veuve*) that she becomes. Furthermore, as readers of *Les rêveries de la femme sauvage* know well, the misnamed dog Fipps returns in the figure of *Le Chien*, Fips. He returns amputated, having lost a letter of his name. Both the name "Fipps" and the name "Fips" are slight alterations on the words for son: *fils*. As such, the dog named Fipps or Fips is both a substitute child and a false or monstrous child. And when the child-substitute Fipps returns as the failed child-dog Fips, he does so with a vengeance. Fips bites back against his host children by demanding recognition for the Algerian-Jewish dog that he might have been by biting his name into the flesh of the one who has failed to name or to love him. One might also say that through this bite, Fips becomes one of the secret signatories of *Les rêveries*.[16] Fips, the unloved dog-child who haunts *Rêveries*, returns to reclaim his right to a name; in fact, in the course of the text, he will be belatedly renamed Job.

In both *Osnabrück* and *Les rêveries de la femme sauvage*, the character of the mother-virgin incarnates the extreme limits of language itself because the world in which she lives—the world of life itself—is a world without beginning or end and hence without death and hence without division and hence without letters and hence without words. Or doors. A world without words is also a world in which doors have no meaning. Eve the mother-virgin of *Osnabrück* never rings the doorbell, while her counterpart the midwife of *Rêveries* is herself a false door who unknowingly repels the advances of the other. In *Osnabrück*, she charges across the threshold without pausing, in *Rêveries* she does not even acknowledge the existence of a threshold. Both versions of the mother-virgin are impermeable, impenetrable, inscrutable, and unstoppable. Like life itself, she arrives unannounced, departs without warning and her abrupt arrivals and departures provoke meaningful events about which she herself remains unaware.

In both books, mother and daughter collide at the threshold. The threshold becomes the privileged site of the on-going primordial drama of their intimacy. There, mother and daughter become entangled in a love-hate, life-death, mute struggle that takes place at the primal frontier that simultaneously binds them together and divides them. Whenever mother and daughter meet at the threshold, they make a scene. Like this epic one:

> C'EST PARCE QU'ELLE NE SONNE PAS. Elle n'arrive pas. Il n'y a pas de porte. Pas de seuil. Pas de pas. . . . Tu viens? Dis-je. Je suis là, dit-elle, je tourne la tête elle est déjà dans la cuisine, déjà dans le frigidaire, dans le tiroir, dans le couloir déjà. . . . Je recommence.—Sonne maman, sonne, supplié-je. Je veux dire je voudrais tant que tu sonnes. . . . Sonne maman je t'en prie, murmuré-je, accorde-nous les dix secondes qui déplient la scène du recevoir. . . . Alors le jour suivant. La clé tourne dans la serrure. Crac. Elle ouvre, entre, avance, fend, passe, pivote, recule, et une main sur la porte crevée, de l'intérieur, sonne.—Sonne AVANT, dis-je. En vain.

> IT'S BECAUSE SHE DOESN'T RING THE DOORBELL. She does not arrive. There is no door. No threshold. No doorstep. . . Are you coming? I say. I'm here, she says, I look round she is already in the kitchen, already in the fridge, in the drawer, in the corridor already. . . . I try again.—Ring, mum, ring, I beg. I mean I'd really like it if you rang. . . . Ring, mum, please ring, I murmur, give us the ten seconds for the welcome scene to unfold. . . . So the next day. The key turns in the lock. Crack. She comes in, moves forward, cuts through, passes, pivots, goes backwards, and with one hand on the broken-open door, from the inside, rings.—Ring BEFORE, I say. In vain.[17]

Whenever mother and daughter meet, they converse in a foreign tongue entirely composed of wordless gestures, alimentary exchanges, and strange sentences in which words are not words at all, but rather embodied actions, events, caresses, and blows. In that ancient arena (also known as a kitchen), every accented inflection becomes engaged in the body-to-body mortal combat that bears witness to their infinitely intimate hostility:

> Cette confiture, s'écrie ma mère, serait aussi bonne si/elle/é/tait/moins/chère. Toutes les deux nous frappons très fort avec des petits marteaux invisibles, nous cassons tout. Puis nous nous asseyons, mais pas dans la cuisine, et nous prenons le petit déjeuner comme s'il n'y avait pas les taches de sang près de l'évier.

> This jam, my mother cries, would be just as good if/it/was/cheap/er. Both of us, we hit hard with little invisible hammers, we break everything. Then we sit down, but not in the kitchen, and we have breakfast as though there were no bloodstains by the sink.[18]

The kitchen (in which neither mother nor daughter ever sits) is the antechamber to the world: It is a sacred temple in which the endless dramas of birth and matricide, death and resurrection, take place. In this scene, which opens *Osnabrück*, the kitchen is a war zone in which the mother's accented exclamations about the price of jam become her way of writing herself into the scene of life at her daughter's expense: ("*s'écrie ma mère*" is also "*s'écrit ma mère*"). Blood is shed. In this matricidal battle between mother and daughter, the blood that is left near the kitchen sink reopens the abyssal wound between them. It is a wound of endless separation that already anticipates the haunting refrain, "*Mutter, kann ich trennen?*" with which the book closes. The blood stains on the kitchen sink that open the book prepare the ground for the onion-laden tears that are shed in the kitchen at its end. Those final tears are the mute response to the primal incantation, "*Mutter, kann ich trennen?*" "*mère, puis-je séparer?*" "Mother, can I separate?" from which the entire novel springs.

I want to invoke one last unforgettable encounter between mother and daughter that takes place over the kitchen sink. This scene, taken from *L'amour du loup*, is a kind of postscript to the tragicomic drama of *Osnabrück*. In a chapter entitled "*Le livre nié*," there is a small anecdote, a living prose poem that is called: "*Inoublier: Des branches de Mimosa*" ("To Unforget: Mimosa Branches"). In this small text, the writer tells a story about how her ninety year-old mother enters her home without her knowledge on a freezing winter day while the writer was locked away in her study, engrossed in a private conversation with the ghost of the dead father. The scene takes place in February, the month in which the dead father had died long ago.

While the writer is with her dead father, and hence is absent from herself and life, the ancient mother crosses the threshold and leaves a bouquet of mimosa on the kitchen sink. This bouquet of flowers is a gift of unforgetting. With that simple gesture, Eve extracts a song composed with the letters of life (*vie*) from the letters that spell the month of death (*février*), and replants that song of life back into the kitchen sink (*évier*). This unspoken and uncalculated gift recalls the writer back to life. The writer reads this scene in life as it was written in life by the mother. And so she thinks:

> Je pense une pensée qui était comme si je la lisais: "Ma mère est venue me déposer des branches de mimosa sur l'évier cet après-midi chez moi." L'évier vivier. C'est rien. Et je sais que ce n'est pas rien. C'est une signature. Vie est. Il n'y a ni un mot ni un geste qui ne soit déjà dans l'ordre de l'inoubliable. La vie qui est faite d'oubli est en même temps porteuse d'innombrables inoubliables, que nous oublions. Eve y est.

> I think a thought that was as though I were reading it: "My mother came to put me some mimosa branches on the sink this afternoon at my place." The sink tank. It's nothing. And I know it's not nothing. It's a signature. Life is. There's neither word nor gesture that's not already in the order of the unforgettable. Life, made of forgetting is at the same time the bearer of innumerable unforgettables, that we forget. Eve is here. (Eve y est.)[19]

By engraving her own given name (Eve) in the kitchen sink (*l'évier*) the ninety-year-old mother gives rebirth to her mourning daughter in the whispered foreign tongue of the language of mimosa. In its muted *mi-mots*, its muttered half-words, the mimosa recalls the writer to the source of the foreign mother tongue. The words are a gift. Written in the unforgettable language of life. Inscribed in a foreign tongue so foreign that it recalls the infinite intimacy of life itself, the mother gives the daughter a gift of writing which comes from the other: the other's life, the other life. And signs it, in life. And then the writer countersigns it, otherwise, with her given name: "Hélène Cixous."

TWELVE

Bit: Mourning Remains in Derrida and Cixous

> One has perhaps to let oneself be taken in a little longer by the words, the morsels of words or dead bits in decomposition that let the writing go a bit more unbridled.
>
> —JACQUES DERRIDA, "Ja or the Faux-Bond"

BIT

Bit. In English, the word is "bit." But which bit is this bit? Is it a noun or a verb? Is it a piece of something torn off with the teeth, or is it an act of biting or having been bitten? According to the *Oxford English Dictionary*, the word "bit" can mean the thing one bites or the act of biting, the cutting edge of a tool, or the biting part of anything. By extension, the dictionary informs us, "bit" also means the "bite" or "sting" of death or disease or anything else that threatens to destroy me from without. This "bit" is a foretaste of my future death. The dictionary also clarifies that the word is so constitutively confused that even when "bit" clearly means the mouthpiece of a horse's bridle, "it is not clear whether the word in this sense signifies that which the horse bites or that which bites or grips the horse's mouth." Biter or bitten, active or passive, inside or outside, the word resists the possibility of deciding. The word "bit" is also a bit of the word "bite."

And it is this bit that designates its aftermath and remainder. The bit is a bit of a bite—its leftover bit—the severed piece that remains—after the event.

In French, the word for "bit" is *mors*. This bit, this *mors*, shares its root with the words *mordre* (to bite), *morsure* (a bite), *morceau* (morsel), and *remords* (remorse). Like the English "bit," all of these words appear to be located in and around the mouth; they all cleave open a confusion between the biter and the bit, the eater and the eaten. But in French, unlike English, the word *mors* also appeals to the ear as well. From its sound, it is indistinguishable from the command *mords* (bite!), the word for death (*mort*), and the words for the dead (*mort* in the masculine singular or *morts* in the plural).

Mors, *mords*, *morceau*, *morts*, *mort*, *morsure*, *remords*: Bit, bite, morsel, dead, death, sting, remorse. Throughout their work, in text after text, Jacques Derrida and Hélène Cixous each put these words to work by tearing them to bits and reworking them differently. For Derrida, the word *mors* returns again and again throughout many (if not most) of his major early writings on the work of mourning and the question of the remainder.[1] As I hope to demonstrate in the pages that follow—even if only schematically—through this word, along with its various decomposed and recomposed elements, Derrida explicitly questions psychoanalytic conceptions of the subject, of sexual difference and of mourning. For Cixous, the *morsure* (bite) is one of the primal sources of writing. Linked to a primal scene (that is to say an event that has happened to me but to which I can never be present) and often, but not always, figured by the bite of Fips the dog, the bite opens an uncloseable wound, and leaves an indelible mark on the body. But more important, perhaps, it bites back, through *remords* (remorse) returning again and again as a trace in me of the one who bit me and hence a trace of that bit of me that will never be part of me but that never lets go of me either. *Remords*. Remorse. Hélène Cixous glosses the word in the opening pages of her book *L'amour du loup et autre remords* (*The Love of the Wolf and Other Remorses*). The first section of the book is called "*Ma conscience me mord la langue avec tes dents*" ("My conscience bites my tongue with your teeth"). This means that my conscience does not belong to me; it is that living bit of you that lives in me and bites back through me. Although *remords* is born from pain, without it there is no writing, no life, and no literature.

Mords (bite!) is the imperative that rings out repeatedly in the pages of Cixous's *L'ange au secret*. "*Suivez aussi le mot 'mors'*" ("Follow too the word *mors*") is the command that reverberates in Derrida's "Cartouches." So I bite the bit and try to track the word through the bodies of their work. But following the bit turns out to be no simple matter, since there are forms of the word *mors* virtually everywhere in both corpuses, and one never encounters exactly the same bit twice. For this reason, to follow the word *mors* necessarily entails both changing the way one reads and acknowledging how that change has, in the same gesture, also transformed the very nature of the work itself. In other words, by reading "bit" by "bit," a certain fiction of the archive begins to fall apart. It is important to stress here that the bit is not a synecdoche—it is not a "part" for the whole. Once detached from the work, bits drift apart, producing new relations and new associative paths. Or, to put it another way, the archive becomes transformed into a labyrinth that is infinitely open to the outside but from which there may be no discernable exit. Following the word *mors* inaugurates a reading process that has no predetermined order, no established given boundaries, no given limits, and no end. Reading bits: analysis terminable and interminable.

What Remained of a Dog Bite . . .

> The signature is a wound, and there is no other origin for the work of art. (*Glas*, 184)

What remained of a dog bite long after the event? This question haunts Hélène Cixous's entire corpus. The barest bones of the narrative are this: One day, when Cixous was a child in Algeria, the family dog bit her on the foot. This skeletal account underwrites the countless poetic renditions of the dog and its bite that traverse the oeuvre. In virtually every text she writes, some trace of this event remains. In some texts, she tells the story of the bite and gives the dog's name: Fips. In others, she alludes merely to the experience of having been bitten, the letter "F," or the bright red colored geraniums that may have been silent flower witnesses to the event. Sometimes, the dog bite on the foot becomes transformed into another sort of wounding event, as in the short text "*Pieds nus*," in which a children's game goes horribly and violently awry when a young Arab boy, pretending to be a shoe shiner, paints one of the narrator's new white sandals bright red.[2] And sometimes, as in *L'ange au secret*, the event remains latent, but palpable, through the numerous references to biting jaws, tearing teeth, and scars that awaken and then blossom into open wounds.[3] Like these awakening scars, Fips the dead dog returns again and again: He comes alive in dreams, appears with the dead son in *Le jour où je n'étais pas là* and is resurrected as a cat in *Messie* and elsewhere.[4] In still other instances, the dog bite lies so deeply buried that it might be impossible to unearth, but that does not mean that it is not secretly at work in the deepest recesses of the text. What matters about the dog bite is that it is an event "worthy of the name." As such, the event could not be experienced at the moment of its occurrence, but only becomes "lived" in its afterlife through writing. Furthermore, because it leaves an indelible trace on the one to whom it happens, and because that trace can only be read retroactively, the bite writes itself on the body and demands to be read in the future by a future body of writing. Alluding to Freud and psychoanalysis, Cixous often refers to such events as "primal scenes" and uses this phrase as the subtitle of her book *Rêveries de la femme sauvage*.[5] But in other texts, she explicitly relates the scene of the dog bite to Jacques Derrida and to some of his emblematic words, such as "signature" and "circumcision."

As a way of opening up a textual relation between Derrida and Cixous through the dog bite, I would like to invoke four different textual renditions of the event. I prefer to speak about more than one bite because although the same dog bite returns again and again, when it returns, it is no longer quite the same bite. *Chaque fois unique*. Each time unique, the bite bites back differently and makes a different difference. The same bite writes itself over and over again differently and each time leaves a unique signature on the text in which it recurs. And, paradoxically, precisely because each text is singular and unique, that singularity emerges most saliently when they are read together through their differences.

Two of these four instances take place in *Messie*. Published in 1996, *Messie* opens with an epigraph from the book of Tobit, in which a son leaves his father and sets off alone in the company of an angel and a dog.[6] The entire text is filled with sacred animals. The specific event of the dog bite, however, is described in two different texts and there are significant discrepancies between them. The first bite is in "États d'août" ("States of August"), and the second is in the text that directly follows it: "Arrivée du chat" ("The Arrival of the Cat").[7] In "États d'août," a cryptic love story of separation and betrayal, the reference to the dog bite occurs toward the very end of the text as the narrator tells about how all the events that have marked her have touched her on her "left" side:

> je suis pour toujours inscrite à gauche dans le corps et dans les événements, quand je suis blessée, c'est à gauche. . . . Le jour où mon pauvre chien m'a déchiqueté l'âme j'avais pour lui, ce fut au pied gauche, j'écris avec la main droite, mais je lui dicte depuis ma bouche intérieure qui est à gauche en bas du cœur, rien ne peut faire changer le cours de ma nature.

> I am forever inscribed on the left in the body and in events, when I am hurt, it's on the left. . . . The day when my poor dog tore apart the soul I had for him, it was on the left foot; I write with the right hand, but I dictate from my inner mouth which is on the left, at the base of the heart, nothing can change the path of my nature.[8]

The left, or "sinister" side is the side that inscribes and *insists*. (The word "sinister" is an anagram of the word *insister*, the title of Hélène Cixous's most recent book devoted to Jacques Derrida.) In this text, the events that do not let go are those that come from the left side and are written on the left, from the side of the heart. In this passage, the wound made by the dog on the left foot is directly linked to the existence of a secret inner mouth, lodged at the base of the heart, which dictates the words that the narrator then writes down with the right hand.

In "Arrivée du chat," however, the description of the actual moment of the dog bite is written in the third person, the dog bites the girl's *right* foot, not the left one, and the focus is on the inner experience of the dog rather than the girl:

> Mais un jour dans la douleur débordante de sa rage d'être lapidé toute la journée pour être né de ce côté-ci du grillage lui qui n'était qu'un bâtard efflanqué, dans un hurlement de désespoir le chien s'était retourné contre celle qui l'aimait inutilement, et il lui avait planté ces crocs dans le pied droit. Meurs et tue-moi, grondait-il enragée, car ceci n'est pas une vie. Pourquoi m'as-Tu crée? De quel infâme défaut dans ta création dois-je témoigner? Pauvre Job, elle aussi, si elle avait pu mordre le pied de Dieu, elle l'aurait fait.

> Once, however, in the limitless grief of his fury at being lapidated all day for being born on this side of the fence, he who was an emaciated bastard, with a howl of despair the dog turned against she who loved him uselessly and

> he planted his teeth in her right foot. Die and kill me, he growled angrily because this is not a life. Why hast Thou created me? Of what vile flaw in your creation do I have to bear witness? Poor Job, she would also have bitten the foot of God if she could have.[9]

The dog's suffering is given a voice of biblical proportions in this text. Because he has been chained up to the wrong side of the fence, he is forced to pay for all of the violence from the world directed toward his family, and, in a fit of despair, rage, and fury, he lashes out at the girl who loved him. Like Job, he is an innocent victim. And, like Job, the voice of his pain is not heard during the time of his suffering. Here, there is no question about the girl's love for the dog. She understands why he bites her, and she identifies him with Job and identifies both with him as Job and with God through the pain she experiences through him and his bite. She shares his pain.

But the event of the dog's bite doesn't end with this moment of tender albeit painful recognition in *Messie*. Fips and the scene of the bite return, with a vengeance, in *Les rêveries de la femme sauvage* and "Stigmata: or Job the Dog."[10] In both of these texts, however, the scene of the dog bite now takes pages and pages to recount. Fips becomes more and more memorable as the actual narrative event of the bite becomes more convoluted and its ongoing significance becomes more and more difficult to read. For reasons that I hope will become clearer later on, I will begin with a discussion of the scene in *Rêveries*, even though it was published after "Stigmata." Each of these extraordinary texts is an infinitely rich prose poem that deserves to be read word by word and line by line.

In *Rêveries* (as in many of the other texts in which he figures), Fips is explicitly presented as the narrator's unacknowledged bastard baby brother. He is a brother because he is the dog child that the father brought home to the other children before he died. But the scene of the event of the bite actually begins pages before she is bitten as she conjures the dog up from the past and, when she recognizes him and calls to him by name, he comes bouncing back from the dead:

> Je te reconnais, Fips, dis-je, tu es un, tu es inoubliable. À ce moment-là il perce d'un bond la frêle buée odorante tendue entre notre maintenant et notre hier, blessure fraîche, plus jeté que galopant, dans l'effort où il fut toujours de franchir les grillages qui le séparaient de la juste vie.

> I recognize you, Fips, I say, you are one, you are unforgettable. At this very moment he jumps through the frail odorous mist stretched taut between our now and our yesterday, a fresh wound, more as if tossed than galloping, straining as he always did to clear the fences between him and the just life.[11]

The past opens up into the present like a fresh wound. That is the meaning of the term "unforgettable." It is a word that Cixous uses in a specific sense, although she glosses it more thoroughly elsewhere.[12] For example, in the passage from "Stigmata" that corresponds to this moment in *Rêveries*, she writes: "I admit, Fips, you are unforgettable, you have attained the rank that was always denied you while you lived, you are the most living of the departed."[13] The name "unforgettable" is thus reserved for that which becomes reclaimed for "life" after life and, in general, things or people designated as "unforgettable" attain this status because they were so forgotten and forsaken in life that they were never remembered enough to be really forgotten in life. But when they return, belatedly, from the nether regions of this limbo state of nothingness, the return itself becomes a living event—we might even call it an event of "hyperlife"—because it resists being put to rest and has no resting place and so opens the past up into the present like a wound. (I fear I have gotten ahead of myself by using the term "hyperlife," so this might be a good time to announce that I hope to be able to relate the figure of Fips and the primal scene of the dog bite to the prefix "hyper" in both Cixous and Derrida later on in this chapter). But at this point we can say that each time the forgotten, forsaken dog Fips returns from the dead, he is hyper-alive and hence "unforgettable."

In the pages that follow this greeting, the narrator goes on to tell the story of the dog's life. She describes how, in his early childhood, the two other children tried to force him to resemble their image of the ideal baby brother by forcing him to sleep in the shoebox cradle that they prepared for him.[14] Some pages later, the narrator explains how, after the father dies, the dog suffers the fate of being doubly victimized for being exactly the dog who he is. Outside the family, he pays the price for the fact that he belongs to a Jewish family. Ironically, however, it turns out that because he belongs to a Jewish family, he doesn't belong at all. He is rejected by the Jewish matriarchy (Eve and Omi) because as Jews, they do not believe that a dog belongs in the family. Dogs inside, it's not kosher, as Eve will say elsewhere.[15] Jew for the non-Jews and non-Jew for the Jews, Fips is aggressed from all sides, and expresses his experience of solitary and miserable exile by quoting from Rousseau's reveries.

But at that time, the girl doesn't hear the dog speaking to her through Rousseau's words because she isn't listening to him. She is not there; she is escaping from that world by reading. And it is while she is lost in her reading that she is interrupted and then bitten. The doorbell rings and in a fury she jumps up and stamps her foot on the floor while running for the door and the dog, startled by her rage, which comes from nowhere, lunges at her from nowhere, and the bite begins.

The bite begins and goes on and on:

> Et dans un grand frisson rauque il se jette sur le pied que je lève sur lui. De cette morsure je vais mourir, car elle me lâche plus elle s'enfonce sans fin et pénètre jusqu'à mon cœur, nous entrons dans l'éternité de la folie pensais-je, la tête environnée de nuées écarlates. Les dents duraient. Nous étions devenus inséparables.
>
> And with a great raucous shudder he pounces on the foot I aim at him. I shall die of this bite, for it doesn't let go of me it digs in and in, penetrating right to my heart, that is where we enter folly's eternity, I thought, my head in a swirl of scarlet clouds. The teeth went on. We had grown inseparable.[16]

Finally, Aïcha beats the dog down. In the aftermath of the bite, the dog that bites becomes bitten. Fodder for fat ticks, he is devoured to death. At the end of his life, the dog's suffering makes him saintly, and the narrator calls him "Job." The narrator says his death is remembered by no one. Speaking about the day her brother disposes of the remains, she says, "*je n'étais pas là.*" *Chaque fois unique*, each day I wasn't there. So the remains of the dog disappear but he leaves his mark on her feet: "*Les cinq bouches cousues sur mes pieds*"—the five sewn-up mouths on my feet.[17] These sewn-up mouths remain from the dog bite. But the stitches on the wounds become undone over time, and the lips of the wounds open up into remorse and writing. And love springs from writing and remorse. Belatedly. Retroactively. The scene of the dog bite in *Rêveries* ends on this note of belated declaration of love: "*et pourtant j'aimais Fips, je le sens encore, mais pas au Clos-Salembier, je l'aimais plus tard*" (and yet I loved Fips, I feel that still, but not in Clos-Salembier, I loved him later on).[18] *Sero te amavi*: "So late have I loved thee."

But what remains of the dog bite in "Stigmata: or Job the Dog"? Although the actual narrative account of the bite is fairly similar to the version that appears in *Rêveries* (despite it being somewhat longer and more detailed), this strange and powerful text (which, to my knowledge, has been published only in English) is subtly and substantially different from its other incarnations. It is certainly the darkest, most obscure and most fertile rendition of the scene. But for the purposes of this discussion, I will be obliged to focus more on the way Cixous frames the story rather than on the text itself. Cixous opens "Stigmata" with some introductory remarks about the status of the figure of the "blessed wound" in Saint Augustine, James Joyce, and Jean Genet. She then explains that when she first encountered the wound in her early work on Joyce, it struck her as a "masculine" and "Catholic" motif. After reading Derrida's "Circonfession," however, she changes her mind about the inherent Catholicism of the blessed wound and begins to wonder about "circumcision" in relation to her own work:

> This text ["Circonfession"] is about circumcision, a wound inflicted on someone who is not present at the scene of his own mutilation. With Derrida the wound is concrete, it is a violent event that took place in reality. . . . Is the fertile wound, I wondered, part of the masculine phantasmal make-up? And is there anything analogous in women's texts? What about my own relation to the inscription on the body of my psychomythical events? I wrote it in a text called *Stigmata, or Job the Dog*. Or else: The *Origin of my Philosophy*. Or else: *First Symptoms of Writing*. Or: *The Opening of the Mouth*.[19]

Cixous here presents "Stigmata" as a kind of written response to "Circonfession." Certainly, it would appear that "Circonfession" is a critical point of reference for Cixous's reading of Derrida as well as for the place that his writing comes to occupy in her work. Although, as is well known and has been well documented, Cixous was an avid and active reader of Derrida for roughly thirty years before "Circonfession" was published (indeed, they first met face to face in 1962 because she wrote to him after reading him), this text seems have a special—perhaps even "primal"—status for her.[20] There would, of course, be many ways of explaining this, beginning with the literary and autobiographical resonances that connect their separate but uncannily "shared" childhood experiences in Algeria.[21] The event of reading "Circonfession" thus becomes an event in Cixous's own writing history and, or so this argument would suggest, it marks a turning point and makes a difference to that history. At this point it might be interesting to recall that in the text "Quelle heure est-il ou la porte (celle qu'on ne passe pas)" ("What is it o'clock? or the door [we never enter]") first presented at Cerisy in 1992 and reprinted in *Stigmata*, Cixous opens the text by describing the scene of her "primal vision" of Jacques Derrida "in 1962" making his way down the crests in Arcachon and then writes: "*Plus tard, j'appelerais ce tableau: Circoncision du monde*" (Later I would call this tableau: "circumcision of the world").[22] The term "circumcision" is hence applied retroactively, in 1992, to describe the effect reading him had on her in 1962. "Circonfession" is thus implicitly implicated as the text behind the "tableau" of the vision (written in a "now" time) that rereads and reimagines the primal scene of her "first" reading of him (then). In any case, it does seem clear that "Circonfession" leads Cixous to think differently about "circumcision" (now put here in quotation marks) and encourages her to explore how different kinds of circumcision might be at work in her own life writing and how they might make a difference to it. In the wake of "Circonfession," Cixous begins to inscribe her reading of Derrida more explicitly into her texts, and there are arguably also some significant changes in the way she writes her own autobiographical "primal scenes" from this time forward.[23] From this perspective, "Circonfession" can be seen as something like a spyhole (or *Judas*) through which Cixous rereads Derrida's entire oeuvre. She begins to stitch bits of that oeuvre back into her own work, marking his phrases with her own idioms all the while attending to the differences between them. Indeed, it should be remembered here that "difference" is precisely what interests her about circumcision as circumcision is precisely about the question of what makes differences and what is made of them. Thus even in the moments when Cixous openly cites Derrida or alludes to him directly, her writing about and through him is actively marked by her attention to their differences; they include (but are not limited to) sexual differences and different relations to death. This may be partly why she makes the connection to "Circonfession" explicit in her preface to the story of Fips in "Stigmata: or Job the Dog." Seen in this light, "Stigmata" can be read as an early autobiographical anticipation of the close reading of "Circonfession" that she will later go on to carry out in *Portrait de Jacques Derrida en jeune saint juif*.[24]

But I actually brought up "Stigmata" in order to show how this text engages in a silent (but audible) conversation with Derrida across the body of a text signed by someone else. And it is this other text that returns us to the haunting question with which we began: "what remained of a dog bite long after the event?" The text in question is, of course, Jean Genet's "What remained of a Rembrandt torn into small, very regular squares and rammed down the shit-hole." Cixous begins "Stigmata" by observing, "for Genet, the wound is the founding secret of all major creation," and then goes on to quote three separate bits from this text. In "Stigmata," Cixous rewrites Genet's text by quoting its bits. Via Genet, and alongside of Genet, she articulates two thoughts which are not present in any of the other narrative accounts of the dog bite we have looked at:

> in our last times I was able to desire that he should die. But I could not say it to myself. But I remember having felt the obscure and impossible desire-without-words. And this desire opened other very nasty wounds behind my heart.
>
> I never even persuaded myself that Fips had any mortal remains. I assigned him the terrible role of holocaust.[25]

And it is these two afterthoughts in the aftermath of the dog bite that most dramatically bring us back, once again, to the questions with which we began: what is the relationship between the bite and the bit; between the "after-bite" of "remorse" and the status of whatever else "remains"? Or, to translate these terms back into the specifically French idioms of Cixous and Derrida, we might want to rephrase this as a question about how to read Cixous's interrogation of the word *mordre* (in all its forms from *morsure* to *remords*) in relation to Derrida's rigorous elaboration of the word *mors* (bit) in *Glas* and elsewhere. As it happens, one way of reading this relation *between* Cixous and Derrida is by reading them together through their respective readings of Jean Genet. Let us recall, after all, that *Glas* begins by quoting the title of the same text by Genet that Cixous cites from in "Stigmata." The Genet column of *Glas* opens with the following sentence: "What remained of a Rembrandt torn into small, very regular squares and rammed down the shithole is divided." But where Cixous interrogates her own relation to remorse through this text, Derrida turns to Genet for help in tearing words and things to bits. And then he looks to the word *mors* to think about what remains, what resists, and what is left over.

Bits and Crypts

When I began this reading, I had naively intended to trace the word *mors* throughout Derrida's oeuvre. It soon became very clear that I had bitten off more than I could chew. I can say that if one were to take up this challenge seriously, it would carve out an interesting path leading from the work on impossible mourning in *Glas*, "*Fors*," and *La verité en peinture* that Derrida published in the mid-1970s, to the many later texts devoted to circumcision, cannibalism, animality, hospitality, the archive, and sacrifice to name only the most salient examples. But there is also literature—and it is not an example among others in this context. There is no thinking about the *mors* (about the bit) in Derrida that is not also an engagement with literature and the literary. All of his writings on the *mors* are concerned with the way the bit cuts up the tongue before it becomes available for conceptual consumption by philosophy, psychoanalysis, or religion. And all three of those discourses give the ingestion of primal morsels (*morceaux*) a role to play in their originary and constituting fables: whether or not those first bits take the form of Plato's *pharmakon*, Freud's totem, or the biting of the first foreskin in circumcision. For Derrida, the *mors* is not a concept; the bit *resists* conceptualization. The *mors* is the trace of that which cannot be fully incorporated and therefore leaves an unassimilated remainder. In "Cartouches," he writes:

> But the introjection of the piece [*morceau*] *in other words of the bit* [*mors*], is interminable, it always ends up by letting drop an absolutely heterogeneous remainder of incorporation. Infinite analysis of mourning, between introjection and incorporation.[26]

Furthermore, as he demonstrates at great length in *Glas*, "*Fors*," and "Cartouches," the *mors* resists conceptualization because it operates on language not merely through words but through bits of words.[27] These bits of language that have been cut off from any determinable philosophical concept, linguistic referent, or proper name drift and disseminate in uncontrollable and unpredictable ways. Some of the bits of language that cannot be assimilated into concepts get spit out as *literature*.

Whenever the word *mors* appears in *Glas*, "*Fors*," and "Cartouches," Jean Genet is not far away. For, as Derrida explicitly points out in the opening pages of *Glas*, *mors* is one of Genet's signatures: a "genet" or jenny is a kind of a horse on which he, Jean Genet, "rides horse(back) on his proper name. He holds it by the bit [*mors*]" (*Il est à cheval sur son nom propre. Il le tient par le mors*).[28] Derrida insists on reading Genet's signature through the word *mors* to show how Genet signs his own texts by tearing his proper name—along with anything else that might be considered "proper"—to bits. In a text called "Countersignature" presented at Cerisy-la-Salle at a conference on Genet in August 2000 in which Derrida discusses his own earlier reading of Genet in *Glas*, he explains:

> Everything in Genet's text begins with a question of the remainder—the signature being precisely a remainder—that, throughout the book and beyond, orders a problematic of remaining [*restance*] that I cannot reconstitute here, but that escapes all ontology, all philosophy that sees in the remainder "what remains," that is, a substance, persistence or even a state. The remaining of the remainder is not a substance that subsists or stays, it isn't a being that resists time.[29]

Once one begins reading the "bits" that punctuate Derrida's oeuvre, there is seemingly no end to the pathways that are opened up by possible associations between them. For example, one could explore the intimate relationship between bits and crypts in Derrida's reading of Genet by following the trace of the word *mors* as it takes us to his three different readings of the "matchbox" (*boîte d'allumettes*) sequence from Jean Genet's *Funeral Rites* (*Pompes funèbres*). Derrida quotes this bit of *Funeral Rites* in *Glas*, then he quotes himself quoting it in "*Fors*," and then in "Cartouches" he quotes himself quoting his quotes of it (while identifying a bit he has possibly misread) in the two earlier versions. It is no accident, of course, that the sequence in question is about a matchbox, made of nested boxes, as Genet's text would have it, that is a portable, miniature repository for his own death. The matchbox is small enough to carry around in a pocket. *Glas* ends with this image of portable, flammable death:

> Comment fait-il? Il a toujours eu son cadavre sur lui, dans sa poche, dans une boîte d'allumettes. Sous la main. Ça s'allume tout seul.

> How does he do it? He is ready. He always has his corpse on him, in his pocket, in a matchbox. Near at hand. It lights up alone.[30]

In "*Fors*," Derrida inserts Genet's matchbox into his reading of Nicolas Abraham and Maria Torok's reading of Freud's Wolf Man case history:

> The crypt is perhaps itself that contract with the dead. The cryptophore engages itself toward the dead, grants the dead, as collateral, a mortgage within itself, a pledge within the body, a cystic pocket both blatant and secret, the spot where a thanato-poetic pleasure can always catch fire again. . . . That supposes that the crytophore, having taken the "bite" (the bit) without being able to digest it, forced to keep it in accessible and impossible reserve, must constantly betray the cipher that seals and conceals it. To keep life safe and put death in one's pocket (in a "matchbox" says Genet in *Pompes funèbres*).[31]

It is worth noting here that Derrida elucidates the figure of the crypt (with which he issues a challenge to psychoanalytic models of mourning based on introjection and/or incorporation), by slipping in a bit of literature.[32] Or, more precisely, he slips in the matchbox bit from Genet to describe the bits that psychoanalysis cannot account for. Derrida turns to Genet to convey the thought that only literature—along with the "thanato-poetic" pleasures found therein, can provide a place—which is not a place—for the indigestible bits of life and death that cannot be assimilated into a self. The "thanato-poetic" pleasure of literature is driven by the impossibility of being able to tell where death begins and life ends. It is also interesting to note here that Freud himself seems to imply that only literature can make life palatable for us by giving us a bit of death. In "Reflections Upon War and Death," he writes:

> It is an inevitable result of all this that we should seek in the world of fiction, in literature and in the theatre compensation for what has been lost in life. There we still find people who know how to die—who, indeed, even manage to kill someone else. There alone too the condition can be fulfilled which makes it possible for us to reconcile ourselves with death: namely, that behind all the vicissitudes of life we should still be able to preserve a life intact. For it is really too sad that in life it should be as it is in chess, where one false move may force us to resign the game, but with the difference that we can start no second game, no return-match. In the realm of fiction we find the plurality of lives which we need.[33]

Literature lets me put my death in a matchbox, lets me play with it in secret hidden places close to me. But to play with literature is to play with fire. No way of telling when it might flare up, no way to contain the flames; no accounting for the bits or knowing what remains.

Or what might return. Curiously, something like the figure of Genet's matchbox shows up again in what might seem to be an unlikely place in Derrida's oeuvre: *Genèses, généalogies, genres et le génie*. But this time, Genet's matchbox turns up in Derrida's text after having passed through Hélène Cixous's subtle and encrypted rewriting of it in *Manhattan*. Derrida does not let on whether or not he is aware that the matchbox is there, buried in her words in the inner recesses of his own text. In the closing pages of *Genèses*, Derrida quotes a very long passage from Cixous's book that, in very uncharacteristic fashion, he doesn't really gloss. This substantial bit of Cixous's text makes a pocket in his text. He lets the long quotation (which runs uninterrupted from page 94 to page 96 of *Genèses*) alone to do its work on his text from within. But he does say, before beginning to quote, that this passage is a "confession" or a "concession" to the secret passions of the archive. In order to show how these texts are embedded in one another, I will tear from Derrida's long quotation a smaller (more digestible) bit by beginning with his last sentence before he quotes from *Manhattan* and then go on to quote him quoting her book:

> Par exemple, cette confession ou cette concession de *Manhattan* sur la passion contrariée de l'archive:
>
> Pourquoi n'ai-je jamais jeté "les pièces de conviction"? Je ne mets jamais un pied ni à la cave ni au grenier, je crains les cartons, les boîtes, les enveloppes, les bêtes allégoriques compactes de taille d'une grosse langouste ou d'une tortue au ventre caparaçonné de blanc au crâne suivi d'antennes téléphoniques, les vieilles valises à retardement qui ressemblent aux cercueils portables, le savon miniature de la taille d'une boîte d'allumettes encore blanc d'ivoire sans doute empaqueté dans son maillot de papier glacé jauni à l'enseigne du King's Crown Hotel.

> For instance, this confession or confession of *Manhattan* about the thwarted passion for the archive:
>
> Why have I never tossed out the "incriminating bits"? I never set foot in either the cellar or the attic, I fear the cardboard boxes, the crates, the envelopes, the compact allegorical beasts big as a good-sized crayfish or an elongated tortoise, belly clad in white skull followed by telephone antennae, old delayed action suitcases that look for all your life like portable coffins, the miniature, matchbox-sized cake of soap still ivory white no doubt still packed in its glossy jaundiced paper vest with the logo of the King's Crown Hotel.[34]

The passage from *Manhattan* is about what remains from a love affair—thirty-six years after its end—with someone who may never have really existed.[35] What remains are bits of "evidence," kept in a crypt, a dark tunnel of the basement that the narrator never enters because she's afraid of cartons, boxes, envelopes, tortoises, old suitcases and anything else that might resemble a "portable coffin." And then, in the midst of this hodgepodge list of cluttered bric-a-brac, wedged between the two phrases "portable coffins" and "size of a matchbox," she retrieves a bit of remaining evidence from the affair: an ivory colored piece of miniature soap, swathed in yellowed wax paper, bearing the insignia of the King's Crown Hotel. Encased by two direct allusions to Genet's matchbox ("portable coffins" and "size of a matchbox"), Cixous transforms the figure of the matchbox into a miniature bar of soap. The matchbox/bar of soap connection is confirmed when, at the end of the book, in the last chapter entitled "Après la fin" ("After the End"), the narrator tells how the whole affair washed away silently; she specifies that it left no *ashes*, nothing but a soap bubble (the most ephemeral of remains)—in its wake:

> Il était plus mort qu'aucun mort ne l'a jamais été, mort sans survie mort d'une mort sans vie sans aucun des restes qui continuent à couver immortellement et au premier souffle de souvenir ranimés comme des vêtements par des mites nous tirent des larmes. Il s'était dissipé sans cendre sans bruit. Une bulle de savon . . .

> He was deader than any dead man had ever been; dead without afterlife dead of a death without life without any remains which continue to brood immortally and at the first breath of memory are reanimated like moth-ridden clothes that draw tears from us. He had dissipated without ashes without sound. A soap bubble . . .[36]

Cixous's lingering soap bubble is the only witness to a mode of death that leaves no trace; for in this rewriting of the matchbox, we encounter "death by water" in place of fire. But the man who is deader than a dead man is a man who is fictively dead and who dies by fiction. (In the book, Gregor steals Kafka's identity, counterfeits his letters, and pretends to be dying.) At the end of *Manhattan*, however, thinking about her fictive lover Gregor, the narrator concludes that perhaps he needed to live a fake life, fake his death, to write fake literature precisely because he had never really been "bit" in life: bit by death, or a dog, or any other form of "blessed wound."

> Ou bien aucun ne lui était jamais arrivé encore des événements violents qui causent la naissance d'une âme vouée à l'alliance littéraire, aucune de ces circoncisions d'une partie du corps spirituel aucune de ces entailles en forme de bouches qui livrent passage aux premières imprécations de l'écriture. . . . Privés du coup de lance et de la plaie qui donne. J'imagine qu'il avait le malheur de n'avoir pas été encore visité d'un malheur. Alors que j'avais déjà eu la *chance négative*, j'avais précocement perdu mon père et par suite le chien fils de mon père et presque tout de suite après j'avais sur le seuil dû laisser mon propre fils, et les perdant chaque fois une fois de plus en chacun reperdant les autres . . .

> Or else: none of those violent events that cause the birth of a soul destined to the literary covenant, none of those circumcisions of a part of the spiritual body, none of those mouth-shaped incisions that grant passage to the first imprecations of writing had ever yet ever happened to him. . . . Deprived of the lance-blow and the wound that gives, I imagine that he had the misfortune of never yet having been visited by a misfortune. Whereas I had already had *negative luck*, I had precociously lost my father and then subsequently the dog son of my father and then almost directly afterwards I had to leave on the doorstep my own son; and each time, losing them one more time and in each one re-losing the others.[37]

Uncut and untouched by death, he is deprived of what remains: the wound of death in life that opens me up to the other and to literature. Comparing herself to Gregor, the narrator concludes that she has been blessed by her "negative fortune"—and she conjures up the successive losses of her father (who died too soon), her father's dog (whom she loved too late), and her dead son (whom she had to "leave on the doorstep"). Each of these bites of death is unique and leaves its unique trace; but the imprint of each one remains in the others and returns in the *remords* that remain.

Resistance, Hyperanalysis, and Hyper . . .

Manhattan opens under the sign of "resistance." The author/narrator doesn't want to go to Certes; she goes to Certes. After roughly thirty pages documenting her war with herself, she explicitly addresses the question of "resistance" and says:

> J'ai toujours fait ce que je ne voulais pas faire. . . . J'ai pris le chemin de Certes par sévérité à l'égard de mes résistances. J'ai toujours résisté durement à mes résistances.

> I always did what I didn't want to do. . . . I took the road to Certes in strict regard for my resistances. I've always rigorously resisted my resistances.[38]

This meditation on "resistance" is, in some sense, a discourse on literary method. Cixous writes by resisting her resistances. As we have seen, she writes through death by resisting her resistance to death. This resistance to the resistance is another name for what we have been calling *remords*. And, as we have seen, *mors* is one of the names Derrida gives for the way literature resists psychoanalytic accounts of mourning. In the essay entitled "Resistances," however, Derrida explicitly challenges psychoanalysis through psychoanalysis by showing that it posits a concept of "resistance" that it then cannot contain, explain and control. Following Freud closely, Derrida argues that the concept of resistance is radically heterogeneous. He shows how Freud struggles with the concept and is obliged to break it down into different kinds of resistance, but ultimately ends up positing a form of resistance more resistant than all of the others. This resistance comes from the unconscious and cannot be reclaimed by the ego. He writes:

> On rencontre une "résistance à l'analyse" qui à la fois figure la plus résistante des résistances, la résistance par excellence, la résistance *hyper*bolique et pourtant celle qui désorganise le principe même, l'idée constitutive de la psychanalyse comme analyse des résistances.
>
> One encounters a "resistance to analysis" that figures *both the* most resistant resistance, resistance par excellence, *hyper*bolic resistance, *and* the one that disorganizes the very principle, the constitutive idea of psychoanalysis as analysis of resistances.[39]

Derrida uses the prefix "*hyper*" to describe the resistance that is both the most tenacious resistance and the one that resists analysis. He then goes on explicitly and repeatedly to link the prefix to the mode of analysis opened up by this resistant resistance and hence to deconstruction as such:

> Qu'est-ce que la déconstruction de la présence, sinon l'expérience de cette dissociation *hyper*analytique du simple et de l'originaire ?
>
> What is the deconstruction of presence if not the experience of this *hyper*analytic dissociation of the simple and the originary?[40]

Finally, at the end of the essay, he proposes that there is a necessity for something that he calls "*hyper*analysis":

> Ce que nous venons d'approcher, c'est *à la fois* une nécessité *hyper*analytique, la loi d'un "il faut analyser sans fin", d'ailleurs "ça s'analyse indéfiniment", donc cela doit s'analyser *hyper*bolythiquement.

> What we have just approached is both a *hyper*analytic necessity—the law of a "one must analyze endlessly," what is more, "it is analyzing itself indefinitely." "It is indefinitely analyzable," therefore it must be analyzed *hyper*bolytically.[41]

"Hyperanalysis," which is derived from hyperresistance, becomes another name for deconstruction. The prefix "hyper" and the notion of "resistance" are also two of the words that Derrida uses when talking about Cixous's writing. In both *HC pour la vie c'est à dire . . .* and *Genèses*, Derrida writes at great length about the way Cixous's writings have been met with resistance. He observes, with evident regret and impatience, that Cixous's texts provoke resistance in some readers. He finds that some readers resist her *because* she is a woman, while others resist her because they need to appropriate her *as* a woman. Both rejection and appropriation are symptoms of the same resistance. At a more interesting level, however, he seems to imply that Cixous's work solicits resistance in those readers who cannot bear to read her inimitable form of literary *hyper*analysis. And, in *HC pour la vie*, he explicitly and repeatedly calls her fiction "*hyperréaliste*."[42] Hyperrealist, that is to say hyperreal, writer of a reality more than real and of a dream book more dream than dream. This hyperreality both brings us closer to the fantasmatic images from which dreams are born and returns us to the question of what remains.

What remains of mourning remains that are encrypted into dream fictions? In two of Cixous's recent works (*Le jour où je n'étais pas là* and *Rêve, je te dis*) we discover two unique but uncannily doubled scenes in which the narrating voice confesses that she has stolen a bit of "pocket-sized" death. Both bits of text are made up of a tissue of citations and self-citations and defy the boundaries between mourner and mourned, between the container and the contained. These intimate instances of "hyper death," lovingly preserved in a dreamscape of writing, are the living remains of the unforgettable:

> Dedans un minuscule coffret de la taille de ma main. Dedans ce coffret une infime motte de terre. Furtive je pris le fragment de mon fils mort. Je brisai

> une miette grosse comme un ongle que j'enveloppai dans un mouchoir. Mon larcin accompli je remis le reste dans le petit coffre et refermai le tout. Je pris l'air innocent. J'enfouis la miette de mon mort dans ma poche. Ce qui ne m'avait pas été donné, je l'avais pris.
>
> Inside: a minuscule casket the size of my hand. Inside this casket a decrepit dead clump of earth. Furtive I took the fragment of my dead son. I broke off a crumb as big as a fingernail that I wrapped up in a tissue. My theft accomplished I put the rest back into the little coffer and I sealed it all up again. I looked innocent. I stuffed the crumb of my dead into my pocket. What had not been given to me, I had taken.[43]
>
> Dedans ce minuscule coffret une infime motte de terre couleur brique. Voilà. La pierre tombale serait argile, terre cuite—ceci était un fragment—peut-être la tombe était-elle déjà. Furtive je pris le fragment. Je brisai une miette grosse comme un ongle que j'enveloppai dans un mouchoir. Mon larcin accompli, je remis le reste dans le petit coffre et refermai le tout. J'avais surpris la dernière demeure. J'ai pris l'air innocent, J'enfouis le fragment de la tombe secrète de J.D. dans ma poche. Ce qui ne m'avait pas été donné, je l'avais pris.
>
> Inside this minuscule casket a decrepit dead brick-colored clump of earth. There it was. The gravestone would be clay, baked earth—this was a fragment—perhaps the tomb already existed. Furtive I took the fragment. I broke off a crumb the size of a fingernail that I wrapped up in a tissue. My theft accomplished, I put the rest back into the little coffer and I sealed it all up again. I had surprised the last resting place. I looked innocent; I stuffed the fragment of the secret tomb of J.D. into my pocket. What had not been given to me, I had taken.[44]

Both scenes are primal scenes of mourning. Each scene is unique and each one reproduces itself in the other. If we look more closely at these "little coffers," we come to recognize that those tiny caskets are placeholders for that which has no proper place. Like a fictive, fantasmatic camera obscura, they give birth to new images that belong neither to the realm of the living nor to that the dead. Their unique mode of reproduction gives new life to inassimilable bits of death. As such, these small black boxes perform an uncanny work of mourning—one that is at once primordially archaic and strangely new. Like Pandora's jar, and the many other unruly reproductive containers (including freezers, case studies, photographs, labyrinths, miniature portraits, dreams, crypts, and tiny coffins) that we have encountered throughout this book, these minuscule caskets both preserve bits of death and reproduce new forms of life from them. As such, they bear the unmistakable signature of the uncanny, uncontainable, and unrecognizable life forms that emanate from the maternal function.

NOTES

INTRODUCTION: PANDORA'S LEGACY

1. For a witty and indispensable treatment of the uncanny, see Nicholas Royle, *The Uncanny* (Manchester: Manchester University Press, 2003). Although the thinking in this book runs parallel in many ways to Royle's, he does not privilege the uncanny status of the mother in the way I am proposing here.

2. Julia Kristeva often uses the term "maternal function" to designate the various operations performed by the mother during the birthing process and in an infant's early life. However, my use of the term differs radically from hers. My understanding of the maternal function is concerned with modes of mechanical repetition as a critical (and traditionally overlooked) part of the development of the subject. For an excellent treatment of Kristeva's understanding of the maternal function, see Kelly Oliver's many writings on Kristeva, including *Reading Kristeva: Unraveling the Double Bind* (Bloomington: Indiana University Press, 1993), *Family Values: Subjects Between Nature and Culture* (New York: Routledge, 1997), and the lucid editorial prefaces in *The Portable Kristeva* (New York: Columbia University Press, 2002).

3. This is a point that Jacques Derrida makes repeatedly. See "*Khōra*," for example, where Derrida writes: "Philosophy cannot speak philosophically of that which looks like its 'mother,' its 'nurse,' its 'receptacle,' or its 'imprint bearer.' As such, it speaks only of the father and the son, as if the father engendered it all of his own." In *Khōra*: *On the Name*, ed. Thomas Dutoit, trans. Ian McCleod (Stanford, Calif.: Stanford University Press, 1995), 126.

4. The mother and the maternal function occupy a major place within feminist philosophy and feminist-inflected psychoanalytic theory. As mentioned in note 2, the maternal function (or the primary importance of the mother and the maternal body) occupies a pivotal place in Julia Kristeva's work. Kristeva's interest in the maternal function is of course greatly indebted to the important work of Melanie Klein. For an excellent introduction to psychoanalytic accounts of

the mother, see Janice Doane and Devon Hodges, *From Klein to Kristeva: Psychoanalytic Feminism and the Search for the "Good Enough" Mother* (Ann Arbor: University of Michigan Press, 1992). See Amber Jacobs, *On Matricide: Myth, Psychoanalysis, and the Law of the Mother* (New York: Columbia University Press, 2008), for an interesting recent examination of the repression of myths of matricide within psychoanalysis. I find Jacobs's discussion of the figure of Metis (the mother of Athena whom Zeus swallows and incorporates) very compelling, but I am not entirely convinced that the problem with the maternal function is best examined through matricide. For me, the mother's relation to birth remains even more of a stumbling block for psychoanalytic theory than the repression of her murder.

5. One of the underlying premises of this book is that real women (and the category of real women includes but is not limited to real mothers) may actually suffer real consequences in the real world from the conflation between the human rights that properly belong to "women" and the uncanny and potentially anxiety-producing properties of the maternal function. Simply put, this book contends that certain kinds of patriarchal efforts to control real women may be traced back to reactive and ineffectual attempts to contain the disturbing and destabilizing effects of the maternal function. Likewise, the confusion between "mothers" and "women" implicitly excludes men from being able to fill the human role of "mother" in the life of a child. Therefore, in addition to all the other good conceptual reasons stated, and for feminist, gay, and queer political reasons as well, I believe that it is important not to conflate real women either with "mothering" or with the "maternal function."

6. One of the names that psychoanalysis gives to the existential predicament and the temporal effects of the psychic phantasy of wanting to be present at the scene of one's own conception is "primal scene." Although I refer to "primal scenes" throughout this book, Chapter 3 explores this concept directly through an examination of the temporal structure of the primal scene and its relation to the event of birth and the maternal function in Freud's case history of the patient known as "Wolf Man."

7. In Chapter 1, I analyze a recent case in French public affairs about a woman who becomes pregnant, denies her pregnancy to herself and her husband, gives birth without his knowledge, strangles the baby, and then preserves the dead baby in a freezer bag, which she keeps in a freezer in the kitchen of the home. Surprisingly, as I discovered when working on this case, the phenomenon of "freezer babies" following denial of pregnancy and infanticide is not uncommon. I argue that this case (and cases like it) points to the ways in which the distinction between the mother and the maternal function can become pathological and how technological inventions (here the freezer) play an important role in the pathology.

8. Avital Ronell, *The Telephone Book: Technology—Schizophrenia—Electric Speech* (Lincoln: University of Nebraska Press, 1989).

9. Hesiod, *Theogony* and *Works and Days*. In *Hesiod*, vol. 1, ed. and trans. Glenn W. Most (Cambridge, Mass.: Harvard University Press, 2006). All references to Hesiod will refer to this edition. Line numbers are indicated in the body of the text.

10. See, in particular, Jean-Pierre Vernant, *Pandora, La Première femme* (Paris: Bayard, 2006) and "The Myth of Prometheus in Hesiod," *Myth and Society in Ancient Greece* (New York: Zone Books, 1990), 183–201; Nicole Loraux, "On the Race of Women and Some of Its Tribes: Hesiod and Semonides," *The Children of Athena: Athenian Ideas About Citizenship and the Division Between the Sexes* (Princeton, N.J.: Princeton University Press, 1993), 72–110; Froma Zeitlin, "Signifying Difference: The Case of Hesiod's Pandora," *Playing the Other: Gender and Society in Classical Greek Literature* (Chicago: University of Chicago Press, 1995), 53–86. See also Geneviève Hoffmann, "Pandora, La jarre et l'espoir," *Etudes Rurales* 97/98 (January–June 1985): 119–132. For a recent feminist reappraisal of the Pandora myth, see Vered Lev Kenaan, *Pandora's Senses: The Feminine Character of the Ancient Text* (Madison: University of Wisconsin Press, 2008).

11. Loraux, "On the Race of Women," 81.

12. Ibid., 74.

13. For a fascinating reflection on prosthesis (in all forms), see David Wills, *Prosthesis* (Stanford, Calif.: Stanford University Press, 1995). Although I share many points of interest in common with Wills's work, his book focuses especially on prosthesis in relation to the father. The chapter "Berchtesgaden, 1929," on Freud, telepathy, and the uncanny is especially relevant to the concerns of this book.

14. Vernant, "Myth of Prometheus," 196.

15. Loraux, "On the Race of Women," 83–84.

16. Zeitlin, "Signifying Difference," 64–66.

17. Ibid., 84.

1. THE SEX OF DEATH AND THE MATERNAL CRYPT

1. Charles Baudelaire, "Le cygne," *Oeuvres complètes*, ed. Claude Pichois (Paris: Gallimard, 1975), 1:85–87.

2. Following G. W. F. Hegel's famous discussion of Antigone in *The Phenomenology of Spirit*, trans. A. V. Miller (London: Oxford University Press, 1977), numerous philosophers and thinkers have written extensively about Antigone. Most notably, see Jacques Derrida, *Glas*, trans. John P. Leavey Jr. and Richard Rand (Lincoln: University of Nebraska Press, 1986); Jacques Lacan,

The Seminar of Jacques Lacan, Book VII: The Ethics of Psychoanalysis, trans. Dennis Porter (New York: Norton, 1992); Luce Irigaray, "The Eternal Irony of the Community," in *Speculum of the Other Woman*, trans. Gillian Gill (Ithaca, N.Y.: Cornell University Press, 1985); George Steiner, *Antigones* (Oxford: Oxford University Press, 1984); Judith Butler, *Antigone's Claim: Kinship Between Life and Death* (New York: Columbia University Press, 2000); Tina Chanter, "Tragic Dislocations: Antigone's Modern Theatrics," *Differences* 10, no. 1 (1998): 75–97; Carol Jacobs, "Dusting Antigone," *MLN* 111, no. 5 (1996): 889–917; Joan Copjec, "The Tomb of Perseverance: On Antigone," in *The Ethics of History* (Evanston, Ill.: Northwestern University Press, 2004), 118–154; Charles Shepherdson, "The Atrocity of Desire: Of Love and Beauty in Lacan's *Antigone*," in *Lacan and the Limits of Language* (New York: Fordham University Press, 2008), 50–80; Samuel Weber, "Antigone's 'Nomos,'" in *Theatricality as Medium* (New York: Fordham University Press, 2004), 121–140. This list of eminent thinkers and writers is hardly exhaustive. I include it here not only as evidence of the pervasive fascination with Antigone, but also because this chapter was, in some sense, motivated by my frustration with the way in which this tradition bears within it certain (often unspoken) assumptions about the gendering of mourning. At the risk of sounding too cryptic (as I cannot develop this idea here), I have never been entirely convinced (in spite of appearances) that Antigone functions as a *feminine* figure.

3. Sophocles, *Electra*, in *The Complete Plays of Sophocles*, ed. Moses Hadas, trans. Richard Claverhouse Jebb (New York: Bantam Books, 1967), 37–74; Euripides, "Electra," in *Ten Plays*, trans. Moses Hadas and John McLean (New York: Bantam Books, 1960), 205–240; Aeschylus, *The Oresteia*, trans. Robert Fagles (New York: Penguin Classics, 1984).

4. There are numerous references to Niobe throughout classical texts. For a superb discussion of Niobe's importance in the ancient world, see Nicole Loraux, *Mothers in Mourning*, trans. Corinne Pache (Ithaca, N.Y.: Cornell University Press, 1998). Nicole Loraux's subtle and important work was a major source of inspiration for this chapter.

5. Nicole Loraux has devoted a good deal of work to this topic. In particular, see *Mothers in Mourning and Tragic Ways of Killing a Woman*, trans. Anthony Forster (Cambridge, Mass.: Harvard University Press, 1987).

6. In *Tragic Ways of Killing a Woman*, Loraux writes: "Not all Athenian women died in their beds, but it was always left to the husband, or at least to the family, to preserve the memory of the dead woman. At the level of social expectations, the city, in effect, had no comment to make on a woman's death, even if she was as perfect as she could be. . . . The glory of a woman was to have no glory. . . . The death of a wife simply drew to a close a life of love and devotion,

of good humor and discretion, and a husband would know, afterward, how "to speak very well" of that life (2–3).

7. I am thinking here primarily of the following: Juliet Mitchell, *Psychoanalysis and Feminism* (New York: Pantheon, 1974); Juliet Mitchell, "Introduction I," *Feminine Sexuality: Jacques Lacan and the École Freudienne*, trans. Jacqueline Rose (New York: Norton, 1982); Jacqueline Rose, *Sexuality in the Field of Vision* (London: Verso, 1986); Jane Gallop, *The Daughter's Seduction: Feminism and Psychoanalysis* (Ithaca, N.Y.: Cornell University Press, 1982); *Between Feminism and Psychoanalysis*, ed. Theresa Brennan (New York and London: Routledge, 1989); *Feminism and Psychoanalysis*, ed. Richard Feldstein and Judith Roof (Ithaca, N.Y.: Cornell University Press, 1989); Luce Irigaray, *Speculum of the Other Woman*, trans. Gillian C. Gill (Ithaca, N.Y.: Cornell University Press, 1983); Luce Irigaray, *This Sex Which Is Not One*, trans. Catherine Porter and Carolyn Burke (Ithaca, N.Y.: Cornell University Press, 1985); Hélène Cixous and Catherine Clément, *The Newly Born Woman*, trans. Betsy Wing (Minneapolis: University of Minnesota Press, 1986); Elizabeth Grosz, *Jacques Lacan: A Feminist Introduction* (New York: Routledge, 1990); Sarah Kofman, *The Enigma of Woman: Woman in Freud's Writings*, trans. Catherine Porter (Ithaca, N.Y.: Cornell University Press, 1985).

8. In this context, see *In Dora's Case: Freud—Hysteria—Feminism*, ed. Charles Bernheimer and Claire Kahane (Ithaca, N.Y.: Cornell University Press, 1985); *Diacritics* 12, no. 2 (Summer 1982); Hélène Cixous, *Portrait de Dora* (Paris: Des Femmes, 1976); Monique David-Ménard, *Hysteria from Freud to Lacan: Body and Language in Psychoanalysis*, trans. Catherine Porter (Ithaca, N.Y.: Cornell University Press, 1989); Parveen Adams, *The Emptiness of the Image: Psychoanalysis and Sexual Difference* (New York: Routledge, 1996).

9. In addition to the texts by Sarah Kofman and Luce Irigaray cited earlier, see Shoshana Felman, *What Does a Woman Want? Reading and Sexual Difference* (Baltimore: Johns Hopkins University Press, 1993).

10. Here I would like to acknowledge the important work by Madelon Sprengnether. See in particular her book *The Spectral Mother: Freud, Feminism, and Psychoanalysis* (Ithaca, N.Y.: Cornell University Press, 1990.) I am also thinking here about much of the work done by and on Julia Kristeva. See, in particular, Julia Kristeva, *Powers of Horror: An Essay on Abjection*, Trans. Leon S. Roudiez (New York: Columbia University Press, 1982) and *Black Sun: Depression and Melancholia*, trans. Leon S. Roudiez (New York: Columbia University Press, 1989). On Kristeva, see Kelly Oliver, *Reading Kristeva: Unraveling the Double-Bind* (Bloomington: Indiana University Press, 1993) and the essays in *Ethics, Politics, and Difference in Julia Kristeva's Writing*, ed. Kelly Oliver and Ewa Ziarek (New York: Routledge, 1993).

11. Janine Chasseguet-Smirgel, "Woman's Social Status as a Reflection of the Internal Relationship to Mother and Father in Both Sexes," *International Forum of Psychoanalysis* (1993): 28.

12. Freud's writings on the figure of the mother traverse his writings from the early work up till the end. However, the mother is most often associated with death, the uncanny, *déjà vu*, and literature. In *the Interpretation of Dreams*, for example, Freud recounts a powerful dream (known as the dream of the "three fates"), in relation to which he recounts the following resonant memory of his own mother teaching him about life returning to death through the act of making dumplings: "When I was six years old and was given my first lessons by my mother, I was expected to believe that we were all made of earth and must therefore return to earth. This did not suit me and I expressed some doubts about the doctrine. My mother thereupon rubbed the palms of her hands together—just as she did making dumplings, except that there was no dough between them—and showed me the blackish scales of epidermis produced by the friction as a proof that we were made of earth. My astonishment at this demonstration knew no bounds and I acquiesced in the belief which I was later to hear expressed in the words: '*Du bist der Natur einen Tod schuldig*' [Thou owest God a death]." *The Interpretation of Dreams*, in *The Standard Edition of the Complete Psychological Works of Sigmund Freud* (hereafter *SE*), trans. James Strachey (London: Hogarth Press, 1966), 4:205.

13. See Jean-Pierre Vernant, "Figures féminines de la mort en Grèce," In *L'individu, la mort, l'amour: Soi-même et l'autre en Grèce ancienne* (Paris: Gallimard, 1989), 131–152.

14. There have been hundreds of references to the "Courjault affair" in newspapers and blogs since the events took place. Virtually every newspaper in Europe (as well as others around the world) published a version of the story. Numerous "experts" have been consulted by the media for their views on the case. One of these experts is Sophie Marinopoulos, author of the book *Dans l'intime des mères* (Paris: Fayard, 2005). Marinopoulos has also published a fictional essay (based on her clinical encounters with women who have killed and abandoned their children) entitled *La vie ordinaire d'une mère meurtrière* (Paris: Fayard, 2008). In an interesting further twist, the illegitimate daughter of former President François Mitterand, Mazarine Pingeot, has also written a novel (*Le cimetière des poupées*) inspired by the case. Finally, it appears that the Courjault case is not particularly unusual. Another shocking case of "freezer babies" surfaced in France in August 2007. In May 2008, three babies were found in a freezer in Wenden, Germany. Since the Courjault affair surfaced, many similar cases have been reported throughout Europe. Curiously, in each case, the babies are strangled after birth, put in a plastic bag, and then put in the freezer.

15. Freud, *SE*, 5:354.

16. Jacques Derrida has discussed this point in "To Speculate—On Freud" in *The Post Card: From Socrates to Freud and Beyond*, trans. Alan Bass (Chicago: University of Chicago Press, 1987), 357–409. On Freud and death, see also Adrian Johnston, "Intimations of Freudian Mortality: The Enigma of Sexuality and the Constitutive Blind Spots of Freud's Self-Analysis," *Journal for Lacanian Studies* 3, no. 2 (2005): 222–246.

17. Freud, *SE*, 14:289.

18. Ibid., 13:142.

19. Here one thinks immediately of Luce Irigaray's famous claim concerning Freud's erasure of a more primal murder of the mother in "Body Against Body: In Relation to the Mother," in *Sexes and Genealogies*, trans. Gillian C. Gill (New York: Columbia University Press, 1993), 7–21. See also Emily Zakin, "Beyond the Sexual Contract: Traversing the Fantasy of Fraternal Alliance," in *Between the Psyche and the Social: Psychoanalytic Social Theory*, ed. Steve Edwin, Kelly Oliver, and Emily Zakin (Lanham, Md.: Rowman & Littlefield, 2002), 159–183.

20. For a more extended discussion of this question, see Chapter 3.

21. Freud, *SE*, 13:126–127.

22. Ibid., 127–128.

23. For a more extended discussion of this point, see Chapter 4.

24. I refer to two of Freud's most famous case histories. For "Rat Man," see "Notes Upon A Case of Obsessional Neurosis," *SE*, 10:151–249, and for "Wolf Man," see "From the History of an Infantile Neurosis," *SE*, 17:3–124. For powerful readings of the relationship between crypts and dead siblings in Freud's case histories, see, in particular, Laurence A. Rickels, *Aberrations of Mourning: Writing on German Crypts* (Detroit: Wayne State University Press, 1988). Writing about the Rat Man, Rickels remarks, "When the sister died, her brother, now carrion bird, consumed the rat he henceforth carried inside. In *Totem and Taboo* Freud refers to a certain Indian tribe in California which preserves the skin and feathers of the buzzard it murders and mourns. Birds do not die; their skin and feathers are stuffed by that which they animate and cover over. . . . Like Wolfman in Abraham and Torok's reading, Ratman was another corpse carrier who found shelter within Freudian analysis" (166–167). For rich work on crypts, the maternal body and the motif of dead siblings, see also Avital Ronell, *The Telephone Book: Technology—Schizophrenia—Electric Speech* (Lincoln: University of Nebraska Press, 1989) and *Finitude's Score: Essays for the End of the Millennium* (Lincoln: University of Nebraska Press, 1994).

25. See Nicolas Abraham and Maria Torok, *The Wolf Man's Magic Word: A Cryptonymy*, trans. Nicholas Rand (Minneapolis: University of Minnesota Press, 1986), and Nicolas Abraham and Maria Torok, *The Shell and the*

Kernel, ed. and trans. Nicholas Rand (Chicago: University of Chicago Press, 1994).

26. Abraham and Torok, *The Shell and the Kernel*, 130.
27. Ibid., 128.
28. Freud, *SE*, 13:116.
29. Ibid., 118.
30. Respectively, *SE*, 12:289–301; 17:217–256; and 18:273–274.
31. Freud ascribes uncanny powers to the figure of the maternal body in *Dream-Work*. In Chapter 9, I discuss how Freud implicitly associates the uncanny properties of the maternal body to photography through a reading of this famous passage from *The Interpretation of Dreams*: "In some dreams of landscapes and other localities emphasis is laid in the dream itself on a convinced feeling of having been there once before. (Occurrences of *déjà vu* in dreams have a special meaning.) These places are invariably the genitals of the dreamer's mother; there is indeed no other place about which one can assert with such conviction that one has been there once before" (*SE*, 5:399).
32. Freud, *SE*, 17:244.
33. Ibid., 12:292.
34. Ibid., 299.
35. Ibid., 301.
36. Ibid.

2. MOURNING, MAGIC, AND TELEPATHY

1. Jacques Derrida, "*Fors*: Les mots anglés de Nicolas Abraham et Maria Torok," in *Cryptonymie: Le verbier de l'homme aux loups* (Paris: Aubier Flammarion, 1976), 7–73. For the English translation of this text, see "*Fors*: The Anglish Words of Nicolas Abraham and Maria Torok," trans. Barbara Johnson, in *The Wolf Man's Magic Word: A Cryptonymy* (Minneapolis: University of Minnesota Press, 1986), xi–xlviii. All subsequent references to "*Fors*" will be to the English translation. See also Jacques Derrida, *Glas*, trans. John P. Leavey Jr. and Richard Rand (Lincoln: University of Nebraska Press, 1986), and *The Truth in Painting*, trans. Geoff Bennington and Ian McLeod (Chicago: University of Chicago Press, 1987).
2. Jacques Derrida, "*Ja*, or the *Faux-Bond*," in *Points: Interviews, 1974–1994*, ed. Elisabeth Weber (Stanford, Calif.: Stanford University Press, 1995), 48.
3. Jacques Derrida, *Specters of Marx: The State of the Debt, the Work of Mourning and the New International*, trans. Peggy Kamuf (New York: Routledge, 1994), 97.
4. Jacques Derrida, "Freud and the Scene of Writing," in *Writing and Difference*, trans. Alan Bass (Chicago: University of Chicago Press, 1978),

196–231; "The Double Session," in *Dissemination*, trans. Barbara Johnson (Chicago: University of Chicago Press, 1981), 173–285; "La parole soufflée," in *Writing and Difference*, 169–195; "The Theater of Cruelty and the Closure of Representation," ibid., 232–250.

5. Derrida refers to a number of works by Nicolas Abraham and Maria Torok. Most often, he invokes *The Wolf Man's Magic Word: A Cryptonymy*, trans. Nicholas Rand (Minneapolis: University of Minnesota Press, 1986) and the essays in *The Shell and the Kernel*, ed. and trans. Nicholas Rand (Chicago: University of Chicago Press, 1994). However, as this essay argues, there are significant differences between the English translation of the *Wolf Man's Magic Word* and the original French text. See also *Cryptonymie*. All further references to these texts are to the English translations indicated here.

6. Jacques Derrida, *The Post Card: From Socrates to Plato and Beyond*, trans. Alan Bass (Chicago: University of Chicago Press, 1987); "Circumfession," in *Jacques Derrida*, trans. Geoffrey Bennington (Chicago: University of Chicago Press, 1993); *Memoires: For Paul de Man*, trans. Cecile Lindsay, Jonathan Culler, and Eduardo Cadava (New York: Columbia University Press, 1986); *Aporias: Dying—Awaiting (One Another at) the Limits of Truth*, trans. Thomas Dutoit (Stanford, Calif.: Stanford University Press, 1993); "Faith and Knowledge: The Two Sources of 'Religion' at the Limits of Reason Alone," trans. Samuel Weber, in *Religion*, ed. Jacques Derrida and Gianni Vattimo (Stanford, Calif.: Stanford University Press), 1–78; *Points: Interviews*, 1974–1994, ed. Elisabeth Weber (Stanford, Calif.: Stanford University Press, 1995).

7. Derrida, *Points*, 321.

8. For an excellent discussion of the crypt in Abraham and Torok's work, see Peggy Kamuf, "Abraham's Wake," *Diacritics* (March 1979): 32–43. See also J. Hillis Miller's discussion of the topography of the crypt: "Derrida's Topographies," *South Atlantic Review* 59, no. 1 (January 1994): 1–25. See also Esther Rashkin's extensive writings on the crypt, literature, and intergenerational trauma in *Family Secrets and the Psychoanalysis of Narrative* (Princeton, N.J.: Princeton University Press, 1992) and *Unspeakable Secrets and the Psychoanalysis of Culture* (Albany: State University of New York Press, 2008).

9. Derrida, "*Fors*," xvi.

10. Sigmund Freud, "Mourning and Melancholia," in *Standard Edition of the Works of Sigmund Freud*, ed. Ernest Jones (London: Hogarth Press, 1966), 14:237–258.

11. Nicolas Abraham and Maria Torok, "Mourning or Melancholia: Introjection *versus* Incorporation," in *The Shell and the Kernel*, 125–138.

12. Ibid., 127.

13. Derrida, "*Fors*," xvii.

14. Ibid.

15. Ibid., xxvi.

16. Ibid., xxv.

17. See, in particular, Derrida's discussion of Freud's "Animism, Magic, and the Omnipotence of Thoughts," in *H.C. for Life, That Is to Say*, trans. Laurent Milesi (Stanford, Calif.: Stanford University Press, 2006), 108–122.

18. Jacques Derrida, "Telepathy," trans. Nicholas Royle, in *Psyche: Inventions of the Other*, *Volume* 1, ed. Peggy Kamuf and Elizabeth Rottenberg (Stanford, Calif.: Stanford University Press, 2007), 226–261; Derrida, "My Chances/Mes Chances: A Rendezvous with Some Epicurean Stereophonies," trans. Irene Harvey and Avital Ronell, in ibid., 344–376.

19. Jacques Derrida, "Me—Psychoanalysis," trans. Richard Klein, in ibid., 129–142; "'Geopsychoanalysis' and the Rest of the World," trans. Peggy Kamuf, in ibid., 318–343.

20. Maria Torok, "Afterword: What is Occult in Occultism? Between Sigmund Freud and Sergei Pankeiev Wolf Man," in *The Wolf Man's Magic Word*, 84–106.

21. Sigmund Freud, "Dreams and Occultism," *SE*, 22:31–56.

22. Nicholas Royle calls attention to the importance of thinking about telepathy through the logic of the foreign body in his reading of Derrida's "Telepathy": "Rather than conceiving telepathy as something supplementary, something added on to the experience of a subject, Derrida situates it in accordance with the logic of the foreign body, as being at once outside-the-subject and at the very heart of the subject." See "The Remains of Psychoanalysis (i): Telepathy," in *After Derrida* (Manchester: Manchester University Press, 1995), 72. For an interesting discussion of the figure of the foreign body in Freud, see Elizabeth Rottenberg, "The Resistance to Interpretation," *Philosophy Today* 50 (2006): 83–89.

23. Torok, "Afterword," 86.

24. Jacques Derrida, *Given Time: I. Counterfeit Money*, trans. Peggy Kamuf (Chicago: University of Chicago Press, 1992), 152.

25. "Télépathie" was first published in *Furor* 2 (1981). It was then republished in *Confrontations* 10 (1983) before being collected into *Psyché: Inventions de l'autre* (Paris: Galilée, 1987), 237–270.

26. Derrida, "Telepathy," 360–361.

27. This telepathic connection was originally detected by Derrida's translator, Nicholas Royle, who adds a translator's note to Derrida's question, "Who is Mr. P?" that refers Derrida's readers to Torok's "Afterword." I would like to take this opportunity to refer readers once again to Royle's own hilarious reading of Derrida's "Telepathy" in his book *After Derrida*. Here, as elsewhere throughout his extensive body of work on telepathy and the uncanny, Royle shows just how funny the magic of telepathy can be. See, in particular,

After Derrida (Manchester: Manchester University Press, 1995) and *The Uncanny* (Manchester: Manchester University Press, 2003). See also Sarah Wood's discussion of telepathy, Derrida, and Abraham and Torok in her review of books by Nicholas Royle and Robert Smith, "Let's Start Again," *Diacritics* 29, no. 1 (Spring 1999): 4–19.

28. In his reading of Derrida's "Telepathy," Michael Naas invokes the figure of the source to describe the strange topology of this text. He writes, "One can read 'Telepathy' either as a small part of the oeuvre of Derrida or as the singular place, the point source, in which, telepathically perhaps, a whole tradition—past, present, and future—comes to well up." See "Lacunae: Divining Derrida's Sources Through 'Telepathy,'" in *Taking on the Tradition: Jacques Derrida and the Legacies of Deconstruction* (Stanford, Calif.: Stanford University Press, 2003), 84.

3. THE SEXUAL ANIMAL AND THE PRIMAL SCENE OF BIRTH

1. As elsewhere, all English references to Sigmund Freud are to the *Standard Edition*. References to the German text here are to Sigmund Freud, *Studienausgabe: Zwei Kinderneurosen*, vol. 8 (Frankfurt: S. Fischer Verlag, 1989).

2. See, in particular, Peter Brooks's now classic discussion of the Wolf Man case history as modern literature in "Fictions of the Wolf Man: Freud and Narrative Understanding," in *Reading for the Plot: Desire and Intention in Narrative* (Cambridge, Mass.: Harvard University Press, 1984), 264–285. For other notable readings of Wolf Man, see Cynthia Chase's insightful "Translating the Transference: Psychoanalysis and the Construction of History," in *Telling Facts: History and Narration in Psychoanalysis*, ed. Joseph H. Smith and Humphrey Morris (Baltimore: Johns Hopkins University Press, 1992), 103–126, and Whitney Davis's compelling derivation of Freud's homosexual engagement with the Wolf Man based on the visual media in the case in *Drawing the Dream of Wolves: Homosexuality, Interpretation, and Freud's Wolf Man* (Bloomington: Indiana University Press, 1995). For an exploration of Freud's psychic investment in Wolf Man that draws upon both Abraham and Torok's work and that of Whitney Davis, see Lawrence Johnson, *The Wolf Man's Burden* (Ithaca, N.Y.: Cornell University Press, 2001). For a fascinating philosophical treatment of eating, animal phobias, and the kinship between humans and animals, see Kelly Oliver, "Psychoanalysis as Animal By-Product: Freud's Zoophilia," in *Animal Lessons: How They Teach Us to Be Human* (New York: Columbia University Press, 2009), 247–276.

3. See Muriel Gardiner, *The Wolf-Man by the Wolf-Man* (New York: Basic Books, 1971), and "The Wolf Man's Last Years," *Journal of the American Psychoanalytic Association* 31 (1983): 867–897; Nicolas Abraham and Maria

Torok, *The Wolf Man's Magic Word: A Cryptonymy*, trans. Nicholas Rand (Minneapolis: University of Minnesota Press, 1986). At the very end of his life, the Wolf Man also engaged in a rather strange relationship with a German journalist, Karin Obholzer, who tracked him down and then published her conversations with him in 1980, a year after his death. Karin Obholzer and Sergius Pankejeff, *The Wolf-Man: Conversations with Freud's Patient, Sixty Years Later* (New York: Continuum, 1982). After his death, in 1981, in her "Afterword" to *The Wolf Man's Magic Word*, Maria Torok claims to have uncovered new evidence in the case by arguing that the patient known as Wolf Man is also none other than the person designated as "Mr. P" in Freud's text devoted to telepathy, "Dreams and Occultism." Because Mr. P. is famously an Anglophone (who apparently owned a large library of English books and provided Freud with an English-language copy of Galsworthy's *Forsyte Saga*) whereas Wolf Man (according to the very reliable testimony of Muriel Gardiner) was incapable of reading even his own autobiography when it was first published in Gardiner's English translation, it seems highly unlikely that Mr. P. is the same person as Wolf Man.

4. See Chase, "Translating the Transference," for an excellent discussion of the question of translation in general and this example in particular.

5. Sigmund Freud, "Analysis Terminable and Interminable," in *Standard Edition of the Works of Sigmund Freud*, ed. Ernest Jones (London: Hogarth Press, 1966) (hereafter *SE*), 23:217–218.

6. Freud, *SE*, 17:10.

7. Here it is worth recalling that, as Whitney Davis reports in *Drawing the Dream of the Wolves*, Otto Rank provoked a "minor tempest" (as Davis calls it) in Freud's inner circle by connecting the dream of "six or seven wolves" to the photographs hanging in Freud's consulting room during the treatment. See pages 61–65 for a discussion of this.

8. There are several important exceptions to this claim. Most notably, Gilles Deleuze and Félix Guattari have famously taken up Freud's treatment of the number of the wolves in *Wolf Man*, in "1914: One or Several Wolves," in *A Thousand Plateaus: Capitalism and Schizophrenia*, trans. Brian Massumi (Minneapolis: University of Minnesota Press, 1987), 26–38. See also Gary Genosko, "Freud's Bestiary: How Does Psychoanalysis Treat Animals?" *Psychoanalytic Review* 80, no. 4 (1993): 603–632; Tom Tyler, "The Quiescent Ass and the Dumbstruck Wolf," *Configurations* 14, no. 1 (2008): 9–28. As stated in note 2, Kelly Oliver also devotes considerable attention to the role that animals play in major philosophical and psychoanalytic texts in *Animal Lessons*.

9. In writing this chapter, I have been greatly aware of the monumental contributions of Jean Laplanche concerning the primal scene and, with it, fantasy, seduction, sexuality, and *Nachträglichkeit*. This chapter is deeply

indebted to Laplanche's extended (and constantly evolving) reflections on these questions. In *Essays on Otherness*, for example, he explicitly criticizes his own earlier claims about the *Wolf Man* in the text written with J-B Pontalis, "Fantasy and the Origins of Sexuality." In thinking about the question about the specificity of human sexuality, I have also been greatly helped by Philippe Van Haute and Tomas Geyskens's book *Confusion of Tongues: The Primacy of Sexuality in Freud, Ferenczi, and Laplanche* (New York: Other Press, 2004). I have also been influenced by André Green's recent writings on sexuality. In this context, it is interesting to recall that Jacques Lacan derives his notion of "foreclosure" (repudiation) from Freud's use of the German word "*Verwerfung*" in the Wolf Man. Although not all of following works are addressed explicitly in this chapter, they are all essential to my overall understanding of the *Wolf Man* case history in particular and the ramifications of the primal scene more generally: Jacques Derrida, "*Fors*," in *Cryptonymie: Le verbier de l'homme aux loups* (Paris: Aubier Flammarion, 1976). Derrida's text is translated by Barbara Johnson as "*Fors*: The Anglish Words of Nicolas Abraham and Maria Torok," in *The Wolf Man's Magic Word* (Minneapolis: University of Minnesota Press, 1986). André Green, *Le temps éclaté* (Paris: Editions de Minuit, 2000); Jean Laplanche, *Problematiques* (Paris: Presses Universitaires de France, 1981); Jean Laplanche and J. B. Pontalis, *Vocabulaire de la psychanalyse* (Paris: Presses Universitaires de France, 1973), *The Language of Psycho-Analysis* (New York: Norton, 1974), *Fantasme originaire: Fantasmes des origines, origines du fantasme* (Paris: Hachette Littératures, 1999); Jean Laplanche, *Essays on Otherness*, ed. John Fletcher (New York: Routledge, 1999).

10. Freud, *SE*, 4:127.
11. Ibid., 131–132.
12. Ibid., 17:147.
13. Ibid., 17:36–39. The German is from *Studienausgabe*, 158.
14. Ibid., 20:125–126.
15. Ibid., 103.
16. Ibid., 17:132.
17. Ibid., 40–41.
18. Ibid., 34.
19. Laplanche, *Essays on Otherness*, 170.
20. Freud, *SE*, 17:96.
21. Ibid., 120.

4. BACK OF BEYOND: ANXIETY AND THE BIRTH OF THE FUTURE

1. Jacques Derrida, *The Post Card: From Socrates to Freud and Beyond*, trans. Alan Bass (Chicago: University of Chicago Press, 1987).

2. Cathy Caruth, *Unclaimed Experience: Trauma, Narrative, and History* (Baltimore: Johns Hopkins University Press, 1996).

3. Sigmund Freud, *Beyond the Pleasure Principle*, in *Standard Edition of the Works of Sigmund Freud*, ed. Ernest Jones (London: Hogarth Press, 1966) (hereafter *SE*), 18:12–13.

4. Although, as is well known, the question of anxiety is extremely important in the work of Melanie Klein and Jacques Lacan, this chapter focuses exclusively on Freud's treatment of anxiety.

5. See the following works on *Inhibitions, Symptoms, and Anxiety* for some notable exceptions to this claim: Richard Boothby, *Death and Desire: Psychoanalytic Theory in Lacan's Return to Freud* (New York: Routledge, 1991); André Green, "Conceptions of Affect," *International Journal of Psycho-Analysis* 58 (1977): 129–156; Jean Laplanche, "A Metapsychology Put to the Test of Anxiety," *International Journal of Psychoanalysis* 62 (1981): 81–89, and *Problématiques*, 4 vols. (Paris: Presses Universitaires de France, 1981); Charles Shepherdson, "Introduction," in *Lacan's Seminar on Anxiety: An Introduction* (New York: Other Press, 2001); Samuel Weber, "Metapsychology—Set Apart," in *The Legend of Freud* (Minneapolis: University of Minnesota Press, 1982), 32–60; Weber, "Beyond Anxiety: The Witch's Letter," trans. Michael Levine, in *Return to Freud: Jacques Lacan's Dislocation of Psychoanalysis* (Cambridge: Cambridge University Press, 1991), 152–182; Weber, *Targets of Opportunity: On the Militarization of Thinking* (New York: Fordham University Press), 2005.

6. Laplanche, "A Metapsychology Put to the Test of Anxiety," 81.

7. Sigmund Freud, *Inhibitions, Symptoms, and Anxiety*, in *SE*, 20:93.

8. Ibid., 97.

9. In this context, it is interesting to note that Jacques Derrida calls attention to the political dimension of the organization of the ego as follows in *Rogues*: "What can a bygone psychoanalysis or one that is still to come tell us about democracy? Is there any democracy in the psychic system? And in psychoanalytic institutions? Who votes, what is a vote, or a voice, in the psychic and political system? In the state, in international institutions, including those of psychoanalysis? . . . I can do little more than simply situate these questions, which would no doubt all have to be put to the test of the autoimmune." Jacques Derrida, *Rogues: Two Essays on Reason* (Stanford, Calif.: Stanford University Press, 2005), 55.

10. Freud, *SE*, 20:132.

11. Ibid., 126.

12. Ibid., 130.

13. Ibid., 162.

5. ON PSYCHO-PHOTOGRAPHY: SHAME AND ABU GHRAIB

1. Léon Wurmser, *The Mask of Shame* (Baltimore: Johns Hopkins University Press, 1981), 55.

2. Since April 2004 there have been many important and compelling commentaries and analyses of the photographs. Here I will limit myself only to referencing some of the most influential and/or original texts: Dora Apel, "Torture Culture: Lynching Photographs and the Images of Abu Ghraib," *Art Journal* 64, no. 2 (2005); Hazel Carby, "A Strange and Bitter Crop: The Spectacle of Torture," *Open Democracy: Free Thinking for the World* (2004); Mark Danner, *Torture and Truth: America, Abu Ghraib, and the War on Terror* (New York: New York Review Books, 2004); Seymour M. Hersh, *Chain of Command: The Road from 9/11 to Abu Ghraib* (New York: HarperCollins, 2004); Julia Lesage, "Abu Ghraib Links," *Jump Cut: A Review of Contemporary Media* 47 (2005); Robert Jay Lifton, "Conditions of Atrocity," *The Nation*, May 31, 2004; Frank Rich, "It Was the Porn That Made Them Do It," *New York Times*, May 30, 2004; Luc Sante, "Torturers and Terrorists," *New York Times*, May 11, 2004; Susan Sontag, "Regarding the Torture of Others," *New York Times* May 23, 2004; Slavoj Žižek, "What Rumsfeld Doesn't Know That He Knows About Abu Ghraib," www.inthesetimes.com (2004).

3. From very early on, the Abu Ghraib photographs moved across boundaries. One of the first (and most provocative) "uses" of the photographs was the exhibition (from September 17 to November 28, 2004) curated by Brian Wallis, *Inconvenient Evidence: Iraqi Prison Photographs from Abu Ghraib* (International Center of Photography, 2004). This exhibition was jointly organized by the International Center of Photography and the Andy Warhol Museum. Other discussions of the "iconic" status of the images and/or their appropriation by artists and activists include: Apel, "Torture Culture"; Sarah Boxer, "Backup of Torture Incarnate, and Propped on a Pedestal," *New York Times*, June 13, 2004; Andy Grundberg, "Point and Shoot," *American Scholar* 74, no. 1 (2005); Adrian Kear, "The Anxiety of the Image," *Parallax* 11 (2005); W. J. T. Mitchell, "Echoes of a Christian Symbol: Photo Reverberates with Raw Power of Christ on Cross," *Chicago Tribune*, June 27, 2004; Rich, "It Was the Porn That Made Them Do It"; Abigail Solomon-Godeau, "On the Image Wars," *Artforum* 2004; Sontag, "Regarding the Torture of Others."

4. See Joan Walsh, *The Abu Ghraib Files*, 2006: http://www.salon.com/news/abu_ghraib/2006/03/14/introduction/.

5. Reed Brody, *The Road to Abu Ghraib* (New York: Human Rights Watch, 2004).

6. Hersh, *Chain of Command*, 25.

7. Robert F. Drinan, *The Mobilization of Shame: A World View of Human Rights* (New Haven: Yale University Press, 2001). See also Thomas Keenan, "Mobilizing Shame," *South Atlantic Quarterly* 103 (Spring–Summer 2004).

8. Hersh, *Chain of Command*, 43.

9. Danner, *Torture and Truth*, xiii.

10. Hersh, *Chain of Command*, 25.

11. This point is in explicit conversation with Linda Williams. See Linda Williams, "Corporealized Observers: Visual Pornographies and the 'Carnal Destiny of Vision,'" *Fugitive Images: From Photography to Video*, ed. Patrice Petro (Bloomington: Indiana University Press, 1995).

12. Antonio M. Taguba and National Public Radio (U.S.), *Article* 15–6 *Investigation of the* 800*th Military Police Brigade* (2004). The "Taguba Report" is also reprinted in Danner, *Torture and Truth*.

13. Ibid., 416.

14. Wurmser, *The Mask of Shame*, 55.

15. Hersh, *Chain of Command*, 38–39.

16. For some critics, the fact that young women were so heavily implicated in the torture and abuse is a defining aspect of the Abu Ghraib photographs. For a compelling treatment of the place of sexuality and sexual difference in understanding the Abu Ghraib photographs, see Kelly Oliver, *Women as Weapons of War: Iraq, Sex, and the Media* (New York: Columbia University Press, 2007).

17. Apel, "Torture Culture," 93.

6. AVITAL RONELL'S BODY POLITICS

1. Avital Ronell, *The Telephone Book: Technology—Schizophrenia—Electric Speech* (Lincoln: University of Nebraska Press, 1989).

2. Avital Ronell, *Finitude's Score: Essays for the End of the Millennium* (Lincoln: University of Nebraska Press, 1994).

3. Ronell, *The Telephone Book*, 115–116.

4. Ronell herself glosses this important passage in Freud in several different ways in *The Telephone Book*. In particular, however, she performs a complex and extraordinary reading of unconscious transmission and its relationship to "organ function" within psychoanalysis in pages 99–106. She writes, for example:

> To tie up some of these loosened wires, it is useful to note that the question of sight-retreat and of unconscious transmissions is articulated in psychoanalysis in terms of citing a telephonics, that is in terms of putting through calls from the unconscious, always subject to being cut off. (99)

> Freud claims that vision can be disrupted by something like an internally punishing voice. The voice gets the upper hand, shutting down visual apprehension, when the eye is felt to be abusing its "organ of sight for evil, sensual pleasures." (100)
>
> The extent to which the telephone feeds into the psychogenic disturbance of which Freud writes, or in fact simulates it, needs to be seriously considered. Understanding the organ as such, in its singular unity, still needs to be determined. But the kind of organ which the telephone duplicates, replaces or protects may itself be subject to multiple displacements (psychoanalysis has argued convincingly for the symbolic exchangeability of anus and ear, for instance). If by this logic, the telephone begins to behave like "an actual genital," we may be opening the shutters on the scandal which accompanied its conception. (104–105)

I have unfortunately been compelled to simplify this discussion in the interests of expository clarity. I urge the reader to consult her texts in order to appreciate how profoundly the richness of her thought is embedded in the poetic density of her writing.

5. For this discussion concerning the openness of the ear, see Jacques Lacan, *The Four Fundamental Concepts of Psycho-Analysis* (London: Hogarth Press, 1977).

6. Ronell, *The Telephone Book*, 193; *Finitude's Score*, 241.

7. The expression comes, of course, from Jacques Derrida. See *The Ear of the Other: Otobiography, Transference, Translation: Texts and Discussions with Jacques Derrida*, ed. Christine McDonald (New York: Schocken Books, 1985).

8. Ronell, *The Telephone Book*, 13.

9. Ibid., 193–194.

10. Ibid., 340.

11. Ibid., 334–345.

12. Ibid., 4.

13. Ibid., 144.

14. Ibid., 341.

15. For an important study on technology and failed mourning, see Laurence A. Rickels, *Aberrations of Mourning: Writing on German Crypts* (Detroit: Wayne State University Press, 1988).

16. Sigmund Freud, "Mourning and Melancholia," *The Standard Edition of the Complete Psychological Works of Sigmund Freud* (London: Hogarth Press, 1944), 14:249–50.

17. See, for example, Janine Chasseguet-Smirgel, *Creativity and Perversion* (New York: Norton, 1984), and "Altglas, Altpapier (Empty Bottles, Waste Paper): Reflections on Certain Disorders of the Superego in Relation to

Houseproud Mothers," *Psychoanalytic Inquiry* 11 (1991): 537–558; Arlene Kramer Richards, "A Romance with Pain: A Telephone Perversion in a Woman?" *International Journal of Psychoanalysis* 70 (1989): 153–164; and Leonard Shengold, "The Symbol of Telephoning," *Journal of the American Psychoanalytical Association* 30 (1982): 461–470.

18. Shengold, "The Symbol of Telephoning," 466.

19. Ibid., 465.

20. Chasseguet-Smirgel, "Altglas, Altpapier," 554.

21. Ronell, *The Telephone Book*, 8.

22. Avital Ronell, *Crack Wars: Literature Addiction Mania* (Lincoln: University of Nebraska Press, 1992), 118–119.

23. For a more detailed engagement with *Madame Bovary* in relation to questions of time and addiction, see my book *Dead Time: Temporal Disorders in the Wake of Modernity (Baudelaire and Flaubert)* (Stanford, Calif.: Stanford University Press, 2001).

24. Ronell, *Crack Wars*, 122.

25. Ibid., 125.

26. Ibid., 106.

27. Jacques Derrida, "The Rhetoric of Drugs," trans. Michael Israel, in *Points*, ed. Elisabeth Weber (Stanford: Stanford University Press, 1995), 228–254.

28. Ronell, *Crack Wars*, 52.

29. Ronell, *Finitude's Score*, 221.

30. Ibid., 210–211.

31. Ibid., 207.

32. Ibid., 300.

7. *BLADE RUNNER*'S MOVING STILL

1. See Guiliana Bruno, "Ramble City: Postmodernism and *Blade Runner*," *October* 41 (Summer 1987): 61–74, and David Harvey, "Time and Space in Postmodern Cinema," in *The Condition of Postmodernity* (Oxford: Basil Blackwell, 1989), 308–323, for their discussions of *Blade Runner* as an example of cinematic postmodernism. While I treat much of the same textual material as Bruno and Harvey, my reading emphasizes *Blade Runner*'s cinematic critique of the status of the human subject. Along different lines, see Constance Penley's discussion of *Blade Runner* as an example of a "critical dystopia" in "Time Travel, Primal Scene and the Critical Dystopia (On *The Terminator* and *La Jetée*)," in *The Future of an Illusion: Film, Feminism and Psychoanalysis* (Minneapolis: University of Minnesota Press, 1989), 121–139. For a wonderful development of some of the questions that my article raises concerning gender, subjectivity, and

photography, see Kaja Silverman, "Back to the Future," *Camera Obscura* 27 (September 1991): 109–132.

2. In "Film Aesthetics, Film History and the Idea of a Film Canon," a paper delivered to the Columbia Film Seminar on September 26, 1991, Peter Wollen cited *Blade Runner* as the only (then) current example of a canonical film from the 1980s.

3. Pauline Kael, "Baby, the Rain Must Fall," *New Yorker*, July 12, 1982.

4. Richard Corliss, "The Pleasures of Texture," *Time*, July 12, 1982.

5. Michael Sragow, "*Blade Runner*: Stalking the Alienated Android," *Rolling Stone*, August 5, 1982.

6. Strictly speaking, the Freudian term "primal scene" cannot be used to describe any filmic representation because, as we have repeatedly said, the primal scene is an event that cannot be represented. But because Freud's account of the Wolf Man case history provides a model for the human subject that is constituted as a knot of memory, sexual difference, and fantasmatic identification with nonhuman figures, the notion of the primal scene enables us to interrogate *Blade Runner*'s treatment of primal memories and human subjectivity. For a more detailed account of the photographic nature of the structure of the primal scene, see Chapter 3.

7. Here it should be clear that I am referring to the "original" film (released in 1982) rather than to the "director's cut" released a decade later.

8. Although I do not want to trivialize the complexity and specificity of the issues that surrounded the Rodney King trial and its traumatic aftermath, I would like to point out that *Blade Runner* asks to be read (at least in part) as an allegory of race relations in the United States. Set in a future Los Angeles, the film explicitly refers to the blade runner unit as an elite branch of the Los Angeles Police Department. The police chief's use of the term "skin jobs" (a slang term for replicants) is likened to that of the term "niggers." In the context of the analysis of the "empathy test," it is chilling to note that the defense lawyers in the King trial established a discourse of "inhumanity" (defense lawyers depicted King rhetorically as an "animal" and as having superhuman strength) that relied on temporal manipulations of the videotape (defense lawyers played the tape repeatedly in slow motion to diminish the sense of reality of the photographic image to prove (simultaneously) that King was "in complete control" and that the tape was not an accurate witness to the event. For a brilliant and compelling analysis of the King trial and the use of the tape as witness, see Avital Ronell, "Traumatic TV: Twelve Steps Beyond the Pleasure Principle," in *Finitude's Score: Essays for the End of the Millennium* (Lincoln: University of Nebraska Press, 1994), 305–327.

9. Roland Barthes, "The Rhetoric of the Image," in *Image, Music, Text*, trans. Stephen Heath (New York: Hill & Wang, 1977), 45. In *Camera Lucida*,

Barthes glosses the difference between photography and film as follows: "in the cinema, no doubt, there is always a photographic referent, but this referent shifts, it does not make a claim in favor of its reality, it does not protest its former existence; it does not cling to me: it is not a specter." Barthes, *Camera Lucida*, trans. Richard Howard (New York: Noonday Press, 1981), 89.

10. Ibid., 76.

8. NOTHING TO SAY: FRAGMENTS ON THE MOTHER IN THE AGE OF MECHANICAL REPRODUCTION

1. See Jean-François Lyotard, "Prescription," trans. Christopher Fynsk, in *Toward the Post-Modern*, ed. Robert Harvey and Mark S. Roberts (New Brunswick, N.J.: Humanities Press, 1993), 176–199. In this text, Lyotard treats the relationship between the body and the law through a close reading of Kafka's "In the Penal Colony." Certainly, there is much more to say about the relationship between Barthes's discussion of the body and Lyotard's treatment of the body in this powerful text.

2. I have included references to Barthes text in both French and English where I believe that language of the French text is particularly important. The English quotations are from *Camera Lucida: Reflections of Photography*, trans. Richard Howard (New York: Noonday Press, 1981). The French quotations are from Roland Barthes, *La chambre claire: Note sur la photographie* (Paris: Gallimard, 1980).

3. There is a wealth of critical writings on *La chambre claire*. I have learned from many of the wonderful readings that exist. See, among others, the many excellent articles collected in Jean-Michel Rabaté, ed., *Writing the Image After Roland Barthes* (Philadelphia: University of Pennsylvania Press, 1997); *Fugitive Images: From Photography to Video*, ed. Patrice Petro (Bloomington: Indiana University Press, 1995); *Signs in Culture: Roland Barthes Today*, ed. Steven Ungar and Betty R. McGraw (Iowa City: University of Iowa Press, 1989). See also Timothy Murray's provocative discussion of fetishism and the maternal body in "Photo-Medusa: Roland Barthes Incorporated," in *Like a Film: Ideological Fantasy on Screen, Camera and Canvas* (New York: Routledge, 1993), 65–97.

4. Barthes, *Camera Lucida*, 5–7; *La chambre claire*, 17–19.

5. Jacques Derrida, "The Deaths of Roland Barthes," trans. Pascale-Anne Brault and Michael Naas, in *Psyche: Inventions of the Other, vol.* 1, ed. Peggy Kamuf and Elizabeth Rottenberg (Stanford, Calif.: Stanford University Press, 2007), 284–285.

6. Barthes, *Camera Lucida*, 115; *La chambre claire*, 176.

7. Barthes, *La chambre claire*, 127; *Camera Lucida*, 81.

8. Barthes, *Camera Lucida*, 88.
9. Ibid., 76–77.
10. Ibid., 88–89.
11. Barthes, *Camera Lucida*, 5.
12. Ibid., 81; *La chambre claire*, 126–127.
13. Barthes, *Camera Lucida*, 13–14.
14. Ibid., 10–11.
15. Ibid., 110.
16. Ibid., 11–12; *La chambre claire*, 25–27.

9. DARKROOM READINGS: SCENES OF MATERNAL PHOTOGRAPHY

1. Roland Barthes, *Camera Lucida: Reflections on Photography*, trans. Richard Howard (New York: Noonday Press, Farrar, Strauss and Giroux, 1981), 40. The original French edition is *La chambre claire: Note sur la photographie* (Paris: Gallimard, Seuil, 1980), 66–68. Among the few critics who have discussed the "Alhambra" passage and/or its accompanying image in depth are Nancy Shawcross, Timothy Murray, Diana Knight, and Gordon Hughes. Curiously, as I will discuss later, Jacques Derrida alludes to the passage, almost invokes it, but does not in fact discuss it directly. See Nancy M. Shawcross, "Correspondences: Baudelaire and Barthes," in *Roland Barthes on Photography* (Gainesville: University Press of Florida, 1997), 46–66; Timothy Murray, "Photo-Medusa: Roland Barthes Incorporated," in *Like a Film: Ideological Fantasy on Screen, Camera and Canvas* (New York: Routledge, 1993), 65–97; Diana Knight, "Return Journey: The South-West," in *Barthes and Utopia: Space, Travel, Writing* (Oxford: Clarendon Press, 1997), 219–243; Gordon Hughes, "*Camera Lucida*, Circa 1980," in *Reflections on Roland Barthes's Camera Lucida*, ed. Geoffrey Batchen (Cambridge, Mass.: MIT Press, 2009), 193–209.

2. See Gordon Hughes and Timothy Murray in particular.

3. Unfortunately, Richard Howard's translation of Barthes's caption here is both poetically tone-deaf and grammatically inaccurate. Barthes's caption is an obvious allusion to and rewriting of the central line in Baudelaire's poem "*La vie antérieure*": "*C'est là que j'ai vécu.*" Barthes retains the first part of the citation "*C'est là*" (It is there) but changes the tense of the verb "*vivre*" (to live) from "*passé composé*," which normally denotes completed action in the past time, to the conditional tense. The conditional is often used (as it is here) as a virtual potential reserve for a desired but unrealized and essentially unrealizable future action. Howard's published translation, "I want to live there," transforms the conditional tense into a direct present indicative, thereby removing the entire tension surrounding the temporality of life itself in Barthes's poetically photographed sentence.

4. Sigmund Freud, *The Interpretation of Dreams*, in *Standard Edition of the Works of Sigmund Freud* (London: Hogarth Press, 1966) (hereafter *SE*), 4:277–278.

5. Determining the precise source of the Freud quotation in Barthes's text is actually even more complicated. The French edition of *La chambre claire*, which, unlike the English edition, includes Barthes's bibliographical references in the margins, indicates that Barthes probably does not quote Freud directly. Instead, he copies the Freud quotation from an article by Jean Thibaudeau and Jean-François Chevrier, "Une inquiétante étrangeté," in *Le Nouvel Observateur*, *Spécial Photo* 3 (June 1978): "Qu'est-ce qu'un paysage? Selon Freud, dans les rêves, une représentation des organes génitaux, et au bout du compte du corps maternel, comme lorsque la vision s'accompagne d'un sentiment de 'déjà vu,' 'il n'est point d'autre lieu dont on puisse dire avec d'autant de certitude qu'on y a déjà été,' sentiment composé d'attirance et d'effroi, qu'il nommera l'inquiétante étrangeté." They have combined and collapsed the two Freud texts into one. They have also introduced the notion of attraction and horror here.

6. Freud, *The Interpretation of Dreams*, *SE*, 5:399.

7. For example, in *The Psychopathology of Everyday Life*, he writes: "To put it briefly, the feeling of '*déjà vu*' corresponds to the recollection of an unconscious phantasy." *SE* 6:266. For a compelling discussion of déjà vu in Freud's work, see Nicholas Royle, *The Uncanny* (Manchester: Manchester University Press, 2003), 172–186. In his chapter "Déjà Vu," Royle performs a brilliant analysis of the relationship between the (mostly repressed) figure of déjà vu as it appears in *The Uncanny* essay and its relation to the "landscape dream déjà vu" passage from the *Interpretation of Dreams*. Royle observes: "If, as Freud maintains, 'there is indeed no other place about which one can assert with such conviction that one has been there before,' it may be equally valid to maintain that there is no other place about which one can assert with such conviction that one cannot possibly know what one is talking about in supposing that 'one has been there before'" (181).

8. In their essay "Notes on Love and Photography," in *Photography Degree Zero: Reflections on Roland Barthes's Camera Lucida*, ed. Geoffrey Batchen (Cambridge, Mass.: MIT Press, 2009), 105–140, Eduardo Cadava and Paola Cortés-Rocca also call attention to the mother's body as darkroom. They write: "The condition of possibility for a process of reproduction that gives something to be seen, the mother's body is at once camera, developer, and photographic darkroom. Giving birth to an image, the mother is another name for photography." Cadava and Cortés-Rocca's essay performs a notably loving and affirmative reading of photographic maternal love in Barthes's book. While I admire the virtuosity of many of their insights, I remain somewhat more reticent than

they about the specific range of positive possibilities they accord to Barthes's conception of photographic love, survival, and futurity.

9. Sigmund Freud, "The Uncanny," *SE*, 5:7.

10. Sigmund Freud, "Negation," *SE*, 19:235.

11. Jacques Derrida, "The Deaths of Roland Barthes," trans. Pascale-Anne Brault and Michael Naas, in *Psyche: Inventions of the Other, vol.* 1, ed. Peggy Kamuf and Elizabeth Rottenberg (Stanford, Calif.: Stanford University Press, 2007), 264–298, at 276.

12. Ibid.

13. For a sustained discussion of photography and the maternal function in *Camera Lucida* with a slightly different focus, see Chapter 8.

14. Barthes, *Camera Lucida*, 93.

15. Although this point exceeds the scope of this essay, I would like to remark that throughout Derrida's essay on Barthes as well as in many of his subsequent writings dealing with photography, Derrida often uses language associated with an interrogation of birth (and/or the maternal function) even when ostensibly writing explicitly about death. Thus, for example, in the very recently republished and newly translated *Athens, Still Remains*, Derrida writes about a sentence-phrase, "we owe ourselves to death" (*nous nous devons à la mort*) that comes to him, photographically, "like an original—or a negative without origin." Describing this photographic sentence, he writes: "We owe ourselves to death. This sentence was right away, as we have come to understand it, greater than the instant, whence the desire to photograph it without delay in the noonday sun. . . . An untranslatable sentence (and I was sure from the very first instant that the economy of this sentence belonged to my idiom alone, or rather to the domesticity of my old love affair with this stranger whom I call the French language), a sentence that resists translation, as if one could only photograph it, as if one instantaneously had to take the image by surprise at its birth, immobile, monumental, impassive, singular, abstract, in retreat from all treatment, unreachable in the end by any periphrasis, by any transfer, by rhetoric itself, by the eloquence of transposition." Jacques Derrida, *Athens, Still Remains: The Photographs of Jean-François Bonhomme*, trans. Pascale-Anne Brault and Michael Naas (New York: Fordham University Press, 2010), 13–16.

16. Throughout this chapter, I have also been trying (albeit obliquely) to engage Derrida's writings on photography to help me think about how to understand the specific status of the "unconscious" in Walter Benjamin's famous, but perhaps insufficiently understood, concept of the "optical unconscious." For his most sustained discussion of the "optical unconscious," see Benjamin's 1931 essay "Little History of Photography," In *Selected Writings*, ed. Michael Jennings, Howard Eiland and Gary Smith (Cambridge, Mass.: Harvard University Press, 1999), 2:507–530. Benjamin writes: "For it is another nature

which speaks to the camera rather than to the eye: "other" above all in the sense that a space informed by human unconsciousness gives way to a space informed by the unconscious. Whereas it is a commonplace that, for example, we have some idea what is involved in the act of walking (if only in general terms), we have no idea at all what happens during the fraction of a second when a person actually takes a step. Photography, with its devices of slow motion and enlargement, reveals the secret. It is through photography that we first discover the existence of this optical unconscious, just as we discover the instinctual unconscious though psychoanalysis. Details of structure, cellular tissue, with which technology are normally concerned—all this is, in its origins, more native to the camera than the atmospheric landscape or the soulful portrait. Yet at the same time, photography reveals in this material physiognomic aspects, image worlds, which dwell in the smallest things—meaningful yet covert enough to find a hiding place in waking dreams, but which, enlarged and capable of formulation, make the difference between technology and magic visible as a thoroughly historical variable" (510–512). Although Derrida (and Eduardo Cadava following him) have pointed to the common historical moment that is shared by both psychoanalysis and photography and to the specific analogies that can be established between photography and psychic processes, the specifically historical dimension of a "photographic unconscious" unbound from the notion of a psychological subject still remains to be thought. Derrida refers to Benjamin's writings connecting photography and psychoanalysis on numerous occasions including "The Deaths of Roland Barthes" and *Right of Inspection*, trans. David Wills (New York: Monacelli Press, 1998). For an excellent discussion of this question, see Eduardo Cadava's chapter "Psyches" in *Words of Light*: *Theses on the Photography of History* (Princeton, N.J.: Princeton University Press, 1997), 97–101. Specifically addressing the status of the unconscious, Cadava writes: "The photograph tells us that when we *see* we are unconscious of what our seeing cannot see. In linking, through the photographic event, the possibility of sight to what he calls "the optical unconscious," to what prevents sight from being immediate and present, Benjamin follows Freud, who, in his own efforts to trace the transit between the unconscious and the conscious, often returns to analogies drawn from the technical media, and in particular from photography" (97).

17. Barthes, *Camera Lucida*, 85–87.
18. Ibid.
19. Ibid., 85.
20. Ibid., 82.
21. Ibid., 91.
22. Ibid., 115.
23. Ibid., 116, 118.

24. Ibid., 5–6.

25. From a psychoanalytic perspective (as Barthes knows well) the fascination with an image of the parents prior to one's own birth clearly conjures up the deferred (and implicitly photographic) temporality of the "primal scene:" "*Nachträglichkeit.*" For a discussion of the photographic aspect of the primal scene, see Chapter 3.

26. Barthes, *Camera Lucida*, 65.

27. Ibid., 3.

28. To my knowledge, I am one of the few critics who have called attention to it. See my "Flat Death: Snapshots of History," in *Dead Time: Temporal Disorders in the Wake of Modernity* (Stanford, Calif.: Stanford University Press, 2001), 86.

29. It seems that Barthes inscribes a kind of subliminal narrative about the 1850s—that is, the inaugural period of the Second Empire and the historical period that coincides with the birth of photography. In this context, it is interesting to note that as Diana Knight observes: "'*La Vie antérieure*' and '*L'Invitation au Voyage*' were first published in 1855, which makes them exactly contemporaneous with Clifford's photograph, dated as 1854 in the text, and as '1854–1856' beneath the reproduction." In *Barthes and Utopia: Space, Travel, Writing*, 221.

30. This section of this chapter is loosely based on a text on Cixous and photography that I originally wrote in French for a conference (organized by Marta Segarra) devoted to the work of Hélène Cixous in Paris in 2008. The French conference paper was published as "*Photolectures*" in *Hélène Cixous: Croire Rêver—Arts de Pensée*, ed. Bruno Clément and Marta Segarra (Paris: Editions Campagne première, 2010), 190–199. I would like to thank Geoffrey Bennington for help with the English translation. For a beautiful reading of the figure of "light writing" in Cixous that runs parallel to the one presented here, see Michael Naas, "*Flicker: réflexions à la lumière de sa veilleuse*," in ibid., 169–181.

31. Hélène Cixous, *So Close*, trans. Peggy Kamuf (London : Polity Press, 2009), 3. For the original French edition, see Hélène Cixous, *Si près* (Paris: Galilée, 2007).

32. Cixous, *So Close*, 3.

33. Ibid., 70.

34. Ibid.; *Si près*, 99.

35. *So Close*, 45; *Si près*, 66.

36. These quotations are from *So Close*, 48.

37. Ibid., 5.

38. Ibid., 2–3.

39. Ibid., 71.

40. Hélène Cixous, *Osnabrück* (Paris: Des femmes, 1999), 37. My translation.

41. Over the last several years, there has been a veritable explosion of interest in Proust and photography. Here it bears mentioning that in Roland Barthes's posthumously published seminar *La préparation du roman* (Paris: Editions du Seuil, 2003), Barthes includes a section called "*Proust et la Photographie*." For a discussion of this final seminar, see Kathrin Yacavone, "Reading Through Photography: Roland Barthes's Last Seminar 'Proust et la Photographie,'" *French Forum* 34, no. 1 (Winter 2009): 97–112. Among the many recent critics who have been working on Proust and Photography (or photographic issues in Proust) see, in particular, Mieke Bal, *The Mottled Screen: Reading Proust Visually*, trans. Anna Louise Milne (Stanford, Calif.: Stanford University Press, 1997), and Elena Gualtieri, "Bored by Photographs: Proust in Venice," in *Photography and Literature in the Twentieth Century*, ed. David Cunningham, Andrew Fisher, and Sas Mays (Newcastle: Cambridge Scholars Publishing, 2005), 25–41.

42. Hélène Cixous, *Benjamin à Montaigne: Il ne faut pas le dire* (Paris: Galilée, 2001), 78–84. The translations are mine, with the help of Geoffrey Bennington.

43. Hélène Cixous, *Reveries of the Wild Woman: Primal Scenes*, trans. Beverley Bie Brahic (Evanston, Ill.: Northwestern University Press, 2006), 84.

44. Hélène Cixous, *Manhattan: Letters from Prehistory, trans. Beverley Bie Brahic* (New York: Fordham University Press, 2007), 112.

45. Cixous, *Benjamin à Montaigne*, 137–138.

46. Ibid., 138.

47. As Derrida points out in "Freud and the Scene of Writing," Freud often invokes photography to describe the relationship between conscious and unconscious processes. See Jacques Derrida, "Freud and the Scene of Writing," in *Writing and Difference*, trans. Alan Bass (Chicago: University of Chicago Press, 1978), 196–231. Derrida cites Freud from "A Note on the Unconscious in Psycho-Analysis (1912)" where Freud writes: "A rough but not inadequate analogy to this supposed relation of conscious to unconscious activity might be drawn from the field of ordinary photography. The first stage of the photograph is the 'negative' every photograph picture has to pass through the 'negative process': and some of these negatives which have held good in examination are admitted to the 'positive process' ending in the picture" (*SE*, 12:264).

48. Hélène Cixous, *L'amour du loup et autres remords* (Paris: Galilée, 2003), 143. My translation.

10. THE MOTHER TONGUE IN *PHÈDRE* AND *FRANKENSTEIN*

1. Racine, *Phèdre*, in *Oeuvres complètes* (Paris: Editions du Seuil, 1962), ll. 249–50. All subsequent quotations refer to this edition, and all line numbers

will be indicated in the text. English translations are my modified versions of *Phèdre*, trans. Margaret Rawlings (New York: Dutton, 1962).

2. Phèdre begins her confession by veiling it as a declaration of love for Theseus: "*Oui, Prince, je languis, je brûle pour Thésée*" (634) ("Yes, Prince, I am languishing, I am burning for Theseus").

3. Barbara Johnson, "My Monster/My Self," in *A World of Difference* (Baltimore: Johns Hopkins University Press, 1987), 151. This text, an earlier version of which appeared in *Diacritics* (Summer 1982), was a major source of inspiration for me. Although Johnson does not explicitly address the mother figures in *Frankenstein*, the implications of her argument led me to begin to ponder the relationship between maternity, monstrosity, and desire.

4. Mary Shelley, *Frankenstein; Or the Modern Prometheus* (New York: New American Library, 1965), vii–xii.

5. See also Margaret Homans, *Bearing the Word: Language and Female Experience in Nineteenth-Century Women's Writing* (Chicago: University of Chicago Press, 1986), 100–119. In some ways, Homans's analysis of the circumvention of the mother runs parallel to the analysis presented here; however, Homans locates desire exclusively in the character of Frankenstein and therefore in a fictive representation of male sexuality. This and other differences of emphasis lead our analyses to somewhat different conclusions, although I find her discussion of the question of literalization extremely suggestive.

6. Sharon Willis has reminded me that the term "immaculate conception" refers to the fact that Mary herself was conceived outside of original sin. It is worth noting that it is not sufficient for there to be a "virgin birth"—the mother herself must be purified of the implicit sin received by her mother.

7. Shelley, *Frankenstein*, 118–119.

8. The relationship, both biographical and textual, between Mary Shelley and her mother, Mary Wollstonecraft, is too complex to be fully explored here. However, we might point out that *Frankenstein* can be read, in its entirety, as both a rewriting and an effacement of Wollstonecraft's *Maria or the Wrongs of Women*. Both of these books are explicitly described as "horror stories"; Frankenstein is a horror tale in which mother/daughter relationships are effaced, whereas Maria delineates the horror that surrounds mother/daughter relationships because of socially repressive conditions for women. In the opening pages, Maria, a woman abused and enslaved by her husband, laments both the loss of her child and the fact that she is a girl. "Still she mourned for her child, lamented she was a daughter, and anticipated the aggravated ills of life that her sex rendered almost inevitable, even while dreading she was no more." Mary Wollstonecraft, *Maria or the Wrongs of Women* (New York: Norton, 1975), 23–24.

9. Shelley, *Frankenstein*, 70.

10. It is interesting to note that in Percy Shelley's preface to *Frankenstein*, he, unlike Mary, does not specify in which language the stories were read: "We . . . occasionally amused ourselves with some German stories of ghosts which happened to fall into our hands."

11. Shelley, *Frankenstein*, 112.

12. David Marshall has written an extraordinary chapter in his book *The Surprising Effects of Sympathy: Marivaux, Diderot, Rousseau and Mary Shelley* (Chicago: University of Chicago Press, 1988), in which he points out that large portions of the monster's "autobiography" are very nearly line-by-line translations of Rousseau's *Rêveries* into English. The difference that emerges between these "autobiographies" is precisely one of translation—for the monster, "autobiography" exists only as translation.

13. Shelley, *Frankenstein*, 113.

14. Ibid., 122.

15. When he reads Plutarch, Racine's historical "authority," the monster displays distaste for the story of Theseus: "I felt the greatest ardour for virtue rise within me, and abhorrence for vice, as far as I understood the signification of those terms. . . . Induced by these feelings, I was of course led to admire peaceable lawgivers, Numa, Solon, and Lycurgus, in preference to Romulus and Theseus." Is Theseus's "vice" that he kills monsters?

16. Shelley, *Frankenstein*, 107.

17. Ibid., 35; emphasis mine.

18. Ibid., 136.

19. Ibid., 137.

20. Ibid.

11. BIRTHMARKS (GIVEN NAMES)

1. Hélène Cixous, *L'amour du loup et autres remords* (Paris: Galilée, 2003), 94; Hélène Cixous, *Stigmata: Escaping Texts*, trans. Eric Prenowitz et al. (New York: Routledge, 1998), 147.

2. Here it bears remarking that the utterance "*il faut que*" demands careful reading throughout Cixous's works. It is no accident, for example, that in the early, famous (and often poorly read text) "Le rire de la Méduse," Cixous opens her call for the invention of "*l'écriture feminine*" by invoking the imperative, affirmative and positive force of this neutral (and unconjugatable) verbal "command" as a means of contesting the oppressive legacy of patriarchal law. The nuanced implications of this opening incantation to "Le rire de la Méduse" have, unfortunately, been lost in translation. Perhaps it is time to return to the French version of this text. See Hélène Cixous, "*Le rire de la*

Méduse," in *L'arc: Simone de Beauvoir et la lutte des femmes* (Marseille: Arc, 1975), 39–54.

3. Cixous, *L'amour de loup*, 84; *Stigmata*, 141–142.

4. Cixous, *L'amour de loup*, 96; *Stigmata*, 148.

5. Hélène Cixous, *OR: Les lettres de mon père* (Paris: Des femmes, 1997), 21; my translation.

6. Hélène Cixous, "De la scène de l'inconscient à la scène de l'Histoire," in *Hélène Cixous: Chemins d'une écriture*, ed. Françoise van Rossum-Guyon and Myriam Díaz-Diocaretz (Paris: Presses Universitaires de Vincennes, 1990), 16. Many of Cixous's most attentive readers have written about the importance of names in her work. See, for example, Mireille Calle-Gruber, "Hélène Cixous's Imaginary Cities: Oran-Osnabrück-Manhattan-Places of Fascination, Places of Fiction," *New Literary History: A Journal of Theory and Interpretation* 37, no. 1 (2006) 135-145; Mairéad Hanrahan, "The Place of the Mother: Hélène Cixous's Osnabrück," *Paragraph: A Journal of Modern Critical Theory* 27, no. 1 (2004): 6–20.

7. Cixous, "De la scène de l'inconscient," 16; my translation.

8. Hélène Cixous, *L'ange au secret* (Paris: Des femmes, 1991).

9. Hélène Cixous, "In October 1991 . . ." trans. Keith Cohen, in *Stigmata*, 43–62. Here is what she says: "My mother has always been a young boy. I could talk to you about her but in a way I'm terrified because she is so young. As for writing about my mother, I've done it with extreme succinctness. What I've done, in fact, amounts to nothing. It seems to me that we can't write about our mother. I'm sure of it. It's one of the limits of writing" (47).

10. Cixous, *Or*; Hélène Cixous, *Osnabrück* (Paris: Des femmes, 1999); Hélène Cixous, *Les rêveries de la femme sauvage: Scènes primitives* (Paris: Galilée, 2000).

11. She is presumably referring here to *Dedans*. Hélène Cixous, *Dedans* (Paris: B. Grasset, 1969).

12. Cixous, *Or*, 169–170.

13. Ibid., 175–76.

14. Cixous, *Osnabrück*, 63.

15. In *l'amour du loup*, Cixous describes the genesis of the book as follows: "*Des lettres sont arrivées d'Algérie. Je les vis virer devant moi: c'était les lettres r, v, des consonnes cherchant leurs voyelles sur mes lèvres . . . . Les lettres relient ravin, rêveries, arriver, rive, vire, rire, et que ça vire*" (Some letters arrived from Algeria. I saw them swerve in front of me: they were the letters r, v, consonants in search of their vowels on my lips. The letters bind together ravine, reveries, arrive, back, swerve, laughter, and it turns).

16. It is interesting to note that there has been considerable critical attention given to "Fips" the dog, although very little has been written about "Fipps."

This is perhaps in part because a version of the story of "Fips" appeared in English in *Stigmata* under the title of "Stigmata or Job the Dog," *Stigmata*, 243–261. For powerful readings of the figure of the dog in Cixous's work see: Hugh S. Pyper, "'Job the Dog': Hélène Cixous on Wounds, Scars and the Biblical Text," *Biblical Interpretation: A Journal of Contemporary Approaches* 11, no. 3–4 (2003): 438–448; Marta Segarra, "Hélène Cixous's Other Animal: The Half-Sunken Dog," *New Literary History: A Journal of Theory and Interpretation* 37, no. 1 (2006): 119–134.

17. Cixous, *Osnabrück*, 83–85.

18. Ibid., 21.

19. Cixous, *L'amour de loup*, 167.

12. BIT: MOURNING REMAINS IN DERRIDA AND CIXOUS

1. The three main texts I will be focusing on here are *Glas*, "*Fors*," and *La verité en peinture*. See Jacques Derrida, "*Fors*," in *Cryptonymie: Le verbier de l'homme aux loups*, ed. Nicolas Abraham and Maria Torok (Paris: Flammarion, 1976), 7–73; *Glas* (Paris: Editions Galilée, 1974); *La vérité en peinture* (Paris: Flammarion, 1978); *Glas* (Lincoln: University of Nebraska Press, 1986); *The Truth in Painting* (Chicago: University of Chicago Press, 1987). For Derrida's own later reprise of this early work, see "Countersignature," *Paragraph* 27, no. 2 (2004): 7–42. In the following passage from *Glas*, Derrida makes it explicit that reading the "bit" is both the object and a method of reading:

> L'objet du présent ouvrage, son style aussi, c'est le *morceau*. Qui se détache toujours, comme son nom l'indique et pour que vous ne l'oubliiez pas, avec des dents. L'objet du présent ouvrage (code de la couturière), c'est ce qui d'une morsure reste dans la gorge: le mors. (*Glas*, 135)

> The object of the present work, and its style too, is the *morsel*. Which is always detached, as its name indicates and so that you don't forget it, by the teeth. The object of the present work (*ouvrage*) (code of the dressmaker) is what remains of a bite, a sure death [*une morsure*], in the throat [*gorge*]: the bit [*mors*]. (*Glas*, 118)

2. Hélène Cixous, "Pieds nus," *Une enfance algérienne*, ed. Leïla Sebbar (Paris: Gallimard, 1997), 55–66.

3. See, for example this passage:

> Je suis dans la gueule du livre, je le sens me mordre de tous les côtés, le dos, la nuque, les pieds. C'est une gueule à plusieurs langues. Je n'en sortirai pas indemne. Mes cicatrices d'antan sont en train de se réveiller. C'est bien ce que je craignais.

La réouverture des lèvres. Retrouver le fer le feu le frère l'espiègle ferveur des dents déchiquetant les innocents, c'est bien ce que je voulais, le rire du fer, le goût du feu, lame glissée droite là-bas dans le coin exigu que fait le passé avec l'oubli, derrière la porte. A l'idée de la peur mortelle que je me promettais, je frissonnais de rire.

Hélène Cixous, *L'ange au secret* (Paris: Des femmes, 1991), 47.

4. Hélène Cixous, *Messie* (Paris: Des femmes, 1996); Hélène Cixous, *Le jour où je n'étais pas là* (Paris: Galilée, 2000).

5. Hélène Cixous, *Les rêveries de la femme sauvage: Scènes primitives* (Paris: Galilée, 2000). *Reveries of the Wild Woman: Primal Scenes*, trans. Beverley Bie Brahic (Evanston, Ill.: Northwestern University Press, 2006).

6. Derrida and Cixous engage in an ongoing exchange about Cixous's reference to the book of Tobit in *Messie*. In *HC pour la vie, c'est à dire*, he refers to having taken a "*morceau*" of her dog Tobie [*sic*]. In *Insister*, she recalls a conversation they had about the dog in Tobit and then goes on to recount a series of his dreams involving dogs and dog bites. Hélène Cixous and Ernest Pignon, *Insister: À Jacques Derrida* (Paris: Galilée, 2006), 109–110.

7. This section of *Messie* was published in English as Hélène Cixous, "The Cat's Arrival," *Parallax* 12 (2006): 21–42.

8. Cixous, *Messie*, 45.

9. Ibid., 85–86.

10. See Hélène Cixous, *Stigmata: Escaping Texts*, trans. Eric Prenowitz (New York: Routledge, 1998). The text in question here is "Stigmata or Job the Dog," 181–194.

11. Cixous, *Rêveries*, 73; *Reveries of the Wild Woman*, 42.

12. See, for example, the section of "Le Livre nié" in *L'amour du loup* entitled "Inoublier: Des branches de Mimosa." Hélène Cixous, *L'amour du loup et autres remords* (Paris: Galilée, 2003), 166–173.

13. Cixous, *Stigmata*, 184.

14. See Marta Segarra's lovely text about this: "Hélène Cixous's Other Animal: The Half-Sunken Dog," *New Literary History* 37, no. 1 (2006): 119–134.

15. In the final passages of "Ce corps étrangjuif," a text included in the volume *Judéités: Questions pour Jacques Derrida*, Cixous brings up the status of Fips in a dialogue between her and her mother on the subject of animals and Jews:

J'interroge ma mère:

— Quel rapport les Juifs ont-ils aux animaux?

— Les juifs n'ont pas de rapport. L'animal est impur dit ma mère . . .

— Mais notre Fips?

— Dans la maison, il reste dehors. Si ton père voulait un chien il n'a pas agi en juif (78).

16. Cixous, *Rêveries*, 80; *Reveries of the Wild Woman*, 46.

17. Beverley Bie Brahic translates this line as "the five mouths stitched to my feet." But I would be more inclined to translate it as "the five sewn-up mouths on my feet."

18. Cixous, *Rêveries*, 82; *Reveries of the Wild Woman*, 47.

19. Cixous, *Stigmata*, 182.

20. For a compelling and comprehensive account of the bibliography of "crossed" intertextual readings between Cixous and Derrida, see Laurent Milesi, "Portraits of H. C. as J. D. and Back," *New Literary History* 37, no. 1 (2006): 65–84.

21. In *Insister*, Cixous suggests that she and Derrida are similarly marked, but "in chiasmus" by their respective "primal scenes" (childhood losses, wounds) in Algeria:

> une de mes hypothèses . . . c'est que nous sommes lui et moi les sujets et résultats de scènes primitives très puissamment différentes et influentes—on dirait surdéterminantes, de ces "premiers chagrins" (dit Kafka), premières mutilations, premières morsures de mort, survenus dans l'enfance, dont les traces mémoriels et inconscients nous marquent ou blessent en chiasme.) (100)

22. Hélène Cixous, "Quelle heure est-il ou la porte (celle qu'on ne passe pas)," in *Le passage des frontières: Autour du travail de Jacques Derrida*, ed. Marie-Louise Mallet et al. (Paris: Galilée, 1994), 83–98.

23. For example, in *L'amour du loup*, Cixous explicitly relates Derrida's shoebox from "Le ver à soie" to the shoebox into which she tries to put Fips to sleep. Both of these boxes are "magic lanterns" in a Proustian sense: cameras of the imagination that project primal images from these small "camera obscura" that emanate from primal places hidden in the unconscious:

> Mais toutes ces pièces sont les lieux d'origine des *visions* primitives. Ce sont des caméra (*Kamera*, *Kammer*), des boîtes à fabriquer des images; et parfois des boîtes à chaussures, comme celle dans laquelle j'ai couché Fips mon chien martyr ou celle dans laquelle Jacques Derrida a élévé son ver à soie. . . . Le livre a la forme d'une boîte à chaussures fossile. (143)

See Chapter 9 for another discussion of this passage.

24. The link between these two texts seems to be confirmed by the following sentence toward the beginning of *Portrait*: "*Si nous n'avions pas en commun la circoncision (je cesse ici de l'entourer d'antonomases)—du moins celle du pénis, car l'autre celle du coeur, je l'ai connue aussi . . . nous avons en miroir un nombre de* stigmates *précis et datés*" (my emphasis). Hélène Cixous, *Portrait de Jacques Derrida en jeune saint juif* (Paris: Galilée, 2001), 12.

25. Cixous, *Stigmata*, 185, 187.

26. Derrida, *The Truth in Painting*, 201.

27. It bears mentioning that all three of these texts are, indeed, bits: Each one is a detachable piece of another textual entity to which it is and is not related. The Genet column is only one side of Glas; "*Fors*" is the detachable preface to the book *The Wolf Man's Magic Word*, written by Nicolas Abraham and Maria Torok; and "Cartouches" is a chapter of *The Truth in Painting* that was initially published as part of a exhibition catalogue entitled *Gérard Titus-Carmel: The Pocket Size Tlingit Coffin*.

28. Derrida, *Glas*, 43 (English translation, 35).

29. Derrida, "Countersignature," 31.

30. Derrida, *Glas*, 260 (English translation, 289).

31. Derrida, "*Fors*," xxxix.

As I argue in Chapter 2, when writing about impossible mourning, Derrida often refers back to "*Fors*."

32. Sigmund Freud, "Reflections Upon War and Death," *SE* 14:290.

33. Hélène Cixous, *Manhattan: Lettres de la préhistoire* (Paris: Galilée, 2002), 74–75; Jacques Derrida, *Genèses, généalogies, genres et le génie: Les secrets de l'archive* (Paris: Galilée, 2003), 94; Derrida, *Geneses, Genealogies, Genres & Genius: The Secrets of the Archive*, trans. Beverly Bie Brahic (New York: Columbia University Press, 2008), 81–82.

34. For a lovely reading of the status of fiction and reality in *Manhattan*, see Eric Prenowitz, "Make Believe: Manhattan's Folittérature," *New Literary History* 37, no. 1 (2006): 147–167.

35. Cixous, *Manhattan*, 237.

36. Ibid., 218.

37. Ibid., 34.

38. Jacques Derrida, *Résistances de la psychanalyse* (Paris: Galilée, 1996), 22, 36.

39. Ibid., 42.

40. Ibid., 46.

41. Jacques Derrida, *H.C. pour la vie, c'est à dire* (Paris, Galilée, 2002), 30, 38; *H.C. for Life, That Is to Say*, trans. Laurent Milesi (Stanford, Calif.: Stanford University Press, 2006).

42. Hélène Cixous, *Le jour où je n'étais pas là* (Paris, Galilée, 2000); *The Day I Wasn't There*, trans. Beverley Bie Brahic (Evanston, Ill.: Northwestern University Press, 2006), 173 (here, my translation).

43. Hélène Cixous, *Rêve je te dis* (Paris: Galilée, 2003); Hélène Cixous and Beverley Bie Brahic, *Dream I Tell You* (Edinburgh: Edinburgh University Press, 2006), 97 (here, my translation).

BIBLIOGRAPHY

Abraham, Nicolas, and Maria Torok. *The Shell and the Kernel: Renewals of Psychoanalysis*. Edited and translated by Nicholas T. Rand. Chicago: University of Chicago Press, 1994.

———. *The Wolf Man's Magic Word: A Cryptonymy*. Edited by Nicholas T. Rand. Minneapolis: University of Minnesota Press, 1986.

Abraham, Nicolas, Maria Torok, and Jacques Derrida. *Cryptonymie: Le verbier de l'homme aux loups*. Paris: Flammarion, 1976.

Apel, Dora. "Torture Culture: Lynching Photographs and the Images of Abu Ghraib." *Art Journal* 64, no. 2 (2005): 88–100.

Bal, Mieke. *The Mottled Screen: Reading Proust Visually*. Stanford, Calif.: Stanford University Press, 1997.

Barthes, Roland. *Camera Lucida: Reflections on Photography*. Translated by Richard Howard. New York: Hill & Wang, 1981.

———. *Image, Music, Text*. Translated by Stephen Heath. New York: Hill & Wang, 1977.

———. *La chambre claire: Note sur la photographie*. Paris: Cahiers du cinéma, 1980.

Batchen, Geoffrey. *Burning with Desire: The Conception of Photography*. Cambridge, Mass.: MIT Press, 1997.

———. *Each Wild Idea: Writing, Photography, History*. Cambridge, Mass.: MIT Press, 2001.

Batchen, Geoffrey, ed. *Photography Degree Zero: Reflections on Roland Barthes's Camera Lucida*. Cambridge, Mass.: MIT Press, 2009.

Bell, David F. "Infinite Archives." *SubStance: A Review of Theory and Literary Criticism* 33, no. 3 (105) (2004): 148.

Benjamin, Walter. *Selected Writings*. Edited by Marcus Paul Bullock and Michael William Jennings. 4 vols. Cambridge, Mass.: Belknap Press, 1996.

Bennett, Andrew. "On Posterity." *Yale Journal of Criticism: Interpretation in the Humanities* 12, no. 1 (1999): 131.

Benvenisti, Meron. *Abu Ghraib: The Politics of Torture*. Berkeley, Calif.: North Atlantic Books, 2004.

Bernheimer, Charles, and Claire Kahane, eds. *In Dora's Case: Freud–Hysteria–Feminism*. New York: Columbia University Press, 1985.

Boothby, Richard. *Death and Desire: Psychoanalytic Theory in Lacan's Return to Freud*. New York: Routledge, 1991.

Bourke, Joanna. "Sexy Snaps." *Index on Censorship* 34, no. 1 (2005): 39–45.

Bowie, Malcolm. *Psychoanalysis and the Future of Theory*. Cambridge, Mass.: Blackwell, 1994.

Boxer, Sarah. "Backup of Torture Incarnate, and Propped on a Pedestal." *New York Times*, June 13, 2004.

———. "Critic's Notebook: Humiliating Photographs As Trophies of War." *New York Times*, May 20, 2004.

———. "Finding Echoes of Iraq War in a Film About Vietnam." *New York Times*, June 17, 2004.

Brassaï. *Proust in the Power of Photography*. Translated by Richard Howard. Chicago: University of Chicago Press, 2001.

Brennan, Teresa, ed. *Between Feminism and Psychoanalysis*. New York: Routledge, 1989.

Brody, Reed. "The Road to Abu Ghraib." *Human Rights Watch*, 2004.

Brooks, Peter. *Reading for the Plot: Design and Intention in Narrative*. New York: Knopf, 1984.

Bruno, Giuliana. "Ramble City: Postmodernism and 'Blade Runner.'" *October* 41 (1987): 61–74.

Butler, Judith. *Antigone's Claim: Kinship Between Life & Death*. New York: Columbia University Press, 2000.

———. "The Pleasure of Repetition." In *Pleasure Beyond the Pleasure Principle*, edited by Robert A. Glick and Stanley Bone, 259–275. New Haven: Yale University Press, 1990.

———. "Theories and Methodologies: Photography, War, Outrage." *PMLA: Publications of the Modern Language Association of America* 120, no. 3 (2005): 822–827.

Cadava, Eduardo. "Toward an Ethics of Decision." *Diacritics: A Review of Contemporary Criticism* 24, no. 4 (1994): 4.

———. *Words of Light: Theses on the Photography of History*. Princeton, N.J.: Princeton University Press, 1997.

Cadava, Eduardo, and Paola Cortés–Rocca. "Notes on Love and Photography." In *Photography Degree Zero: Reflections on Roland Barthes's Camera Lucida*, edited by Geoffrey Batchen, 105–140. Cambridge, Mass.: MIT Press, 2009.

Calle-Gruber, Mireille. "Hélène Cixous's Imaginary Cities: Oran-Osnabrück-Manhattan–Places of Fascination, Places of Fictions." *New Literary History* 37, no. 1 (2006): 135–145.

Carby, Hazel. "A Strange and Bitter Crop: The Spectacle of Torture." *Open Democracy: Free Thinking for the World* 11 (October 2004), www.openDemocracy.net.

Caruth, Cathy. *Unclaimed Experience: Trauma, Narrative, and History*. Baltimore: Johns Hopkins University Press, 1996.

Chanter, Tina. "Eating Words: Antigone as Kofman's Proper Name." In *Enigmas: Essays on Sarah Kofman*, edited by Penelope Deutscher and Kelly Oliver, 189–202. Ithaca, N.Y.: Cornell University Press, 1999.

———. *Ethics of Eros: Irigaray's Rewriting of the Philosophers*, New York: Routledge, 1995.

———. "Tragic Dislocations: Antigone's Modern Theatrics." *Differences: A Journal of Feminist Cultural Studies* 10, no. 1 (1998): 75–97.

Chanter, Tina, and Ewa P. Ziarek, eds. *Revolt, Affect, Collectivity: The Unstable Boundaries of Kristeva's Polis*. Albany: State University of New York Press, 2005.

Chase, Cynthia. "Translating the Transference: Psychoanalysis and the Construction of History." In *Telling Facts: History and Narration in Psychoanalysis*, edited by Joseph H. Smith and Humphrey Morris, 103–126. Baltimore: Johns Hopkins University Press, 1992.

Chasseguet-Smirgel, Janine. "Altglas, Altpapier: (Empty Bottles, Waste Paper): Reflections on Certain Disorders of the Superego in Relation to Houseproud Mothers." *Psychoanalytic Inquiry* 11 (1991): 537–558.

———. *Creativity and Perversion*. New York: Norton, 1984.

Cixous, Hélène. *Benjamin à Montaigne: Il ne faut pas le dire*. Paris: Galilée, 2001.

———. "Castration or Decapitation?" *Signs* 7, no. 1 (1981): 41–55.

———. *Dedans*. Paris: B. Grasset, 1969.

———. "From the Scene of the Unconscious to the Scene of History." In *The Future of Literary Theory*, edited by Ralph Cohen, 1–18. New York: Routledge, 1989.

———. *Insister: à Jacques Derrida*. Paris: Galilée, 2006.

———. *L'amour du loup et autres remords*. Paris: Galilée, 2003.

———. *L'ange au secret*. Paris: Des femmes, 1991.

———. *Le jour où je n'étais pas là*. Paris: Galilée, 2000.

———. *Les rêveries de la femme sauvage: Scènes primitives*. Paris: Galilée, 2000.

———. "Letter to Zohra Drif." *Parallax* 4, no. 2 (1998): 189–196.

———. *Manhattan: Letters from Prehistory*. Translated by Beverley Bie Brahic. New York: Fordham University Press, 2007.

———. *Manhattan: Lettres de la préhistoire*. Paris: Galilée, 2002.

———. *OR: Les lettres de mon père*. Paris: Des femmes, 1997.

———. *Osnabrück*. Paris: Des femmes, 1999.

———. *Portrait de Dora*. Paris: Des Femmes, 1976.

———. *Reveries of the Wild Woman: Primal Scenes*. Translated by Beverley Bie Brahic. Evanston, Ill.: Northwestern University Press, 2006.

———. *Si près*. Paris: Galilée, 2007.

———. *So Close*. Translated by Peggy Kamuf. Cambridge, Mass.: Polity, 2009.

———. *Stigmata: Escaping Texts*. New York: Routledge, 1998.

Cixous, Hélène, and Jacques Derrida. *Veils*. Translated by Geoffrey Bennington. Stanford, Calif.: Stanford University Press, 2001.

Cohen, Tom. *Jacques Derrida and the Humanities: A Critical Reader*. New York: Cambridge University Press, 2001.

Copjec, Joan. *Read My Desire: Lacan Against the Historicists*. Cambridge, Mass.: MIT Press, 1994.

———. "The Tomb of Perseverance: On Antigone." In *The Ethics of History*, edited by David Carr, Thomas R. Flynn, and Rudolf A. Makkreel, 118–154. Evanston, Ill.: Northwestern University Press, 2004.

Crary, Jonathan. *Techniques of the Observer: On Vision and Modernity in the Nineteenth Century*. Cambridge, Mass.: MIT Press, 1990.

Danner, Mark. *Torture and Truth: America, Abu Ghraib, and the War on Terror*. New York: New York Review of Books, 2004.

David-Ménard, Monique. *Hysteria from Freud to Lacan: Body and Language in Psychoanalysis*. Ithaca, N.Y.: Cornell University Press, 1989.

Davis, Whitney. *Drawing the Dream of the Wolves: Homosexuality, Interpretation, and Freud's Wolf Man*. Bloomington: Indiana University Press, 1995.

Dean, Tim. *Beyond Sexuality*. Chicago: University of Chicago Press, 2000.

Deleuze, Gilles, and Félix Guattari. "1914: One or Several Wolves." In *A Thousand Plateaus: Capitalism and Schizophrenia*, 26–38. Minneapolis: University of Minnesota Press, 1987.

Derrida, Jacques. *Apories: Mourir—s'attendre aux "limites de la vérité."* Paris: Galilée, 1996.

———. *Archive Fever: A Freudian Impression*. Chicago: University of Chicago Press, 1996.

———. "The Deaths of Roland Barthes." In *Psyche: Inventions of the Other*, edited by Peggy Kamuf and Elizabeth Rottenberg, 264–298. Stanford, Calif.: Stanford University Press, 2007.

———. *Etats d'âme de la psychanalyse: L'impossible au-delà d'une souveraine cruauté*. Paris: Galilée, 2000.

———. "Fors: The Anglish Words of Nicolas Abraham and Maria Torok." In *The Wolf Man's Magic Word: A Cryptonomie*, xi–viii. Minneapolis: University of Minnesota Press, 1986.

———. "Fors: Les mots anglés de Nicolas Abraham et Maria Torok." In *Cryptonomie: Le verbier de l'homme aux loups*, 7–73. Paris: Aubier Flammarion, 1976.

———. *Genèses, généalogies, genres et le génie: Les secrets de l'archive*. Paris: Galilée, 2003.

———. *The Gift of Death*. Chicago: University of Chicago Press, 1995.

———. *Glas*. Lincoln: University of Nebraska Press, 1986.

———. *Glas*. Paris: Editions Galilée, 1974.

———. *H.C. for Life, That Is to Say*. Translated by Laurent Milesi. Stanford, Calif.: Stanford University Press, 2006.

———. *H.C. pour la vie, c'est à dire*. Paris: Galilée, 2002.

———. *La carte postale de Socrate à Freud et au-delà*. Paris: Flammarion, 1980.

———. *On the Name*. Translated by Thomas Dutoit. Stanford, Calif.: Stanford University Press, 1995.

———. *The Post Card: From Socrates to Freud and Beyond*. Translated by Alan Bass. Chicago: University of Chicago Press, 1987.

———. *Psyche: Inventions of the Other*. Stanford, Calif.: Stanford University Press, 2007.

———. *Résistances de la psychanalyse*. Paris: Galilée, 1996.

———. *Resistances of Psychoanalysis*. Translated by Peggy Kamuf, Pascale-Anne Brault, and Michael Naas. Stanford, Calif.: Stanford University Press, 1998.

———. *Rogues: Two Essays on Reason*. Stanford, Calif.: Stanford University Press, 2005.

———. *Specters of Marx: The State of the Debt, the Work of Mourning, and the New International*. Translated by Peggy Kamuf. New York: Routledge, 1994.

———. *The Truth in Painting*. Chicago: University of Chicago Press, 1987.

———. *Voyous: Deux essais sur la raison*. Paris: Galilée, 2003.

———. *Without Alibi*. Edited by Peggy Kamuf. Stanford, Calif.: Stanford University Press, 2002.

———. *The Work of Mourning*. Translated by Pascale-Anne Brault and Michael Naas. Chicago: University of Chicago Press, 2001.

———. *Writing and Difference*. Translated by Alan Bass. Chicago: University of Chicago Press, 1978.

Derrida, Jacques, and Gil Anidjar. *Acts of Religion*. New York: Routledge, 2002.

Derrida, Jacques, and Jean-François Bonhomme. *Athens, Still Remains: The Photographs of Jean-François Bonhomme*. Translated by Pascale-Anne Brault and Michael Naas. New York: Fordham University Press, 2010.

Derrida, Jacques, and Anne Dufourmantelle. *Of Hospitality*. Stanford, Calif.: Stanford University Press, 2000.

Derrida, Jacques, and Christie McDonald. *The Ear of the Other: Otobiography, Transference, Translation—Texts and Discussions with Jacques Derrida*. New York: Schocken Books, 1985.

Derrida, Jacques, and Marie-Françoise Plissart. *Right of Inspection*. Translated by David Wills. New York: Monacelli Press, 1998.

Derrida, Jacques, and Elisabeth Weber. *Points: Interviews, 1974–1994*. Stanford, Calif.: Stanford University Press, 1995.

Deutscher, Penelope. "Mourning the Other, Cultural Cannibalism, and the Politics of Friendship (Jacques Derrida and Luce Irigaray)." *Differences: A Journal of Feminist Cultural Studies* 10, no. 3 (1998): 159–184.

de Vries, Hent, and Samuel Weber, eds. *Violence, Identity, and Self-Determination*. Stanford, Calif.: Stanford University Press, 1997.

Didi-Huberman, Georges. *Images malgré tout*. Paris: Minuit, 2003.

Dimock, George. "Anna and the Wolf-Man: Rewriting Freud's Case History." *Representations* 50 (1995): 53–75.

Doane, Janice L., and Devon L. Hodges. *From Klein to Kristeva: Psychoanalytic Feminism and the Search for the "Good Enough" Mother*. Ann Arbor: University of Michigan Press, 1992.

Drinan, Robert F. *The Mobilization of Shame: A World View of Human Rights*. New Haven: Yale University Press, 2001.

Eng, David L., and David Kazanjian, eds. *Loss: The Politics of Mourning*. Berkeley: University of California Press, 2003.

Fedida, Pierre. "The Relic and the Work of Mourning." *Journal of Visual Culture* 2, no. 1 (2003): 62.

Feldman, Allen. "Abu Ghraib: Ceremonies of Nostalgia." *Open Democracy: Free Thinking for the World* (2004), www.openDemocracy.net.

Feldstein, Richard, and Judith Roof, eds. *Feminism and Psychoanalysis*. Ithaca, N.Y.: Cornell University Press, 1989.

Felman, Shoshana. *What Does a Woman Want? Reading and Sexual Difference*. Baltimore: Johns Hopkins University Press, 1993.

Felman, Shoshana, and Dori Laub. *Testimony: Crises of Witnessing in Literature, Psychoanalysis, and History*. New York: Routledge, 1992.

Fish, Stanley. "Withholding the Missing Portion: Power, Meaning and Persuasion in Freud's The Wolf-Man." In *The Linguistics of Writing: Arguments Between Language and Literature*, edited by Nigel Fabb, Derek Attridge, Alan Durant, and Colin MacCabe, 154–172. New York: Methuen, 1987.

Forrester, John. *The Seductions of Psychoanalysis: Freud, Lacan, and Derrida*. New York: Cambridge University Press, 1990.

Freud, Sigmund. *The Standard Edition of the Complete Psychological Works of Sigmund Freud*. 24 vols. London: Hogarth Press, 1966.

———. *Studienausgabe*. Edited by Alexander Mitscherlich, Angela Richards, James Strachey, and Ilse Grubrich-Simitis. 11 vols. Frankfurt: Fischer Taschenbuch, 2000.

———. *The Wolf-Man: With the Case of the Wolf-Man*. Edited by Sergius Pankejeff, Ruth Mack Brunswick, and Muriel Gardiner. New York: Basic Books, 1971.

Gallop, Jane. *The Daughter's Seduction: Feminism and Psychoanalysis*. New York: Cornell University Press, 1982.

———. *Reading Lacan*. Ithaca, N.Y.: Cornell University Press, 1985.

Gebhardt, James F., and U.S. Army Command and General Staff College. Combat Studies Institute. "The road to Abu Ghraib US Army detainee doctrine and experience." Combat Studies Institute Press, http://purl.access.gpo.gov/GPO/LPS59576.

Genosko, Gary. "Freud's Bestiary: How Does Psychoanalysis Treat Animals?" *Psychoanalytic Review* 80, no. 4 (1993): 603–632.

Ginzburg, Carlo. *Myths, Emblems, Clues*. London: Hutchinson Radius, 1990.

Gordon, Max. "Abu Ghraib: Postcards from the Edge." *Open Democracy: Free Thinking for the World* 14 (October 2004), www.openDemocracy.net.

Green, André. "Conceptions of Affect." *The International Journal of Psycho-analysis* 58 (1977): 129–156.

———. *Le temps éclaté*. Paris: Editions de Minuit, 2000.

Green, André, and Catherine Chabert. *Sur la théorie de la séduction*. Paris: In Press Editions, 2003.

Greenberg, Karen J. *The Torture Debate in America*. New York: Cambridge University Press, 2006.

Greenberg, Karen J., and Joshua L. Dratel. *The Torture Papers: The Road to Abu Ghraib*. New York: Cambridge University Press, 2005.

Grosz, E. A. *Jacques Lacan: A Feminist Introduction*. New York: Routledge, 1990.

Grundberg, Andy. "Point and Shoot." *American Scholar* 74, no. 1 (2005): 105–109.

Gualtieri, Elena. "Bored by Photographs: Proust in Venice." In *Photography and Literature in the Twentieth Century*, edited by Andrew Fisher David Cunningham and Sas Mays. Newcastle: Cambridge Scholars, 2005.

Gunning, Tom. "Phantom Images and Modern Manifestations: Spirit Photography, Magic Theater, Trick Films, and Photography's Uncanny." In *Fugitive Images: From Photography to Video*, edited by Patrice Petro, 42–71. Bloomington: Indiana University Press, 1995.

Halpert, Eugene. "Lermontov and the Wolf Man." *American Imago: A Psychoanalytic Journal for Culture, Science, and the Arts* 32 (1975): 315–328.

Hanrahan, Mairéad. "Of Altobiography." *Paragraph: A Journal of Modern Critical Theory* 23, no. 3 (2000): 282–295.

———. "Oublire: Cixous's Poetics of Forgetting." *Symposium: A Quarterly Journal in Modern Literatures* 54, no. 2 (2000): 77–89.

———. "The Place of the Mother: Hélène Cixous's Osnabrück." *Paragraph: A Journal of Modern Critical Theory* 27, no. 1 (2004): 6–20.

Harari, Roberto. *Lacan's Seminar on "Anxiety": An Introduction*. New York: Other Press, 2001.

Harvey, David. *The Condition of Postmodernity: An Enquiry Into the Origins of Cultural Change*. Cambridge, Mass.: Blackwell, 1989.

Hersh, Seymour M. *Chain of Command: The Road from 9/11 to Abu Ghraib*. New York: HarperCollins, 2004.

Hesiod. *Hesiod*. 2 vols. Cambridge, Mass.: Harvard University Press, 2006.

Hoffmann, Geneviève. "Pandora, la jarre et l'espoir." *Etudes Rurales* 97/98 (January–June 1985): 119–132.

Homans, Margaret. *Bearing the Word: Language and Female Experience in Nineteenth-Century Women's Writing*. Chicago: University of Chicago Press, 1986.

Hughes, Gordon. "*Camera Lucida*, Circa 1980." In *Reflections on Roland Barthes's Camera Lucida*, edited by Geoffrey Batchen, 193–209. Cambridge, Mass.: MIT Press, 2009.

Independent Panel to Review DoD Detention Operations. "Final Report of the Independent Panel to Review DOD Detention Operations." Independent Panel to Review DoD Detention Operations, http://purl.access.gpo.gov/GPO/LPS53245.

Irigaray, Luce. *Sexes and Genealogies*. New York: Columbia University Press, 1993.

———. *Speculum of the Other Woman*. Translated by Gillian Gill. Ithaca, N.Y.: Cornell University Press, 1985.

Jacobs, Amber. *On Matricide: Myth, Psychoanalysis, and the Law of the Mother*. New York: Columbia University Press, 2007.

Jacobs, Carol. "Dusting Antigone." *MLN* 111, no. 5 (1996): 889–917.

Jagodzinski, Jan. "The Trauma of the Image: Prisoner 'Abuse' in Abu Ghraib Prison." *Simile* 6, no. 1 (2006): 3–3.

Johnson, Barbara. "My Monster/My Self." *Diacritics: A Review of Contemporary Criticism* 12, no. 2 (1982): 2–10.

Johnson, Lawrence. *The Wolf Man's Burden*. Ithaca, N.Y.: Cornell University Press, 2001.

Johnston, Adrian. "Intimations of Freudian Mortality: The Enigma of Sexuality and the Constitutive Blind Spots of Freud's Self-Analysis." *Journal for Lacanian Studies* 3, no. 2 (2005): 222–246.

Jonte-Pace, Diane. "At Home in the Uncanny: Freudian Representations of Death, Mothers, and the Afterlife." *Journal of the American Academy of Religion* 64, no. 1 (1996): 61–88.

Kamuf, Peggy. "Abraham's Wake." *Diacritics* 9, no. 1 (1979): 32–43.
———. "To Give Place: Semi-Approaches to Hélène Cixous." *Yale French Studies* 87 (1995): 68–89.
Kear, Adrian. "The Anxiety of the Image." In *Parallax*, 107–116. Routledge, 2005.
Keenan, Thomas. "Mobilizing Shame." *South Atlantic Quarterly* 103 (Spring/Summer 2004): 435–439.
Knight, Diana. *Barthes and Utopia: Space, Travel, Writing*. Oxford: Clarendon Press, 1997.
———. "Roland Barthes, or the Woman Without a Shadow." In *Writing the Image after Roland Barthes*, edited by Jean-Michel Rabaté, 132–143. Philadelphia: University of Pennsylvania Press, 1997.
Kofman, Sarah. *The Childhood of Art: An Interpretation of Freud's Aesthetics*. New York: Columbia University Press, 1988.
———. *The Enigma of Woman: Woman in Freud's Writings*. Translated by Catherine Porter. Ithaca, N.Y.: Cornell University Press, 1985.
Krauss, Rosalind E. *The Optical Unconscious*. Cambridge, Mass.: MIT Press, 1993.
———. "Reinventing the Medium." *Critical Inquiry* 25, no. 2 (1999): 289–305.
Kristeva, Julia. *Black Sun: Depression and Melancholia*. Translated by Leon S. Roudiez. New York: Columbia University Press, 1989.
———. *Intimate Revolt: And, The Future of Revolt*. New York: Columbia University Press, 2002.
———. *Powers of Horror: An Essay on Abjection*. Translated by Leon S. Roudiez. New York: Columbia University Press, 1982.
Kristeva, Julia, and Kelly Oliver. *The Portable Kristeva*. New York: Columbia University Press, 1997.
Lacan, Jacques. *Écrits*. Paris: Éditions du Seuil, 1966.
———. *Écrits: A Selection*. New York: Norton, 1977.
———. *The Seminar of Jacques Lacan, Book VII: The Ethics of Psychoanalysis*, 1959–1960. Translated by Dennis Porter. New York: Norton, 1992.
Lane, Christopher. "Review: The Testament of the Other: Abraham and Torok's Failed Expiation of Ghosts." Review of Abraham and Torok, *The Shell and the Kernel*, vol. 1. *Diacritics* 27, no. 4 (1997): 3–29.
Lansky, Melvin R., and Andrew P. Morrison. *The Widening Scope of Shame*. Hillsdale, N.J.: Analytic Press, 1997.
Laplanche, Jean. *Essays on Otherness*. Translated by John Fletcher. New York: Routledge, 1999.
———. *Life and Death in Psychoanalysis*. Baltimore: Johns Hopkins University Press, 1976.
———. "A Metapsychology Put to the Test of Anxiety." *International Journal of Psychoanalysis* 62 (1981): 81–89.

———. *Problématiques*. 4 vols. Paris: Presses Universitaires de France, 1981.

Laplanche, Jean, and J. B. Pontalis. *Fantasme originaire: Fantasmes des origines, origines du fantasme*. Paris: Hachette Littératures, 1999.

———. *The Language of Psycho-analysis*. New York: Norton, 1974.

Lesage, Julia. "Abu Ghraib Links." *Jump Cut: A Review of Contemporary Media*. http://www.ejumpcut.org/archive/jc47.2005/links.html.

Lev Kenaan, Vered. *Pandora's Senses: The Feminine Character of the Ancient Text*. Madison: University of Wisconsin Press, 2008.

Lewis, Helen Block. *Shame and Guilt in Neurosis*. New York: International Universities Press, 1971.

Lewis, Michael. *Shame: The Exposed Self*. New York: Free Press, 1992.

Lifton, Robert Jay. "Conditions of Atrocity." *The Nation*, May 31, 2004.

Lippit, Akira Mizuta. *Electric Animal: Toward a Rhetoric of Wildlife*. Minneapolis: University of Minnesota Press, 2000.

Loraux, Nicole. *Born of the Earth: Myth and Politics in Athens*. Ithaca, N.Y.: Cornell University Press, 2000.

———. *The Children of Athena: Athenian Ideas About Citizenship and the Division Between the Sexes*. Princeton, N.J.: Princeton University Press, 1993.

———. *The Divided City: Forgetting in the Memory of Athens*. New York: Zone Books, 2002.

———. *The Invention of Athens: The Funeral Oration in the Classical City*. Cambridge, Mass.: Zone Books, 2006.

———. *Mothers in Mourning*. Ithaca, N.Y.: Cornell University Press, 1998.

———. *The Mourning Voice: An Essay on Greek Tragedy*. Ithaca, N.Y.: Cornell University Press, 2002.

———. *Tragic Ways of Killing a Woman*. Cambridge, Mass.: Harvard University Press, 1987.

Lyotard, Jean François. *Toward the Postmodern*. Edited by Robert Harvey and Mark S. Roberts. Atlantic Highlands, N.J.: Humanities Press International, 1993.

MacMaster, Neil. "Torture: From Algiers to Abu Ghraib." *Race & Class* 46, no. 2 (2004): 1–21.

Mahony, Patrick. *Cries of the Wolf Man*. New York: International Universities Press, 1984.

Major, René. *Etats généraux de la psychanalyse*. Paris: Aubier, 2003.

———. *La démocratie en cruauté*. Paris: Galilée, 2003.

Malabou, Catherine. "L'imprenable en question ou se prendre à mourir." *Etudes Françaises* 38, no. 1–2 (2002): 135–144.

Mannoni, Octave. *Un si vif étonnement: La honte, le rire, la mort*. Paris: Editions du Seuil, 1988.

Marder, Elissa. *Dead Time: Temporal Disorders in the Wake of Modernity (Baudelaire and Flaubert)*. Stanford, Calif.: Stanford University Press, 2001.

Marshall, David. *The Surprising Effects of Sympathy: Marivaux, Diderot, Rousseau, and Mary Shelley*. Chicago: University of Chicago Press, 1988.

Meeropol, Rachel, and Reed Brody. *America's Disappeared: Detainees, Secret Imprisonment, and the "War on Terror."* New York: Seven Stories Press, 2005.

Michaud, Ginette. "Derrida & Cixous: Between and Beyond, or 'What to the Letter Has Happened.'" *New Literary History: A Journal of Theory and Interpretation* 37, no. 1 (2006): 85–106.

Milesi, Laurent. "Portraits of H. C. as J. D. and Back." *New Literary History: A Journal of Theory and Interpretation* 37, no. 1 (2006): 65–84.

Miller, J. Hillis. "Derrida's Topographies." *South Atlantic Review* 59, no. 1 (1994): 1–25.

Mirzoeff, Nicholas. "Invisible Empire: Visual Culture, Embodied Spectacle, and Abu Ghraib." *Radical History Review* 95 (2006): 21–44.

Mitchell, Juliet. *Psychoanalysis and Feminism*. New York: Pantheon Books, 1974.

Mitchell, W. J. T. "Echoes of a Christian Symbol: Photo Reverberates with Raw Power of Christ on Cross." *Chicago Tribune*, June 27, 2004.

———. "Sacred Gestures." *Afterimage* 34, no. 3 (2006): 18–23.

Morrison, Andrew P. *The Culture of Shame*. New York: Ballantine Books, 1996.

———. *Shame: The Underside of Narcissism*. Hillsdale, N.J.: Analytic Press, 1989.

Murray, Timothy. "Photo-Medusa: Roland Barthes Incorporated." In *Like a Film: Ideological Fantasy on Screen, Camera and Canvas*, 65–97. New York: Routledge, 1993.

Naas, Michael. *Derrida from Now On*. New York: Fordham University Press, 2008.

———. *Taking on the Tradition: Jacques Derrida and the Legacies of Deconstruction*. Stanford, Calif.: Stanford University Press, 2003.

Nägele, Rainer. *Reading After Freud: Essays on Goethe, Hölderlin, Habermas, Nietzsche, Brecht, Celan, and Freud*. New York: Columbia University Press, 1987.

Nathanson, Donald L. *The Many Faces of Shame*. New York: Guilford Press, 1987.

———. *Shame and Pride: Affect, Sex, and the Birth of the Self*. New York: Norton, 1992.

Niman, Michael I. "Strange Fruit in Abu Ghraib: The Privatization of Torture." *Humanist* 64, no. 4 (2004): 18–23.

Obholzer, Karin, and Sergius Pankejeff. *The Wolf-Man: Conversations with Freud's Patient, Sixty Years Later*. New York: Continuum, 1982.

Oliver, Kelly. *Animal Lessons: How They Teach Us to Be Human*. New York: Columbia University Press, 2009.

———. *The Colonization of Psychic Space: A Psychoanalytic Social Theory of Oppression*. Minneapolis: University of Minnesota Press, 2004.

———. *Family Values: Subjects Between Nature and Culture*. New York: Routledge, 1997.

———. *Reading Kristeva: Unraveling the Double-Bind*. Bloomington: Indiana University Press, 1993.

———. *Subjectivity Without Subjects: From Abject Fathers to Desiring Mothers*. Lanham, Md.: Rowman & Littlefield, 1998.

———. *Witnessing: Beyond Recognition*. Minneapolis: University of Minnesota Press, 2001.

———. *Women as Weapons of War: Iraq, Sex, and the Media*. New York: Columbia University Press, 2007.

Panofsky, Dora, and Erwin Panofsky. *Pandora's Box: The Changing Aspects of a Mythical Symbol*. New York: Pantheon Books, 1962.

Penley, Constance. *The Future of an Illusion: Film, Feminism, and Psychoanalysis*. Minneapolis: University of Minnesota Press, 1989.

Petro, Patrice. *Fugitive Images: From Photography to Video*. Bloomington: Indiana University Press, 1995.

Prenowitz, Eric. "Make Believe: Manhattan's Folittérature." *New Literary History: A Journal of Theory and Interpretation* 37, no. 1 (2006): 147–167.

Pucci, Pietro. *Hesiod and the Language of Poetry*. Baltimore: Johns Hopkins University Press, 1977.

Pyper, Hugh S. "'Job the Dog': Hélène Cixous on Wounds, Scars and the Biblical Text." *Biblical Interpretation: A Journal of Contemporary Approaches* 11, no. 3–4 (2003): 438–448.

Rabaté, Jean-Michel. *Writing the Image After Roland Barthes*. Philadelphia: University of Pennsylvania Press, 1997.

Racine, Jean. *Phèdre*. Paris: Gallimard, 1999.

Rashkin, Esther. *Family Secrets and the Psychoanalysis of Narrative*. Princeton, N.J.: Princeton University Press, 1992.

———. "Nicolas Abraham and Maria Torok (1919–75 and 1925–98)." In *The Columbia History of Twentieth-Century French Thought*, edited by Lawrence D. Kritzman, Brian J. Reilly, and M. B. DeBevoise, 377–379. New York: Columbia University Press, 2006.

———. "Tools for a New Psychoanalytic Literary Criticism: The Work of Abraham and Torok." *Diacritics: A Review of Contemporary Criticism* 18, no. 4 (1988): 31–52.

———. *Unspeakable Secrets and the Psychoanalysis of Culture*. Albany: State University of New York Press, 2008.

Regard, Frédéric. "On Cixous's Tongue (Beyond Scopic Desire)." *Angelaki* 9, no. 1 (2004): 179–187.

Rich, Frank. "It Was the Porn That Made Them Do It." *New York Times*, Sunday, May 30, 2004.

Richter, Gerhard. "Unsettling Photography." *CR: The New Centennial Review* 7, no. 2 (2007): 155–173.

Rickels, Laurence A. *Aberrations of Mourning: Writing on German Crypts*. Detroit: Wayne State University Press, 1988.

Ronell, Avital. *Crack Wars: Literature Addiction Mania*. Lincoln: University of Nebraska Press, 1992.

———. *Dictations: On Haunted Writing*. Bloomington: Indiana University Press, 1986.

———. *Finitude's Score: Essays for the End of the Millennium*. Lincoln: University of Nebraska Press, 1994.

———. *Stupidity*. Urbana: University of Illinois Press, 2002.

———. *The Telephone Book: Technology–Schizophrenia–Electric Speech*. Lincoln: University of Nebraska Press, 1989.

———. *The Test Drive*. Urbana: University of Illinois Press, 2005.

Rose, Jacqueline. *Why War? Psychoanalysis, Politics, and the Return to Melanie Klein*. Cambridge, Mass.: Blackwell, 1993.

Rottenberg, Elizabeth. "The Resistance to Interpretation." *Philosophy Today* 50 (2006): 83–89.

Royle, Nicholas. *After Derrida*. Manchester: Manchester University Press, 1995.

———. *Deconstructions: A User's Guide*. London: Palgrave, 2000.

———. *Jacques Derrida*. New York: Routledge, 2003.

———. "Portmanteau." *New Literary History: A Journal of Theory and Interpretation* 37, no. 1 (2006): 237–247.

———. *Telepathy and Literature: Essays on the Reading Mind*. Cambridge, Mass.: Blackwell, 1991.

———. *The Uncanny*. Manchester: Manchester University Press, 2003.

Sante, Luc. "Torturers and Terrorists." *New York Times*, May 11, 2004.

Schwab, Gabriele, ed. *Derrida, Deleuze, Psychoanalysis*. New York: Columbia University Press, 2007.

Segarra, Marta. "Hélène Cixous's Other Animal: The Half-Sunken Dog." *New Literary History: A Journal of Theory and Interpretation* 37, no. 1 (2006): 119–134.

Shawcross, Nancy M. "The Filter of Culture and the Culture of Death: How Barthes and Boltanski Play the Mythologies of the Photograph." In *Writing the Image After Roland Barthes*, edited by Jean-Michel Rabaté, 59–70. Philadelphia: University of Pennsylvania Press, 1997.

———. *Roland Barthes on Photography: The Critical Tradition in Perspective*. Gainesville: University Press of Florida, 1997.

Shelley, Mary. *Frankenstein: Or the Modern Prometheus*. New York: New American Library, 1965.

Shengold, Leonard. "The Symbol of Telephoning." *Journal of the American Psychoanalytical Association* 30 (1982): 461–470.

Shepherdson, Charles. "The Elements of the Drive." *Umbr(a): A Journal of the Unconscious* 1 (1997): 131.

———. "The Gift of Love and the Debt of Desire." *Differences: A Journal of Feminist Cultural Studies* 10, no. 1 (1998): 30.

———. "Introduction." In *Lacan's Seminar on Anxiety: An Introduction*. New York: Other Press, 2001.

———. "Of Love and Beauty in Lacan's Antigone." *Umbr(a): A Journal of the Unconscious* 1 (1999): 63.

Silverman, Kaja. "Back to the Future." *Camera Obscura: A Journal of Feminism, Culture, and Media Studies* 27 (1991): 109–132.

Solomon-Godeau, Abigail. "On the Image Wars." *Artforum*, 2004.

———. *Photography at the Dock: Essays on Photographic History, Institutions, and Practices*. Minneapolis: University of Minnesota Press, 1991.

Sontag, Susan. "Regarding the Torture of Others." *New York Times*, May 23, 2004.

Sophocles. *The Complete Plays of Sophocles*. Edited by Richard Claverhouse Jebb and Moses Hadas. New York: Bantam Books, 1982.

Stevens, Christa. *L'ecriture solaire d'Hélène Cixous: Travail du texte et histoires du sujet dans Portrait du soleil*. Amsterdam: Rodopi, 1999.

Strasser, Steven. *The Abu Ghraib Investigations: The Official Reports of the Independent Panel and the Pentagon on the Shocking Prisoner Abuse in Abu Ghraib*. New York: Perseus Books, 2004.

Tester, Keith. "Reflections on the Abu Ghraib Photographs." *Journal of Human Rights* 4, no. 1 (2005): 137–143.

Tisseron, Serge. *La honte, psychanalyse d'un lien social*. 2nd ed. Paris: Dunod, 2007.

———. *Le mystère de la chambre claire: Photographie et inconscient*. Paris: Flammarion, 1996.

Tyler, Tom. "The Quiescent Ass and the Dumbstruck Wolf." *Configurations* 14, no. 1 (2008): 9–28.

United States Department of the Army. Office of the Chief of Public Affairs. "Investigation of Intelligence Activities at Abu Ghraib." http://purl.access.gpo.gov/GPO/LPS53415

van Haute, Philippe. *Against Adaptation: Lacan's "Subversion of the Subject."* New York: Other Press, 2002.

van Haute, Philippe, and Tomas Geyskens. *Confusion of Tongues: The Primacy of Sexuality in Freud, Ferenczi, and Laplanche*. New York: Other Press, 2004.

van Rossum-Guyon, Françoise, and Myriam Díaz-Diocaretz, eds. *Hélène Cixous, chemins d'une écriture*. Amsterdam: Rodopi, 1990.

Vernant, Jean Pierre. *La mort dans les yeux: Figures de l'autre en Grèce ancienne, Artémis, Gorgô*. Paris: Hachette, 1985.

———. *Myth and Society in Ancient Greece*. New York: Zone Books, 1990.

———. *Myth and Thought Among the Greeks*. Boston: Routledge & Kegan Paul, 1983.

———. *Pandora, la première femme*. Paris: Bayard, 2006.

Vernant, Jean Pierre, and Pierre Vidal-Naquet. *Myth and Tragedy in Ancient Greece*. Cambridge, Mass.: Zone Books, 1988.

Virilio, Paul. *The Vision Machine*. Bloomington: Indiana University Press, 1994.

———. *War and Cinema: The Logistics of Perception*. New York: Verso, 1989.

Wallis, Brian. "Inconvenient Evidence: Iraqi Prison Photographs from Abu Ghraib." International Center of Photography, 2004.

Walsh, Joan. "The Abu Ghraib Files." Salon.com, http://www.salon.com/news/abu_ghraib/2006/03/14/introduction.

Weber, Samuel. *The Legend of Freud*. Stanford, Calif.: Stanford University Press, 1982.

———. *Mass Mediauras: Form, Technics, Media*. Edited by Alan Cholodenko. Stanford, Calif.: Stanford University Press, 1996.

———. *Return to Freud: Jacques Lacan's Dislocation of Psychoanalysis*. New York: Cambridge University Press, 1991.

———. *Targets of Opportunity: On the Militarization of Thinking*. New York: Fordham University Press, 2005.

———. *Theatricality as Medium*. New York: Fordham University Press, 2004.

Williams, Linda. "Corporealized Observers: Visual Pornographies and the 'Carnal Destiny of Vision.'" In *Fugitive Images: From Photography to Video*, edited by Patrice Petro, 3–41. Bloomington: Indiana University Press, 1995.

———. *Hard Core: Power, Pleasure, and the "Frenzy of the Visible."* Berkeley: University of California Press, 1989.

Willis, Sharon. "Mis-Translation: Vivre l'orange." *SubStance: A Review of Theory and Literary Criticism* 16, no. 1 (1987): 76–83.

Wills, David. *Matchbook: Essays in Deconstruction*. Stanford, Calif.: Stanford University Press, 2005.

———. *Prosthesis*. Stanford, Calif.: Stanford University Press, 1995.

Wood, Sarah. "Review: Let's Start Again." *Diacritics* 29, no. 1 (1999): 4–19.

Wurmser, Leon. *The Mask of Shame*. Baltimore: Johns Hopkins University Press, 1981.

Yacavone, Kathrin. "Reading Through Photography: Roland Barthes's Last Seminar 'Proust et la photographie.'" *French Forum* 34, no. 1 (2009): 97–112.

Zakin, Emily. "Beyond the Sexual Contract: Traversing the Fantasy of the Fraternal Alliance." In *Between the Psyche and the Social: Psychoanalytic Social Theory*, edited by Kelly Oliver and Steve Edwin, 161–174. Lanham, Md.: Rowman & Littlefield, 2002.

Zeitlin, Froma I. *Playing the Other: Gender and Society in Classical Greek Literature*. Chicago: University of Chicago Press, 1995.

Žižek, Slavoj. "What Rumsfeld Doesn't Know That He Knows About Abu Ghraib." *In These Times*, May 21, 2004.

INDEX

Abraham, Nicolas, and Maria Torok
  "Mourning or Melancholia," 30, 41, 259*n*11
  Le verbier de l'homme aux loups, 46–47, 54, 258*n*1, 262–63*n*9, 280*n*1
  The Wolf Man's Magic Word, 40, 44, 47, 50, 54–55, 257*n*25, 258*n*1, 259*n*5, 260*n*20, 261–62*n*3, 262–63*n*9, 283*n*27
Abu Ghraib photographs, 6, 92, 94–109
Adams, Parveen, 255*n*8
Aeschylus, 254*n*3
affect, photographic, 96, 109
Afghanistan, 98, 105
Algeria, 184, 186–87, 191, 231, 237, 279*n*15, 282*n*21
Alhambra, photograph of the, 164, 166–67, 172–73, 175, 177–81, 271*n*1
animal phobia, 28–29, 59, 67–69, 74–75, 87, 261*n*2
animals, 28–29, 31–32, 59–60, 63–73, 76, 132, 232
animism, 29, 45
Antigone, 19, 20, 253–54*n*2
Antonioni, Michelangelo, 146, 177
anxiety, 3, 5, 6–7, 13, 15, 24, 60–61, 67–68, 74, 78–88, 92–96, 103–4, 109, 120–21, 134, 148, 177
  automatic anxiety, 82, 88
  shame anxiety, 92, 108
  signal anxiety, 82, 88
Apel, Dora, 107, 109, 265*n*2
Augustine, Saint, 237

Bal, Mieke, 276*n*41
Barthes, Roland, 7, 109, 118–19, 137–38, 149–58, 163–69, 172–83, 189, 194, 269–70*n*9
Baudelaire, Charles, 19, 50, 154, 164, 165–67, 169, 172, 253*n*1, 271*n*3
Bell, Alexander Graham, 115–16
Benjamin, Walter, 9, 91, 150, 154, 181, 190–93, 218, 273–74*n*16
Bennington, Geoffrey, 275*n*30
Bernheimer, Charles, 255*n*8
birth, concept of, 1–10, 15, 24–26, 29–33, 35, 37, 58–59, 81, 87–88, 116–17, 148–49, 153, 156, 158, 164, 170, 174–75, 180, 184, 186–91, 193, 196, 198, 204–5, 209–10, 217, 219, 227, 245, 248
Blade Runner, 7, 130–40, 143, 146, 147body, foreign, 41, 46–52, 58, 111, 126, 128, 260*n*22
body, maternal, 1–3, 5, 7, 10, 12, 22, 33, 148, 150, 152, 156, 164–67, 170–74, 177, 251, 257*n*24, 258*n*31, 270*n*3
Boothby, Richard, 264*n*5
box, 96, 220. *See also* casket; coffer; coffin
Boxer, Sarah, 265*n*3
Brody, Reed, 265*n*5
Brooks, Peter, 261*n*2
Bruno, Guiliana, 268*n*1
Brunswick, Ruth Mack, 54–55
Butler, Judith, 253–54n2

Cadava, Eduardo, 272–73*n*8, 273–74*n*16
Calle-Gruber, Mireille, 279*n*6

camera obscura, 3, 163, 194, 248, 282*n*23
cannibalism, 30, 42, 240
Carby, Hazel, 109, 265*n*2
Caruth, Cathy, 77, 264*n*2
casket, 33–35, 248. *See also* box; coffer; coffin
castration, 28–29, 59–60, 67–70, 75, 87, 121–22, 134
certainty, 4, 7, 165, 169–71, 176–79
Chanter, Tina, 253–54*n*2
Chase, Cynthia, 261*n*2
Chasseguet-Smirgel, Janine, 22, 121, 122, 256*n*11, 267–68*n*17, 268*n*20
Chevrier, Jean-François, 272*n*5
circumcision, 232, 237–38, 240
Cixous, Hélène, 8, 21, 182–84, 190–94, 214–20, 228–39, 243–47
  L'Amour du loup et autres remords, 193, 220, 227, 230
  L'Ange au secret, 218, 231–32
  Benjamin à Montaigne: Il ne faut pas le dire, 190–91
  Les Commencements, 219
  Dedans, 219, 247–48
  Dream I Tell You (*Rêve, je te dis*), 247
  "Inoublier," 227
  Manhattan, 192, 243, 244–45
  Messie, 232, 234
  OR: Les lettres de mon père, 219, 220
  Osnabrück, 187, 190–92, 219–20, 224–27
  "Pieds nus," 231
  Portrait de Jacques Derrida en jeune saint juif, 238
  "Quelle heure est-il ou la porte," 238
  Reveries of the Wild Woman (*Rêveries de la femme sauvage*) 191, 219, 224, 232
  So Close, 183–89
  "Stigmata or, Job the Dog," 234–35, 237–39
  Vivre l'orange, 218
Clifford, Charles, 164, 167
coffer, 248. *See also* box; casket; coffin
coffin, 33, 244, 249. *See also* box; casket; coffer
Copjec, Joan, 254
Corliss, Richard, 130, 269*n*4
Cortés-Rocca, Paola, 272–73*n*8
Courjault, Véronique, 24, 25, 26, 36
crypt, 6, 23, 26, 29, 30–31, 36–37, 39–42, 44–50, 52, 54, 119, 242, 244

danger, 68, 78–79, 82, 86–87, 92–94
Danner, Mark, 100, 265*n*2, 266*n*9
Darby, Joseph M., 99–102, 104
David-Ménard, Monique, 255*n*8
Davis, Whitney, 261*n*2, 262*n*7
deferred action (*Nachträglichkeit*), 6, 60, 262*n*9, 275*n*2
déjà vu, 6, 163–64, 169–71, 175–76, 178, 182, 256*n*12, 258*n*31, 272*n*5
Deleuze, Gilles, 262*n*8
Derrida, Jacques, 6, 8, 19, 37–39, 40–52, 77, 88, 111, 113, 125, 151, 152, 173–76, 193, 229–43, 246–47, 251
  Aporias, 39, 259
  Athens, Still Remains, 163, 176
  "Cartouches," 231, 240–41
  "Circonfession," 237–38
  "Countersignature," 241
  "The Deaths of Roland Barthes," 151, 163, 173
  demi-deuil, 38
  "The Double Session," 39
  "Faith and Knowledge," 38
  "Fors," 38–40, 42, 46–48, 50, 52, 240–42
  "Freud and the Scene of Writing," 39, 193
  Genèses, généalogies, genres et le génie, 243
  "Geopsychoanalysis and 'The Rest of the World'," 46
  Given Time, 50
  Glas, 19, 38–39, 231, 239–41
  H.C. for Life, That Is to Say, 45
  "Ja, ou le faux-bond," 38, 229
  Memoires for Paul de Man, 39
  "My Chances," 45–46
  Points . . ., 39
  The Post Card, 19, 39, 45–46, 52, 77
  Psyche, 46
  Resistances, 246
  "The Rhetoric of Drugs," 111, 125
  Rogues, 77

Specters of Marx, 38–39
"Télépathie," 51
The Truth in Painting, 38
Writing and Difference, 39
disavowal, 71, 126, 156
Doane, Janice, and Devon Hodges, 251–52*n*4
dreams, 3, 5, 23, 54, 62–63, 116, 168–73, 184, 194, 232, 247, 249, 258*n*31, 273–74*n*16, 281*n*6
dreamwork, the, 59, 63, 168
Drinan, Robert F., 266*n*7
drive, technological, 116, 122, 125
drugs, 111, 123–25

ear, 112–18, 120, 215, 230, 267
Elpis (Hope), 13, 15–16, 88
Euripides, 195, 254*n*3

Felman, Shoshana, 21, 255*n*9
Ferenczi, Sandor, 263
Frankenstein. *See* Shelley, Mary
freezer, 24–26, 33, 35, 252*n*7, 256*n*14
Freud, Sigmund, 1, 6, 19, 21–35, 39, 41, 45–88, 92–93, 113, 119, 120–21, 134, 164–72, 193, 232, 240, 242, 246
"Analysis Terminable and Interminable," 55
Beyond the Pleasure Principle, 77–82, 93, 116
"Dora" case history, 21
"Dreams and Occultism," 47–48, 50–51
"Fausse reconnaissance," 55
"Fetishism," 55, 71
Inhibitions, Symptoms and Anxiety, 29, 32, 55, 67–8, 82–3
The Interpretation of Dreams, 25, 32, 63–64, 168–69, 171
"Little Hans" case history, 67–70
"Medusa's Head," 32
"Negation," 171
"The Occurrence in Dreams of Material From Fairy Tales," 55
"Project for a Scientific Psychology," 93
"Rat Man" case history, 29
"Remembering, Repeating and Working Through," 55
"Repression," 55
"The Splitting of the Ego in the Process of Defence," 55
"The Theme of the Three Caskets," 32–35
"Thoughts for the Times on War and Death," 27, 242
Totem and Taboo, 27–29, 31, 45, 58, 67
"The Uncanny," 1, 32–33, 55, 166, 170–71
"Wolf Man" case history (*From the History of an Infantile Neurosis*), 29–30, 32–33, 40, 43–51, 53–76, 81, 134–35, 242
fright, 78–79, 82, 93
future, the 5, 6, 9, 15, 33, 39, 46, 49, 77–78, 80–88, 91–94, 101, 110, 112, 120, 172, 175, 182, 186, 188, 191, 193, 194, 229, 232, 261*n*28

Gallop, Jane, 21, 255
Gardiner, Muriel, 54, 261–62*n*3
Genet, Jean, 237, 239–41, 242
Genosko, Gary, 262*n*8
Geyskens, Tomas, 262–63*n*9
Green, André, 262–63*n*9, 264*n*5
Grosz , Elizabeth, 255*n*7
Grundberg, Andy, 265*n*3
Gualtieri, Elena, 276*n*41
Guantanamo Bay, 105
Guattari, Félix, 262*n*8

Hanrahan, Mairéad, 279*n*6
Harvey, David, 268*n*1
Hegel, Georg Wilhelm Friedrich, 253*n*2
Hersh, Seymour M., 99, 101, 106, 265*n*2, 265*n*6, 266*n*8, 266*n*10, 266*n*15
Hesiod, 9, 10, 12, 14–15, 253*n*9
Hippolytus, 195, 198, 203
Hoffmann, Geneviève, 9
Homans, Margaret, 277
home, concept of, 4, 11, 13, 20, 24–25, 85, 165, 170–71, 177, 205, 227, 234
Hughes, Gordon, 271*n*1
Human Rights Watch, 98–99, 265*n*5
hysteria, 21, 59, 63

image, fantasmatic, 62, 163, 168–69, 171–73, 247
incorporation, 38–40, 42–44, 52, 54, 60, 119–20, 127, 240, 242. *See also* introjection
infanticide, 24–5, 207, 212, 252*n*7
introjection, 38–43, 52, 119, 240, 242. *See also* incorporation
Iraq war, 91, 94, 128
Irigaray, Luce, 21, 253*n*2, 255*n*7, 257*n*9

Jacobs, Amber, 252*n*4
Jacobs, Carol, 253–54*n*2
jar, 8, 13–16, 33, 88, 148, 248. *See also* Pandora
Johnson, Barbara, 47, 204, 263*n*9, 277*n*3
Johnson, Lawrence, 261*n*2
Johnston, Adrian, 257*n*16
Joyce, James, 237

Kael, Pauline, 130, 269*n*3
Kahane, Claire, 255*n*8
Kamuf, Peggy, 259*n*8
Kear, Adrian, 265*n*3
Keenan, Thomas, 266*n*7
Klein, Melanie, 251*n*4, 264*n*4
Knight, Diana, 271, 275*n*1
Kofman, Sarah, 21, 255*n*9
Kristeva, Julia, 21, 251*n*4, 255*n*10

Lacan, Jacques, 21, 70, 87, 113, 253–54*n*2, 262–63*n*25, 264*n*4, 267*n*5
Laplanche, Jean, 71–72, 75, 79–80, 262–63*n*9, 264*n*6
legacy, maternal, 198–99, 202, 204–6
Lev Kenaan, Vered, 253*n*10
Lifton, Robert Jay, 265*n*2
Limbaugh, Rush, 109
Loraux, Nicole, 9, 11, 12, 14, 20, 253*n*10, 253*n*11, 253*n*15, 254*n*4, 254*n*5, 254–55*n*6
Lyotard, Jean-François, 149–50, 270*n*1

magic, 37, 41–46, 49–50, 52, 155, 218, 260*n*27, 274*n*16
magical thinking, 6, 29, 155
Marder, Elissa, 268*n*23, 275*n*28
Marinopoulos, Sophie, 256*n*14
Marshall, David, 278*n*12
matchbox, 241–44
maternal function, 2–9, 12, 15–16, 22, 24–26, 29–32, 116–18, 120, 148, 150, 159, 163, 176, 181–83, 194, 249, 251*n*2, 251–52*n*4, 252*n*5, 252*n*6, 252*n*7, 273*n*13
matricide, 227, 251–52*n*4
McGraw, Betty R., 270*n*3
mechanical reproduction, 3, 5, 9, 11, 16, 94, 120, 150, 170
memory, involuntary, 172, 177
metapsychology, 6, 22, 28, 45, 46, 59, 81, 92
metis, 251–52*n*4
Michelet, Jules, 180–81
Milesi, Laurent, 282*n*20
Miller, J. Hillis, 259*n*8
Mitchell, Juliet, 21, 255*n*7
Mitterand, François, 36, 256*n*14
mors, 230–31, 239–41, 246, 280*n*1
Most, Glenn, 13, 253*n*9
mother tongue, 154, 198, 200–5, 208–9, 228
mourning, 6, 19, 20, 23, 25–26, 29–31, 35–46, 50, 59, 114, 116, 118–20, 123, 129, 150, 175, 181, 228, 230, 240, 242, 246, 247, 248, 254*n*2, 283*n*31
  failed, 6, 24, 26, 37, 40, 54, 118, 123, 267*n*15
  work of, 37–39
mouth, 15, 30, 31, 114, 120, 206, 229–30, 233
Murray, Timothy, 270*n*3, 271*n*1

Naas, Michael, 261*n*28, 275*n*30
Niobe, 19, 20, 254*n*4

Obholzer, Karin, 261–62*n*3
Oliver, Kelly, 251*n*2, 255*n*10, 261*n*2, 262*n*8, 266*n*16

Pandora, 1, 8–16, 33, 88, 148, 248
Pankeiev, Sergei, 46, 50–51, 54
Patai, Raphael, 106
paternity, 32
Penley, Constance, 268*n*1
Petro, Patrice, 266*n*11, 270*n*11

photograph, psychic, 58
photographic writing, 7, 163–64, 179, 182–83
photography, 1, 3, 5–6, 7, 9, 62, 91, 96, 97, 99–100, 103, 106–8, 118–19, 137–38, 148–59, 163, 165–66, 169, 174, 176–91, 194
photography, involuntary, 178, 181, 189–90
Pingeot, Mazarine, 256*n*14
Plutarch, 209, 278*n*15
Pontalis, Jean-Baptiste, 262–63*n*9
Powell, Colin, 92
pregnancy, denial of, 24, 252*n*7
Prenowitz, Eric, 215, 283*n*34
primal scene, 6, 57–62, 64–66, 70–76, 81, 110, 134–36, 140, 148, 163, 190, 216, 219, 221, 230, 232, 235, 238, 248
prosthesis, 14, 115, 118, 120, 122, 123, 131, 187, 253*n*13
prosthetic maternal, 7, 118–19, 150
Proust, Marcel, 172, 177–78, 183, 189–93, 276*n*41
Psycho-Photography, 91, 94
Pucci, Pietro, 9
punctum, 109, 153, 165. See also *studium*

Rabaté, Jean-Michel, 270*n*3
Racine, Jean, 8, 195–205, 214, 276–77*n*1, 278*n*15
Rand, Nicholas, 46–47
Rashkin, Esther, 259*n*8
Reagan, Ronald, 92
remainder, the, 39, 52, 143, 153, 182, 230, 240–41
replicant, 9, 117, 131–42, 145, 147, 148
resistance, 116, 193, 245–47
Rich, Frank, 265*n*2
Rickels, Laurence, 257*n*24, 267*n*15
Ronell, Avital, 7, 111–28, 164, 253*n*8, 257*n*24
Rose, Jacqueline, 21, 255*n*7
Rottenberg, Elizabeth, 260*n*22
Rousseau, Jean-Jacques, 236, 278*n*12
Royle, Nicholas, 251*n*1, 260*n*22, 260–61*n*27, 272*n*7
Rumsfeld, Donald, 99

Sante, Luc, 265*n*2
Segarra, Marta, 275*n*30, 279–80*n*16, 281*n*14
sexual difference, 10, 21, 23, 30, 60, 65–67, 69–71, 76, 116, 134–35, 140, 142, 230, 238
shame, 6, 7, 92, 94, 96–97, 99, 102–8
Shawcross, Nancy M., 271*n*1
Shelley, Mary, 8, 195, 196, 204–13, 277*n*4, 277*n*8
Shengold, Leonard, 121, 267–68*n*17, 268*n*18
Shepherdson, Charles, 253–54*n*2, 264*n*5
Silverman, Kaja, 268–69*n*1
Solomon-Godeau, Abigail, 265*n*3
Sontag, Susan, 99, 265*n*2
Sophocles, 254*n*3
Sprengnether, Madelon, 255*n*10
Steiner, George, 253–54*n*2
studium, 153. See also *punctum*
superego, anal-sadistic, 121–22

Taguba, Major General Antonio M., 103–5, 266*n*12
techno-analysis, 112, 116
techno-maternal, the, 118
telepathy, 6, 48, 49–52, 253*n*13, 260*n*22, 260–61*n*27, 261*n*28
telephone, 6, 7, 112, 113, 115–24, 127, 164, 187, 243, 266–67*n*4
time, utopian, 165, 167, 172–75
Tobit, book of, 232, 281*n*6
Torok, Maria, 6, 29–30, 39–55, 242, 257–63. *See also* Abraham, Nicolas
torture, 97–99, 103, 105, 107, 108, 222, 266*n*16
totem animal, 27, 31, 64
toxic maternal, the, 123
translation, 3, 44, 46–47, 50, 54, 195–96, 206, 208–9, 214–15, 219
trauma, 30, 42, 54, 56–57, 77–82, 85, 87–8, 93–94, 108, 120, 259*n*8

uncanny, the, 1, 5–9, 16, 22, 31–35, 49–51, 58, 81–86, 94, 148–50, 154–58, 166, 170–72, 175, 177, 182, 186, 189, 194, 248, 249

Ungar, Steven, 270
Unheimlich. *See* uncanny
utopia, 163, 172–75

Van Haute, Philippe, 263
Vernant, Jean-Pierre, 9, 13–14, 253*n*10, 253*n*14, 256*n*13

Wallis, Brian, 265*n*3
Walsh, Joan, 265*n*4
Weber, Samuel, 253–54*n*2, 264*n*5
Williams, Linda, 108, 266*n*11
Willis, Sharon, 277*n*6
Wills, David, 253*n*13
winter garden, photograph of, 173, 175
wolf dream, 58, 60–64, 73, 134
Wollen, Peter, 269*n*2
Wollstonecraft, Mary, 206, 277*n*8
Wood, Sarah, 260–61*n*27
Wurmser, Léon, 104, 265*n*1, 266*n*14

Yacavone, Kathrin, 276*n*41

Zakin, Emily, 257*n*19
Zeitlin, Froma, 9, 14, 15, 16, 253*n*10, 253*n*16
Ziarek, Ewa, 255*n*10
Žižek, Slavoj, 265*n*2